Essential Questions in Adolescent Literacy

■ ■ ■

Teachers and Researchers Describe What Works in Classrooms

Edited by
Jill Lewis

Foreword by Elizabeth Birr Moje

THE GUILFORD PRESS
New York   London

© 2009 The Guilford Press
A Division of Guilford Publications, Inc.
72 Spring Street, New York, NY 10012
www.guilford.com

Printed in the United States of America

This book is printed on acid-free paper.

Last digit is print number: 9   8   7   6   5   4   3   2   1

Library of Congress Cataloging-in-Publication Data

Essential questions in adolescent literacy : teachers and researchers describe
what works in classrooms / edited by Jill Lewis.
    p. cm.
  Includes bibliographical references and index.
  ISBN 978-1-60623-268-2 (hardcover)–ISBN 978-1-60623-267-5 (pbk.)
  1. Language arts (Middle school)   2. Language arts
(Secondary)   I. Lewis, Jill, Ed.D.
  LB1631.E86 2009
  428.0071′2—dc21

2008047684

To David
with love

About the Editor

Jill Lewis, EdD, is Professor of Literacy Education at New Jersey City University. Previously she taught high school English in public schools and directed a reading lab at a community college. She has published numerous articles, chapters, and books on adolescent literacy, content-area reading, professional development, and advocacy, and presents her work widely in the United States and internationally. Dr. Lewis is a past member of the Board of Directors of the International Reading Association and a recipient of its Special Service Award.

Contributors

Laura Azcoitia, MA, Larkin High School, Elgin, Illinois

Rita M. Bean, PhD, Department of Instruction and Learning, School of Education, University of Pittsburgh, Pittsburgh, Pennsylvania

Tom Bean, PhD, Department of Curriculum and Instruction, College of Education, University of Nevada Las Vegas, Las Vegas, Nevada

Deanna Birdyshaw, PhD, School of Education, University of Michigan, Ann Arbor, Michigan

Kathryn E. Carroll, EdD, Pittsburgh Lincoln K–8, Pittsburgh Public Schools, Pittsburgh, Pennsylvania

Avivah Dahbany, PhD, private practice, East Brunswick, New Jersey

Barbara Davis, BSEd, Ninety Six High School, Ninety Six, South Carolina

Benita Dillard, MA, Odyssey High School, Las Vegas, Nevada

Mary Dillingham, PhD, Wren High School, Piedmont, South Carolina

Fabiola P. Ehlers-Zavala, PhD, Department of English, Colorado State University, Fort Collins, Colorado

Francine Falk-Ross, PhD, Department of Literacy Education, School of Education, Pace University, Pleasantville, New York

April Ficklin, MA, Adult and Graduate Studies, Southern Wesleyan University, Central, South Carolina

Victoria Ridgeway Gillis, PhD, Department of Teacher Education, Eugene T. Moore School of Education, Clemson University, Clemson, South Carolina

Leigh Haltiwanger, MA, Upper Savannah Mathematics and Science Regional Center and Lander University, Greenwood, South Carolina

Helen Harper, PhD, Department of Curriculum and Instruction, College of Education, University of Nevada Las Vegas, Las Vegas, Nevada

Lisa Hoffman, MA, Farmington High School, Farmington, Michigan

Shannon Hurst, MA, Unity West Junior High School, Cicero, Illinois

Jacy Ippolito, EdM, Graduate School of Education, Harvard University, Cambridge, Massachusetts

Bill Jones, BA, Roselle Public Schools, Roselle, New Jersey

Lori Kelsey, MS, Rancho Santa Fe Middle School, Rancho Santa Fe, California

Kendall Kiser, MEd, Monroe Middle School, Monroe, North Carolina

William Kist, PhD, Department of Teaching, Leadership and Curriculum Studies, College of Education, Health, and Human Services, Kent State University, Kent, Ohio

Jill Lewis, EdD, Department of Literacy Education, College of Education, New Jersey City University, Jersey City, New Jersey

Pamela A. Mason, EdD, Language and Literacy Program, Harvard Graduate School of Education, Cambridge, Massachusetts

Lauren Bosworth McFadden, EdD, Department of Educational Studies, College of Education and Human Services, Seton Hall University, South Orange, New Jersey

Shannon Mitchell, MEd, Annenberg School of Education, University of Southern California, Los Angeles, California

William Dee Nichols, PhD, Department of Elementary and Middle Grades Education, Western Carolina University, Cullowhee, North Carolina

Tanya Reader, MEd, Carl Sandburg Middle School, Glendora Unified School District, Glendora, California

William H. Rupley, PhD, Department of Teaching, Learning, and Culture, College of Education and Human Development, Texas A&M University, College Station, Texas

Jim Ryan, BSEd, Highland Middle School, Barberton, Ohio

Nancy Walker, PhD, Teacher Education Program, College of Education and Organizational Leadership, University of La Verne, La Verne, California

Jennifer Wimmer, MA, Department of Curriculum and Instruction, College of Education, University of Nevada Las Vegas, Las Vegas, Nevada

Thomas DeVere Wolsey, EdD, Richard W. Riley College of Education and Leadership, Walden University, Minneapolis, Minnesota

Foreword

When I began teaching in 1983, I thought I would invite young people into an exciting exploration of ideas, concepts, and relationships through our study of biology and history. Like most high school teachers, I loved the subjects I had studied for so long. I also loved the idea of engaging others in conversations about ideas. What could be better than teaching high school students and engaging them in analyses of natural phenomena or the causes and effects of historical events and relationships? My ideals were dashed pretty quickly when I encountered what I thought was my students' lack of interest in or proficiency with reading and writing the texts of biology and history.

It was this struggle that led me to the study of literacy. Like the authors of *Essential Questions in Adolescent Literacy: Teachers and Researchers Describe What Works in Classrooms*, I wanted to find ways not only to engage my students with the texts of the disciplines but also to scaffold their comprehension and composition relative to those texts. Like the authors of this book, my path as both a teacher and a researcher has been multidimensional. I have looked closely at classroom practices, at young people's literacy practices, at the people and contexts that motivate them to read, and at the texts of instruction.

This path of adolescent literacy research has also been long and winding. When I entered the field, scholars talked about *content-area reading*, which emphasized the application of generic cognitive reading strategies in the content areas. A decade later, the lexicon shifted to *secondary school literacy*, a move that attempted to account for the contexts of secondary schooling, with changing class periods and different disciplinary influences. We next moved to *adolescent literacy*, with its focus on the literacy practices of youth themselves. Two decades later, in a new millennium, we have entered a new period, a sea change of sorts, in which people who were never before interested in the reading and writing of adolescents seem suddenly focused on measuring and (re)mediating youth literacy skills. This is a time when policy initiatives seek best practices, and many authors write of strategy instruction in secondary schools as if it is a new and singular solution to the challenges of adolescent literacy development.

This book, however, challenges many of these notions. What makes this book compelling is that it brings these different critical dimensions of adolescent and secondary school literacy together in one volume. From chapters that focus on the value of understanding young people's experiences to chapters that discuss how to assess youth literacy and subject-area learning, the book offers a wide array of perspectives on the teaching and learning of literacy with and for adolescents. In many ways, the book serves as a compendium of the different paths taken in the study of literacy teaching and learning in the secondary school (for a useful review of this path, see Phelps, 2005).

The authors—both researchers and classroom teachers—use portraits of classrooms to illustrate complexities that teachers and students face in secondary school subject-matter areas, review literature relevant to those complexities, and offer teaching *practices*—not just an alphabet soup of strategies—that put the adolescent learner front and center in the quest for developing literate proficiencies. These chapters acknowledge the topics and texts that interest youth, the differences in their experiences and in their development, and the many new texts and media that may or may not engender new literate practices. But more than that, the authors in this volume seek to make connections from those experiences, developmental trends, texts, and literacies of youth to the teaching and learning in classrooms. They are not content merely to explicate theories or to marvel at youth literacies outside of school; these authors seek to integrate the findings of a multidimensional approach to studying adolescent literacy into a multidimensional approach to teaching adolescent literacy in actual secondary school classrooms.

Our field—and the adolescent students we serve—need this integrated and multidimensional approach. Without it, we cannot hope to make the kind of change needed to support adolescents' literacy development in the 21st century. Without it, adolescent literacy policy will be merely rhetoric. I commend this volume to readers as an important step forward in shifting the ways we think, talk, read, write, and practice adolescent literacy.

ELIZABETH BIRR MOJE, PhD
University of Michigan

Reference

Phelps, S. F. (2005). *Ten years of research on adolescent literacy, 1994–2004: A review* (No. ED-01-CO-0011). Naperville, IL: Learning Point Associates.

Preface

Essential Questions in Adolescent Literacy: Teachers and Researchers Describe What Works in Classrooms has been designed to bridge what too often is a gap between research-based theory and effective classroom practices in adolescent literacy. Each chapter, coauthored by teacher educators and teachers who have worked with middle and secondary school students, uses both theory and current research-based best literacy practices to inform each other and to address key questions about adolescent literacy. This dual approach for each chapter ensures that the theory and research are supported by the teacher's voice.

The questions addressed in this volume are key to developing adolescent literacy, because they require deep reflection about the learner, the learning context, the role of school in American society, and school resources. Together they can spark our curiosity to delve further into this field, to initiate new applications grounded in research, and to consider the multiple perspectives that might be available for answering them.

With the recent attention to adolescent literacy, many universities are beginning to redesign their literacy education courses to move away from the traditional "reading in the content areas" approach to one that looks more broadly at the adolescent learner in in-school and out-of-school contexts, as well as schoolwide literacy initiatives in middle and secondary schools, integrating new literacies, and differentiating instruction for English language learners and struggling readers. The topics in this book have been written with this fresh approach to adolescent literacy instruction in mind.

The organization of this book has been designed to make evident the practical applications of the research and theory. Each chapter begins with a vignette (Classroom Portrait) welcoming the reader into the classroom (or school) and transitions to a discussion of how the vignette illustrates the question being addressed in the chapter. Unless otherwise specified, all names in each chapter, including those in the Classroom Portrait, are fictitious. The Portrait is followed by a brief description of the chapter authors' backgrounds, after which the teacher educator typically provides a theoretical research base that addresses the chapter question. The classroom teacher then describes how the theory is realized in classroom instruction. In some chapters an alternating dialogue approach is used, whereas in others the classroom teachers' discussion of practical application follows an introduction to theory and research relevant to the chapter question. Each chapter concludes with several Questions for Reflection that encourage the reader to consider how discussion points and applications in the chapter might be pertinent to his or her teaching or student experience and teaching goals. Questions are designed with the assumption that whereas some of our readers are receiving their first teaching certification, others may have already taught in classrooms.

Essential Questions in Adolescent Literacy: Teachers and Researchers Describe What Works in Classrooms is divided into three parts. In Part I, Getting Personal: Connecting Adolescent Literacy Instruction with Students' Lived Experiences, we emphasize the need to teach to the student, not to a test. We focus on the learner as an individual and consider ways to connect that individual meaningfully to the school context. In Chapter 1, "How Can What We Know about Adolescent Learners Be Used to Benefit Our Literacy Instruction?," Lewis and Jones offer research on the cognitive and social–emotional development of the adolescent and illustrate how this information can be used to design literacy instruction that is considerate of the developmental needs of adolescents, using a Promoting Adolescent Literacy (PAL) framework. Chapter 2, by Dahbany and McFadden, discusses the question, "How Can Motivation and Self-Efficacy Theory Inform Adolescent Literacy Teaching Practices?" and describes different types of motivation applicable to different age groups, and how these can be used specifically to target learning cohorts for a more successful engagement in the reading process. In Chapter 3, "How Can Adolescents' Literacies Outside of School Be Brought into the Classroom?," Kist and Ryan address attempts to translate adolescents' out-of-school literacy skills and interests into the experiences of a new high school teacher and introduce us to new literacies as they are incorporated into classrooms in both alternative and more traditional settings. Chapter 4, "Adolescent Literacy and Democratic Life: What's Politics Got to Do with It?," by Harper and Mitchell, moves outside the text per se and discusses the political nature of education and how, in a democratic society, strategies used to engage adolescents in the reading process should reflect, and thus reinforce, the democratic process.

Part II, Connecting Adolescent Literacy Instruction to Students' Personal Goals, continues the focus on the individual, especially struggling readers and adolescents who have met with little success thus far in their school careers. In Chapter 5, Lewis and Reader address the question "How Can We Help Adolescent Readers Meet the Challenges of Academic Text?" They focus on *academic literacy*, the skills and social dispositions that, according to national standards in several content fields, are particular to successfully understanding and interpreting of types of text that the adolescent encounters in the school setting. Ehlers-Zavala and Azcoitia consider academic literacy for adolescent English language learners (ELLs) and provide foundational knowledge that all teachers need, as well as practical teaching suggestions, in Chapter 6, "How Can Teachers Help Adolescent English Language Learners Attain Academic Literacy?" In Chapter 7, "How Can We Use Adolescents' Language and Classroom Discourse to Enhance Critical Thinking Practices?," Falk-Ross and Hurst examine classroom dialogue and how these conversations can be used in content-area classes to promote critical thinking and critical literacy. In Chapter 8, Nichols, Rupley, and Kiser discuss the question, "How Can Vocabulary Instruction Be Made an Integral Part of Learning in Middle and High School Classrooms?" These authors offer six principles to help teachers introduce in meaningful ways the large amount of new vocabulary that students must learn in content-area classes. "How Does Creative Content-Area Teaching Work with Adolescents?" is the focus of Chapter 9, by Bean, Walker, Wimmer, and Dillard. They examine research on new literacies involving multimedia and the Internet, and how teacher creativity can incorporate these digital literacies into both traditional and nontraditional high school settings. With concern for adolescents' writing, Wolsey and Kelsey tackle the question "How Can We Help Adolescents Think about Content through Writing?" in Chapter 10. They explore the concept that writing, which in the classroom setting most often involves students demonstrating what they have learned, is in fact a way *of* learning, and a powerful tool to help students acquire content. They illustrate effective instruction for developing adolescents' writing, especially argumentation. Chapter 11, "How Can Content-Area Teachers Differentiate Instruction for Their Students to Improve Student Learning?," by Birdyshaw and Hoffman, examines the obstacles to differentiating instruction for academically diverse students in middle and secondary school, and recounts steps that have been taken to address this issue and create a successful learning environment. Chapter 12, "How Can Assessment Evaluate Student Learning, Inform Instruction, and Promote Student Independence?," draws from research on self- and peer-evaluation studies. Gillis, Halti-wanger, Ficklin, Dillingham, and Davis discuss how learning can be accomplished both in the assessment, by students using teacher-developed evaluation criteria, and in the collaborative development of course rubrics with the teacher.

In Part III, Building School Communities for Adolescent Literacy Instruction, the reader is moved from inside the classroom to the larger school context, specifically to consider how other school personnel can contribute to adolescents' literacy development. Chapter 13 provides research and firsthand experiences that address the question "What Do Middle Grades and High School Teachers Need to Know about Literacy Coaching?" Here Bean and Carroll provide guidelines for working with a coach and share how varied the coaching experience can be with different teachers. Mason and Ippolito, in Chapter 14, "What is the Role of the Reading Specialist in Promoting Adolescent Literacy?," discuss the requirements of the reading specialist (as differentiated from the literacy coach), and the contributions that reading specialists can make in the current literacy crisis in grades 5–12.

Because there is remarkable agreement among researchers about what needs to be done to address literacy issues in middle and high school classes, several themes cut across all of the research cited and the classroom strategies suggested:

- The importance of valuing and considering the uniqueness of the adolescent learner when planning literacy instruction.
- The importance of considering adolescents' in-school and out-of-school literacies when planning instruction.
- The need to motivate and engage students in their literacy development.
- The need to involve adolescents actively in making meaning from text.
- The benefits of integrating technology for literacy development.
- The benefits of schoolwide decision making and curriculum planning for promoting adolescent literacy across content areas.
- The interrelatedness of all aspects of language arts literacy: reading, writing, speaking, listening, and thinking.

We trust that our readers will enjoy the teachers' personal stories, benefit from the research we offer, and reflect with others on the questions we raise both in the chapter titles and end-of-chapter questions. In spite of the considerable agreement among researchers and policymakers about what must be done to improve adolescent literacy, less clear is the extent to which these ideas reach classrooms. We hope this book will make a difference.

Acknowledgments

I would like to thank the editorial team at The Guilford Press, especially Craig Thomas, for their diligence and thoughtful contributions to this book. I also wish to thank the many authors of the chapters in this book, who contributed generously of their time and whose collaboration with me and with each other made this project so personally gratifying. My deepest appreciation also goes to my dear friends, especially Diane Szumski and Avivah Dahbany, for their love and support. My dear children, Miles and Allison, are also to be recognized for teaching me a great deal about adolescence and communication. I also wish to thank New Jersey City University for granting me release time to work on this project.

Contents

PART III. BUILDING SCHOOL COMMUNITIES FOR ADOLESCENT LITERACY INSTRUCTION

PART I

■   ■   ■

Getting Personal

Connecting Adolescent Literacy Instruction with Students' Lived Experiences

■ ■ ■

CHAPTER 1

How Can What We Know about Adolescent Learners Be Used to Benefit Our Literacy Instruction?

JILL LEWIS
BILL JONES

CLASSROOM PORTRAIT

As Kevin Abbott prepares for his first year as a seventh-grade reading teacher, he reviews the textbook his students will be using for the upcoming school year. He is excited to see that it includes a personal essay by author Alex Haley, "My Furthest-Back Person." It tells the story of how Haley was inspired to write his best-known work *Roots: The Saga of an American Family*. Remembering how important it is for students to make connections to what they are reading, Kevin believes this essay is perfect for his students. For starters, most of his students are African American and have most likely heard of the story already. Also, many students may have heard personal accounts from family members of ancestors whose stories mirror those in Haley's book. Kevin also remembers watching the much acclaimed television miniseries based on the novel, and fondly recalls the vivid storytelling and vibrant characters that made the show one of the most watched programs in the history of television. Recalling this, Kevin decides that he will show part of the movie after his students are finished reading Haley's essay.

After creating a number of lessons around "My Furthest-Back Person," Kevin introduces the story to his students. To his chagrin, many of them seem disinterested in the essay. Several voice their displeasure, saying they are tired of reading stories about slaves or tales from the "olden" days. Kevin also detects that many of his students are having difficulty comprehending the text, and he comes to the realization that the story is written above their instructional reading level. He is further dismayed when his colleague brings up a major concern about an extension activity that Kevin has planned in connection with the essay, to create a family tree. The colleague mentions that it might not be a good idea to have the students research their family trees to reflect Haley's work, noting that some students currently live in foster homes, and bringing up the family tree topic may make them feel extremely uncomfortable. She also remarks that such a project requires students to interview a number of family members whom students may not be able to reach in such a short time. Kevin's coworker further comments that some parents may not want to have such personal information written about in a school project.

All of these concerns and issues have put a damper on Kevin's outlook for the school year. A once-promising series of lessons has turned out to be a less than perfect class activity, and a lesson in getting to know one's students. How can he help students connect texts to their lives and simultaneously develop their literacy achievement? Why is everything he attempts to do with his students fraught with complex considerations?

MySpace, YouTube, eating disorders, tattoos … what's going on? Adolescence, of course! Kevin Abbot is not alone as a teacher who feels that adolescents are a challenge to teach. When we examine what we know about adolescent development, it is easy to understand why. Although it is difficult to pinpoint an exact age when adolescence begins, and it varies for different individuals, it is usually considered to begin at puberty and continue through maturity, that is, approximately between ages 11 and 21. This age group was first studied by G. Stanley Hall (1916), who described adolescence as a period of *Sturm und Drang*, storm and stress. Today's researchers would agree with this view, noting that during this dynamic period of life between childhood and adulthood, the individual experiences rapid physical and social changes. Furthermore, during this period of normal life progression, important psychological changes occur, relating particularly to the way adolescents perceive themselves, and these perceptions tend to fluctuate between feelings of superiority and inadequacy (Kellough & Kellough, 2008; Scales, 2003; Wiles, Bondi, & Wiles, 2006). Adolescence can be a turbulent phase of life, something that adolescents may not realize until after they have reached adulthood. In fact, think back to your own teen years. Would you want to relive them? Most adults to whom we have posed this question have given a resounding NO! Distance has added perspective. Adolescence is, and always will be, one of the most frightening, confusing yet exhilarating periods of one's life.

Teachers in middle and high school sometimes find themselves colliding with their students, struggling to get them to focus on school when their attention is on just about everything but school. Youth culture is distinctive and sometimes difficult for "outsiders," including teachers, to understand. Teens look for something new that will make a statement about who they are—that will give them a personal identity and also lead to peer acceptance. What frequently emerges from this creative search is distinctive ways of dressing or unique hairstyles and unconventional preferences, including music preferences; we may hear or see words used in new and perhaps incomprehensible ways to "outsiders," such as e-mail-ese. Adolescents sometimes exhibit risky behavior in their search for identity. It is during adolescence that boys and girls also start to discover their special talents, perhaps in art, leadership, music, academics, or sports, and that they become engaged in activities in which they can demonstrate caring for others, perhaps through volunteer work and community service. They set personal goals and sometimes have to make difficult decisions. They learn how to interact with diverse individuals and gradually to accept, albeit often reluctantly, society's norms. Development of other identities, including gender and ethnic identities, is also constructed during adolescence.

Developing students' literacy is especially complicated during this phase of life. Although some literacy skills, such as listening and speaking, develop without formal instruction in early childhood, learning to read is something that students have been practicing since the earliest grades, perhaps even in preschool or before, with a parent or teacher's assistance. Thus, by the time they reach middle and high school, students are expected to have mastered basic literacy skills. Unfortunately, this is not the case for many students, and for most, even greater maturity is needed for the kinds of texts they will read in middle and high school classes, including the ability to read with a critical eye, to observe and evaluate carefully, to note bias and perspectives, and to deal with metaphor and abstraction. In adolescence, most students have a growing capacity to handle such sophistical reading expectations. But for students who struggle with reading assignments, peer pressure and humiliation in front of peers exacerbate their sense of inadequacy, leading to feelings of total defeat. We need solutions to keep these students from spiraling downward and experiencing the sense of helplessness and depression that is so common in adolescence. We also need to continue to refine the literacy abilities of all students, so they can use their literacies in ways they find purposeful and joyful.

One way we can increase our teaching successes with all students is to look less at the texts and more at the students. Who is it we are teaching? What is it we need to know about them that may have a positive bearing on how and what we teach? In this chapter we discuss the adolescent learner from a psychosocial perspective to offer some answers to these questions. Our responses are informed by research, as well as by our practice as teachers. Jill Lewis, now primarily a teacher-educator and professor at New Jersey City University, taught Language Arts to grades 7–12 in New York and Virginia for several years. She has also spent more than three decades providing professional development on adolescent literacy to teachers and teaching underprepared college freshmen, students whose literacy skills never fully developed in the middle and secondary grades. Most recently she was involved in a 5-year project, working with secondary grade teachers and students in the Republic of Macedonia's vocational/technical schools. She found startling the similarities in youth culture around the world! Bill Jones, currently a sixth-grade Reading teacher at Grace Wilday Junior High School in Roselle, New Jersey, has taught secondary students in Reading and Language Arts for the past 5 years. In addition, he has taught reading and writing courses at Middlesex County College and Mercer County Community College in New Jersey. He is currently completing his master's as a Reading Specialist at New Jersey City University.

Literacy Transitions

As already noted, the literacy expectations that teachers have for adolescents are greater than those held for students in earlier grades. We see this in a host of ways, including the types of texts and textual supports provided to younger readers, the kinds and formats of assessments, and the time on direct instruction versus independent work in lower grades compared to middle and secondary grades. If we examine the grade-level standards in the 1996 *Standards for the English Language Arts*, developed collaboratively by the International Reading Association (IRA) and National Council of Teachers of English (NCTE), or those of individual states, we can see a gradual shift from fairly basic to very complex expectations, such as from being able to read one's own name (kindergarten) to being able to discuss characterization in a Shakespearean play (upper grades). These differences in expectations are appropriate, for just as adolescence is a period of social–emotional–physical transition, so too is it a period when literacy abilities become more mature.

Literacy development is a lifelong process, and adolescents are developing along the continuum. Researchers offer some examples of how these literacy transitions are evident in children of different ages (Allington & Cunningham, 1996; Burns, Griffin, & Snow, 1999; Clay, 1991; Holdaway, 1979; McGee & Richgels, 1996; Strickland & Morrow, 1988; Teale & Sulzby, 1986). From birth to age 3, children typically speak their first holophrases and then sentences, start to recognize pictures in books, may turn pages, and by age 3 may do some "play reading." More sophisticated literacy skills, including interactions with texts, occur by age 5, when milestones might include speaking in sentences, retelling familiar stories, understanding that print carries a message, and even writing one's own name or a story using invented spelling. We see some children at this age recognizing letters and even whole words. We can expect that by age 7, most children use writing for different purposes and are enthusiastic about learning to read. They become less egocentric and begin to show interest in other times and places. They also enjoy sharing books with other children. In the years leading up to early adolescence, ages 7–11, we see children working cooperatively and enjoying challenges. They learn new words quickly and show greater variety in reading preferences, and they are able to use a variety of reading strategies to comprehend text and relate text to their personal lives. As children enter adolescence we witness more communication between individuals, often through blogs and text messaging, and songs and magazines specifically targeted to teens offer avenues for personal identity and growth. Choice becomes key, and comprehension becomes more sophisticated and analytical. Such developmental shifts in purposes for interacting with texts, and skills needed for comprehending them, are complemented by changing classroom activities, and expectations for comprehension and literacy responses.

Psychosocial Transitions in Adolescents

In the same way that we see gradual modifications in a student's literacy goals and abilities from very early school experiences into adolescence, we can identify changes in an individual's social–emotional–physical characteristics that correspond to the transition from childhood to adolescence. Vygotsky (1978) added to our knowledge base of adolescent behavior by noting the importance of the cultural and historical contexts of children's lives and the contributions of their social experiences to learning and psychological development. For adolescents of the 21st century, as with any generation, societal characteristics affect their social behaviors, lifestyles, interactions with adults, and thoughts about their futures. "Today's teenagers, sometimes referred to as Millennials (Howe & Strauss, 2000), or Generation Y, live in more diverse communities; are fluent in the language, customs, and values of the digital world; often grow up in one-parent families, and expect to go to college" (Lewis & Dahbany, 2008, p. 9). Our literacy instruction can benefit from our knowledge of the hallmarks of some of the psychosocial transitions in adolescents.

Cognitive Development

Although cognitive changes during adolescence are less apparent than physical changes, many such transitions are evident in classrooms. Specifically, adolescents' thinking becomes more analytical, and they are increasingly capable of *metacognition*, or thinking about their thinking, in ways they could not when they were younger (Flavell, 1963; Kellough & Kellough, 2008; Manning, 2002; Scales, 2003). Piaget (1969/2000) report that during the *concrete operational stage*, approximately between ages 7 and 11, children can think inductively, reasoning from the specific to the general, but only about things within their own experiences. But as Lewis and Dahbany (2008) explain, between ages 11 and 15, during the period that Piaget refers to as the *formal operational stage*, adolescents can

> think about possibilities that are outside their experiences. They develop deductive reasoning, where they can start with an idea and use their logic to develop specific conclusions. They can test hypotheses and reason logically.... Adolescents can now assess how to accomplish a task and the best way to complete it. They can monitor their own performance as they work on a task, and adjust their performance to complete it successfully. (p. 11)

There is also a shift during this period to more emotional or intuitive thinking. Adolescents' preoccupation with concerns about how others perceive them is key to understanding their behavior. During this period of development and increased self-awareness, there is also a tension between adolescents' dependence on parents or caregivers, and their desire for independence and autonomy. Such conflicting feelings can also be seen in classrooms, where teens simultaneously want and resist teacher assistance.

Social-Emotional Development

Erikson (1968) saw eight stages in human social-emotional development, with adolescents shifting from the *industry versus inferiority stage* (6–12 years of age) into the *identity versus role confusion stage* (12–18 years of age). In the former, parental influences are still significant, albeit decreasing; during the latter, peer influence is much greater, and the search for the answer to "Who am I?" is paramount. We can observe adolescents experimenting with identities, shifting peer groups, and sometimes totally rejecting societal norms only to embrace them at other times. As Lewis and Dahbany (2008) note, "Probably the best process of finding one's identity is to have an identity moratorium. This enables the adolescent to try out various identities or possible selves" (p. 14).

Adolescence and Motivation

Motivation (or lack of it) is frequently cited by investigators as a key issue when working with adolescents (Gottfried, 1990; Guthrie, Wigfield, & Perencevich, 2004; Hidi & Harackiewicz, 2000; Wigfield & Guthrie, 1997). Ryan and Pintrich (1997) suggest that adolescents who are motivated to succeed in school might be so for a variety of reasons: to master a subject (mastery goals), to be seen as better than others (relative goals), or to get a reward or avoid punishment (extrinsic goals). If motivated, and if students feel successful at what they've accomplished, ongoing positive results can ensue; that is, a sense of self-efficacy, or belief that they can accomplish a goal, can result in self-perpetuating motivation. Bandura (1978, 1986) explained that an individual's interpretation of his or her accomplishments guides, informs, and alters his or her environment and self-beliefs, which in turn inform and alter subsequent performances.

Teachers can cultivate motivation. Giving adolescents opportunities to express preferences regarding their assignments can play an important role in the motivation to do schoolwork. This seems logical, but results from a large-scale study by Pitcher and colleagues (2007) revealed that student experiences with academic reading and writing did not match their interests and needs. Reflective teachers give needed attention to motivating their adolescent students.

Using What We Know for Effective Adolescent Literacy Instruction

These attributes of the psychosocial development of adolescents are critical considerations for designing literacy instruction for our students. No trait by itself can affect the totality of a student's reading achievement. Yet each must be taken into account as we plan literacy lessons.

A Developmentally Considerate Framework for Promoting Adolescent Literacy (PAL)

Lewis and Dahbany (2008) recently suggested that teachers could achieve greater literacy success with adolescent learners by using a developmentally considerate framework as the basis for our lessons. In this way, positive classroom environments are created where individual developmental differences are respected and supported.

The Promoting Adolescent Literacy framework (Lewis & Dahbany, 2008), as originally conceived, comprised five themes drawn from hallmarks of adolescent development: literacy for developing cognition, literacy for self-assessment and self-monitoring, literacy for understanding multiple perspectives and flexible thinking, literacy for building relationships, and literacy for developing autonomy and identity. In this section the original framework is expanded with one additional theme, literacy for building confidence and engagement, and each theme is elaborated from PAL's original design. When considered together, these six themes offer a plan for promoting adolescent literacy, with full consideration for the developmental nature of adolescence and how teachers of middle and secondary school students can use the shifts during this phase of life effectively. They also take into account the social and cultural context in which adolescents develop and provide opportunities for teachers to value the uniqueness of each student and the contributions he or she can make to society. In this section each theme is explained. Bill Jones then elaborates on how these themes are realized through his adolescent literacy instruction.

PAL Theme 1: Literacy for Developing Cognition

As explained earlier in this chapter, adolescence is a period of cognitive maturation, including adolescents' developing ability to think about possibilities outside their personal experiences. They question more and draw more logical conclusions from the texts they encounter. Adolescents are starting to become skeptical of things they hear and read, and they don't merely accept every idea presented to them. They realize that just because something appears in print, it doesn't mean it is true. They can also evaluate how well an argument is substantiated or how clearly ideas are stated or represented. As they mature, adolescents are increasingly able to make text-to-world and text-to-text connections, and to explore concepts deeply and broadly. They may also see more connections between text ideas and other forms of representation, such as those between an essay about the Depression in the United States and photographs of this period in American history. They can identify themes that occur in diverse texts and can synthesize ideas well beyond simple recall of facts. These increased cognitive abilities may be strengthened with instructional opportunities that attend to these maturing skills, as described later in this chapter.

PAL Theme 2: Literacy for Self-Assessment and Self-Monitoring

This second feature of the PAL framework is reflective of adolescents' increasing self-analysis and ability to use metacognitive processes while engaged with texts. Because they are more capable of judging their performance, students also need an opportunity to set criteria by which they can be judged. This may be one of the more difficult areas for teachers to accept, because some teachers may view it as leading to their own loss of control. However, for students to design meaningful assessments successfully, they need scaffolded instruction (Vygotsky, 1978), and the teacher's role in this is key. Teachers also need to guide students through metacognitive processes that result in students' recognizing when comprehension has not occurred and how to adjust their approach to the text to fix the problem. In the following section, Bill Jones illustrates how this theme is realized in his classroom.

PAL Theme 3: Literacy for Understanding Multiple Perspectives and Flexible Thinking

With more advanced cognitive abilities, adolescents are better able to consider alternative perspectives in texts, perhaps modifying their original beliefs. Students may be able to appreciate how their own perspectives may have evolved from their culture, knowledge, role, experience, and belief systems; and understand the power literacy holds on individuals (Freire, 1984). Through carefully planned activities, including rich discussions and debate, teachers "can guide students to the realization that there is more than one way to think about something, and that alternative perspectives do not necessarily make one idea right or wrong" (Lewis & Dahbany, 2008, p. 27).

Studying development of cognition among college students, Perry (1970) found that students transition through nine positions regarding authoritativeness of ideas they read and hear, moving from the view that there are clearly right and wrong ideas, answers, or choices, to a position in which ambiguity and multiple possibilities existed. Furthermore, these students eventually realized that although they (like others) had to commit to ideas, their positions could be flexible and conceived of as temporary or as holding true for them until they found preferred alternatives. The development of such flexibility in thought can be facilitated in middle and high school classrooms, as the instructional examples in the next section illustrate.

PAL Theme 4: Literacy for Building Relationships

Whereas peer pressure is a hallmark of adolescence, so too is the importance of developing friendships and learning to interact in positive ways with others. From an economic perspective, according to the National Center for Education Statistics (2005), jobs in the service sector are outpacing many other areas in terms of job growth, and these jobs require strong communication skills. Furthermore, employers depend heavily on the ability of their employees to work collaboratively, and successful collaboration requires effective communication. Increasingly, the workplace requires collaboration between experts from many different fields. As Costa (n.d.) notes,

> Cooperative humans realize that all of us together are more powerful—intellectually and/or physically—than any one individual. Probably the foremost disposition in our post industrial society is the heightened ability to think in concert with others; to find ourselves increasingly more interdependent and sensitive to the needs of others. Problem solving has become so complex that no one person can go it alone. No one has all the data needed to make critical decisions; no one person can consider as many alternatives as several people can. (p. 13)

Building communities in classrooms contributes significantly to students' preparation for working with diverse individuals in other settings, empowering individuals for an independent life. Brainstorming and problem solving with classmates foster critical thinking and respect for the ideas, talents, skills, and values of others, and develop recognition of and appreciation for interdependence. The research on teamwork is clear about its value in several ways. Johnson and Johnson (1986) found persuasive evidence that cooperative teams achieve at higher levels of thought and retain information longer than do students who work quietly as individuals. Students are capable of performing at higher intellectual levels when asked to work in collaborative situations than when asked to work individually (Vygotsky, 1978). Lewis (2008) notes that "Equally, teamwork can provide the means for developing leadership, building relationships, and enhancing communication skills" (p. 330). Bill Jones later suggests strategies for building teamwork in classrooms.

PAL Theme 5: Literacy for Developing Autonomy and Identity

"Teenagers are like people who express a burning desire to be different by dressing exactly alike." This anonymous comment captures one of the tensions during adolescence: the need for acceptance, especially peer acceptance, versus the need to create a personal identity. Adolescents are forming their psychosocial identities (gender, sexual, ethnic), while also making career and educational plans, and trying to gain control of their own lives. We have witnessed teens identifying with particular groups in almost hero-worship-like fashion, some more healthy than others (i.e., church groups vs. gangs), as they are attempt to work out their position in the world, including power relationships within the different groups to which they belong.

The adolescents in our classrooms are waiting to become recognized as mature adults, and we have at least some influence over what kind of adults they will be. It is important that teachers provide a diversity of models in the texts they select for students to study, as well as opportunities for students to discuss them freely.

Using this PAL framework theme, literacy instruction incorporates discussion about differences between students, including ethnic, religious, and value differences, in ways that honor these differences and help students with ego development that is so critical during adolescence. We can guide students through identity areas, where there are so many options: vocation; ideological and relationship values; sex role values and forms of sexual expression; and family structure. We can help students to understand how their personal identities are changing and to work toward building positive self-esteem. Students also benefit if we offer experiences that guide them toward learning how their identities have thus far been formed. A second tension during adolescence occurs between dependence and autonomy. As Steinberg (1999) notes,

> Although we often use the words autonomy and independence interchangeably, in the study of adolescence they mean slightly different things. Independence generally refers to teens' capacity to behave on their own. The growth of independence is surely a part of becoming autonomous during adolescence, but autonomy means more than behaving independently. It also means thinking, feeling, and making moral decisions that are truly your own, rather than following along with what others believe. (p. 276)

Steinberg's explanation suggests that teachers will want to give their adolescent students opportunities for self-governance to develop self-reliance.

PAL Theme 6: Literacy for Building Confidence and Engagement

As adolescents mature, they develop a better understanding of themselves and can identify personal strengths, as well as weaknesses. They are also more able to compare their achievements alongside those of others. Feelings of inadequacy lead to low self-esteem; believing that one knows what to do, and that one has the skills and strategies to accomplish one's goal leads to confidence. This positive view of oneself is especially problematic for struggling adolescent readers, who face increasingly complex texts and concepts in middle and high school classrooms. Clearly, teachers' literacy lessons can contribute in important ways to developing adolescents' confidence in themselves, reciprocally leading students to greater literacy achievement.

Teachers who are aware of individual student strengths can create opportunities for all students to succeed. They can set achievable expectations for students and encourage them to trust themselves as they tackle new learning challenges. Risk taking is critical to literacy success; students must feel confident to guess word meanings, establish relevance, identify point of view, draw conclusions, and make connections with texts. They must also have the confidence to share their ideas with others. Teachers can listen to what their students say and allow them to feel that their ideas are valued. Characteristically, during adolescence, students develop the ability to respond more positively to criticism from their elders, and even more so from their peers. Teachers can contribute to this development by incorporating guided peer critiquing into their literacy instruction.

As Bill Jones illustrates in the next section, each theme outlined in the PAL framework can be realized through carefully planned adolescent literacy instruction.

The Teacher's Voice: Using the PAL Framework in Adolescents' Classrooms

I teach reading in a middle school classroom in a northern, semiurban New Jersey school district. It is a bedroom community of mostly single-family homes and converted multiple-unit dwellings adjacent to a large urban center. The school houses the district's sixth and seventh grades, and serves a mostly minority, highly transient population. Most students are African American and Latino, and 55% come from low-income families who have emigrated from Haiti, Ghana, Nigeria, Jamaica, the West Indies, the Dominican Republic, and Mexico. Quite a few have passed through the district's English as a second language (ESL) program and now attend regular classes.

The 2007 school report card issued by the state of New Jersey indicates that 58% of my district's sixth and seventh graders had a proficient rating on the 2007 Language Arts portion of New Jersey's Statewide Assessment. In an effort to boost test scores, administrators and teachers have created a number of programs for students. Many teachers offer before- and afterschool tutoring for their struggling students. Students also attend test-besting classes three times per week that introduce various test-taking strategies and skills to enable students to perform better on future standardized tests. The district has also established an afterschool program that offers small-group instruction by its teaching staff. Furthermore, the school's Title I program allows parents to enroll their students in tutoring programs offered by private firms.

Four of my reading and language arts (writing) classes are heterogeneous, with students of varying abilities. The fifth comprises gifted and talented students. In all classes we read different genres in a literature anthology textbook that I supplement with novels, magazines, newspapers, pamphlets, and other texts. My instruction is differentiated, based on students' needs, interests and skills. The PAL framework calls for teachers to organize their literacy instruction around six themes of adolescent psychosocial development. Here I describe how each PAL theme is addressed through instructional strategies I have used successfully with my sixth- and seventh-grade students who meet with me for 43 minutes each school day.

Theme 1 in the Classroom: Literacy for Developing Cognition

As discussed earlier in this chapter, adolescent readers are developing their ability to analyze texts. They realize that reading is an interactive process that requires them to think about what they have experienced, read, heard, or seen, and to question claims made in texts. They also have begun to expand their capacity to dissect arguments and evaluate multiple viewpoints.

ANTICIPATION GUIDES

An anticipation guide (Herber, 1978) is an effective prereading and postreading activity that promotes reflection. The guide is a set of teacher-created statements that probe students' knowledge or beliefs about a topic and that may be revised after students read text on this topic. For example, before my classes read *Stargirl*, by Jerry Spinelli (2000), I ask students to react to a number of statements about peer pressure and its relationship to self-image, two of the book's prevailing themes. After students respond to each statement, we discuss how those themes impact adolescents, both in and out of school. I redistribute the guides after we finish the novel. Students then reread the statements to determine whether any of their opinions about the topics have changed. Quite often I hear comments such as "I still don't believe peer pressure impacts me that much; I will always be my own person." But anticipation guides do have an impact on many students' thinking. I was surprised to hear one student say, "I never realized how much what others say affects me, but it's true; I always dress like my friends to be cool. I would never dress crazy like Stargirl. Everyone would make fun of me." This comment came from a young man who didn't seem to be interested in the book but was obviously paying attention to the characters and how they reacted to each other. More importantly, he was able to associate a literary theme to his own life and make a personal connection to the book.

INQUIRY QUESTIONS

The inquiry questions strategy (Unrau, 2004) has students formulate their own questions about what they are reading. Recently my students developed their own inquiry questions while they were reading *The Skin I'm In* by Sharon Flake (1998). As part of an author study assignment, the students had to write questions they would ask the author about the characters and the events that take place in the book. I provided an Inquiry Questions Guide that included sample questions, such as "How does the author's personal and cultural background tie into the storyline?" and "Why did the author choose to write this novel?" Students had to generate questions about matters related to the book, and each question had to involve deep thinking, and not just simple recall of facts. They then searched for answers to their questions, using as a starting point a list of websites I supplied that contained information about the author.

Many students liked this activity because it gave them an opportunity to learn more about the writer of a book they enjoyed. One of my students said that she found reading about Flake so interesting that she bought another of the writer's books to read over spring break. I was also impressed by the complexity of the questions the students created. Many focused on the topics of discrimination, bullying, and urban life—three themes featured in the novel. One question concerned a character whose face was discolored by a skin condition. The student wanted to ask the author whether she would ever recommend that such a person undergo plastic surgery. Another student wanted to know why Flake thought bullying was such a pervasive problem, despite the proliferation of character education and antibullying programs in schools. Still another student asked why the author wrote books for an adolescent audience, and what impact she hoped to have on her readers. I thought all of these questions illustrated higher-level thinking skills and demonstrated that students not only were making personal connections to the text but also were connecting the text to real-life issues and the world around them.

QUESTIONS TAXONOMY

Bloom's taxonomy (1956), updated by Anderson and Krathwohl, (2001), offers categories of questions, moving from very basic recall questions to those that require more sophisticated thinking. The Analysis, Synthesis, and Evaluation components of the taxonomy are particularly helpful for creating classroom activities that stretch students' cognitive development. The Analysis feature calls on students to identify and comprehend elements of a process. My students might compare and contrast the writing style of two authors from the same time period, such as Paul Zindel and Walter Dean Myers. The Synthesis element calls for opportunities that foster original, creative thinking. In my class, students create video news reports, board games, or reader's theater plays about topics and concepts discussed in class. The Evaluation facet of the taxonomy requires students to determine how closely a concept or idea is consistent with personal standards or values. I incorporate this with student activities such as critiquing a government policy (e.g., the recent gun ownership ruling by the U.S. Supreme Court), then defending their personal stance by creating an alternative policy of their own. I keep the taxonomy in mind while I plan instruction to ensure that my students have opportunities to develop higher-level thinking skills.

DRAW

DRAW (Draw, Read, Attend, and Write; Agnew, 2000) is one more classroom activity that promotes cognitive development. With DRAW, students work in small groups to discuss a piece of literature and respond to questions that involve critical thinking. As the first step, a member of each group draws from a container a question the teacher has prepared. After group members read the assigned article, they answer their question, then report their answer back to the class. This procedure promotes class discussion, and students are expected to attend to the discussion, because they are responsible for learning the information that each group presents.

I often use DRAW when my students are reading informational texts or nonfiction articles. In one instance, I asked my students to read an article about bats and how they are often misunderstood because of long-believed myths and legends. After students learn that bats are not the dangerous creatures that popular legend has made them out to be, each student group is asked to answer a different inferential question. One group is asked, "Now that you know that bats are friendly animals that can often be trained, would you be willing to adopt one as a pet? Why or why not?" Another is asked, "How can informed people help save bats from the harm they face in light of the public misperception about them?" When I write these questions, I try to make them as thought-provoking as possible to stir student interest. Once the groups receive their questions, students have 15 minutes to formulate a written response, after which each group shares its question and response. Others are encouraged either to voice their support for the group's response or challenge the answer. A lively discussion often ensues. This process is repeated until each group is given an opportunity to present its question and response, and receive feedback from the other students. DRAW not only encourages critical thinking but it also enhances collaboration and increases student motivation. Postactivity remarks support this view; students comment that they not only learn new and interesting information, but they also have fun while doing it. One student in my class summed it up rather succinctly when she wrote, "BATS RULE!"

PROBLEMATIC PERSPECTIVES

Improving problem-solving skills is a large part of critical thinking abilities, and teachers need to guide their students through this process. Problematic Perspectives (Vacca & Vacca, 2005) presents a problem and asks students to solve it, while they work within a group. This activity can be used for a prereading assignment or as an extension exercise during reading to create student interest in the text. For instance, before I have my students read an excerpt from the nonfiction book *Exploring the Titanic* by Robert Ballard (1988), I have them consider a situation in which they are on a sinking ship. The scenario calls for them to collect 10 items that they and five other survivors will need as they board a lifeboat in the middle of the frigid Atlantic Ocean. Each group has 15 minutes to create this list and afterward must justify the reason for each item. Members from other groups have the opportunity to comment or to challenge items on their classmates' lists. As with the previous DRAW activity, Problematic Perspectives often generates a spirited class discussion. In fact, in one instance, students argued whether old-fashioned flares or modern-day laser pointers would be more appropriate to bring onto the raft. I believe this strategy not only builds problem-solving and critical thinking proficiencies, but the group work also allows students to learn about negotiation and collaboration, two important life skills.

Theme 2 in the Classroom: Literacy for Self-Assessment and Self-Monitoring

As noted earlier, as students move into adolescence, their ability to use self-analysis and metacognitive processes increases. Teachers can encourage this maturation through instruction that has students evaluate or judge their own performance. Such self-assessments empower students to take ownership of their learning and become better students.

EXIT PASSES

One of the easiest ways to involve students in assessing their own learning is through *exit passes* or *exit slips*. Fisher and Frey (2004) explain that these can effectively document student learning, give students opportunities to think about what they have learned and how it can be used in the real world, help students reflect on their learning process, and enable teachers to evaluate the effectiveness of their instruction. At the end of a class period, I ask students to write on exit slips one or two pieces of information that they have learned during class, as well as any questions they may have about the subject that was discussed. They might also note any ideas about the topic that occurred to them and that they did not get to mention during class time, an idea that was particularly interesting to them, or something related to the topic they would like to explore further. This practice has students review what they have learned and also assists the teacher in determining what concepts or strategies need to be reviewed. Sometimes I find that students have misinterpreted something we discussed, and without using exit slips, this might not be so readily apparent to me. Student responses on exit slips can also point me in new directions for discussion or class projects.

A variation of the exit slip that I use is the *admit slip*. The procedure is the same, but students complete their writing at the start of class or as an "admission ticket" to class. On the admit slip students might comment on a homework assignment or something we discussed the previous day. Sometimes my students use these to make connections between what we have done in class and something they read, saw, or heard outside of class.

SUMMARY SHEETS

This form of self-assessment requires more detailed responses than exit slips. During the last 10 minutes of class, students list three main points about the subject discussed in class and any new vocabulary that was introduced, along with a definition, if possible. Because *summary sheets* are completed individually, they provide both student and teacher specific information about learning that has occurred and concepts that have to be revisited during the next class. This activity gives students practice in summarization and in distinguishing between major and minor details. I return these sheets to students, so that they will have them for future reference, perhaps as study aids before an exam.

In the book *I Read It, But I Don't Get It*, Chris Tovani (2000) suggests using a type of summary sheet during sustained silent reading (SSR), and I have modified her suggestions to fit my students and classroom purposes. In the top section of my sheet, students identify what they have read, perhaps a newspaper, magazine, or book, along with page or section numbers. The middle section asks students to write a brief paragraph summarizing this text. The bottom section of the form asks students to make text-to-self, text-to-text, or text-to-world connections. This SSR form serves a number of purposes. First, it allows students to self-assess what they have read and assists them in identifying connections they have made, which boosts their comprehension and interpretation of the literature.

We know that students, especially struggling students, often need explicit instruction in summarization. They have difficulty distinguishing between important and unimportant ideas, and tend to confuse paraphrasing with summarizing. Sometimes they critique ideas rather than summarizing them. By providing explicit instruction in summarization, along with opportunities for students to practice the skill through these self-assessment tools, I am able to determine whether further instruction is needed, while students simultaneously monitor their learning.

LEARNING LOGS

I encourage students to think of a *learning log* as a diary or a journal, but with a focus on their literacy activities in school. They write about what they have learned in class, why they think it is important or not important, and how they can apply the learned concepts to other classes and to life in general. For example, if, after reading a novel, the class discusses the personality traits of different characters, students might write about that as their daily entry in their learning log. They might also write about how they felt that knowledge would assist them in analyzing characters in other novels and, in essence, make them better readers. Sometimes they explain how the character gave them insight about someone they know and don't understand, such as a parent, sibling, or friend. While reading the book *Seedfolks* by Paul Fleischman (1997), my student Amir wrote about a personal connection he made regarding one of the characters and his own grandmother. He noted that he never understood why his grandmother was still afraid to go outside at night, years after she was robbed. His thinking changed, however, after he read about the character in the novel named Sae Young, an older woman who owns a dry cleaning store and recalls how she lived in fear for years after being robbed at gunpoint. Amir wrote in his learning log that he never realized it could take months and even years for a person to recover from such an incident. But after reading Sae Young's personal account, Amir was finally able to understand how fear can paralyze a person for a long time. He also wrote that he hoped he could help his grandmother become less afraid, much the way Sae Young was able to in the book.

I generally assign learning logs when the class is reading about important events, such as the civil rights movement, or learning about new reading strategies or study skills, and collect them a few days later, so I can comment on students' work, get a glimpse into what they are learning, and find out how they feel about the new topic. This feedback helps me to determine whether I need to redirect my efforts and alter my lessons to fit the needs of my students. In one instance, a student used her log to express her frustration at being unable to decipher analogies, despite numerous class lessons on the subject. Although I knew Kimmie didn't like solving the word comparisons, it wasn't until I read her personal account that I realized I needed to take additional steps to assist her. I provided additional instructions and assigned Kimmie a study buddy, a fellow student who was proficient at solving analogies and was willing to help. Eventually, Kimmie was able to decode analogies successfully on her own. Without learning logs, I might not have met Kimmie's needs.

COLLABORATION FOR SELF-ASSESSMENT

Even though self-assessment is usually considered an individual effort, that doesn't have to be the case. Collaboration and group activities can play an active role in self-assessment. Before a test or a quiz, I often have my students team up to review the concepts on which they will be evaluated. This allows students to assess what they know compared to their classmates' knowledge. It also helps them learn from their fellow students and gain insight into how others gain information and understanding.

JEOPARDY AS A SELF-ASSESSMENT TOOL

My students also self-assess during a collaborative game of *Jeopardy* that I often use for review before a test or exam. However, unlike the TV version, I have my students create the questions for the game. A few days before the game, the class decides what categories should be included in the review. I then place students in different groups, where they write questions for each category, after which I select questions that I believe are most pertinent for review. On the day of the game, the class is divided into two teams that play against each other, using a board that has questions compiled from all of the groups. I find that students almost always enjoy this activity. Giving the students the opportunity to write the questions gives them a personal stake in the review process, and they often create probing questions that challenge their classmates to think critically.

Theme 3 in the Classroom: Literacy for Understanding Multiple Perspectives and Flexible Thinking

This theme calls for teachers to conduct lessons that promote *critical literacy*, a thinking process that is essential for educating citizens of a free and democratic society. Through such lessons, students expand their thoughts and opinions and take into consideration other viewpoints on controversial issues. Classroom teachers can promote critical literacy by having students utilize different types of texts to analyze and evaluate alternative viewpoints, as well as recognize their own point of view on an issue. Teachers who rely too heavily on a single textbook may find that it doesn't adequately address a controversial topic, but instead gives a one-sided view of a multidimensional subject. This practice shortchanges students by giving them a biased view of the world around them.

DIVERSE AND AUTHENTIC TEXTS

My students are introduced to diverse viewpoints through multiple primary and secondary resources, including newspapers, magazines, journals, novels, pamphlets, film, and other types of texts. For instance, when studying the woman's suffrage movement, I often bring in newspaper accounts, magazine articles, photographs, and other material to supplement the narratives in our textbook and provide multiple viewpoints on the topic. Viewing authentic literature, such as copies of newspaper articles and pamphlets from that time period, as well as photographs of the most significant individuals involved in the movement, makes the subject more real for students and allows them to see the issue in a different light. For example, after reading the book of short stories called *The Circuit* by Francisco Jiménez (1997), a narrative that recounts the trial and tribulations of a migrant farm family, we discuss U.S. immigration policy. To prepare students for this conversation, we read essays by people who support a more liberal immigration policy, and by those who want to keep a tighter reign on the U.S. borders. We discuss how immigration impacts different aspects of the country, such as the economy, public services, taxes, and the labor market. The discussion culminates in students debating the positive and negative aspects of current U.S. immigration policy.

USING MUSIC

Popular music and familiar songs are woven into my lessons to promote critical literacy. Music that connects to adolescents' lives can be an effective means of getting students to consider complex matters. For instance, when my class studies the work of Dr. Martin Luther King, Jr. and the civil rights movement, I introduce my students to the song "Pride (In the Name of Love)" by the rock band U2 (1984). I also use the song, which pays homage to the work of Dr. King, to discuss issues my students might consider worth dying for, such as going to war to fight for their country or euthanasia. Such discussions often result in spirited debate as students probe deeply inside themselves and begin to question societal norms and government policies. I feel these explorations of ideas are important, because students need to learn that such questioning is a vital part of a free and democratic society.

COMMUNITY SURVEYS

This strategy calls for students to investigate a controversial topic by interviewing community residents about the issue. We design the survey by considering possible points of view and framing one or more questions that allow for responses that reflect diverse opinions. Students gather information from people of all ages, races, and walks of life. If students find that they cannot get a good cross-section of opinion, they can widen their base of respondents by going outside of the local community. Recently, my students conducted such a survey after they read a biography about the early life of President Abraham Lincoln. Because he is credited with holding the country together during the Civil War and many historians consider him one of the nation's greatest Presidents, I thought it would be the perfect time to discuss current politics. Students asked at least 10 community members, "Do you believe the upcoming presidential election will have any direct impact on your life?," and compiled their findings in a report. This activity gave them an opportunity to hear myriad opinions about a topic that evokes strong opinions and to synthesize this information to formulate their own opinions about the topic.

Theme 4 in the Classroom:
Literacy for Building Relationships

Research informs us that adolescents are social beings who learn best when working with their peers and others. We also know that teamwork is key to success, whether in higher education or workplace environments. Thus, students need to practice frequently their collaborative skills for working with groups, and cooperative learning is one of the cornerstones of the PAL framework. A wide range of activities can assist students in building their relationship skills while simultaneously developing their literacy.

DAY PLANNER ACTIVITY

I first heard of this strategy while attending a workshop, and I have been using the day planner ever since. In this cooperative learning strategy, students select four class members with whom they will individually address certain questions based on the topic we are studying. Students first draw a clock in their notebooks, or day planner. Inside the face of the clock they write the numbers 12, 3, 6, and 9, and they draw a line either underneath or by the side of each number. Once students have created their day planners, they make appointments with classmates for the four times specified on their clocks. After approximately 2 minutes for appointment scheduling, I give students a question to ponder and tell them to meet with one of their appointments. Rather than moving the activity along in a clockwise fashion, I randomly select a meeting time, thus identifying the first partner with whom a student will meet to discuss the first question; this creates an atmosphere of spontaneity. After a few minutes, I tell the students to get ready for their next question and to meet with their next appointment. This process continues until all of the questions that need to be addressed have been discussed. Questions are designed to promote discussion and to address adolescents' common concerns. For instance, in a recent day planner activity, after the class read an article about Internet safety and expressed some concern about the topic, students were asked to discuss the kinds of precautions they should take when they take part in instant messaging, visit chat rooms, and log onto social networking websites. The students were also asked to consider what parents, schools, and Web server system administrators can do to protect young people when they go online. This topic spurred a thought-provoking class session in which students expressed their desire to associate freely with others online and how they felt about their parents' concerns and possible restrictions on teen Internet usage. It also helped to develop relationships among class members, especially for students who are shy at first, or who do not have many friends in class, because the day planner provides opportunities for them to share ideas and meet other students.

TEXT MESSAGING

Most students today are familiar with cell phones and text messaging, so I sometimes have my students create text messages on a cell phone template to respond to a scene from a novel. For instance, after reading a scene about an incident in the school cafeteria in the book *The Skin I'm In* (Flake, 1998), my students wrote text messages to friends describing what they visualized while reading the book. In another technology-driven activity, students pose as characters from a novel or short story and go online to send instant messages to a student who is posing as another character, as they did for *The Skin I'm In*, wherein they simulated an online conversation between two of the lead characters. Their messages deal with a scene from the story in which one girl tries to convince another not to report her for her part in setting fire to a teacher's classroom.

STRUCTURED ACADEMIC CONTROVERSY TO BUILD CONSENSUS

Because my students will encounter the need for teamwork, including work with diverse individuals, whether in college or the workforce, I often arrange class activities that require listening (and respecting) multiple viewpoints of classmates. Structured Academic Controversy works particularly well, because it requires eventual consensus among group members. Developed by Johnson and Johnson (1995), in this activity, students investigate the different views surrounding a controversial topic, synthesize information on the subject, and develop a consensus position. Reaching consensus is key to effective teamwork.

Recently, after my students read an article about renewable resources, they participated in a Structured Academic Controversy activity originally designed for teachers participating in professional development in Macedonia (Lewis, 2004). After talking about some of the decisions that planners for the international Olympic Games had to make, my students had to decide whether the next Olympic Games should use paper or Styrofoam cups for refreshments. First, I divided the students into groups of four, then assigned each student a partner within his or her group with whom to read an article containing ideas related to the question. One pair was to find support for the paper cup, whereas the other had to find support for the Styrofoam cup. The short reading selection included principles of both chemistry and economics related to the choice of cups. After reading the material, the partners wrote a list of reasons that supported their assigned position. Once the pairs completed their lists, each presented its position to the other pair, with as much conviction as possible. Each had to challenge the opposing pair's list of reasons and to defend its own reasoning from attack.

To the surprise of the students, each pair then had to change positions on the question, such that the pair that once supported paper cups was now in favor of Styrofoam cups, and vice versa, with each pair again making a list of reasons from the text supporting the new position, and presenting and defending the new position, to the opposing pair. After both pairs argued for the opposing positions, each team of four had to reach consensus on which cup they would choose for the Olympic games and write a brief report advocating their consensus position.

Once each team finished its report, the class was polled to determine how many groups supported each type of cup, including their reasons for their choices. After each point was written on a comparison chart, we discussed how reading and collaboration helped each team with decision making, and how consensus building might be a useful skill in adult life.

Theme 5 in the Classroom: Literacy for Developing Autonomy and Identity

In their study of third, fourth, and fifth graders, Skinner and Belmont (1993) found that students who believe that teachers are providing meaningful choices for them show an increase in effort, attention, and interest in classroom reading and writing tasks. In an environment that supports autonomy, adolescents have the opportunity to choose what they wish to do, such as which books to read during independent reading time, or which research projects to undertake, while teachers provide guidance that is informational rather than controlling (Ryan, Connell, & Deci, 1985). As adolescents struggle for autonomy, they are motivated when they recognize that the locus of control can be internal rather than external. I address autonomy in my literacy lessons throughout the year in a variety of activities that include student choice. We move back and forth from whole-class to small-group to independent assignments.

JIGSAW TO DEVELOP AUTONOMY FOR ALL STUDENTS

Through scaffolded instruction, struggling students feel competent to take on learning challenges that they might otherwise be reluctant to pursue. Once students are able to perform a task with a small group, they then have the opportunity to demonstrate learning independently. One example of such an approach is the Jigsaw activity, first created by Elliot Aronson and his graduate students for use in Austin, Texas, public schools, and later described by Aronson and Bridgeman (1979). In Jigsaw, students start with a home group, which is responsible for learning a complete reading assignment. The home group is then separated into expert or jigsaw groups, with one member from each home group assigned to an expert group. Each expert group is given responsibility for learning and being prepared to teach its home group a portion of the text. For instance, the students in expert group *A* may be responsible the first two pages of a text, while students in expert group *B* have the next two pages, and so on. Expert or jigsaw groups might summarize their reading section or write five interesting facts from what they have read, or they might create a visual to represent the information. Once each jigsaw group is finished, students go back to their home groups to explain what they have learned from their respective portion of the text.

I recently used Jigsaw with informational text on music, software, and video piracy via illegal Internet downloads. After dividing the class into home groups of four students, I assigned each student a jigsaw group. The first of these groups read about the proliferation of illegal downloads through the Internet; the second read about the repercussions of violating copyright laws through online piracy; the third, about how authorities use sophisticated technology to track down folks who abuse the Internet for such practices; and the fourth, about how people may legally download material through subscription fees, and so forth. Each jigsaw or expert group had to list five important facts from its assigned section, then students returned to the home groups to share the information they gathered in their jigsaw groups. My students, especially the struggling readers, enjoy participating in this scaffolded approach, because they do not feel overwhelmed by reading large portions of text and they are encouraged to work together to comprehend reading material they might otherwise find difficult to learn. It is a unique opportunity for them to be perceived as "experts." All students are also developing their identities as they shift back and forth between the role of observer and active contributor, from listener to leader.

LITERACY RÉSUMÉS FOR DEFINING ONESELF

One way to integrate identity development into literacy lessons is to have students create their own literacy résumés. Moore and Onofrey (2007) note that literacy résumés give students the opportunity to "celebrate their reading and writing and promote their literacy identities"

(p. 290). Student résumés may include information from a number of areas, including titles of books, magazines, and other literature that students like to read, to the topics that interest them. They may also summarize students' reading history, information on how often they read, the reasons why they read, and a synopsis on their daily reading habits. Creating a literacy résumés also makes students more aware of the roles that reading and writing play in their lives. Other kinds of résumés (e.g., for part-time jobs or volunteer work) provide an additional avenue for my students to assess what they have done and to identify strengths, as well as potential areas for personal development.

GOAL SHEETS TO FOSTER STUDENT AUTONOMY, SELF-DIRECTION, AND IDENTITY

The goal sheets I've created ask students to set literacy goals for themselves. For example, goals may include reading one book per marking period, developing more effective comprehension strategies, or increasing vocabulary through word games and other word power methods.

Goal attainment should be measurable and may be mutually agreed upon by individual students and their teachers. I conference with each student to refine the goals and standards for his or her success. Some students are overly ambitious, and it is self-defeating if their yardsticks for measuring achievement are unrealistic. Thus, we keep the number of goals to a minimum and make sure that all are achievable; we also establish a time frame for reaching them. At the end of that designated time period, the students and I conference to determine progress, identify new goals, and set new time frames, thereby maintaining momentum and motivation. When students achieve what they have set out to do on the goal sheets, they feel a sense of accomplishment and are ready to complete new challenges. They recognize that they are able to take control of some aspects of their lives and are more clear about what they want to do, and how to accomplish it.

READER RESPONSE LOGS

Another activity aimed at advancing student identity involves using *reader response logs*. Unlike the previously described learning logs, reader response logs are used by students to write reactions to text. Pages in student notebooks are divided into two columns: On the left, students note ideas from the text that caught their attention; on the right, students write their reaction or comments about the reading. In addition to responding to specific ideas the text, students might comment on aspects of the text, such as illustrations or other graphics, conclusions the author draws, definitions given, symbolic expressions used, or conclusions drawn. Sometimes I give students specific questions that address identity formation, such as "Which character is most like–unlike you? Why or how might you have solved the problem faced by (character)?" Students may also consider ways in which the text reminds them of other things they have heard, read, or seen. Furthermore, it is possible to consider the texts from other perspectives, such as that of a younger–older person, someone of the opposite sex, or someone in a position of authority. This activity encourages students to think about what the text means to them both personally and intellectually as they make distinctions between their own identities and those of others. I also encourage my students to vary the types of responses they include, and suggest that they might respond by illustrating their ideas or writing a response poem, thus making the assignment more creative and giving students more opportunities to experiment with writing genre.

Theme 6 in the Classroom: Literacy for Building Confidence and Engagement

As noted earlier in this chapter, research suggests that students who are presented with materials that engage their interest will be motivated to continue reading. Relevance of curricular materials and topics is essential to student success, requiring teachers to know about their students' interests (Greenleaf, Jiménez, & Roller, 2002).

INTEREST INVENTORIES

Teachers can determine their students' interests through class discussions, reflective journals, and interest inventories. At the beginning of each school year, my incoming students complete an *interest inventory,* in which they list the types of materials they like to read, subjects they like to read about, and their favorite authors. The inventory also asks students to list their favorite TV shows, movies, sports, and musical groups. This information enables me to develop lessons that feature texts that are relevant to my students, that motivate them to read and learn more about topics or stories that appeal to them, and to be sure that I have material in my classroom library that appeals to diverse student interests.

Wigfield (2004) notes that teachers who create opportunities for students to choose among assignments and texts find students less resistant to completing their work. As teachers, we often forget that adolescents live in a world of rules—*take out the garbage, clean your room, take your little sister to the mall with you,* and many others—imposed on them by adults. Teachers can give their students a sense of empowerment by allowing them to make their own decisions in the classroom. For instance, when assigning homework, I often give students the option of answering even- or odd-numbered questions from our anthology. At other times, I may provide a series of questions I've developed or that have come from students' learning logs or class discussion, and students choose half of the questions to answer. When we create projects, students have several options. After students finished reading the novel *Stargirl* (Spinelli, 2000), for instance, they could either choose an alternative name for themselves and write a narrative about the new moniker (Stargirl isn't the main character's real name), create an interactive Venn diagram explaining the similarities and differences between themselves and Stargirl, design a pseudo MySpace or Facebook page for Stargirl, or produce a new line of greeting cards to reflect Stargirl's personal credo of love and thoughtfulness for others. I also give my students a voice in how they will be graded on the project by having them participate in the creation of an assessment rubric. Since adopting this philosophy of choice, I find that more of my students complete their assignments and, better yet, more students seem to enjoy doing them.

Teachers have choice in the types of classroom activities that students do, and, to be honest, some are more engaging than others for students. The inclusion of technology in literacy activities has been found to contribute in important ways to student motivation. Kamil, Intrator, and Kim (2000) found that when computers are used in literacy activities such as reading and writing, student participation and collaboration increase. My students work on computer programs such as Study Island (*www.studyisland.com*), a program that provides interactive exercises and gauges their literacy skills through various assignments and quizzes. We use the technology to do research projects, to produce final drafts, and to do e-mail and text messaging activities described earlier. Later chapters in this volume offer many other possibilities for infusing technology into adolescent literacy instruction.

Concluding Thoughts

Since the inception of No Child Left Behind, we have heard many criticisms that there is too much "teaching to the test." We wholeheartedly agree. In fact, what we argue for is teaching to the student, which requires deep knowledge of student development. We have described how understanding adolescent psychosocial development can be used to organize instruction in developmentally considerate ways. The PAL framework outlines six themes that, if utilized for planning literacy instruction, ensure that each aspect of the adolescent's psychosocial development is addressed. As our teaching examples illustrate, each theme lends itself to teaching many strategies that promote students' literacy achievements. But strategies should not be taught in isolated fashion or simply because they are needed "for the test." They are useful because of what they offer to adolescents in helping with text comprehension, and because they take into account adolescents' maturing cognitive, emotional, and social needs. We have selected only a few strategies for illustrative purpose. There are many others, of course, that address PAL's six themes. The point is to think about students' development first, and then decide which of the entire range of effective strategies also meet students' developmental needs.

Working to improve adolescents' literacy offers teachers myriad opportunities, as well as challenges. By understanding why adolescents behave and think as they do we can be more considerate of them when we teach. Our teaching will be more needs-driven, and our students' literacy will mature to the point that it will serve them well in adulthood. We believe that teaching to the student should not be an option.

Questions for Reflection

1. The PAL framework includes six themes. Which themes do you believe are the most important in improving adolescent literacy? Why?

2. In what ways might supervisors or administrators assist in advancing the PAL framework in today's secondary classrooms? What impact would their involvement have on advancing literacy skills among students?

3. The second half of this chapter outlines a number of classroom activities correlated with the PAL framework. Which of these do you foresee implementing in your classroom? What other activities would fit into the PAL framework?

4. Today's adolescents are often bombarded through various media with messages that include profanity, graphic violence, and explicit sexual images. How does exposure to those messages impact today's literacy activities with students? Should teachers take steps to counter those messages through literacy experiences? Or do you think teachers should somehow accept those messages as part of the real world and try to incorporate their spirit into classroom lessons? Explain your viewpoint.

References

Agnew, M. L. (2000). DRAW: A motivational reading comprehension strategy for disaffected readers. *Journal of Adolescent and Adult Literacy, 43*(6), 574–576.

Allington, R. L., & Cunningham, P. (1996). *Schools that work.* New York: HarperCollins.

Anderson, L. W., & Krathwohl, D. R. (Eds.). (2001). *A taxonomy for learning, teaching, and assessing: A revision of Bloom's taxonomy of educational objectives.* New York: Longman.

Aronson, E., & Bridgeman, D. (1979). Jigsaw groups and the desegregated classroom: In pursuit of common goals. *Personality and Social Psychology Bulletin, 5,* 438–446.

Ballard, R. (1988). *Exploring the titanic.* Toronto: Scholastic/Madison Press.

Bandura, A. (1978). The self system in reciprocal determinism. *American Psychologist, 33,* 344–358.

Bandura, A. (1986). *Social foundations of thought and action: A social cognitive theory.* Englewood Cliffs, NJ: Prentice-Hall.

Bloom, B. S. (Ed.). (1956). *Taxonomy of educational objectives. Handbook I: Cognitive domain.* New York: David McKay.

Burns, M. S., Griffin, P., & Snow, C. E. (Eds.). (1999). *Starting out right: A guide to promoting children's reading success.* Washington, DC: National Academy Press.

Clay, M. (1991). *Becoming literate: The construction of inner control.* Portsmouth, NH: Heinemann.

Costa, A. L. (n.d.). *Components of a well developed thinking skills program.* Retrieved January 14, 2007, from *www.newhorizons.org/strategies/thinking/costa2.htm.*

Erikson, E. H. (1968). *Identity, youth and crisis.* New York: Norton.

Fisher, D., & Frey, N. (2004). *Improving adolescent literacy: Strategies at work.* Upper Saddle River, NJ: Merrill/Prentice-Hall.

Flake, S. (1998). *The skin I'm in.* New York: Jump at the Sun.

Flavell, J. H. (1963). *The developmental psychology of Jean Piaget.* Princeton, NJ: Van Nostrand Reinhold.

Fleischman, P. (1997). *Seedfolks.* New York: HarperCollins.

Friere, P. (1984). *Pedagogy of the oppressed.* New York: Continuum.

Greenleaf, G. L., Jiménez, R. T., & Roller, C. M. (2002). Reclaiming secondary reading interventions: From limited to rich conceptions, from narrow to broad conversations. *Reading Research Quarterly, 37*(4), 484–496.

Gottfried, A. E. (1990). Academic intrinsic motivation in young elementary school children. *Journal of Educational Psychology, 82*(3), 525–538.

Guthrie, J. T., Wigfield, A., & Perencevich, K. C. (Eds.). (2004). *Motivating reading comprehension: Concept-oriented reading instruction.* Mahwah, NJ: Erlbaum.

Hall, G. S. (1916). *Adolescence* (2 vols.). New York: Appleton.

Herber, H. L. (1978). *Teaching reading in the content areas* (2nd ed.). Englewood Cliffs, NJ: Prentice-Hall.

Hidi, S., & Harackiewicz, J. M. (2000). Motivating the academically unmotivated: A critical issue for the 21st century. *Review of Educational Research, 70,* 151–179.

Holdaway, D. (1979). *The foundations of literacy.* Sydney, Australia: Ashton Scholastic.

Howe, N., & Strauss, W. (2000). *Millennials rising: The next great generation.* New York: Vantage Books.

International Reading Association & the National Council of Teachers of English. (1996). *Standards for the English language arts.* Newark, DE and Urbana, IL: Author.

Jiménez, F. (1997). *The circuit: Stories from the life of a migrant child.* Albuquerque: University of New Mexico Press.

Johnson, D. W., & Johnson, R. T. (1986). *Circles of learning: Cooperation in the classroom.* Edina, MN: Interaction.

Johnson, D. W., & Johnson, R. T. (1995). *Creative controversy: Intellectual challenge in the classroom* (3rd ed.). Edina, MN: Interaction.

Kamil, M. L., Intrator, S., & Kim, H. S. (2000). The effects of other technologies on literacy and literacy learning. In M. Kamil, P. Mosenthal, P. D. Pearson, & R. Barr (Eds.), *Handbook of reading research* (Vol. III, pp. 773–778). Mahwah, NJ: Erlbaum.

Kellough, R. D., & Kellough, N. G. (2008). *Teaching young adolescents: Methods and resources for middle grades teaching* (5th ed.). Upper Saddle River, NJ: Pearson/Merrill/Prentice-Hall.

Lewis, J. (Ed.). (2004). *Learning through projects* (Module 2, Secondary Education Activity Project). Newark, DE: International Reading Association/ USAID.

Lewis, J. (2008). "But I'm not going to college!": Developing adolescents' literacy for the 21st-century workplace. In S. Lenski & J. Lewis (Eds.), *Reading success for struggling adolescent learners* (pp. 311–340). New York: Guilford Press.

Lewis, J., & Dahbany, A. (2008). What do we know about the adolescent learner and what does it mean for literacy instruction? In S. Lenski & J. Lewis (Eds.), *Reading success for struggling adolescent learners* (pp. 9–36). New York: Guilford Press.

Manning, M. L. (2002). *Developmentally appropriate middle level schools* (2nd ed.). Olney, MD: Association for Childhood Education International.

McGee, L. M., & Richgels, D. J. (1996). *Literacy beginnings: Supporting young readers and writers.* Needham Heights, MA: Allyn & Bacon.

Moore, D., & Onofrey, K. (2007). Fostering literate academic identities during the first days of school. In J. Lewis & G. Moorman (Eds.), *Adolescent literacy instruction: Policies and practices* (p. 286–303). Newark, DE: International Reading Association.

National Center for Education Statistics. (2005, July). Indicator 20: School completion. In *Youth indicators, 2005: Trends in the well-being of American youth* (NCES 2005-050). Washington, DC: Author. Retrieved February 6, 2007, from *nces. edu.gov/programs/youthindicators/Indicators.asp?PubPageNumber = 20.*

Perry, W. G., Jr. (1970). *Forms of intellectual and ethical development in the college years: A scheme.* New York: Holt, Rinehart & Winston.

Piaget, J. (2000). *The psychology of the child.* New York: Basic Books. (Original work published 1969)

Pitcher, S. M., Albright, L. K., DeLaney, C. J., Walker, N. T., Seunarinesingh, K., Mogge, S., et al. (2007). Assessing adolescents' motivation to read. *Journal of Adolescent and Adult Literacy, 50*(5), 378–396.

Ryan, A. M., & Pintrich, P. R. (1997). "Should I ask for help?": The role of motivation and attitudes in adolescent's help seeking in math class. *Journal of Educational Psychology, 89,* 329–341.

Ryan, R. M., Connell, J. P., & Deci, E. L. (1985). A motivational analysis of self-determination and self-regulation in education. In C. Ames & R. Ames (Eds.), *Research on motivation in education: Vol. 2. The classroom milieu* (pp. 13–51). New York: Academic Press.

Scales, P. C. (2003). Characteristics of young adolescents. In National Middle School Association (Ed.), *This we believe: Successful schools for young adolescents* (pp. 43–51). Westerville, OH: National Middle School Association.

Skinner, E. A., & Belmont, M. J. (1993). Motivation in the classroom: Reciprocal effects of teacher behavior and student engagement across the school year. *Journal of Educational Psychology, 85,* 571–581.

Spinelli, J. (2000). *Stargirl.* New York: Knopf.

Steinberg, L. (1999). *Adolescence* (5th ed.). Boston: McGraw-Hill.

Strickland, D. S., & Morrow, L. M. (1988). New perspectives on young children learning to read and write. *Reading Teacher, 42*(1), 70–71.

Teale, W., & Sulzby, E. (1986). *Emergent literacy: Writing and reading.* Norwood, NJ: Ablex.

Tovani, C. (2000). *I read it, but I don't get it.* Portland, ME: Stenhouse.

U2. (1984). Pride (in the name of love). In *The unforgettable fire* [CD]. New York: Island Records.

Unrau, N. (2004). *Content area reading and writing: Fostering literacies in middle and high school cultures.* Upper Saddle River, NJ: Merrill/Prentice-Hall.

Vacca, R. T., & Vacca, J. L. (2005). *Content area reading: Literacy and learning across the curriculum.* Boston: Pearson/Allyn & Bacon.

Vygotsky, L. (1978). *Mind in society: The development of higher psychological processes.* Cambridge, MA: Harvard University Press.

Wigfield, A. (2004). Motivation for reading during the early adolescent years. In D. S. Strickland & D. E. Alvermann (Eds.), *Bridging the literacy achievement gap, grades 4–12* (pp. 56–69). New York: Teachers College Press.

Wigfield, A., & Guthrie, J. T. (1997). Motivation for reading: Individual, home, textual, and classroom perspective. *Educational Psychologist, 32,* 57–135.

Wiles, J., Bondi, J., & Wiles, M. T. (2006). *The essential middle school* (4th ed.). Upper Saddle River, NJ: Pearson/Prentice-Hall.

CHAPTER 2

■ ■ ■

How Can Motivation and Self-Efficacy Theory Inform Adolescent Literacy Teaching Practices?

AVIVAH DAHBANY
LAUREN BOSWORTH McFADDEN

CLASSROOM PORTRAIT

Mr. Judd was not a new teacher; in fact, he was something of an icon in the district. He had been there for 10 years and had enjoyed much success. Parents and students alike spoke very highly of him. He had always planned engaging lessons while covering the necessary curriculum. He utilized various teaching strategies, knowing that this would aid him in meeting the needs of various learners. This year, however, something was different. His students were not excited about learning. In fact, the majority of his students were just going through the motions in his class. Where was the spark? Where was their passion for the literature?

Mr. Judd did what he thought he should do, continuing with the district-mandated texts and the lesson plans that had worked so well in the past. In addition, he dressed up, acted out various scenes, and even invited the author of one of the novels the class was reading to come speak to the class. Nothing seemed to work.

As another day ended, Mr. Judd, determined not to give up on his students or his desire to engage his students in the subject he loved, acknowledged, "I must be missing something. I'm just not sure what?"

> The important thing is not so much that every
> child should be taught, as that every child
> should be given the wish to learn.
> —Attributed to SIR JOHN LUBBOCK (1834–1913)

As the Classroom Portrait illustrates, teachers are sometimes frustrated because students do not appear motivated to learn, in spite of considerable instructional planning, careful focus on standards, and use of what seem to be effective teaching practices. Often, motivating students and enhancing their self-concepts are the factors that most affect their achievement. Having a working knowledge of motivation theories helps teachers understand the complexity of successfully engaging our students, especially our struggling adolescents.

But, regrettably, there is not "one grand motivation or self-concept theory" that encompasses everything (Weiner, 1990). Motivation is a complex trait with many definitions, theories, concepts, and variables. Understanding several different motivation orientations can help teachers select the particular theory, concept, or variable that best suits their personality, teaching style, and beliefs. When strategy suggestions are offered to motivate students, teachers can identify their theoretical basis or orientation. Once teachers adopt a motivation orientation, they can research and develop strategies that are grounded in that orientation to help their students. Teachers can then consistently apply strategies, based on an orientation, that address motivational issues in the classroom. If one strategy does not work, teachers can return to that orientation, see why it did not work, and revise their strategy to be more successful.

Whereas teachers need to identify their motivational orientation preference, it would also benefit teachers to learn all of the orientations, so that they can change approaches should their preferred one not work with an individual student.

In this chapter, Avivah Dahbany, a school psychologist, discusses motivational and self- efficacy theories that will enable you to select the ones most relevant to your teaching style and students. Lauren McFadden, a teacher-educator who recently completed teaching in the public schools for 5 years, then links these theories with instructional activities that not only are relevant to adolescents but also narrow the gap between in-school literacy activities and those in which students engage at home.

Theories about Motivation

Defining Motivation

There are several definitions of motivation. The common theme that runs through each, however, is that individuals who are motivated have a purpose or direction for what they do. We can understand individuals' behavior better when we determine their motives for particular behaviors. According to Lee (2005),

> Motivational theories help to explain people's achievements as well as their failure to achieve. They provide a way of understanding accomplishments and success, especially in the face of challenge and adversity. They also help to explain unexpected outcomes such as lackluster performance of talented individuals or the triumph of an underdog who exceeds all expectations. (p. 330)

If students do not have a purpose or a valued reason for engaging in a particular behavior, then they will not be motivated to achieve. Although this sounds like common sense, it becomes more complicated when we examine different theories of motivation and recognize that *motives*, or reasons for doing something, as well as desired outcomes, vary from individual to individual.

An underlying theme of most theories about motivation is that an individual's needs (or wants) cause certain individual behaviors that produce a particular satisfaction or reward. But because we teach individuals, teachers must consider multiple needs, and rewards must be varied, since not all students have the same goals. As we examine these theories, consider your own motivations, perhaps your motivation for teaching. Consider, too, the kind of behaviors you believe will bring about the results (rewards) you desire, and what those rewards might be. Then ask yourself how your own belief system corresponds to each theory described. Knowing these things about yourself can assist you in considering your students' motivations and the kinds of rewards each student might value.

Humanistic Theories

One of the most applicable theories for understanding student motivation in the classroom is Maslow's (1954, 1971) seven-step hierarchy of human needs. He posited that needs have to be fulfilled at each step before one moves on to the next step. There are four lower, deficiency needs that must be satisfied before one can move on to growth needs: (1) physiological needs (e.g., breathing, hunger, thirst); (2) safety/security needs, which means feeling safe in one's environment; (3) needs for belonging and love, which means being accepted by family and friends; and (4) esteem, or the need to feel competent, to be able to achieve, and to gain the approval and recognition of others. After the deficiency needs are fulfilled, one can work toward satisfying three growth needs: (1) the need to know and understand; (2)

the aesthetic need (i.e., to be surrounded by beauty, organization, and symmetry); and (3) *self-actualization,* which means achieving one's potential. Another need added later (Maslow & Lowery, 1998) is *self-transcendence,* which means to help others achieve their own potential. Teachers do this on a daily basis. Maslow's theory is readily applied to both the school and the classroom. Free breakfast and lunch programs satisfy the most basic of needs. Classroom activities are often designed to satisfy other needs.

Intrinsic and Extrinsic Motivation Theories

Intrinsic motivation generally refers to one's natural curiosity and resulting activity levels. It is formally defined as "an incentive to engage in a specific activity that derives from the activity itself (e.g., a genuine interest in a subject studied), rather than because of any external benefits that might be obtained (e.g., course credits)" (VandenBos, 2007, p. 498). In contrast, *extrinsic motivation* is defined as "an external incentive to engage in a specific activity, especially motivation arising from the expectation of punishment or reward. An example of extrinsic motivation for studying is fear of failing an examination" (VandenBos, 2007, p. 360).

Research has shown that younger children are motivated to achieve by their efforts, mastery of concepts, and social reinforcement (praise) from their teachers. If they do not do well, they believe that with their effort and ability, they will achieve success in the future. However, as children enter adolescence, their confidence in their perception of their abilities declines due to changes in their cognitive development. Adolescents begin to differentiate between effort and ability, and they perceive high effort on easy assignments as low ability, and low effort on a difficult assignment as high ability. They also begin to compare their skills to those of their peers and to objective standards, such as results of standardized tests and obtaining scholarships (Stipek & Daniels, 1988; Stipek & MacIver, 1989). Therefore, research has revealed that intrinsic motivation declines from elementary to middle school (Eccles, Wigfield, & Schiefele, 1998), and from elementary school to high school (Gottfried, Marcoulides, Gottfried, Oliver, & Wright-Guerin, 2007). Schools may use an increasing number of tangible rewards with adolescents to promote academic achievement, such as pizza parties, tickets to sporting events, and discounts at local stores. Nevertheless, teachers of adolescents continually work to increase intrinsic motivation, so that students will value what they are learning for its own sake rather than for such prizes.

Behavioral Theory

Behavioral theory posits that you can increase desired behaviors and decrease undesirable behaviors by the consequences that follow the behaviors. Thorndike's *law of effect* (Nevin, 1999) states that people are more likely to repeat behaviors followed by satisfying consequences that strengthen those behaviors, and less likely to repeat behaviors followed by unsatisfying consequences that weaken those behaviors. *Reinforcement* is defined as any consequence that increases the behavior, and *punishment* is any consequence that decreases the behavior.

We have seen application of behavioral theory in every school throughout the country, with the most serious consequences, such as expulsion or failing a grade, and the most valuable monetary rewards, such as college scholarships, applied more often in high school. However, these rewards and consequences do not matter to every adolescent. The caveat for attempts to apply behavioral theory successfully to classrooms or schools is that you need to know what students consider to be a reinforcement or punishment.

To use consequences effectively, teachers should refer to the consequence hierarchy (Hyman et al., 1997), which suggests a transition from positive reinforcement, as the first step, to presentation punishment, as the final step, as follows:

1. Positive reinforcement
2. Negative reinforcement
3. No reinforcement
4. Removal punishment
5. Presentation punishment

Positive reinforcement is giving students something they like or want (e.g., praise, good grades). *Negative reinforcement* is taking away something that students do not like or want (e.g., homework passes). *No reinforcement* is planned ignoring of students' behavior, which many teachers find difficult to implement in the classroom, although it is effective over time. *Removal punishment* is taking away something that students want or like (e.g., participation in a favorite activity), and last, *presentation punishment* is giving students something that they do not like (e.g., extra homework). Note that if teachers start modifying students' behavior with the punishment consequences, they lose their opportunity to provide the positive environment and student–teacher relationships needed to enhance positive student growth.

There is a debate among psychologists about the use of rewards because of the concern that they may reduce intrinsic motivation (Cameron & Pierce, 1996; Kohn, 1996; Lepper, Keavney, & Drake, 1996). In a classic study (Lepper, Greene, & Nisbett, 1973), children who liked to draw were placed into three groups: Members of the first group were told they would be given a reward for drawing a picture; members of the second group were given a reward as a surprise; and members of the third group did not receive any rewards. Researchers monitored the students' drawing activities during free-play period and found that the group that received a reward spent half as much time drawing after receiving the rewards than the other two groups. A meta-analysis (Cameron & Pierce, 1994) revealed that rewards do not decrease intrinsic motivation. Verbal praise (i.e., social rewards) and performance feedback (evaluation of one's performance on a task) seems to increase intrinsic motivation. However, it appears that if you give tangible rewards (i.e., a token or an activity) to people for just doing a task, without feedback regarding their performance, intrinsic motivation decreases when persons return to the task after the reward is removed. Therefore, it appears that teachers should always consider making activities as intrinsically interesting as possible, and using rewards only when they are needed.

Expectancy–Instrumental Value Theory

The expectancy–instrumental value theory (Atkinson, 1957) is also applicable to adolescent learners. It posits a formula that one's effort and motivation is based on whether or not one thinks he or she will be successful in achieving a goal, and the value of reward one expects from completing the goal. Wigfield (1994), and Eccles and Wigfield (1995), expanded and refined this theory to include four components: *competence beliefs* (whether or not people think they have the skills to accomplish the task); *expectations for success* (whether or not they will be able to complete the task); *subjective task values*, including attainment, intrinsic, usefulness; and *cost of the task*. In a recent study, Durik, Vida, and Eccles (2006) found that "ability beliefs and task values predicted literacy behaviors over time, from fourth grade to high school" (p. 392), thus supporting the expectancy–value model of motivation.

When teachers communicate confidence in their students, they are providing them with the support needed to internalize expectations of being successful. Alternatively, when teachers communicate lower expectations of their students, this too is internalized and results in lack of competence, expectation of failure, and low value and cost of the activity to the adolescent. These expectations in part contribute to the achievement gap between urban and suburban students (Ferguson, Clark, & Stewart, 2002).

Achievement Motivation and Goal Theories

According to McClelland (1987), individuals have three types of needs: achievement, authority/power, and affiliation. How are these needs evident in middle and high school classrooms? Achievement-oriented people attempt challenging tasks, have realistic goals, and seek advancement. They need to feel a sense of accomplishment, and they require feedback from others regarding their progress and achievement efforts. Do you recognize this type of individual in the classes you teach or in classes you attend?

Authority-motivated people need to make an impact, to feel influential and effective, and to increase their personal prestige and status. They like to have their ideas accepted, and they have a strong desire to lead others. You can recognize these students in school leadership positions, such as class president or club leader.

Affiliation-motivated people desire social relationships and like to interact with others. They need to be popular and liked, and they are good team players. Students with affiliation needs do well with small-group activities. Many teachers are active in professional associations, such as the International Reading Association, or their local and state reading councils, to satisfy their need for affiliation.

McClelland (1987) also posited an avoidance motive that is caused by anxiety. If people avoid tasks, they may have fears of failure, rejection, success, or power. Atkinson (1964) expanded McClelland's theory and indicated that people either seek success or seek to avoid failure. When success seekers fail at a task, their motivation is increased, and they try again. When failure avoiders fail, they decrease their efforts.

These multiple theories of motivation provide the background for teachers to think about when developing activities for their students. But we also have to look at fostering adolescents' self-perception and self-efficacy to enhance their ability and desire to learn, and to stay with a difficult task until mastery is achieved.

Promoting Positive Self-Perception and Self-Efficacy in Adolescents' Classrooms

A defining characteristic of adolescents is their need to develop *self-efficacy*, or the belief that they can accomplish things on their own. Teachers often develop this sense of efficacy during literacy instruction by scaffolding their instruction, moving from what students know to what is yet to be learned. As students acquire new knowledge, they perceive themselves as learners and develop a positive view of themselves.

In this section we look at three theories concerning self-perception, so we may understand that the ways we respond to students influence their beliefs about themselves as learners.

Attribution Theory

Most people strive to maintain a positive self-concept. Behaviors or actions that are contrary to people's opinions of themselves create *cognitive dissonance* (Festinger, 1957), "an unpleasant psychological state resulting from inconsistency between two or more elements in a cognitive system.... Cognitive dissonance creates a motivational drive in an individual to reduce the dissonance" (VandenBos, 2007, p. 189).

When students' performance does not match their opinions of themselves or those of their peers, students seek an explanation of their behaviors that reduces their cognitive dissonance. Rotter (1966) indicated that, based on personality traits, people attribute their success or failure to internal or external factors, which he named *locus of control*. Individuals with an internal locus of control believe that something they did accounted for their success or failure. Those with an external locus of control believe that their success or failure was the result of factors outside their control. When students blame a bad test grade on the teacher, their parents, the class environment, and so forth, they are demonstrating belief in an external locus of control.

Weiner (1994, 2000) elaborated on this point, noting that when people have an internal locus of control and succeed, they attribute their success both to their ability ("I'm smart"), which is a stable characteristic, and to effort ("I tried hard"), which is an unstable characteristic. If they fail, their attributions are that they are stupid (ability/stable) and did not try hard enough (effort/unstable). They are motivated to repeat the task and to try harder. On the other hand, people with an external locus of control attribute their success to easy tasks (stable) and luck (unstable). When they fail, they attribute their failures to a difficult task (stable) and to bad luck (unstable), and tend to give up.

Learned Helplessness

When people develop a consistent internal, stable explanation for their failures, they start to believe they are stupid and that they will always fail no matter what they do (Maier & Seligman, 1976; Seligman, 1972). *Learned helplessness* is defined as "lack of motivation and failure to act after exposure to unpleasant events or stimuli over which the individual has no control (e.g., noise, crowding). Individuals learn that they cannot control their environment, and this may lead them to fail to make use of any control options that are available" (VandenBos, 2007, p. 529). Abramson, Seligman, and Teasdale (1978) further elaborated on the theories of Rotter (1966) and Weiner (1994) by adding universal–personal, global–specific, and chronic–acute helplessness. The first of these asks whether the behavior would occur in anyone under the same circumstances, or just to this person. The second component asks whether the person's behavior occurs in all situations or in just this one situation. Finally, acute helplessness is easier to overcome than is chronic helplessness. Since that time, greater emphasis has been placed on positive aspects of psychology (Seligman & Csikszentmihalyi, 2000), which, for our purposes, focus on self-efficacy, self-regulation, and self-determination theories.

Self-Efficacy and Self-Regulation Theories

Bandura (1982, 1993) posits that human motivation is most strongly mediated by "people's beliefs about their capabilities to exercise control over their own level of functioning and over events that affect their lives. Efficacy beliefs influence how people feel, think, motivate themselves and behave" (1993, p. 118). The ability to set goals is based on people's perceived ability to accomplish them. People who have high levels of self-efficacy set high goals and display greater commitment. To succeed, they also need to have self-regulation skills, which include "the control of one's own behavior though self-monitoring of the conditions that evoke desired and undesired behaviors, structuring the personal environment to facilitate desired behavior and circumvent situations the tend to elicit undesired behavior, self-evaluation and self-administration of punishments and rewards, or some combination of these" (VandenBos, 2007, pp. 832–833). The five stages of a self-regulation model include "problem identification, commitment, execution, environmental management, and generalization" (p. 833).

Teachers can foster self-efficacy by encouraging students to assess their own strengths and weaknesses, and guiding them through the self-regulation model until they are able to accomplish it on their own. This also reinforces adolescents' development of an internal locus of control.

Self-Determination Theory

The final theory we examine was developed by Ryan and Deci (2000). *Self-determination theory* indicates that self-motivation requires three things: relatedness, autonomy, and competence. *Relatedness* is having satisfying relationships with family, peers, and others, and *autonomy* is the ability to initiate, manage, and control one's own behaviors. Students, especially adolescents, have a great need for relationships, especially with their peers, as well as autonomy, as they develop their identities. *Competence* is the belief that one knows how to do a task and can accomplish it.

Many studies related to student achievement support the notion of relatedness and motivation. In one longitudinal study (Wentzel, 1997), adolescents described teachers who cared as "demonstrating a democratic interaction style, developing expectations for student behavior in light of individual differences, modeling a 'caring' attitude toward their own work, and providing constructive feedback" (p. 411). Wentzel (1998) assessed the social relationships between adolescents and their parents, teachers, and peers, and the effects on students' school/class interest, academic goal orientation, and social goal pursuits. As might be predicted, parent support was a good predictor of school interest and academic goal orientation; teacher support was a good predictor of school/class interest; and peer support was a good predictor of social goal pursuits.

> Adolescents report that they work harder for teachers who treat them as individuals and express interest in their personal lives outside of school. Caring teachers, they report, are also honest, fair and trusting.... These teachers grant students some autonomy and opportunities for decision making—for example, by giving them choices in assignments, engaging them in developing classroom rules, and encouraging them to express their opinions in classroom discussions. (Stipek, 2006, p. 46)

As noted in the section on intrinsic and extrinsic motivation, research has shown that younger children are motivated to achieve by their efforts, concept mastery, and social reinforcement. However, as children grow, their achievement motivation declines, especially at 6 and at 12–13 years of age (Stipek, 1984). Eccles, Midgley, and Adler (1984) also found that students' motivation changes with age, cognitive development, and classroom practices. Older students differentiate between effort and ability, compare themselves with others, and need to develop greater self-efficacy skills. However, classroom practices place more emphasis on adhering to structure and routine than on providing students with opportunities for decision making and developing strategies that enhance their autonomy.

> As children mature, they become more skilled, knowledgeable, and competent: they become better able to take responsibility, make decisions, control their lives. They also feel more able to take responsibility and to make academic decisions. One would hope that with increasing grade

level, students would assume greater autonomy and control over their lives and learning. In addition, one would hope that schools would provide an environment that would facilitate task involvement rather than ego involvement, particularly as children enter early adolescence. Unfortunately, there is evidence that just the opposite is true. As students progress through the grades, the classroom is characterized by a decrease in student autonomy and an increase in processes which enhance ego involvement at the expense of task involvement. (pp. 322–323)

Knowing the theoretical background of adolescent motivation and self-efficacy is a start. But the ability to apply this information to classroom practices is the goal. What follows are some practical suggestions to help you apply this information to actual classroom activities.

Applying Theories of Motivation and Self-Efficacy Development in the Classroom

Today's adolescents have grown up in a fast-paced world—fast food, video games, cellular phones, laptops, wireless Internet, and text messaging. This is their reality, one that cannot be ignored. How, then, do we as teachers compete with this reality, motivate our students to read, and inspire them in our classrooms with the same intensity and superfluity of their out-of-school online and text messaging conversations, or encourage them to express themselves and their knowledge through their writing?

Having worked as a middle grades teacher for 5 years and a full-time college professor for 3, I (McFadden) have grappled with this question for years. Rather than attempt to answer it on my own, I have routinely sought the expertise of my fellow teachers and the opinions of my students. It is this information, gathered informally over the years in conversation and through trial and error, that informs my contribution to this chapter.

Motivating adolescents toward literacy requires more than merely assigning the reading of a text or the writing of a paper. Actually motivating the students requires a great deal more, including creativity, ingenuity, and knowledge of an individual student's strengths, weaknesses, and interests. As teachers, we should immerse ourselves in the subject matter we teach and find innovative ways to bring our love of the subject to our students. No matter how much we plan, however, if we do not know our students' strengths, weaknesses, and interests, we have planned in vain. For each student we also must answer the question, "What will motivate and enhance his or her self-efficacy?", because, as we know, individual students have distinct and different needs to be satisfied and rewards that they desire. As we saw earlier in this chapter, many studies indicate that students' intrinsic motivation decreases from elementary school to high school. We need to pay attention to this and do all we can to reignite the passion and thirst for knowledge that is so characteristic of young children.

So how do we as teachers make it "cool" to be lifelong learners and active participants in class? The answer lies in creating activities that are meaningful and of interest to our students, and in narrowing the gap between in-school literacy activities and those in which students engage at home. Thus, what follows are suggestions for motivating adolescents during literacy instruction. Each description includes an explanation of how the activity reinforces some of the theories of motivation and self-concept development we discussed in the first part of this chapter.

Integrating Technology with Digital Stories

Digital storytelling is a great way to integrate technology and literacy instruction, while offering students the autonomy and self-determination they crave (Ryan & Deci, 2000). In a digital story, students use graphics, animation, text, and audio (their own voices; previously recorded audio or digital music, or a combination of these) to tell a story and share it electronically. According to Robin (2005), who has created a website to educate others about digital storytelling, the 10 essential elements of a digital story are (1) overall purpose of the story; (2) narrator's point of view; (3) a dramatic question or questions; (4) choice of content; (5) clarity of voice; (6) pacing of the narrative; (7) meaningful soundtrack; (8) quality of the images; (9) economy of the story detail; and (10) good grammar and language usage.

A quick glance at these elements provides an argument for infusing them into your curriculum. If you're not convinced yet, view some of the amazing work that students across the country have posted on the Internet. When I was discussing the use of digital storytelling in the K–12 classroom with my sophomores who are studying to be teachers, I used stories created by elementary and middle school students. My students were astounded by the impact these digital stories had on them. They were even more dumbfounded that students between the ages of 5 and 14 had created them.

The one digital story that stood out the most was a poem by a fourth grader in the Scott County School District in Georgetown, Kentucky. His poem about September 11, 2001, may be found on that website dedicated to digital storytelling (2006). Not only were my students amazed by the fact that this topic was chosen by a fourth grader, whom they considered far removed from the events of September 11, 2001, but more importantly they were also impressed with the serious tone, music, and graphics selection, and how all of these elements worked together to create a touching remembrance of such a tragic event. In addition to discussing which digital storytelling elements were present in this poem and the role of each in helping the observer to truly understand the thoughts, feelings, and emotions of the creator, my students also realized the overwhelming power of this medium as tears streamed down their faces.

My students then had the task of creating a culminating digital storytelling assignment for a unit of study to be implemented in a K–8 classroom. In addition, they created an exemplary example of what would be expected of their students. Sharing these "exemplars" in class allowed my own students to see the infinite number of topics that can be addressed through digital storytelling, as well as the power of using digital images and music along with their own voices to share their stories. Stories ranged from a look at the Roaring '20s to a biography of Beethoven, to a closer look at the solar system, to a history of the Carlisle Indian School, to a personal narrative on one student's heritage and culture.

My students also saw how far they had come in such a short time in learning to use this new medium (expectancy–instrumental value theory). Successfully completing one's own digital story or WebQuest aids in the development of self-efficacy (Bandura, 1982, 1993). With proper support and encouragement, once-difficult and challenging tasks become second nature to our adolescents.

Blogs

Although blogs are often referred to as personal diaries, because this is how the phenomenon started, they can be much more. In the traditional sense, a blog is a website created to be a collaborative space, where anyone who reads the postings can add to what has been said. Most teachers who read this may be leery of opening up a class discussion to the millions of people who have access to the Web, and this hesitation is warranted. However, newer blogging sites, such as *blogger.com*, allow the blog author to control the type of access for each blog. Thus, teachers can limit the use of the blog to students in their own classes.

I have seen blogs used to continue discussions started in class, to give students the opportunity to begin new discussions on course-related content, to pose open-ended questions on the current class novel, or to provide a central posting location for information that students access, add to, or commented on.

One of the major benefits of this open forum is the ability and often the requirement for all students to be active participants. Blogs, therefore, can motivate students who have affiliation needs (McClelland, 1987). In addition, unlike the rapid fire questioning that often intimidates struggling or shy students during the typical school day, posted questions can be thought about for extended periods of time before the student has to post a reply. Further, this style requires that the ideas and thoughts of each and every student are voiced and heard.

WebQuests to Motivate Students

Developed by Dodge (2007), "a WebQuest is an inquiry-oriented lesson format in which most or all the information that learners work with comes from the web" (paragraph 3). Teachers can either create WebQuests or find thousands of examples on the Web. One of the most famous Web-Quest resources, *webquest.org*, allows teachers to search through thousands of WebQuests by narrowing their search to the subject area they are interested in covering and the appropriate grade level. WebQuests are suitable for a range of grade levels and often are conducive to cross-curricular study. One of the major difficulties with using a WebQuest created by someone else is the links. Make sure that the links are live (still working) before assigning students to the WebQuest. Inherent in the structure of most WebQuests are the following: an introduction that grabs the student's attention, the assignment of an authentic task, cross-curricular content, group work, and the completion of an authentic product.

Inherent in any good WebQuest is a task that will pique students' genuine interests, thus providing the incentive to engage in the activity, a vital element to enhancing students' intrinsic motivation (VandenBos, 2007). Before beginning a WebQuest on the topic of *decades*, my students had to select the three decades they were most interested in studying. I used their choices to form groups, and each group was given the challenge of planning the "party of the decade."

What adolescent wouldn't love to be given this opportunity? As every good party planner knows, a guest list must be written, food must be planned, music must be selected, acceptable attire must be established, and invitations must be sent. All of these elements had to reflect the decade. Because the party would be "thrown" in class, my students also had to create the conversations the guests would have. These conversations had to be inspired by current events, including major sporting events and science/technology advancements, popular culture, and the politics of the time. To create authentic conversations, students were required to research the following: major historical developments, nations at war, famous political figures, scientists, artists, musicians and athletes, as well as clothing styles, television shows, and so forth. The guests and their interests would also inspire the conversation. The guest list had to include important people from the selected decade. Once the guest list was in place, each member of the group had to select one guest whose identity he or she would assume at the party. At least one political figure or leader, one scientist, one athlete, and one person from the arts had to be represented at the party and in the conversation. Within this WebQuest, students honed their skills in the following areas: researching, reading, writing, speaking, listening, working cooperatively, and party planning, all while learning a plethora of new information and having fun.

Motivating with Movies

Many teachers motivate their students to read using extrinsic rewards, such as viewing the movie version of a novel that the class has completed. Even without such a reward, opportunities to explore similarities, differences, and how literary elements were developed in both the book and the movie versions can be a very powerful exercise. In fact, according to Sweeney (2006), using movies in the class allows students to "identify with characters and empathize with situations ... [and to] become more aware of the power structures from which their language has come" (p. 28). In addition, it allows students to make connections between their own experiences, those of the characters in the movie, and other texts they have previously encountered. Teachers can also help students to uncover the structure of a film and compare it to a text they are reading. Analyzing and comparing plot, setting, theme, and portrayals of protagonists and antagonists are just a few of the observations that students may make.

Building a Great Classroom Library

Creating a great classroom library may not happen in a single year. In fact, it may take a few years; don't be afraid to ask for donations (from the friends and the families of the students you teach), because having an extensive library available to your students helps, at the very least, with building fluency, vocabulary, and comprehensions skills. At its best, this library will pique the natural curiosities and genuine interests of your students, playing on their intrinsic motivation. Making sure that your library appeals to various levels of readers, as well as to both genders, is paramount. Boys are often cited as struggling in the area of literacy, but a recent study of the secret reading lives of approximately 50 boys revealed that boys were reading nonfiction, game manuals, comic books, and catalogs (Kenney, 2007). In addition, Black (2005) suggests that the way to pique male interest in reading is by "focusing on computers, magazines, CD-ROMs, videos, card collections and hobbies when expanding the texts that students read and write [about] in our classroom" (p. 59). Developing your classroom library collaboratively with students ensures that you are giving students a voice and a choice in what they want to read—key factors in motivation.

Working Collaboratively with the School Librarian/ Media Specialist

Increasingly, it is unusual for a school to have a librarian. In fact, most schools have *media specialists*, librarians who not only run the library but also teach classes into which they infuse technology. Whatever the title of the person running your school library, it is essential that you work collaboratively with this person to promote students' literacy.

Students from a local school district rave about a mystery unit that the middle school media specialist plans for seventh-grade students each year. To get the students interested in reading mysteries, he opens to the most exciting point in the book, reads a blurb, and slams the book shut. Then, he explains the challenge to the students: to read three mysteries in 3 weeks. He also has activities to go along with the readings and a nightly log to record student readings. The seventh-grade English teachers monitor student logs and the completion of activities. For each book they complete, students enter their names into a drawing at the end of the unit. Students then come together at the end of the unit to celebrate and to see who won the prizes. These rewards appeal to students who have achievement goals. Year after year, students are astounded at how exciting they find mysteries, and how reading can actually be fun. The English teachers love how involved the students become as they recommend and discuss with peers the books they are reading.

Though this unit is extremely popular, it is not the only unit to which students are exposed, nor is it the only time that English teachers and media specialists work together. Another popular tradition is the celebration held at the end of the year for students who read 21 or more books. Each student receives a plaque that is displayed in the library for all to see. A luncheon is also held to honor the students, who are encouraged to bring family members and as many as five friends. Wilhelm (1996, cited in Guth & Heaney, 1998), found that many adolescents rank reading for pleasure at the bottom of many reading and writing attitude surveys, and when asked to comment about reading, often respond that "reading is for someone with no life." The students in this school, however, would beg to differ. Furthermore, though extrinsic rewards often initially capture the interest of the students, the excitement and passion that continue long after the contests are the real rewards.

Tantalizing with Tidbits

Who among us isn't intrigued by at least one of the movie trailers we preview while waiting for the feature film to begin? This powerful strategy to spark viewers' interest can be effective in our own classrooms. Last year, a middle school teacher used this approach to whet her students' appetites for reading by revealing that one of the books in the curriculum actually had the narrator as the murderer. This simple statement caused a flurry of discussion among students, appealing to their affiliation goals (McClelland, 1987). They were determined to figure out which book it could be, despite the fact that this would require them to read multiple selections.

It is true that not every book has such an unusual twist. Nevertheless, with some creative thinking, teachers and students can write tantalizing tidbits about any book, thus awakening the innate curiosity and desire to read.

Best-Seller List

The *New York Times* Best-Seller List and Oprah's Book Club inspire many adults to read. Displays in some bookstores are created for these selections alone. Building upon this concept in our own classrooms is easy. When we provide probing questions for students to answer once they have read a book, questions that help students to think critically about the selection they have read, students can then decide whether this book would be a hit with other students their age. This fulfills the self-determination needs of our adolescent students (Ryan & Deci, 2000). Individual student critiques and ranking of the book should be shared with other students and/or displayed where others have easy access to the information. Students may share these critiques through a simple question-and-answer technique or become more creative by becoming movie critics, like Siskel and Ebert have done with their own television shows or newspaper columns.

Book Clubs

Many books clubs are formed informally by groups of friends, colleagues, or associates who have an interest in reading. Members of the club read the same selection and meet to discuss sections or chapters of the book. Book clubs are not just for adults. In fact, we should encourage students to form them. We can model the formation of book clubs within our own classrooms. This does not mean that we select the text and organize the groups for our students. Instead, students should be given more control, which allows for self-determination needs. To avoid having students simply pick their groups based on who their friends are, a teacher can conduct an informal survey in which the students respond to questions that elicit information about their interests. Using the information provided, teachers can then group students accordingly and allow each group to select a text that piques students' interest, thus fostering adolescent affiliation needs. To avoid having groups that are unable to come up with an appropriate text, teachers should show students how and where to find books that are appropriate for their interests and reading abilities. If selections need to be content specific, then teachers can add more parameters. Teachers in districts with required reading lists or a limited list of acceptable books from which the students must choose should offer those selections. If these books don't appeal to students, perhaps it is time to have a districtwide discussion about revamping the list to make it more appealing to students.

We also want to encourage independent reading, apart from in-class reading clubs. One of the initial assignments for my college sophomores who are studying to be teachers is to interview a student or noneducator about what makes an effective teacher and what they wish teachers to know. Each year, the overwhelming response to what students wish teachers to know is that students have lives outside of the classroom and that a given teacher's class is not the only class they have. Students today are overscheduled, rushing from school to their next activity as soon as the school bells rings at the day's end. Students are often overwhelmed and overscheduled. Is it surprising, then, that many students complain that they barely have time to do the homework we assign, let alone to read or write for pleasure?

This situation can be addressed by providing time within the school day for our students to read or write for pleasure. Drop Everything and Read, or DEAR (n.d.), time is popular in many middle and high schools. This is a set amount of time, often scheduled at the same time each day, for students to sit and read quietly. When teachers make time for these activities in their classrooms, they are modeling the expectancy–instrumental value of reading to their students. Many teachers also allow their students to use this time to free-write, if that is what they choose to do. During this time, students are often encouraged to read for pleasure and are dissuaded from reading class texts. Sometimes students' choices for independent reading become recommendations for class book clubs.

Music Fridays

Students must be the primary focus of every lesson that we plan and teach. Making sure that the content we teach is relevant to their lives is one way to ensure that students are the focus. Current events that affect adolescents, popular magazines that target teens, and current television shows and hit movies are all fertile ground for relevance in classrooms. By making connections to students' lives and interests, we motivate students to engage in content areas that enhance their growth needs (Maslow, 1954, 1971).

Alvermann, Moon, and Hagood (1999, cited in Sweeney, 2006) argue for infusing popular culture into the curriculum, and suggest that doing so affirms "the expertise that students bring to the learning environment, the pleasure that popular culture produces for students, and the multiple readings that students produce from popular culture" (p. 29). This expertise is often essential when working with students from less advantaged homes "who have greater knowledge of popular culture than they do the academic subject matter for with they are considered unready" (p. 29). In fact, relating to popular culture helps these students feel empowered in class and enhances their self-efficacy skills. "Combining popular culture with the academic provides a wonderful way to help students play on their other intelligences or strengths and use non-traditional learning styles to navigate new worlds in and out of the classroom" (p. 36).

A friend who teaches high school English introduced Music Fridays to her classes as a way to integrate popular culture with literacy. She believes the relevance and appeal is evident everywhere. iPods and MP3 players are the rage. Pass a teenager on the road in your car, and it isn't unusual to hear the radio blaring and to see the driver singing along. On Music Fridays, students listen to a song that relates to the novel the class is currently reading. The first time it plays, students simply listen to the lyrics. The second time, students have to determine how the music relates to the novel's characters, themes, or time period. Some of the lyrics used have been from such artists as Metallica, Linkin Park, Frank Sinatra, and John Mayer. Students are also encouraged to come up with lyrics related to the current novel and share them with the class. With this activity, students can think about class novels more deeply as they make these text-to-world connections.

Concluding Thoughts

As you reflect on motivation and self-efficacy theories, which ones appeal to you and to your teaching philosophy? Which ones help you understand the behaviors of students in your class who are not motivated to achieve? Can you think of ways to apply these theories, using the instructional strategies provided to enhance your students' motivation? Can you think of other strategies that may help you narrow the gap between literacy activities in school and those in which your students engage at home?

Dewey argued against the student being a "passive receptacle whose only function is to receive the structured subject matter which scholars have codified" (as cited in Flanagan, 1994, paragraph 24). He said, "The child is the starting point, the centre, and the end.... Personality, character, is more than subject matter. Not knowledge or information, but self-realization, is the goal. To lose all the world of knowledge and lose one's own self is as awful a fate in education as in religion" (paragraph 24). As you prepare each day to impact positively the lives of your students, do not lose sight of what Dewey said. In addition, think about the motivational and self-efficacy theories, and the practical ideas presented. Doing so will make a difference in your teaching (making it more engaging) and in the lives of your students. Make it a goal each day to inspire your students' love of learning and reading. Most importantly, love what you do and remember that the goal of education is to prepare our students for the real world—a world where hard work and perseverance pay off.

Questions for Reflection

1. If Mr. Judd came to you for advice, what motivation theory would you suggest that he adopt for his classroom and students? Why? Would you recommend the adoption of a different theory if he had a seventh-grade class? A 12th-grade class?

2. What self-efficacy theory would be applicable to Mr. Judd's classroom and students? Why? Would you recommend adoption of a different theory if he had a seventh-grade class? A 12th-grade class?

3. Using the motivation and self-efficacy theories you selected for Mr. Judd, develop a lesson plan for his classroom, using the activities noted in the chapter for a seventh-grade class and a 12th-grade class.

4. What motivation and self-efficacy theories would you adopt in your own classroom for your students? Why?

References

Abramson, L. Y., Seligman, M. E. P., & Teasdale, J. (1978). Learned helplessness: Critique and reformulation. *Journal of Abnormal Behavior, 87*(1), 49–74.

Atkinson, J. W. (1957). Motivation determinates of risk taking behaviors. *Psychological Review, 64*(6), 359–372.

Atkinson, J. W. (1964). *An introduction to human motivation.* Princeton, NJ: Van Nostrand.

Bandura, A. (1982). Self mechanism in human agency. *American Psychologist, 37*(2), 122–147.

Bandura, A. (1993). Perceived self-efficacy in cognitive development and functioning. *Educational Psychologist, 28*(2), 117–148.

Black, S. (2005). Reaching the older reader. *American School Board Journal, 192*(4), 50–70.

Cameron, J., & Pierce, W. D. (1994). Reinforcement, reward and intrinsic motivation: A meta-analysis. *Review of Educational Research, 64*(3), 363–423.

Cameron, J., & Pierce, W. D. (1996). The debate about rewards and intrinsic motivation: Protests and accusations do not alter the results. *Review of Educational Research, 66*(1), 39–51.

Digital storytelling presented by our students in the Scott County Schools (Georgetown, Kentucky). (2006, March 27). Retrieved September 27, 2007, from *www.dtc.scott.k12.ky.us/technology/digitalstorytelling/studentstories. html.*

Dodge, B. (2007). *Webquest.org* home page. Retrieved September 27, 2007, from *webquest.org/index.php.*

Drop Everything and Read. (n.d.). Retrieved September 27, 2007, from *www. dropeverythingandread.com.*

Durik, A. M., Vida, M., & Eccles, J. S. (2006). Task values and ability beliefs as predictors of high school literacy choices: A developmental analysis. *Journal of Educational Psychology, 98*(2), 382–393.

Eccles, J. S., Midgley, C., & Adler, T. F. (1984). Grade related changes in the school environment: Effects on achievement motivation. In J. G. Nicholls (Ed.), *The advances in motivation and achievement: Development of achievement motivation* (Vol. 3, pp. 282–331). Greenwich, CT: JAI Press.

Eccles, J. S., & Wigfield, A. (1995). The mind of the actor: The structure of adolescents' achievement task values and expectancy related beliefs. *Personality and Social Psychology Bulletin, 21*(3), 215–225.

Eccles, J. S., Wigfield, A., & Schiefele, U. (1998). Motivation to succeed. In W. Damon & N. Eisenberg (Eds.), *Handbook of child psychology: Social, emotional, and personality development* (Vol. 3, 5th ed., pp. 1017–1095). New York: Wiley.

Ferguson, R. F., Clark, R., & Stewart, J. (2002). *Closing the achievement gap in suburban and urban school communities* (Report No. NCREL-13). Naperville, IL: North Central Regional Education Laboratory. (ERIC Document Reproduction Service No. ED473122)

Festinger, L. (1957). *A theory of cognitive dissonance.* Stanford, CA: Stanford University Press.

Flanagan, F. (1994). *John Dewey.* Retrieved September 27, 2007, from *www.ul.ie/~philos/vol1/dewey.html.*

Gottfried, A. E., Marcoulides, G. A., Gottfried, A. W., Oliver, P.M., & Wright-Guerin, D. (2007). Multivariate latent change modeling of developmental decline in academic intrinsic math motivation and achievement: Childhood through adolescence. *International Journal of Behavioral Development, 31*(4), 317–327.

Guth, N., & Heaney, P. (1998, October). A challenge for school administrators: Motivating adolescents to read *NASSP Bulletin, 82,* 34–40. Retrieved July 3, 2008, from ProQuest Education Journals database (Document ID: 34650098).

Hyman, I. A., Dahbany, A., Blum, M., Weiler, E., Brooks-Klein, V., & Pokalo, M. (1997). *School discipline and school violence: The teacher variance approach.* Needham Heights, MA: Allyn & Bacon.

Kenney, B. (2007). Is there really a problem? *School Library Journal, 53*(9), 11.

Kohn, A. (1996). By all available means: Review of Cameron and Pierce's defense of extrinsic motivators. *Review of Educational Research, 66*(1) 1–5.

Lee, S. W. (Ed.). (2005). *Encyclopedia of school psychology.* Thousand Oaks, CA: Sage.

Lepper, M. R., Greene, D., & Nisbett, R. E. (1973). Undermining children's intrinsic interest with extrinsic rewards: A test of the overjustification hypothesis. *Journal of Personality and Social Psychology, 28,* 129–137.

Lepper, M. R., Keavney, M., & Drake, M. (1996). Intrinsic motivation and extrinsic rewards: A commentary on Cameron and Pierce's meta-analysis. *Review of Education Research, 66*(1), 5–32.

Maier, S. F., & Seligman, M. E. P. (1976). Learned helplessness: Theory and evidence. *Journal of Experimental Psychology: General, 105,* 3–46.

Maslow, A. (1954). *Motivation and personality.* New York: Harper.

Maslow, A. (1971). *The farther reaches of human nature.* New York: Viking Press.

Maslow, A., & Lowery, R. (Ed.). (1998). *Toward a psychology of being* (3rd ed.). New York: Wiley.

McClelland, D. C. (1987). *Human motivation.* New York: Cambridge University Press.

Nevin, J. (1999). Analyzing Thorndike's Law of Effect: The question of stimulus–effect bonds. *Journal of Experimental Analysis of Behavior, 72*(3), 447–450.

Robin, B. (2005). *Educational uses of digital storytelling.* Retrieved September 27,

2007, from *www.coe.uh.edu/~brobin* with link to *fp.coe.uh.edu/brobin/homep-age/SITE05.ppt.*

Rotter, J. (1966). Generalized expectancies for internal versus external control of reinforcements. *Psychological Monographs, 80*(Whole No. 609).

Ryan, R., & Deci, E. (2000). Self-determination theory and the facilitation of intrinsic motivation, social development, and well-being. *American Psychologist, 55*(1), 68–78.

Seligman, M. E. P. (1972). Learned helplessness. *Annual Review of Medicine, 23,* 407–412.

Seligman, M. E. P., & Csikszentmihalyi, M. (2000). Positive psychology: An introduction. *American Psychologist, 55*(1), 5–14.

Stipek, D. J. (1984). The development of achievement motivation. In R. Ames & C. Ames (Eds.), *Research on motivation in education: Student motivation* (Vol. 1, pp. 145–174). New York: Academic Press.

Stipek, D. J. (2006). Relationships matter. *Educational Leadership, 64,* 46–49.

Stipek, D. J., & Daniels, D. H. (1988). Declining perceptions of competence: A consequence of changes in the child or in the educational environment? *Journal of Educational Psychology, 80*(3), 352–356.

Stipek, D. J., & MacIver, D. (1989). Developmental change in children's assessment of intellectual competence. *Child Development, 60,* 521–538.

Sweeney, L. (2006). Ideas in practice: Theoretical bases for using movies in developmental coursework. *Journal of Developmental Education, 29*(3), 28–36.

VandenBos, G. R. (Ed.). (2007). *American Psychological Association dictionary of psychology.* Washington, DC: American Psychological Association.

Weiner, B. (1990). History of motivational research in education. *Journal of Educational Psychology, 82*(4), 616–622.

Weiner, B. (1994). Integrating social and personal theories of achievement striving. *Review of Education Research, 64,* 557–573.

Weiner, B. (2000). Intrapersonal and interpersonal theories of motivation from an attributional perspective. *Educational Psychology, 12*(1), 1–14.

Wentzel, K. R. (1997). Student motivation in middle school: The role of perceived pedagogical caring. *Journal of Educational Psychology, 89*(3), 411–419.

Wentzel, K. R. (1998). Social relationships and motivation in middle school: The role of parents, teachers and peers. *Journal of Educational Psychology, 90*(2), 202–209.

Wigfield, A. (1994). Expectancy value theory of achievement motivation: A developmental perspective. *Educational Psychology Review, 6*(1), 49–78.

CHAPTER 3

How Can Adolescents' Literacies Outside of School Be Brought into the Classroom?

WILLIAM KIST
JIM RYAN

CLASSROOM PORTRAIT

It is the first day of school and the butterflies are back. My room is set, and I am very comfortable with where I will begin as far as lesson plans are concerned, but I can't shake the butterfly stomach that appears on the first day of school. My only consolation is that, as my students arrive, I quickly notice that they too are a little nervous. I quickly discovered that I was about to learn one of many valuable lessons this year.

One of the most important lessons is the value of gauging where your students are and trying to take them to the next level (and not just academically). I assumed that my students could master their lockers with ease and was ready to move to the next, exciting first-day activity of getting to know each other. But there I was, standing in the middle of the hallway full of new sixth graders, all struggling to work their combination locks and put their things away in their lockers. "Mr. Ryan, how do you do that again? Is it left, right, left or right, left . . . ? I need help!" Wow, I really messed up! How am I going to infuse my classroom with new literacies if my students can't even work a simple combination lock?

In the days that followed I observed that whereas my students might not have been able to work their combination locks, they were plugged in in other ways. As my students left the building for the day, I noticed several pulling out cell phones and iPods. I heard students checking in with parents, making plans with other students, and checking voice mail. I also heard several conversations about students using Facebook and MySpace. But I had made

---

> the mistake of assuming that my students would not be able to interact with technology instead of observing where my students were with it and taking them to the next level. Maybe I won't have to scratch my plans for infusing new literacies into my classroom after all.

Bringing New Literacies into Adolescent Classrooms

This excerpt is from a journal that Jim Ryan (one of the coauthors of this chapter) kept during the first 2 years of his classroom-teaching career. The portrait that Jim provides of sixth graders and their out-of-school literacies is not uncommon. For a variety of reasons, many of our students are cut off from their out-of-school worlds during the school day, only to be set loose at the end of the day to resume their Internet surfing, networking, and communicating with friends and associates around the globe. Unfettered online communication among children and teens worries educators and parents, and this has led to the challenges that many teachers face when they want to bridge the gap between students' out-of-school and in-school literacies. With a public reeling from (and watching, strangely, in great numbers) shows such as *Dateline NBC*'s "To Catch a Predator," and with 21 states having filtering laws that apply to schools and libraries (National Council of State Legislatures, 2007), many districts have put in place multiple filters and policies that effectively prevent students at school from taking part in any kind of literacy lives that are not prescripted and protected, even as kids continue to find ways to outsmart these filters (Olsen, 2006).

In this chapter we do not take sides in this debate; statistics and anecdotes may be cited on either side of the Internet safety question. Rather, we present the real-life dilemma faced by new teachers who want to include more of their students' out-of-school literacies in the classroom.

Of course, even before the onset of the Internet and other new media, educators were arguing for a school literacy life that is more meaningfully integrated with "real life"—the way people read and write in the outside world (Dewey, 1899/1980, 1934/1980; Rosenblatt, 1938/1995; Willinsky, 1990). Decades ago, theoreticians such as Vygotsky (1934/1986, 1978) also argued for viewing literacy more as a *social process*—that one's background and life experiences influence one's construction of meaning from a text just as much as the text itself does.

Ironically, the onset of new technology, much of which is more interactive than earlier media, led scholars in the 1990s to take a fresh look at these older ideas and begin to broaden our conception of reading and writing to include multiliteracies (New London Group, 1996) and a more screen-based rather than a page-based view of literacy (Kress, 2003). Education literacy journals are now filled with descriptions of educators' attempts to infuse their classrooms with these new literacies.

But is there an increasing gap between what is accomplished by superstars, such as Teacher of the Year award winners or recipients of the Apple Distinguished Educator award, and what is accomplished by the everyday classroom teacher? And what about the most vulnerable teachers of all—the new ones? These teachers are often expected to carry the profession forward, but they are at the weakest point in terms of institutional power and influence (Anhorn, 2008). Although new teachers may express a desire to continue developing their own out-of-school literacies, even at risk to their careers (Kist, 2008), many are probably stymied in their ability to wed students' out-of-school and in-school literacies by institutional policies and procedures, such as outright bans on Internet usage or such rigorous filtering that new media use is virtually impossible.

The authors of this chapter met when Jim Ryan was a student in Bill Kist's methods class at Kent State University in the fall of 2004. Bill, a former middle school and high school English teacher and curriculum supervisor who became interested in new media when he used video extensively in his own classroom, assigned his high school students the task to make video versions of canonical texts and, using silent films such as *The Kid* (Chaplin, 1921), to talk about story structure, mood, and tone—to name a few examples. Jim has come to teaching as a second career after working as a school and commercial photographer. His own interest in nonprint media made him naturally want to bring alternative media into his classroom.

The methods course in which Jim was a student included an overview of literacy theory, including the relatively new developments in the field known as *new literacies.* One of Bill's goals for the class was to include some examples of assignments and assessments that used new literacies, and that his students in turn could use as they moved into student teaching and the first years of classroom teaching. These activities were presented in the overarching context of a dialogue about exactly what *literacy* means in this new century.

Bill and Jim stayed in touch after Jim graduated and have kept talking about these issues, preserving their dialogue by archiving their e-mails and meeting occasionally, with Bill preserving the conversation via note taking. In this chapter, we provide an overview of Jim's first 2 years of teaching and the dialogue that Jim and Bill had throughout. The remainder of this chapter is presented by our alternating voices, just as our dialogue has been over these past few years.

Year 1 of Teaching: Bridging New and Old Literacies

Jim: I began my teaching career at age 39, with a small group of eighth-grade students. I was assigned to teach them language arts and social studies in an alternative education setting that closely resembled a school within a school. Through a process of evaluating test scores, teacher recommendations, and parent requests, a select number of students was identified to be in the program. The total for this particular year was 28. (The number fluctuated from year to year and was not to exceed 30.) My students were identified as needing more individualized instruction to help them achieve. They did not qualify for special education services, but they were labeled as individuals who likely would not reach their potential without some kind of intervention. They were generally bored with school, bored with teachers' trying to save their educational careers, and just plain bored. It was very difficult trying to motivate those lacking in motivation.

I team-taught with another teacher. I taught language arts and social studies, while the other teacher taught math and science. We were also required to handle all of the other duties typically found in a regular school day, including counseling, discipline (both in our class and during specials), and even home visits to speak with parents/guardians. The premise of the program was to catch some of the students that fall through the cracks in a typical public school system.

While I was teaching in this alternative setting, I was also trying to incorporate all of the great ideas I learned during my undergraduate studies, not to mention complete my Praxis III requirements (a gatekeeping licensure assessment used by the state of Ohio), and be accepted by my fellow teachers. As if this weren't enough, my district was embroiled in contract negotiations that were less than friendly. The teachers were about 6 hours from striking at the beginning of the school year, and it seemed that my first teaching job would end with me walking a picket line. Luckily, cooler heads prevailed. Little did I realize that I would face such challenges in attempting to link students' out-of-school and in-school literacies.

Bill: Jim definitely had a few obstacles as a first-year teacher, but in our conversations, it seemed as if he handled them remarkably well. Of course, at this early point in his career, Jim felt successful just getting through each day. The alternative setting had its advantages and drawbacks. An advantage to the kinds of new pedagogies he wanted to try was that he could work with small class sizes. He also had five networked computers in the back of his room. A disadvantage was that Jim had been told that he could only use these computers to run educational software. I noticed that Jim talked about wanting to include some of the new literacies assignments we had discussed in class, but that he was hampered by his limited ability to use his classroom computers. He settled on an essence of new literacies that was not dependent upon technology. As Jim elaborates below, he allowed students to represent their knowledge using multiple genres, similar to the famous multigenre paper assignment in which students research a topic but instead of writing a typical research paper, present their synthesis of the research in the form of multiple genres (Romano, 2000).

Jim: Although, as Bill described, I did encounter some roadblocks to implementing new literacies in my classroom, I was able to hone in on my students' interests and strengths by breaking away from some of the more traditional assignments and assessments. I noticed that some of my students were very talented in the visual arts. I supported this by creating assessments in which students could show me what they knew by creating a visual or project. Early on, I could tell that I had some really talented artists in my class, and I wanted them to be able to incorporate elements of design in my assignments to reach them.

One such assignment required students to create a movie poster advertising the book that they had just completed for independent reading, chosen from various selections from my classroom library. The rubric we used to grade their poster detailed all of the elements of a typical movie poster, including interesting graphics, actors/actresses, rating, and a little teaser about the content of the book. To create the rubric, I had students brainstorm these elements of movie posters and what makes a good or bad movie poster, using examples from the Internet and local newspapers (see Figure 3.1).

We began our dialogue by looking at examples of movie posters from the newspaper and online. We brainstormed elements of a good poster, including eye-catching photography, easy-to-read text, and ability to create "buzz" or interest in the movie it is advertising. We then looked at various books from our classroom library. Again, we went back to the whole-group discussion format to talk about the similarities and differences between these two pieces of print media.

The students loved this project! I didn't have to remind them continually of the deadlines or keep them on task. They started looking critically at their work and actually helped each other with their posters. During this assignment, my classroom was buzzing with actively engaged students discussing their books. Some of my students also recognized the artistic abilities of others in the group and asked them for help. My students were collaborating with each other about this project, and the dialogue was meaningful and authentic. The culminating element of this project was a gallery walk, where we hung up the movie posters,

Teacher Name: **Mr. Ryan**

Student Name: _____

CATEGORY	10–8	7–5	4–2	1–0
Graphics— Clarity	Graphics are all in focus, and the content is easily viewed and identified from 6 feet away.	Most graphics are in focus, and the content is easily viewed and identified from 6 feet away.	Most graphics are in focus, and the content is easily viewed and identified from 4 feet away.	Many graphics are not clear or are too small.
Graphics— Originality	Several of the graphics used on the poster reflect an exceptional degree of student creativity in their creation and/or display.	One or two of the graphics used on the poster reflect student creativity in their creation and/or display.	The graphics are made by the student but are based on the designs or ideas of others.	No graphics made by the student are included.
Graphics— Relevance	All graphics are related to the topic and make it easier to understand. All borrowed graphics have a source citation.	All graphics are related to the topic and most make it easier to understand. All borrowed graphics have a source citation.	All graphics relate to the topic. Most borrowed graphics have a source citation.	Graphics do not relate to the topic *or* several borrowed graphics do not have a source citation.
Required Elements	The poster includes all required elements, as well as additional information.	All required elements are included on the poster.	All but one of the required elements are included on the poster.	Several required elements are missing.
Content— Accuracy	At least seven accurate facts are displayed on the poster.	Five to six accurate facts are displayed on the poster.	Three to four accurate facts are displayed on the poster.	Less than three accurate facts are displayed on the poster.
Attractiveness	The poster is exceptionally attractive in terms of design, layout, and neatness.	The poster is attractive in terms of design, layout, and neatness.	The poster is acceptably attractive, though it may be a bit messy.	The poster is distractingly messy or very poorly designed. It is not attractive.

(continued)

FIGURE 3.1. Making a movie poster to promote your book.

CATEGORY	10–8	7–5	4–2	1–0
Title	Title can be read from 6 feet away and is quite creative.	Title can be read from 6 feet away and describes content well.	Title can be read from 4 feet away and describes the content well.	The title is too small and/ or does not describe the content of the poster well.
Mechanics	Capitalization and punctuation are correct throughout the poster.	There is one error in capitalization or punctuation.	There are two errors in capitalization or punctuation.	There are more than two errors in capitalization or punctuation.
Use of Class Time	Used time well during each class period. Focused on getting the project done. Never distracted by others.	Used time well during each class period. Usually focused on getting the project done and not being distracted by others.	Used some of the time well during each class period. Some focus on getting the project done but occasionally distracted by others.	Did not use class time to focus on the project or often distracted by others.
Knowledge Gained	Student can accurately answer all questions related to facts in the poster and processes used to create the poster.	Student can accurately answer most questions related to facts in the poster and processes used to create the poster.	Student can accurately answer about 75% of questions related to facts in the poster and processes used to create the poster.	Student appears to have insufficient knowledge about the facts or processes used in the poster.

FIGURE 3.1. *(continued)*

then had an exhibition. The students brought in snacks and enjoyed talking with each other about their work. I borrowed this idea from my days as a photography student, when this procedure was commonplace.

The results of this assignment were awesome! It gave me the confidence to forge ahead with trying to incorporate new literacies into my classroom. It also did wonders for this group of usually unmotivated students. Once I saw how enthusiastic students were while doing this poster project, I was able to give them more latitude in how they represented the nonfiction writing assignment that I assigned next.

As a culminating project for social studies that year, students worked in pairs to design quilt squares dealing with sections of the U.S. Constitution. Each section was to explain a particular portion of the

Constitution in images, adding perhaps a word here or there. Once completed, we sewed these squares together to create a full-size quilt that was displayed in the classroom. The project was a resounding success! The students labored over their squares for days, trying to find just the right images, then placing them on the fabric. I was amazed by their comprehension of some very difficult concepts. The students were also very proud of the finished product that we hung in the classroom.

Bill: During his first year, Jim was doing his best to offer assignments that mimicked new literacies, without using much technology. It was ironic that Jim ended up returning to some old media within a new literacies paradigm, all with an eye toward helping to better unite his students' out-of-school and in-school literacies. In the somewhat restrictive alternative placement that, for some students, was the end of the line, Jim was able to cross barriers and open up some spaces within his classroom to explore the curriculum with his students in a nonstandard, new literacies fashion.

Year 2: New Obstacles for Integrating New Literacies

Jim: As I began my second year of teaching I was faced with a brand new curriculum and age group of students. My second-year assignment was a switch from eighth-grade to sixth-grade social studies and language arts. I also changed buildings within my district. So, in year 2 I found myself working with a completely different staff and creating new lesson plans for a different set of state standards, as well as a different level of student—younger and not placed in an alternative setting.

As I tried to fit in with a new group of administrators and teachers, I quickly discovered an entirely new set of obstacles, the first one being our district Ohio Achievement Test scores. Our building needed to raise test scores or face some serious consequences, including replacement of staff/administration. We formed grade- and subject-level teams to attack this issue. Early on in my second year of teaching, I was immersed in discussions pertaining to raising achievement scores. These discussions, although very good at targeting skills such as test-taking strategies, answering extended response questions, and reading between the lines of test questions in an attempt to decipher just what is being asked of students, were not student-centered. We never discussed new literacies or how we might attempt to link students' out-of-school literacies with those typically used in school. How was I to build on my limited successes from the previous year and continue to incorporate new literacies into my classroom when the mood of the building was so focused on standardized test scores?

My second year of teaching hit another snag with regard to technology. I was excited to learn that my classroom would be equipped with five new computers, complete with Internet access. The only problem was that we would be required to start the year without them. We were reassured that they would be "up and running" sometime in September. September came and went, with no computers. The problem we encountered was a bureaucratic quagmire. We were receiving special funding from the state of Ohio to obtain these computers, and the process was tied up in red tape. A new time line was established, and we were told that the computers would probably be ready to go by November. Again, November came and went, with no computers. We still had computer access within the building via the library (which was always full). Many teachers simply placed new literacies on the shelf due to the fact that access to technology was limited.

Nevertheless, during the early part of the year, I still tried to replicate some of the assignments that had worked for me in my first year, and I relied initially on these early teaching experiences as a guide. I continued to allow students some choices: The students' assignment was to research world civilizations, and they could represent the results of their research in many different forms. Students were to work in groups and uncover details about early civilizations in an effort to identify similarities and differences between ancient and current civilizations. They looked at a civilization's government, religion, geography, culture, and achievements. Each group member was responsible for a portion of this project, presenting the research both in print and visually. Although collaboration on individual documents was limited, I was able to set up a kind of modified WebQuest—one of the students' tasks was to spend some time at the computer researching their topics.

I also, fortunately, had a projector in my classroom that I could hook up to my computer. I used this piece of technology about once a week, usually researching websites that corresponded to the topics we were studying in social studies, including geography, cultures, and architecture. Although my students were reading nonprint texts from my computer, I knew that to really engage students with the curriculum, I needed to get keyboards in their hands.

Toward the end of my second year, I was able to make much greater use of technology, in spite of the lack of computer access for students in my room. By February I had received five ThinClient computers. These computers from Hewlett Packard have no hard drive. They require less maintenance than regular desktops, and they are more secure than desktops or laptops, because information is stored directly onto a server, not on the computer itself. With the arrival of the computers, our district provided us with a kind of Intranet—a website that allowed students to have e-mail accounts on a secure server. Teachers could then link up with other classrooms around the state or around the world, or they could use the site to dialogue with students about various items of interest within their own classrooms and school. An Intranet basically mimics an Internet environment, securely within an organization's computer network, without the risks of being out on the World Wide Web. In this case, our district linked up with other districts' Intranets to form a bigger, safe and secure network. Despite having only the five computers, I was able to implement this technology toward the end of the year in my classroom. The e-mail assignments I used gave me a much clearer window into the out-of-school literacies of my students. My students really enjoyed this new venue of communication. I began very simply. At first I used the student e-mail accounts to cut down on some of the assignments I had made using the paper communication I had utilized in my classroom all year. I sent writing prompts to my students, asking them to respond via e-mail. Not only were these responses easier for me to grade/respond to but it was also fun for me and for the students! My students would enter the classroom each morning saying things like, "Can I check my e-mail?" and "Do we have another writing prompt on the computers?"

My first prompt was as follows:

> Hey Group:
>
> O.K., let's try our new e-mail system. Please respond to the following writing prompt. Do you have any big plans for this summer? If so, what are you going to do? Do you have a summer job? Are you going on vacation? Also, how do you like the opportunity to communicate with me using e-mail instead of paper and pencil? Do you currently use e-mail outside of school?

Most of the students wrote about typical plans, such as going to an amusement park or some other summer destination spot. At this point, I noticed that only one student used text-message speak:

> TYRONE: hi Mr.Ryan its Tyrone and i have lots of things 2 do this summer i plan on going to Florida 4 the summer 2 see the Dayton 500 thats a Nascar race.... My summer J.O.B is baby sitting 4 some extra money 4 things like grifts pool or shoping.Im going to Dayton, Florida.i like talking to u cause u wont lie to us like some other people will cause they dont want 2 hurt your feeling but it ok cause u wont lie to us. Right?lol

I wondered about this lack of text-message speak. I had given my students the opportunity to write e-mails, and, for the most part, they wrote in standard English. Was it because it was being turned in to their teacher? I decided to ask them directly about this issue:

Hey Class!

Great job yesterday with the responses! Hey, this is kinda fun!

Here is your new assignment. We "older" folks often call how you "younger" folks communicate "invented spelling." This is when you use slang or initials to stand for certain words, ex. lol (laugh out loud). Please write to me using these invented spellings. Then, write to me the same message using plain, old English. Please remember to keep it school appropriate and have fun! If you have no idea how to write to me using "invented spelling" just write me a message anyway. Remember, have fun and show me the many ways students communicate with each other.

Thanks,

Mr. Ryan

Interestingly, some of the students were stumped by this prompt and just repeated the example I gave them (lol) in their messages. As I look at the student responses to this assignment, I can make some assumptions about their out-of-school literacies. Although many of my students "plugged-in" as they left the school building each day, I think they were at least initially somewhat intimidated or uncomfortable using these same writing forms in school. The e-mail assignments also showed me that although my students are growing up in a time when technology is all around them, there still exists a wide span of familiarity and skill with regard to these technologies.

One student even admitted that he typed slang into Google just so he could come up with some examples of text-message speak to use in his response. There were really only two students who used text message speak in their messages.

TYRONE: wat it is mr.ryan we is the best kids u had right mi dogg. we is sooooooooooooooooooooooooo colish we can blow away any 1 away how thinks they better right mr.ryan . . . lol, so wat is u doin this summer??? do u plan to do things with your kids so r u thinking about taking them 2 caliharie i dont no how 2 spell it butt its ok. i no lots of things that im going 2 b doin. like 2 start of with the summer im going 2 griffits pool. .like alsome right . . .

SARAH K: mr r waz up. how you doin. i think it's realy kool that ur lettig us write to a e-mail like this hows ur summer gona be like. r u going anywhere special that's i got 2 say. waz up mr r. this is sam. u r kool 4 trin to learn our lang

As I finished out the year, I decided to close with a couple good-bye prompts, again in an attempt to link a school assignment to their outside-school lives.

> Hello again from the front of the room! Many of you are doing a great job responding to my e-mails (the invented spelling was fun although you didn't write very much). Great job! As we finish the year let me ask you a couple of questions. What was your favorite part of this school year (any class, teacher, experience, it is your decision)? What has been your least favorite memory of this year? What are your hopes for next year? Thanks, I can't wait to read your responses . . .
>
> What a great time I have had with you all this year! You are a great bunch of students. I am proud of your accomplishments and hope you continue to work hard next year. I remember how nervous some of you were at the beginning of the year about coming to the middle school. That quickly changed. Have a great summer and please be safe. Also, come and see me next year when you get a chance.
>
> C U L8TR!
>
> Mr. Ryan

Students seemed to open up more in response to these last prompts, with several admitting that what they won't miss about sixth grade was being "picked on." Only a few students used text-message speech to any considerable degree, with Amanda winning the prize for alternative uses of punctuation.

> ABIGAIL: well my favorite teachers are Mrs.,Mason, Mr.,Watson and you. My favorite classes were read 180, choir, and computer tech!!!!!!!!!!!!!!!!! so far my favorite school memory is enjoying a nice school year with all my friends and teachers!! My hopes for next year are that I have classes with all my friends and have another great year at Highland Middle School!!!!!!!!!and I hope we leave the 6th grade drama behind us because it just turning us against each other.(lol) ha ha ha ha ha ha ha ha ha ha ha ha ha ha ha!!!!!!!!!!!!!! !!!!!!!!!!!!!!!!!!!!!!!!!!!!!:):):):):):)
>
> I forgot to tell you my most favorite subject of all is choir!!!!!!!!!!!!!!!!!!!!!!:) :) :) :) :) :) :) :) :) :(:(:(:(:(:(:(i don't want to leave all my friends behind

Whether it was just the end of the year or what, students seemed to be a little nostalgic and were apparently free to express their feelings in e-mail. Several students mentioned that they were indeed nervous at the beginning of the year (starting classes in a new building as the youngest in the school). Many expressed that they had enjoyed the class and would come back to visit. Perhaps the most poignant response was from Ethan.

ETHAN: i will miss u

This Intranet technology allowed the students and me to engage in an atmosphere that imitated the kinds of communicating students do when they leave school, even if they didn't fully take advantage of it. Again, although I observed many of my students "plugging in" as they left the building each day, some of them struggled finding the right words when talking to their teacher via e-mail. I believe that maybe some of the difficulty experienced by my students stemmed from the lack of opportunities they had in blending the two worlds together. But is that such a surprise, given how much difficulty we teachers have in blending the outside and inside literacies?

At least, in a small way, my students were plugging in as they arrived at school instead of when they left—one more small step toward the classroom I envisioned while I was studying to become a teacher. I felt that the e-mail assignment, limited as it was, gave me a glimpse into the possibilities I hope to pursue in coming years.

Bill: Jim ran into more familiar constraints during his second year of teaching, perhaps because he was no longer teaching in an alternative setting. He was now on the front lines of being a typical classroom teacher, with all the pressures of preparing for standardized tests and the stresses of trying to fit into an already established team structure. Still, with all of these pressures, Jim tried to find space for some alternative assignments. Interestingly, it was a technology initiative of the district (installing an Intranet system) that allowed Jim to begin a series of e-mail exchanges with his district. This can serve to demonstrate the power that central district office leaders have to enable teachers to do more innovative projects. Perhaps there is only so much a new teacher, or any teacher, can do without at least some structural supports in place.

It is interesting that when Jim was able to send e-mails to and from his students, they tended to stick to Standard English usage within their messages. Perhaps students are so used to "doing school" (McLaren, 1989) by the time they're in sixth grade, they realize what is the proper discourse when communicating with a teacher. Or perhaps they were just too young, as sixth graders, to have gotten into texting outside of school. Still, there are probably many students in other, perhaps more socioeconomically well-off districts who would have sent thousands of text messages by the age of 12. The Pew Internet and American Life Project (2008) reports that 85% of young people between ages 12 and 17 engage at least occasionally in some form of electronic personal communication.

In the case of Jim's classroom, perhaps assuming that all young people are proficient in these new communication forms is following a faulty stereotype. We have all seen the spam e-mail that gives a list of things that people born after 1985 have never heard of, such as record players or black-and-white television. But even if the students are "digital natives" (Prensky, 2005), there is no guarantee that they have truly absorbed the culture. There is no guarantee that Jim's students have had access to new media, just as there is no guarantee that they have had no access to print literacy. As we talk about bringing closer together students' out-of-school and in-school literacies, Jim's experience demonstrates that we shouldn't automatically assume that students' out-of-school literacies are necessarily technologically rich. In fact, one might argue that it is mostly for those students who are behind in their "new literacies" experiences that we need to make sure our classrooms allow them to have these online experiences that are commonplace for students who are lucky enough to be wired from a very young age.

Year 3: Planning for Future Integration of New Literacies with Gifted Students

Jim: As of this writing (fall 2008), I will be the Gifted Specialist teacher for our two middle schools for the coming school year. I began taking classes to obtain my license to teach gifted students at the beginning of my second year of teaching, and I am very excited about this new direction in my teaching career. Our district's gifted program currently serves students through fifth grade. Once our identified gifted students reach middle school, they are placed in honors classes for language arts and math. The district is trying to increase the educational opportunities for our gifted students, and this is where I come in.

Again, I am wondering how I will fit into this new environment. I will be expected to team with many different, typical classroom teachers in two different buildings. How will I inform teachers with many more years of teaching experience than I have about the needs of their gifted students? How can I incorporate new literacies into classrooms that are not mine, when I have found it a struggle to incorporate them into my own classroom? Will I be able to help our gifted student population, or will I inhibit their growth and success? Will I have opportunities to use the new literacies to engage students in meaningful conversations about content-area topics? Clearly, as I write about my experiences and expectations, I have many more questions than answers. One thing I know for sure is that incorporating new literacies into the classroom is possible. Not only that, it is good for students. I am convinced that bringing new literacies into the classroom helps to break that divide between school and students' out-of-school world. I have seen firsthand students engaging in the curriculum instead of just passively viewing the material that crosses their desks. I have also witnessed students talking to each other about the curriculum when they've had alternative means to represent their ideas. This may seem like a small feat, but it is certainly not the norm in all classrooms, and technology increases students' alternatives.

So how will I take some of my students' early successes into year 3? I guess I will just start small and try to "tweak" what teachers are already doing in their classes not only to help our gifted population but also to encourage the use of new literacies. I look forward to the challenge. I wonder what is in store for me this year and beyond!

Support for New Literacies in Beginning Teacher Classrooms

Bill: In preparing this chapter, it has again become clear how much "stuff" new teachers have to cope with just to survive from one year to another, without even considering their attempt to implement some very basic foundational elements of new literacies. Jim faced organizational barriers, technological barriers, institutional barriers, and just the challenges of being new (now starting his third year in his third different position in the district). Is it any wonder that 20–30% of teachers leave the profession in the first 5 years (Darling-Hammond, 2001)?

In the end, however, there will always be teachers like Jim who manage the struggle and are able to negotiate space for students' out-of-school literacy lives or for their desired ones. Ironically, Jim's work did pay off in part with greater student engagement in his mandated curriculum. Jim actually heard students enter his room saying, "Can we check our e-mail today?" There is probably not a teacher anywhere who has ever heard a student enter the room asking, "Can we check our textbooks today?" But more than just using the *new literacies* as the "spoonful of sugar to make the print go down" (Kist, 2005, p. 9), Jim also attempted to make the classroom work relevant, not just to the mandated curriculum, but to students' lives, so that students were not forced to unplug from the outside world in his classroom but could take steps toward plugging back in, in a time when we are moving increasingly toward round-the-clock communication.

In summary, Jim made attempts to link his students' out-of-school and in-school literacies in several ways. From the first days of his teaching career, he allowed students to have alternatives, both in research subject matter and in form of representation. Although students didn't have complete freedom to read and write whatever they wanted, they had much more latitude relative to their research subject matter and form of representation than they had in traditional classrooms. Jim's students were given permission to "read" and "write" nonprint texts, both in his social studies and in his language arts classes. This was a first step in his alternative classroom. Jim's students were given choices, something that has also been shown to be beneficial to students' print literacy lives (Hunt, 1996). In this case, Jim's students were given choices of topics and forms of representation. Eisner (1994, 1997) has suggested that when we limit our students' ability to communicate by using print only, we are in essence limiting their thought. Setting aside the need to prepare students for 21st-century literacy, if we set up our classrooms to be completely dominated by a traditional, print-centric literacy, we are cutting students off from their literacy lives outside of school, and we are sacrificing what John-Steiner (1997) has called "cognitive pluralism" in our classrooms.

In his classroom, Jim openly discussed the features of different forms of communication, comparing, for example what is done within the genre of movie posters and what are the idiosyncrasies of text message speech. Students were able to talk about what one can "say" in a movie poster that one cannot "say" in a book. And they used these different characteristics to co-construct a rubric that was used to assess their ability to present their work in this alternative medium. This discussion was held in an atmosphere that didn't hierarchize texts but honestly discussed the affordances of different symbol systems (New London Group, 1996).

When confronted with barriers, Jim worked around them to use assignments that allowed for much social networking in person. And when the teachers did gain access to an Intranet, Jim took advantage of it. In his second year, his compromise (and that of his district) to cope with Internet safety concerns by allowing his students to communicate via e-mail within the protections of an Intranet was an important step; even if the students weren't permitted to check out blogs from around the world, they were at least allowed to communicate with each other.

Jim's students worked on a balance of individual and collaborative activities, which, according to John-Steiner (1997) in her study of 50 creative artists, was reported as a key component of their development.

It's important to note that Jim was able to negotiate the dangerous waters of being a new teacher, yet still incorporate some attempts to link his students' in-school and out-of-school literacies. He worked within the set boundaries of a fairly traditional curriculum but found ways to incorporate some simple ideas that were still transformative. He started small, perhaps just adding on a choice element to a preexisting assignment, and added on more new media choices as they became available to him.

Now Jim prepares to rethink his curriculum and instruction as he enters the field of gifted education, so that in his first 3 years of teaching he will have taught in an alternative classroom, in a typical classroom, and in a gifted inclusion program. No small feat for a new teacher!

Concluding Thoughts

Recently, I attended a Cleveland Indians baseball game. I was seated behind what looked to be a boy about 14 years old. I noticed that he seemed to be engrossed in something other than the game. Indeed, I could see that he was texting someone, or multiple people, throughout almost the entire game. One part of me felt sorry that he wasn't in the moment, just enjoying the game. But then I wondered whether there has ever been a time in history when a teenage boy would sit during a baseball game writing to people. Regardless of whether he was using Standard English, he was going through his life, communicating with others. It was really irrelevant what I thought of it, anyway, because he was intent on communicating in this way, just as the future teachers with whom I work resist giving up their participation in social networking sites. But more than likely, the young man I observed will be forced to shut down his Blackberry or cell phone upon entry into his school. And, of course, there are scores of teenagers who aren't forced to unplug upon entry to school, because they can't afford new media tools.

For these students—the digitally precocious and the digitally left behind, and all the students in between—our classrooms must find ways to encourage greater links between students' out-of-school and in-school literacies, and our schools must find ways to support new practices, even when (especially when) they are attempted by the rookie teachers. Or, like the record player or black-and-white television, our schools run the risk of becoming fossilized antiques, increasingly out of touch with the outside world and increasingly marginalized in terms of being meaningful parts of young people's lives.

Questions for Reflection

1. How can educators more systemically overcome barriers to include new literacies in their classrooms? What are some actions that can be taken at the school or even district levels?

2. What are some examples of assignments that can unite students' out-of-school and in-school literacies but use very little technology?

3. If we move to a less-filtered environment, how can students be kept not only safe but also on task, working on what has been assigned?

4. How can teachers work proactively in their school communities to help students, colleagues, and parents support more unification between students' out-of-school and in-school literacies?

References

Anhorn, R. (2008). The profession that eats its young. *Delta Kappa Gamma Bulletin, 74*(3), 15–21, 26.

Chaplin, C. (Director). (1921). *The Kid* [Motion picture]. Los Angeles: First National Pictures.

Darling-Hammond, L. (2001). The challenge of staffing our schools. *Educational Leadership, 58*(8), 12–17.

Dewey, J. (1980a). *Art as experience.* New York: Perigee Books. (Original work published 1934)

Dewey, J. (1980b). *The school and society.* Carbondale: Southern Illinois University Press. (Original work published 1899)

Eisner, E. (1994). *Cognition and curriculum reconsidered* (2nd ed.). New York: Teachers College Press.

Eisner, E. (1997). Cognition and representation: A way to pursue the American dream? *Phi Delta Kappan, 78,* 349–353.

Hunt, L. C., Jr. (1996). The effect of self-selection interest, and motivation upon independent, instructional, and frustrational levels. *The Reading Teacher, 50,* 278–282.

John-Steiner, V. (1997). *Notebooks of the mind: Explorations of thinking* (rev. ed.). New York: Oxford University Press.

Kist, W. (2005). *New literacies in action: Teaching and learning in multiple media.* New York: Teachers College Press.

Kist, W. (2008). I gave up MySpace for Lent: New teachers and social networking sites. *Journal of Adolescent and Adult Literacy, 52,* 245–247.

Kress, G. (2003). *Literacy in the new media age.* London: Routledge.

McLaren, P. (1989). *Life in schools: An introduction to critical pedagogy in the foundations of education.* New York: Longman.

National Council of State Legislatures. (2007). *Children and the Internet: Laws related to filtering, blocking, and usage policies in schools and libraries.* Retrieved September 6, 2008, from *www.ncsl.org/programs/lis/cip/filterlaws.htm.*

New London Group. (1996). A pedagogy of multiliteracies: Designing social futures. *Harvard Education Review, 66*(1), 60–92.

Olsen, S. (2006). *Kids outsmart web filters.* Retrieved September 6, 2008, from news.cnet.com/kids-outsmart-web-filters/2009-1041_3-6062548.html.

Pew Internet and American Life Project. (2008). *Writing, technology and teens.* Retrieved September 6, 2008, from *www.pewinternet.org/ppf/r/247/report_display.asp.*

Prensky, M. (2005). Listen to the natives. *Educational Leadership, 63*(4), 8–13.

Romano, T. (2000). *Blending genre, altering style.* Portsmouth, NH: Heinemann.

Rosenblatt, L. (1995). *Literature as exploration.* New York: Modern Language Association. (Original work published 1938)

Vygotsky, L. (1978). *Mind in society: The development of higher psychological processes.* Cambridge, MA: Harvard University Press.

Vygotsky, L. (1986). *Thought and language.* Cambridge, MA: MIT Press. (Original work published 1934)

Willinsky, J. (1990). *The new literacy: Redefining reading and writing in the schools.* New York: Routledge.

CHAPTER 4

■ ■ ■

Adolescent Literacy and Democratic Life

What's Politics Got to Do with It?

HELEN HARPER

SHANNON MITCHELL

CLASSROOM PORTRAIT

Mrs. G. sighed. Her department head had selected William Golding's *Lord of the Flies* (1962) from the list of texts approved as *the* core novel for all 10th graders, including her class. As in previous years, the students in her 10th-grade class were white, working-class kids, with a few African American and Hispanic students thrown into the mix. As a weird effect of registration, male students were in the majority. Many of these students came from what euphemistically at her school were referred to as "disadvantaged" homes, and all were bussed in from a neighborhood some distance away from the school— geographically, culturally, and economically. Many of the students in this class struggled with reading, although Mrs. G. was convinced that there were at least one, or perhaps two, unacknowledged gifted students whose grades belied the fact they read well above grade level. A couple of the students were recent immigrants who, although also academically talented, were definitely not fluent in English. Many—sometimes Mrs. G. felt that nearly all students— were disaffected from school. *Lord of the Flies* would not have been her choice for this class, and she was fairly certain it would not have been the choice of the students.

Mrs. G. had made the case with her department head and with her principal, and with anyone else who would listen, that a core text of any kind, let alone this one, was not appropriate for the varied interests and abilities represented by the students in her class, and she had argue for some degree of student choice. In doing so, Mrs. G. cited statistics and research findings, and

---

quoted various position statements from the International Reading Association (IRA), the National Council of Teachers of English (NCTE), and the National Reading Conference (NRC). But for this year, her argument had no effect on what had been decided long before the school year began.

Mrs. G. considered what she could do with *Lord of the Flies* and what was possible, what was necessary for this class. She would need to offer much of the usual support to her struggling and/or her not-so-struggling readers—lots of media support (e.g., film versions, read-alouds, vocabulary development activities, plot graphs, and maybe some key translation or abbreviated texts for the English language learners [ELLs]). She also knew she would work extensively with the students' individual and collective responses, questions, and comments about characters, storylines, and themes to focus class discussion. This was all well and good, but Mrs. G. also knew that she needed to think in some deep way about the students' inevitable question, "Why are we reading this stuff?"—at least she hoped they would say "stuff."

Mrs. G. thought about how the novel and its representation of life could be used to help her students think about their lives now, and the private and public lives they would live in the future, and because she was an English teacher, what effects and connections their personal narratives might have relative to the text. Considering the class, she thought about a couple of possible themes she wanted to discuss with her students: The survival aspect of the novel could be connected with other print and media fiction and nonfiction texts about survival, and the class could consider what different representations of survival and extreme conditions said about the human nature. Mrs. G. was already listing the so-called "supplementary" contemporary texts that she and the students could discuss in relation to Golding's novel. Somehow they would also need to talk about the kind of society that the boys attempted to create in the novel and how authority was organized. Maybe they could discuss social rules and political organization, including perhaps something about current or future school organization. Maybe she should talk to the civics teacher about this. Mrs. G. also thought there would need to be something about social class, and the positioning of working-class Piggy and his particular dialect in relation to the other characters in the text. Piggy's use of the "N" word needed to be addressed in relation to language and racism. The construction of childhood and of masculinity, the lack of female characters, and the British focus would need attention. Discussion about the nature of evil and criminality was also possible, and how this novel related to various contemporary conceptions operating in their community. Maybe Mrs. G. might include something from the news. Also, she wondered what kind of project in and outside of the classroom might be possible with this novel.

How to draw from this and inject it into the students' interests and their initial responses to the text would be a trick, but at the heart of all this, if asked, Mrs. G. would say that she wanted her students to think critically about how they and others are represented in life and in text, and how and how they—as students, as citizens, as workers—might name and promote other realities in forwarding a better individual and collective life, locally and nationally. A colleague, with whom Mrs. G. shared these thoughts, commented about how impossible it all sounded, and more importantly, how political it all sounded. With some surprise, Mrs. G. reacted: "What's politics got to do with it?"

In this chapter, we begin by invoking Tina Turner's famous line "What's love got to do with it?" and ask in a similar tone, "What's politics got to do with it?"—that is, with adolescent literacy. In some respects politics would seem to have little to do with adolescent literacy, and with classroom literacy lessons more particularly, or it *should* have little to do with it. This follows in much the same way that the song line suggests "love" has nothing to do with "it," despite insistent demands that it does. But, as we will argue, if not insist, politics (and love) have much to do with what happens, and can happen, in our literacy classrooms and in the field of adolescent literacy more generally, whether we like it or not, whether we realize it or not.

The two of us come to this question of adolescent literacy and politics through different routes and at different times in our lives and careers. Helen Harper is a professor of English Education and Cultural Studies, with 15 years of university teaching and research. She is a former high school English teacher, who worked in northern and rural Canada. Her teaching and research is heavily informed by critical sociology. Shannon Mitchell was a Teach for America educator. She taught English in a high needs, urban high school for 2 years. No longer a classroom teacher, she has begun work on a graduate degree in strategic public relations. The aim of her studies is to engage public and political representatives in a critical examination of public schools, with concrete solutions and a vision for the future of education. Our voices appear at times together, at times separately throughout this chapter, interrupting the text with personal thoughts, insights, and experiences. These comments are a bit like staff room or water cooler talk, but however casual it may sound, both of us are deeply invested in the political nature and issues of literacy education.

By politics we refer in this chapter to (1) *cultural politics:* the promotion of a particular worldview, including what constitutes the good life, the good citizen, a good education, the good person, and so forth, and related to this is (2) *formal politics:* the machinations of particular governments and other civic institutions. In our experience, both of these notions of politics are often problematic for educators. Although teachers see themselves as making a difference in the lives of their students, most do not see themselves as agents of the state, or as politically motivated or involved, at least in the context of their professional lives. Indeed, most of the teachers with whom we have worked, or whom Helen has taught, are careful not to promote their own political views with their students, and in fact make concerted attempts to maintain an air of neutrality on sensitive political or social issues, whether or not they have been instructed to do so. Indeed, this neutrality is often viewed as a sign of their professionalism.

In our experience, many beginning teachers enter the profession speaking not of politics but of love, specifically, their love of children and of their subject area. English/language arts/literacy teachers often speak of their love of books and their desire to share their pleasure, so that students, too, can develop appreciation for literature, or at least print. These teachers are also deeply aware that being able to read and write is key to improving life opportunities. Often literacy in and of itself is seen as the key to a better life. It may be idealistic, but it is often deeply felt.

As a Teach for America teacher, Shannon wished not only to introduce her students to her subject area but also to improve the education and life circumstances of urban youth. She entered the profession with a mission:

> "I remember sitting in one of my undergraduate English classes when a Teach for America recruiter came in and gave a 3-minute speech that changed my life. He said that third-grade students growing up in inner-city schools were already three grade levels behind their suburban counterparts. By the time these inner-city students went to high school, half wouldn't graduate. This statistic forcefully reminded me of my own reality. I'd grown up in one of these suburban school districts. I had been blessed with an education that overprepared me. These kids deserved nothing less. My goal was to give children the opportunity to have a seat at the table of this country's American Dream. I wanted to teach them the power of writing and how important critical reading skills are to success."

For Shannon, the ideal public education should provide all students with an education that "overprepares them," one that guarantees that they have commensurate voice and opportunity with anyone else in America: a seat at the table like everyone else. Helen and others agree, but others might make a more politically neutral love of learning, love of literature, or lifelong learning the classroom priority.

> "From what teachers tell me [Helen] these days what English/language arts teachers seem to treasure most are those moments with

students and texts where the class comes together in the reading of a particularly moving piece of literature or a dramatic performance; where discussion is intense; where emotions run high; where working with text moves from a chore to a joy, and both students and teacher are changed by the experience. For struggling readers and their teachers, it is the moment when the reading suddenly becomes fluid, meaningful, and pleasurable. Time seems to slow down, and there is a kind of warmth and intimacy—just you, your students, and the text, lying quite outside the noise of the 'everyday' just beyond the classroom door.

"However, what I have long come to realize is that those moments with students and text were, and are, never so private and perhaps not always so wonderful; that the political and the public were infused throughout in the selection of text, in the reading lens or protocols, in the language and linguist classroom practices, and in the assessments used. What became apparent, and what we explain throughout this chapter, is that for all of us, and perhaps especially for the English/language arts teacher, teaching is a very public and political enterprise, even in those seemingly private moments with students and text, and perhaps especially in the intense desire of which Shannon speaks to make children's lives better. Cultural politics is there, as is the politics of the state; and it always has been."

In this chapter we discuss what politics and democratic life have to do, or might have to do, with the contemporary field of adolescent literacy and our teaching, but we begin by briefly exploring the historical political and democratic nature of literacy education in America at its very beginning.

From the Very Beginning: The Politics of Literacy Education

Whether the politics of education is as obvious as it is with Shannon, who came to her teaching with a particular mission, or more subtly, as with Helen, where politics infuses classroom lessons and life whether the teacher is or is not aware of it, political life—specifically, democratic life—and literacy education have long been intimately connected in America and elsewhere. In the United States, Thomas Jefferson initiated the public school system but infused it with a political agenda. He insisted that citizenship in a democracy demanded literacy skills, and that publicly funded schools would be sites for the development of such skills. Jefferson stated: "If a nation expects to be ignorant and free, in a state of civilization it expects what never was and will never be ... I propose schooling in reading and writing, arithmetic, and history at common expense to all" (cited in Shannon, 2001, p. 10). For Jefferson and the colonial Founding Fathers, the primary goal of schooling was to improve the minds of the people, to render them sage, so that they could be trusted with the vote. Jefferson's words were translated into action, and 3 years of publicly supported schooling were provided in the fundamentals of reading, arithmetic, and history.

Jefferson's proposal placed public schooling and literacy education at the center of American democratic life. Thus, literacy education, at least within the context of the public school, was always intertwined with politics and politicians, specifically, with the development of the nation, and within competing notions of democratic life and citizenship. Teachers, parents, community members, and others might wish to instill a love of learning, a love of literature, or, for that matter, lifelong learning in their children that is somehow free from the machinations of government, political systems, and contemporary social life. But in the United States, as in many other countries, literacy education, whatever else it might do, is bound to civic interests and has been so from the very beginning.

As radical and revolutionary as Jefferson's notion was at the time, a number of conditions severely limited the power of public education and of literacy education to influence all citizens. First and foremost, access to public schooling was limited. The politics of the day restricted public schooling to full citizens or to those who would become full citizens, which effectively excluded Native Americans and slaves, and included, in only a limited way, white females. Second, only a select number of students was permitted to continue schooling past the 3-year limit, and then, only at their family's expense. According to Jefferson, a natural aristocracy would develop from this select group, and they would govern the country. Whatever else it might do, Jefferson's efforts ensured that extended education would be a luxury for older, less affluent but intellectually capable students.

In addition, the 3 years of literacy education offered to at least some of America's youth provided only the very rudiments of literacy; indeed, it was an education intended to ensure that only those who would be voting could understand the arguments of this natural aristocracy. Teaching and learning basic literacy at this time, and indeed some might argue, in our own time, involved a great deal of drill and memorization, designed so that students might absorb, repeat, and later recall information.

Although public schooling and the literacy it provided in colonial times were limited and limiting to many children and adolescents, this would change in various ways and to various degrees. With political activism, public schooling would become more inclusive and expand to support students through high school. Also, literacy itself would be broadened. However, this did not change the basic constitution of public education. It has always been public and political: always about what constituted a good citizen; always part and parcel of democracy, part and parcel of nation building. And basic literacy, understood as the simple decoding and encoding of text, limited as that might be, remained, although often forgotten, a key part of public schooling as a requirement of democratic participation and citizenship. So, in part, the answer to the question "What does politics have to do it?" is that literacy education had and has everything to do with serving national interests, specifically, with creating democratic citizens. But more than democratic citizens, literacy education was also important to securing the economic prosperity of the nation. And this, too, is political.

As the country has grown, and as capitalism has become more entrenched, basic literacy has been attached to employment prospects, which then have become aligned with developing the economic strength of the country. Contemporary neoliberalism speaks of America's need for an educated and flexible workforce that can compete in the global markets, thus ensuring America's ongoing power in the world. A good citizen, then, must be employed or at least easily employable (because capitalism requires surplus labor). Thus, the economic interests of the country become a second argument for literacy education. From this perspective, adolescents must have basic literacy as a part of the necessary job skills to ensure the viability of country.

"When I [Helen] was an English teacher working in rural Alberta, I taught the General-level track (or stream), those students who did not intend to go to university. The vast majority of my students were white and working class. There were a few minority students, and a few who were recent immigrants. Many of the students in this track were very poor readers. My preparation to become a secondary school teacher did not include strategies to assist struggling adolescent readers. I am appalled and embarrassed now at how little help I was to my students, and how irritated I was that the elementary teachers had failed in some cases so miserably to teach basic literacy to my students. Moreover, had I been asked about the importance of basic literacy to my students, I would have spoken about their own personal employment prospects, unrelated to the country's economic state; and certainly not about their citizenship, not about their public voice. Yet, as I think of it now, my students were already marginalized by their school program, marginalized by their rural status, and some were marginalized by their social class, race, and ethnicity. They, more than anyone, needed the knowledge and power of literacy to ensure their political and economic participation in the community and in the country. While this was a failing on my part, it also has been a failing in our schools, and my teacher education program."

At the time that she was teaching, Helen did not see the meaning of her literacy lessons in terms of the development of economic and political citizenship. Had she done so, Helen might have pressed harder in her lessons, argued more forcefully for her program, and demanded more support from administrators, parents, and the community. Like many of us, she wishes she had known then what she knows now, for certainly she, unlike Shannon, had more autonomy in her classroom and more control over the literacy curriculum.

Shannon, a recent graduate from the Teach for America program and from an MEd program, perhaps had the benefit of better teacher education than Helen, but Shannon had less curricular freedom. For Shannon, as for many beginning teachers, the politics and the power dynamics in her literacy classroom were most evident in the obvious constraints she experienced in designing curriculum. In answering the question "What has politics got to do with it?" it is evident that politics has much to do with the literacy curriculum and school practices that are accepted and validated, and most obviously who decides. Shannon was surprised by the curricular limits placed upon her:

"What I came across in my teaching was widely different than anything I'd ever imagined. What I saw and experienced were low expectations, rigid curriculum, scripted lessons, and mandates from state boards that seemed out of touch with the needs and realities of my students and my classroom."

Similarly, in speaking about her efforts to meet the needs of her second language learners, Shannon comments:

"What I admired most about my ELLs was their immense dedication toward learning English. And it wasn't easy. Thrust into high school–level coursework each day, the students (many of whom had been in the country for less than 2 years) had to find ways to learn English—fast. They were always the hardest working students, so it was important to me that I help them in whatever way I could. Unfortunately, finding how to help them was a constant struggle. My school's solution was a scripted program. It went step by step through the reading process: learning vocabulary, reading the passage out loud together, reading the passage alone, identifying the main idea, responding to sentence starters, and repeating the same sequence with every reading passage. My students became robotic, and I became frustrated with myself as a so-called teacher. How could I send these students into any other English classroom and expect them to succeed, let alone become critical thinkers who actively participate in their communities? Moreover, the state evaluates a student's reading comprehension through a test with 45 multiple-choice questions. For so many of my students, this high-stakes test became a recurring nightmare in the quest for a high school diploma. Literacy for them was just another test in a long series of tests that they would face again and again."

Shannon was clearly frustrated by the macro-level politics of the school and the school board, as well as state authorities and federal mandates that dictated what curriculum would look like in her classroom. Like many of Helen's former students, Shannon was feeling the effects of an ongoing battle over who would control, and to what degree, the literacy curriculum, and more generally what would constitute a "good" literacy education. This is not new. As noted by Singh, Apple, and Kenway (2005),

> Education policies, pedagogies and politics have, at least since the state-sponsored rise of mass industrial education … involved major conflicts, contradictions, and compromises among groups with competing visions of "legitimate" knowledge, what counts as *good* teaching and learning, and what is a "just" nation state and world order. (p. 10)

At the moment it seems that those who control curriculum believe that teachers cannot be trusted with determining *legitimate* knowledge or *good* teaching, or, in this instance, what literacy is and how it should be tested.

For Shannon and for Helen, and many others, basic literacy is not sufficient for democratic citizenship. Critical literacy is also needed in democratic life (Cherland & Harper, 2007; Comber & Nixon, 2001; Freire , 1998, 1970/2000; Lankshear & McLaren, 1993). *Critical literacy* involves the ability to analyze texts and reading practices for their ideological content: to determine what and how particular versions of the world and the good life are promoted, and how particular populations and individuals are represented, and to what effect. This approach to texts allows students to assess and to "talk back" to the text, not simply to accept it, let alone love it. Democratic citizens need to be able to read and to critique the various texts that affect not only their voting decisions but also all forms of democratic activity in economic, cultural, and civic spheres, locally, nationally, and, arguably, internationally. It is a critical and political reading of text, and of textual practices, carefully and thoughtfully informed by the prospect of expanding and deepening democratic citizenship.

An education in basic and potentially critical literacy is tied to what is necessary for democratic citizenship. In addition, public schooling has been charged with the responsibility to develop moral, patriotic citizens (i.e., citizens who not only are capable of participating in democratic and economic life of the country but also endeavor to do so, willingly). As with basic literacy, developing character, and in particular a love of country, has been a long-standing though often unacknowledged task of the public school teachers. In terms of the English/language arts teacher, this responsibility has been tied to the teaching of the national (canonical) literature and the national language, English. The contention is that engagement with literature written by and about Americans ensures that students will have powerful identification with the country and its iconic narratives; thus, students will learn to love their country. This was part of colonial education, evident in Noah Webster's 1783 immensely popular school textbooks, of which he wrote, "Education should be adopted and pursued, which implants in the minds of American young the principles of virtue and of liberty and inspires them with an attachment to their country" (cited in Shannon, 2001, p. 13). Moreover, it was thought that exposure to the nation's literature might ensure the development of citizens who could transcend individual, local, or regional affiliations, literacies, and languages to acknowledge the common good and ensure unity in the nation. The Americanization of citizens through a patriotic literary education has been considered crucial during periods of intense immigration or whenever fear of the foreigner arises in the American psyche.

Another aspect of this argument is that the language of school literary texts, canonical or otherwise, should be taught and written in English. In a country of immigrants, the language of instruction and of texts used in the classroom has been and remains a difficult issue. One view is that the unity of the country depends on a common language, referred to as Standard English, and a common literature, that is, Anglo-American writing. Alternatively, it is argued that ensuring multilingual and multiliterate citizens will keep the country strong nationally and internationally; that is, an expertise in other languages and a large repertoire of various literate and literary practices for use in and outside the country is key to wider communication and the development of national economic prosperity. Moreover, democracy demands many voices and different perspectives; otherwise, choice and critical thought are not possible. There has been and always will be a tension between strengthening national unity and ensuring freedom of thought, speech, and action, so there is debate about what should be emphasized in public education and the literacy classroom.

There are many contentious battles over what constitutes the best literacy education. But to return to our question, "what's politics got to do with it?", adolescent literacy education is a public and political endeavor, because literacy education itself is and always has been a highly political project infused with civic, economic, and patriotic goals, and with competing visions over what best serves the nation and the common good of its citizens. Although the field of adolescent literacy is a part of this, it also has its own particular political terrain.

The Politics of Adolescent Literacy

Adolescent literacy is a field that developed and formalized in large measure through the advocacy efforts and, indeed, the political work of a number of individuals and organizations, most notably, the IRA and its creation of the Commission on Adolescent Literacy in the mid-1990s. Although interest in the reading skills of teenagers goes back to the early part of 20th century, and research in the content-area literacy of adolescents to the 1970s, by the 1990s, these areas of research and scholarship have been largely subsumed by the category of "adolescent literacy" and the work has only intensified since then (Alvermann, Hinchman, Moyre, Phelps, & Waff, 2006).

One goal of those involved in the field of adolescent literacy has been to focus energies on the adolescents who have not attained basic literacy, that is, on striving or struggling teenage readers. As noted in Alvermann and colleagues (2006), until recently, "the emphasis on the development of 'reading and writing' skills by political leaders, state and local school boards of education, and policymakers focused almost exclusively on literacy learning and teaching in the early grades and in elementary school" (Alvermann et al., 2006, p. vii). In the IRA's position statement on adolescent literacy (Moore, Bean, Birdyshaw, & Rycik, 1999, p. 1) Carol Santa, then president of the IRA, stated bluntly, "Adolescents are being short-changed. No one is giving adolescent literacy much press. It is certainly not a hot topic in educational policy or a priority in schools. In the United States, most Title I budgets are allocated for early intervention—little is left over for the struggling adolescent reader." In 1997, the IRA established a Commission on Adolescent Literacy that has pressed for public attention to the literacies of adolescents. Pressure from the IRA and other groups and organizations (NRC, the NCTE, etc.), along with attention to the ongoing low rates of literacy for adolescents learners, has ensured that now "policymakers are finding it increasingly difficult to ignore these groups' concerted call for improved literacy teaching and learning in the upper grades" (Alvermann et al., 2006, p. ix).

In earlier comments in this chapter, we certainly spoke of our own lack of preparation for teaching older students who have limited literacy skills and/or English literacy skills. Increasing attention to the teaching and learning of literacy in the middle and secondary schools is important for expanding and deepening democratic citizenship. This echoes down to us from Thomas Jefferson at the very beginning of this country and indeed from many other countries. It is not something we can instill only in academically talented student-citizens. It is not simply that "literacy promises to enhance individuals as well as society" (Moore et al., 1999, p. 7); rather, it is a specific and necessary part of the renewal of democratic life that must occur in every generation if democracy is to continue (Harper & Bean, 2006). Although easy to accept, it is also easy to forget or to underplay, leaving one of the strongest arguments for increasing attention to adolescents' literacy often unstated. Despite the tremendous advocacy work of the IRA and other organizations supporting adolescent literacy, the political arguments concerning democratic citizenship are unstated or, at best, implied.

What's Politics Got to Do with It?: Texts for Adolescents

The second area of focus in the field adolescent literacy has been the changing nature of teens' literacy practices, particularly with regard to their use of the new and emerging communication technologies. Adolescents, as a group, have embraced and made integral to their lives the various communication and media modalities. In response to the changing nature of students' literacy, many educators have pressed for expanding the limited range of texts offered to adolescents in schools. For example, the IRA Commission on Adolescent Literacy (Moore et al., 1999) insists that adolescents deserve "access to a wide variety of reading materials that they can and want to read" (p. 4). This suggests that we teach not only the canonical texts but also include all forms of texts, particularly those clearly within the abilities and interests of adolescents. To accomplish this, student choice is key. The Commission further notes that adolescents want the independence of selecting "age-appropriate materials they can manage and topics and genres they prefer," which means including "reading materials tied to popular television and movie productions; magazines about specific interests, such as sports, music or cultural backgrounds; and books by favorite authors" (p. 5). Similarly, the NCTE (2004) states that adolescents need "sustained experience with diverse texts in a variety of genres and offering multiple perspectives on real life experiences. Although many of these texts will be required by the curriculum, others would be self-selected and of high interest to the reader" (p. 3; see also *NCTE Principles of Adolescent Literacy Reform*, 2006). Both the NCTE and the IRA insist on a wide selection of texts: "Texts should be broadly viewed to include print, electronic, and visual media" (NCTE, 2004, p. 3). Pushing further, the IRA suggests combining reading material (textbooks, paperbacks, magazines, websites, etc.), with the goal that teen readers, by improving and extending their reading, might "expand and strengthen their grasp of the world … and nourish their emotions and psyches as well as their intellects" (Moore et al., 1999, p. 5).

Knowledge of one's external world and of one's internal world is of importance to the individual, as suggested by IRA, and also to the country. Thoughtful and informed decision making requires access to a wide range of information and a diversity of thought, opinion, and feeling. Beyond information and knowledge, choice is also key to democratic decision making. Without choice, there are no grounds on which to exercise individual and collective freedom. Developing strong expectations for and comfort with choice needs to be a part of democratic schooling and can be used to defend expansion of the range of texts available to adolescents. Thus, although not explicitly stated by the IRA or NCTE, these requirements for democratic life can be used to support efforts to increase the range of texts made available to adolescents and, importantly, to allow adolescent learners greater choice (i.e., freedom) in selecting their texts.

A related focus in the field of adolescent literacy has been on young adult literature, that is, on contemporary literature written specifically for teens and popular with teens, and that usually features teenage protagonists contending with contemporary social and political issues. Using this literature may help to motivate students to read, but since much of this literature has a political and/or social issue emphasis, there are opportunities to address the condition of society. Indeed, Helen and her colleague Tom Bean have found that some of this literature offers powerful opportunities for students and teachers to consider issues of social equity and justice, and the possibility of a broader, more profoundly democratic life (Bean & Harper, 2006; Harper & Bean, 2006).

Although texts themselves may allow for deep discussion of social and political issues, the literary approach taken by teachers is also a part of the implicit political dynamic of the English/language arts classroom. What has become more and more apparent to literacy scholars is that there is no neutral way to engage with or analyze text. We bring our own learned perspectives to text. Reader response, new criticism, feminist criticism, Marxist criticism, postcolonial and critical theories among others, named or not, all offer a particular lens, with particular worldviews, through which to "read" the text (Leggo, 1997; O'Neill, 1993). What we read and how we read, that is, what we have been taught to privilege in our reading of text, can be considered forms of cultural politics. These ways of reading text may ultimately inform how we read the world (Freire, 1998, 1970/2000) and how we teach particular texts.

> "When I [Helen] was teaching my General-level high school students, I offered them opportunities to read self-selected books for independent reading projects and for free-reading during class time—which, despite their reading levels, they loved. But all the common core texts we studied came from British, American, and Canadian lists of canonical texts deemed appropriate for adolescents. I was glad my students read Canadian literature: It was good, surprisingly good, and I thought it would make them proud of being Canadian. It did not occur to me to question with my students which and whose Canada was being represented in the literature they read for my class or how they and others were positioned in this literature. What was particularly troubling for my General-level students was the kind of novels offered to them. By and large, the literature spoke of those striving with lost hopes and dreams, with physical rather than psychological challenges, including a surprising number of those with intellectual challenges. So my General-level students read Steinbeck's *Of Mice and Men* and Keyes's *Flowers for Algernon* as opposed to Charles Dickens's *Great Expectations* in the academic stream. Years later, I know and cringe at what messages my students might have consciously or unconsciously received in my not-so-simple and innocent literature lessons. I should have made them aware of the messages that threaten to undermine their intellectual confidence and their ambitions."

Similarly, Shannon speaks of text selection made available in her context:

"In my first week of teaching I was given a list of available texts my school had acquired, and I was told I could pick anything from my assigned grade level. I was, however, strongly advised to pick choices under the section 'boy novels.' My school, in an attempt to raise failing test scores, had divided the freshmen and sophomore core classes (English, history, math, and science) into all boys' and all girls' sections. I was given the boys and was therefore directed to the 'boy novels.' Who had selected which novel was for boys and which was for girls was anyone's guess. It's safe to say I didn't understand the reasoning or concept behind a 'boy' book.

"The other point I want to make is that a literature lesson is more than just reading a book. For me it was always about engagement. If I could get the boys invested in something, I could push them further. My greatest fear when I first started was that my students were so negative about reading and writing, and being in this all-boys class, that they wouldn't even attempt to learn. So I made it something we did together, talked about together, and explored together. We had conversations about current events, how students felt about school policies, as well as, and sometimes related to, themes in *Lord of the Flies*. It was more about making them overall learners, readers of the language in their world, than just about choosing books from a departmental list. I was forced to play a role in picking what we read, but I tried my best not to define *how* we read it."

Shannon's efforts speak to a desire to return the teen reader to the center of textual interpretation. Her attempts are supported by scholars in the field of adolescent literacy. According to the NCTE, adolescents need "conversations/discussions regarding texts that are authentic, student initiated, and teacher facilitated. Such discussion should lead to diverse interpretations of a text that deepen the conversation" (2004, p. 3). The emphasis is on the interpretive power of the reader, wherein power shifts away from the authoritative reading of critics and educators to the individual reader, thus providing, some would suggest, a more democratic space as well as a more effective pedagogical strategy (Rosenblatt, 1938/1995; Willinsky, 1992).

Yet, as Helen and others would argue, we need to press further, to introduce students to critical and diverse readings of texts that students may not, on their own, have heard of or experienced (Caughlan, 2007; Cherland & Harper, 2007). Critical questions of texts may help students to see how the world is represented in the text, who is missing, and how the reader is positioned in and by the text. The NCTE position statement (2004) acknowledges some of this, stating that a critical examination of text allows adolescents to "question and investigate various social, political and historical content and purposes within texts" and to "make connections between texts, and between texts and personal experiences to act on and react to the world" (p. 3). Furthermore, NCTE's 2006 statement suggests the need to engage students in critical examinations of texts as "they dissect, deconstruct, and re-construct in an effort to engage in meaning making and comprehension processes" (p. 6). Of course, the question is, deconstructing and reconstructing text for what? What is the point of critically analyzing texts and engaging in meaning making?

We would add that there is a need to highlight not only the world in the text but also the text in the world. In the case of *Lord of the Flies*, how is it that this novel of British schoolboys gone wild is seen as entirely appropriate reading for our contemporary students in Shannon's example, for her class composed entirely of males, and more particularly, almost entirely of Latino and African American young men?

Not to ask such questions of the text is to leave unexamined whatever commonsense but value-laden notions of the world, self, and others that adolescent readers, their classmates, and their teacher might hold. Moreover, the purpose of these questions is not simply to "deepen conversation" or to increase reading comprehension, but to expand on the critical consciousness of adolescent readers and their teachers in support of a more profoundly democratic way of life, what John Dewey (1916) named an *associated way of living*, a life lived with others.

The Politics of Diversity and Difference in Adolescent Literacy Lessons

The contemporary field of adolescent literacy has placed a strong emphasis on adolescent readers as a diverse and dynamic population. The IRA Commission on Adolescent Literacy speaks of individual differences, stating that adolescents deserve "teachers who understand the complexities of individual adolescent readers, respect their differences, and respond to their characteristics (Moore et al., 1999, p. 8). Moore and colleagues note as well that "factors such as family heritage, language, and social and economic position contribute to the variation that students regularly display during reading and writing activities" (1999, p. 8).

With specific reference to instruction, Moore and colleagues (1999) state, "Adolescents deserve more than a centralized, one-size-fits-all approach to literacy" (p. 8). This suggests that literacy educators must be comfortable pedagogically with complexity and plurality. Such an approach is clearly at odds with mandated scripted lessons, standardized testing, and accountability measures, some of which Shannon referred to earlier.

The position taken by the IRA Commission is supported by the extensive ethnographic studies of adolescents and their literacy practices. These studies, while naming adolescents as a category of study, trouble the category, revealing how individual adolescents and various social and economic groups of adolescents use literacy in and out of school to name themselves and their world in dynamic ways, many of which lie outside stereotypical views of the adolescent (Blackburn, 2003; Fecho, 2004; Finders, 1997; Moje, 2000; Obidah & Marsh, 2006; O'Brien, Springs, & Stith, 2001). Who we define as the "adolescent" and what we mean by it is critical, because difference, diversity, and complexity, rather than similarity, describe adolescents and their literacy practices. Therefore, literacy educators need to find ways to work with the diversity and complexity of their literacy learners. Although respecting individual and cultural differences, and providing instruction based on knowledge of differences may provide more specific and targeted literacy instruction, and presumably improved literacy learning, more will be needed if we are "to challenge policymakers [and others] who believe that adolescent literacy can be improved solely by imposing accountability measures on schools and teachers" (Lewis & Moorman, 2007, p. xii).

Better policies and more resources, along with more creative and local initiatives, are needed to support the variety of adolescent learners and literacies that enter our contemporary classrooms. The connection between literacy and democratic life can be employed effectively to gain this support. The focus on acknowledging and responding to difference and an insistence on diversity support a literacy program committed to democratic life. Democracy as opposed to totalitarianism is identified by a respect for and, indeed, a need for diversity in thought. If we were all the same, and all thought and acted the same, we would neither have nor would we need democracy. John Dewey (1916) once described *dissent* as the engine of democracy. Acknowledging, respecting, and responding to difference is not just an act that reflects good humanistic teaching in efforts to promote literacy, but a necessary attitude/skill required but often forgotten in democratic life.

"I [Helen] do support the notion of recognizing and responding pedagogically to difference. However, as a teacher-educator I am concerned about the pathologizing of difference—that is, the rigid and permanent labeling of individuals, and the literacy and literacy instruction they will receive. I tell future teachers to plan for and assume that difference and diversity will be evident in their secondary literacy classrooms, but to remain open to fluidity and complexity in their students, and the hybrid and dynamic cultures present in their classrooms; and, most importantly, to be suspicious of any easy categorization of learners and the instructional remedies that are seemingly required. Sound literacy education for democratic life certainly demands this care and attention from us. Finally, I do not believe that merely allowing students to voice their opinions goes far enough in moving students or teachers to a critical consciousness of text and its workings in the world. If we are to increase a commitment to social justice, and the expansion and deepening of democratic life, we need to offer and to allow for critical questions to ourselves and to text that might unsettle our commonsense notions of the self, the other, and the world."

Adolescent Literacy beyond the Classroom, beyond the Nation-State

In *Effective Literacy Instruction for Adolescents*, commissioned by the NRC, Donna Alvermann (2001) suggests that "many adolescents of the Net Generation find their own reasons for becoming literate—reasons that go beyond reading to acquire school knowledge of academic academics texts" (p. 2). She iterates the need to "address the implications of youth's multiple literacies for classroom instruction" (p. 2). The NCTE (2004) states, "It is important for teachers to recognize and value the multiple literacy resources students bring to the acquisition of school literacy" (p. 1). It further acknowledges that adolescents have literacy lives outside of school; therefore, the teachers of adolescents need "continued support and professional development that assist them to bridge between adolescents' rich literate backgrounds and school literacy" (p. 3). Recognizing the out-of-school literacies that students bring to the classroom, and acknowledging a wider range of interests and purposes for literacy, has been a part of the work of scholars and educators in adolescent literacy. In doing so, more relevant, meaningful, and effective literacy lessons are possible.

Literacy communities outside the classroom can be acknowledged, and these communities can, with the advent of the new technologies, range far and wide. Dynamic and multiple affiliations are possible, unencumbered by physical proximity in these times. A student's primary affiliations and identifications need not be with school or neighborhood community. Bridging in-school and out-of-school literacies and for the diversity of students that enter our classrooms becomes a formidable task for the teacher. Certainly, bringing the many worlds of our students into our literacy classrooms, and our literacy classrooms into their worlds, changes the nature of our work and our roles as teachers. Rather than insisting on a single, unified national literacy, the adolescent literacy classroom becomes the site for engagement with, study, and critique of a multiplicity of literacies and communities. Such work hints at the possibility that the literacy of the democratic nation-state needs to expanded and refigured as global literacies in a global democracy. This endeavor may be more in tune with the increasingly interdependent and interconnected world of our students' lives and their digital (computer-generated) literacies.

"If we are truly going to engage teenagers, then we have to open our classrooms to new materials, new goals, and new modes of literacy. If I [Shannon] were to step back and assess my classroom experience, I see that my students were craving a new and different type of literacy: something other than print literacy. My students were and are confronted with information from all types of places and sources via the Internet. They have 24-hour news channels and have grown up watching reality television. A teacher's bookshelf is no longer the only place to find inspiration for them."

"The graduate students at my [Helen's] institution and the teachers I work with in the field continue to educate me about the new communication technologies. Without these students and teachers, my work would suffer enormously. Certainly, my sense of community has expanded with these technologies. My colleagues from across the globe are as close as my e-mail. Moreover, my sense of myself as a Canadian working outside the country is both reconfirmed and reshaped as a result of the technologies that allow me easy access to my family, friends, and colleagues—I can be here and there."

Concluding Thoughts

Politics of various sorts seem to have much to do with adolescent literacy. Whether acknowledged or not, our most basic literacy lessons; our most sophisticated literary texts; our bravest efforts to acknowledge and respond to social, cultural, and individual difference; and our ultramodern attempts to provide the newest and slickest technology for our adolescent literacy learners are informed by and speak implicitly or explicitly to the politics of our work as literacy educators. Indeed, politics seems to have everything to do with it. We think this means embracing the political nature of literacy and, more generally, of schooling in the lives of literacy learners, their teachers, and their communities, and, of course, ourselves. It calls for us to acknowledge the democratic underpinnings of adolescent literacy and the possibilities it offers to advocate for students, for their literacy education, and for our lives lived together on this planet.

Questions for Reflection

1. What are the obvious and not so obvious ways in which the politics of adolescent literacy are evident in your classroom and teaching practice, or in teaching practices you have observed?

2. How might the study of young adult literature forward the development and preparation of students for their lives now and in the future as national–global citizens?

3. What accounts for the difficulty some people have in accepting the political nature of public education and of literacy education in particular?

4. Examine at least three current newspapers and identify (a) images conveyed about the progress/success of public education and (b) expressed goals of public education. How do these accounts compare to your own thoughts on these topics?

References

Alvermann, D. (2001). *Effective literacy instruction for adolescents* [Executive summary and paper commissioned by the National Reading Conference]. Chicago: National Reading Conference.

Alvermann, D., Hinchman, K., Moore, D., Phelps, S., & Waff, D. (Eds.). (2006). *Reconceptualizing the literacies in adolescents' lives* (2nd ed.). Mahwah, NJ: Erlbaum.

Bean, T., & Harper, H. (2006). Exploring notions of freedom in and through young adult literature. *Journal of Adolescent and Adult Literacy, 50*(2), 96–104.

Blackburn, M. (2003). Exploring literacy performances and power dynamics at The Loft: Queer youth reading the world and the word. *Research in the Teaching of English, 37,* 467–490.

Caughlan, S. (2007). Competing cultural models of literature in State content standards. In D. Rowe, R. Jiménez, D. Compton, D. Dickinson, Y. Kim, K. Leander, et al. (Eds.), *The 56th yearbook of the National Reading Conference* (pp. 178–190). Oak Creek, WI: National Reading Conference.

Cherland, M., & Harper, H. (2007). *Advocacy research for literacy education: Seeking higher ground.* Mahwah, NJ: Erlbaum.

Comber, B., & Nixon, H. (2001). *Negotiating critical literacies in classrooms.* Mahwah, NJ: Erlbaum.

Dewey, J. (1916). *Education and democracy.* New York: Macmillan.

Fecho, B. (2004). *"Is this English?": Race, language and culture in the classroom.* New York: Teachers College Press.

Finders, M. (1997). *Just girls: Life and literacy in junior high.* New York: Teachers College Press.

Freire, P. (1998). *Pedagogy of freedom: Ethics, democracy, and civic courage.* New York: Rowman & Littlefield.

Freire, P. (2000). *Pedagogy of the oppressed.* New York: Continuum. (Original work published 1970)

Golding, W. (1962). *Lord of the flies.* New York: Coward-McCann.

Harper, H., & Bean, T. (2006). Fallen angels: Finding adolescents and adolescents literacy in a renewed project of democratic citizenship. In D. Alvermann, K. Hinchman, D. Moore, S. Phelps, & D. Waff (Eds.), *Reconceptualizing the literacies in adolescents' lives* (2nd ed., pp. 147–160). Mahwah, NJ: Erlbaum.

Harper, H., & Bean, T. (2007). Literacy education in democratic life: The promise of adolescent literacy. In J. Lewis & G. Moorman (Eds.), *Adolescent literacy instruction: Policies and promising practices* (pp. 319–335). Newark, DE: International Reading Association.

Lankshear, C., & McLaren, P. (1993). *Critical literacy: Politics, praxis, and the postmodern.* New York: State University of New York.

Leggo, C. (1997). *Teaching to wonder: Responding to poetry in the secondary classroom.* Vancouver: Pacific Educational Press.

Lewis, J., & Moorman, G. (Eds.). (2007). *Adolescent literacy instruction: Policies and promising practices.* Newark, DE: International Reading Association.

Moje, E. (2000). "To be part of the story": Literacy practices of gangsta adolescents. *Teachers College Record, 102,* 651–690.

Moore, D. W., Bean, T. W., Birdyshaw, D., & Rycik, J. A. (1999). *Adolescent literacy: A position statement for the Commission on Adolescent Literacy of the International Reading Association.* Newark, DE: International Reading Association.

National Council of Teachers of English. (2004). A call to action: What we know about adolescent literacy and ways to support teachers in meeting students' needs: A position statement from NCTE's commission on reading. Retrieved September 4, 2008, from *www.ncte.org/about/over/positions/category.literacy/118622.htm.*

National Council of Teachers of English. (2006). *NCTE principles of adolescent literacy reform: A policy research brief.* Urbana, IL: Author.

Obidah, J., & Marsh, T. (2006). Utilizing student's cultural capital in the teaching and learning process: "As if" learning communities and African American students' literate currency. In D. Alvermann, K. Hinchman, D. Moore, S. Phelps, & D. Waff (Eds.), *Reconceptualizing the literacies in adolescents' lives* (2nd ed., pp. 107–127). Mahwah, NJ: Erlbaum.

O'Brien, D., Springs, R., & Stith, D. (2001). Engaging at-risk students: Literacy learning in a high school literacy lab. In E. B. Moje & D. O'Brien (Eds.), *Constructions of literacy: Studies of teaching and learning in and our of secondary schools* (pp. 105–123). Mahwah, NJ: Erlbaum.

O'Neill, M. (1993). Teaching literature as cultural criticism. *English Quarterly, 25*(1), 19–25.

Rosenblatt, L. (1995). *Literature as exploration.* New York: Modern Language Association. (Original work published 1938)

Shannon, P. (2001). *Becoming political, too: New readings and writings on the politics of literacy education.* Portsmouth, NH: Heinemann.

Singh, M., Kenway, J., & Apple, M. (2005). Globalizing education: Perspectives from above and below. In M. Apple, J. Kenway, & M. Singh (Eds.), *Globalizing education: Policies, pedagogies, and politics* (pp. 1–29). New York: Peter Lang.

Willinsky, J. (1992). *The triumph of literature/the fate of literacy: English in the secondary school curriculum.* New York: Teachers College Press.

■   ■   ■

PART II

Connecting Adolescent Literacy Instruction to Students' Personal Goals

CHAPTER 5

■ ■ ■

How Can We Help Adolescent Readers Meet the Challenges of Academic Text?

JILL LEWIS

TANYA READER

CLASSROOM PORTRAIT

Mr. Bowers, a seventh-grade social studies teacher, recently attended a professional development workshop on teaching summarization skills that emphasized how much this ability contributes to students' comprehension of content texts. His students have summarized text before, though not with much success. He realizes the critical role that comprehension plays in student achievement in social studies, and in life. Thus, Mr. Bowers has decided to try teaching this skill again, following workshop suggestions to begin instruction with easy text that is familiar to students. But as the lesson begins, students' faces suggest fatigue and uncertainty, as though students in this class of varying abilities are thinking suspiciously, "Here is another 'strategy' that is supposed to help me, but why should it be any more successful than the rest?"

Using an overhead transparency with four key words printed on it: *Someone, Wants, But,* and *So,* Mr. Bowers asks the students to identify a story that they think everyone in class will know. Students suggest several current movies, but Mr. Bowers has to confess that he has neither heard of nor seen these. He then suggests that students name fairytales. Nearly every hand then goes up and after several familiar tales are named, the class decides to work with *Cinderella* for this activity. Students complete each section of the transparency, naming Cinderella as the *Someone,* and noting that Cinderella *Wants* to go to the ball with the prince. Under Mr. Bowers's guidance, one student recognizes that what gets in Cinderella's way of going to the ball is that "her wicked stepmom and sisters won't let her go because they're jealous of how pretty she is!" Finally, the class discusses the story: "So, what happened?"

They relate that Cinderella went to the ball with the prince and lived—well, you know. After putting all these pieces together, Mr. Bowers explains that this is not a summary, but merely the framework for one. Their next task is to turn this framework, or skeleton, into a summary.

After students successfully complete the summary for *Cinderella*, they move on to their social studies textbook. Working with a section of a chapter, they develop another framework that may be used as a basis for a summary, using the same set of key words they used for *Cinderella*. The text introduces global warming by discussing how this climate change affected one community. This shift to academic text seems to provoke discomfort in the students. Now, a textbook differs from a fairytale, of course, but Mr. Bowers believes this section of the social studies textbook lends itself well to this activity, because events are written in narrative form, a structure with which students are extremely familiar. However, students have a difficult time responding to the four key words for the framework, even though this is a unit review.

Mr. Bowers is disappointed. He doesn't know where the fault lies. In his teaching? In students' reticence? Students' lack of experience with thinking about text beyond simple recall of details? He does know that without the ability to comprehend academic text successfully, students will struggle throughout high school and have limited opportunities for successful futures. He will continue, as he always has during his 12 years of teaching, to look for ways to improve students' ability to comprehend academic text.

Starting with a fairytale seems like a reasonable way to ease students into the frequently needed and important skill of learning to summarize. Though teachers assign this type of task frequently, it is an arduous one, because students must be able to determine what is important and what is less so, and what pieces of information should be synthesized with others, in addition to how to write the summary in a cohesive manner. This is the crux of academic literacy: The information may be familiar, but if students do not know how to access it, then it is not really theirs.

Students' difficulties with comprehending text are not new problems for teachers and schools. Like Mr. Bowers, many teachers who work with adolescents have an unwavering commitment to do all they can to promote student achievement. They hone their craft by participating in teacher study groups, professional development workshops, and conferences; reading professional materials; and conducting action research in their own classrooms. Yet they don't always succeed, and the public perception is that teachers and schools are not doing enough to raise student achievement to high enough levels to compete in what is often referred to as the "global marketplace." In fact, for some time now, the American public and business sector have bemoaned adolescents' low results on standardized assessments such as that of National Assessment of Educational Progress (NAEP, 2005, p. 1), on which "the average reading score for high school seniors was 286 on a 0–500 scale." These scores also indicated that eighth- and 12th-grade students struggle in particular with the ability to analyze, infer, and synthesize information in content-area texts (Heller & Greenleaf, 2007). Only small gains have been made in more than 15 years. Just three points separated eighth graders tested between 1992 and 2007: "The score in reading for literary experience increased from 259 in 1992 to 262 in 2007, and the score in reading for information increased from 261 to 264 over the same period. The score for reading to perform a task showed no significant change in comparison to the score in 1992" (National Assessment of Educational Progress, 2007, p. 26). Gaps between scores of minorities (African American and Hispanic) and those of whites persisted.

Adolescents in the United States have not fared any better on international assessments. The most recent Programme for International Student Assessment (PISA) in-depth assessment of reading literacy and skills among 15-year-olds included 41 participating countries in 2001. In the literacy assessment, students are compared in their abilities to "use literacy knowledge and skills to meet real-life challenges" (Organisation for Economic Co-operation and Development [OECD], 2001, p. 16). Students from the United States scored only at the average OECD level when compared internationally, scoring ninth, with an average score of 542; the international average was 500, with Sweden ranking first internationally at an average of 562 (Whetton & Twist, 2003, p. 4).

In response to concerns raised by these various indicators of student academic progress, Achieve (2008) was created as a bipartisan, nonprofit organization by the nation's governors and business leaders to help "states raise academic standards, improve assessments and strengthen accountability to prepare all young people for postsecondary education and training, careers, and citizenship" (p. i).

One might argue for several reasons, however, that criticizing adolescents and their teachers for these assessment results is actually a case of blaming the victim. First, by the time students reach fourth grade, much formal reading instruction has ended; this is certainly true by sixth or seventh grade, when students typically attend a host of content classes taught by different teachers, most of whom have taken few, if any, courses that focus on developing students' literacy in their subjects. As noted by the International Reading Association (2003),

There is tremendous variation in the content and experiences provided across the 1,150 teacher preparation programs in the United States. Some programs require as little as one three-semester course in reading methods, while others offer as many as 18 semester hours in reading coursework that covers topics ranging from the structure of English to teaching reading comprehension. Some programs offer no practicum hours in public schools with supervised, "hands-on" experiences in reading, while others offer as many as 50 to 60 hours every semester. (p. 2)

Thus, we can well understand Mr. Bowers's situation. Many teachers of middle and secondary grade adolescents have not been prepared adequately to develop the kind of literacy students need to do well on either national or international assessments. This observation includes middle grade and high school English or Language Arts teachers, who are perhaps prepared to teach the fine points of literature, film, and writing but have not had sufficient preparation to help struggling readers with literacy skills that will serve them well in a variety of academic subjects, or meet their post–high school literacy needs in college or the workplace.

Teachers and future teachers need more information about literacy demands of their teaching field and how to address them with students. This chapter examines several content-area subjects with regard to both their unique and common literacy requisites and offers strategies for developing students' literacy. Some suggestions are generic and others are specific to particular content areas. We have been developing students' literacy across disciplines for some time. Jill Lewis, a professor at New Jersey City University, teaches graduate students studying for master's degrees in reading. For more than 30 years she has also taught "underprepared" college freshmen who must improve their literacy skills before they can pursue college-level studies. Her book *Academic Literacy: Readings and Strategies* (2007b) is now in its fourth edition. She has also coedited two books on adolescent literacy. Tanya Reader, currently a sixth-grade English teacher at Carl Sandburg Middle School, has taught secondary students in English and reading for the past 12 years. In addition, she teaches preservice teachers and master's degree candidates at the University of La Verne. She is currently pursuing her doctorate at Claremont Graduate University.

Defining Academic Literacy

We begin our conversation by considering the term *academic literacy,* the focus of this chapter. Adolescents have multiple literacies; they use different ones in different communities, including peer groups, church, family. Literacies are always situated within specific social practices within specific Discourses (Gee, 1996). Some of these literacies are better developed than others, and competence is relative to specific contexts, communities, and practices (Kern & Schultz, 2005). Today's adolescents communicate well with their peers and, in fact, develop uses of language, such as "rap," that are quite unique. There is evidence, however, that middle grade and high school students are not as accomplished in terms of academic literacy, the kind of literacy needed for achievement on traditional school tasks and standardized assessments (Lewis, 1996).

The research indicates a few disheartening things about students' preparation for coping with the demands of academic literacy. In 2004, 1.2 million high school graduates took the American College Testing, Inc. (ACT) assessment, but only 22% achieved scores that would deem them ready for college in all three basic academic areas—English, math, and science. A similar ACT report in March 2006 revealed that only 51% of students were prepared for college-level reading.

This lack of preparation may well result, at least in part, from students' out-of-school experiences, many of which are divorced from the rigor of college-level reading or problem solving in academic subjects. According to Bourdieu (1977b), cultural capital derives from one's *habitus*, "a system of lasting, transposable dispositions which, integrating past experiences, functions at every moment as a matrix of perceptions, appreciations, and actions" (pp. 82–83). One's habitus comprises those cultural signals, dispositions, attitudes, skills, references, formal knowledge, behaviors, goals, and competencies that are rewarded within particular contexts, such as school, to achieve particular outcomes, such as high achievement or high aspirations (Bourdieu, 1977a). The culture of schooling requires academic literacy. It includes particular student–student and teacher–student interactions; formal skills and knowledge, including academic vocabulary and linguistic patterns; expectations for attention and participation; and a reward structure for academic success. Influences outside of school, especially adolescents' peers and family, affect students' habitus and shape their approaches to schooling (Lewis, 2007b).

Lewis (2007b) notes that when our students come face-to-face with more traditional forms of learning (e.g., school learning), they need to use specialized academic literacy skills to comprehend and communicate about texts that are often *decontextualized*, disconnected from many students' experiences. According to Marzano (2004), academic knowledge has a narrower scope than an individual's general knowledge. Depending on a students' prior experience, including subjects taken in school and the quality of teaching experienced in those subjects, students may or may not have the *topic* and *domain knowledge* (Alexander & Jetton, 2000) needed for success in a particular academic environment.

Students who do not plan to attend college also need academic literacy. According to the American Diploma Project (2004) and ACT (2004), the skills required for workforce training beyond high school are similar to those expected of a first-year college student.

Reading and Thinking about Academic Subjects

The first time I (Lewis) meet my undergraduate teacher education students enrolled in an adolescent literacy education course, I ask them to think about the subject in high school or college that was most difficult for them and to list the features of the course reading that were problematic. Regardless of which subjects the students pick, they never fail to comment on the same issues: vocabulary, lack of interest in the subject, complexity of ideas, and inadequate background knowledge. So we accept that these "givens" are potential problem areas for students in all their academic subjects. There are, however, some unique differences between fields of study and in the next few pages we examine these. If you are teaching, or planning to teach, one of these subjects, pay particular attention to not only the academic literacy needs in that discipline but also the requirements in other fields. This knowledge will broaden your understanding of why adolescents are struggling with academic texts.

Throughout this section, we refer to the content standards developed for different content-area subjects, especially those standards that depend on literacy accomplishments. They define what students need to know and need to be able to do in each field. Although every state has developed content-area standards for all grade levels in a variety of subjects, we focus here on the national standards of professional associations. These were developed by experts in the field, including classroom teachers and researchers, and provided guidance to many states in developing their own standards to address local needs.

Reading and Thinking about Social Studies

Some researchers estimate that as much as 75–90% of what students learn in social studies classes comes from their textbooks (e.g., Tyson & Woodward, 1989). In addition, social studies teachers often make use of supplemental material, such as CD-ROMs, newspapers, atlases, guest speakers, encyclopedias, videos and films, field trips, supplemental handouts, primary source documents, and the World Wide Web. This is a considerable amount of text for students to negotiate, and those who teach social studies to adolescents, or who serve as reading coaches to social studies teachers, need to familiarize themselves with the kind of thinking processes students need to use to comprehend such texts.

In 1992, the primary membership organization for social studies educators, the National Council for the Social Studies (NCSS, 2004, paragraph 4), adopted a formal definition that identified two characteristics that distinguish social studies as a field of study: (1) It is designed to promote civic competence, and (2) it is integrative, incorporating many disciplines, such as anthropology, archaeology, economics, geography, history, law, philosophy, political science, psychology, religion, and sociology, as well as appropriate content from the humanities, mathematics, and natural sciences.

The Council elaborates on the integrative nature of social studies and the key role that understanding perspectives plays in successful comprehension of social studies texts. Its standards note:

> Each person experiences life in an individual way, responding to the world from a very personal perspective. People also share common perspectives as members of groups, communities, societies, and nations—that is, as part of a dynamic world community. A well-designed social studies curriculum will help each learner construct a blend of personal, academic, pluralist, and global views of the human condition. (NCSS, 2004, paragraph 17)

With such a broad range of disciplines connected to social studies, teachers may well need a vehicle for ensuring that students can comprehend and use information both independently and when working with others to achieve the goal of civic responsibility that is central to social studies standards. Thus, in 1994, the Council developed an organizing framework, the Essential Skills Framework, to assist teachers with planning and integrating instruction in their social studies classes. It comprises three categories: (1) Acquiring Information/Gathering Data, (2) Organizing and Using Information, and (3) Interpersonal Relationships and Social Participation (NCSS, 1994, Appendix A.). Literacy strategies are available for realizing each of these elements of the framework, as illustrated later in this chapter. They involve development of literacy skills and dispositions, such as prediction, analysis, interpretation, comparison, and critical literacy. Students need to be able to recognize patterns used to organize information, such as sequential, cause and effect, or problem–solution patterns.

Reading and Thinking about Mathematics

Math texts used in middle and secondary schools are quite dissimilar to those found in the social studies classrooms. Unlike social studies, mathematics (at least the in-school math studied by most adolescents) is not culturally bound. The principles and formulas studied as part of the mathematics curriculum in grades K–12 are universal; personal, global, or pluralistic perspectives are seldom considered. There are other differences, too. In social studies texts, ideas from previously studied material may be repeated in later text, but comprehending one page of mathematics text, or one concept in mathematics, is usually dependent on comprehending the ideas or text material that precede it. For instance, can one really understand (or do) multiplication without first knowing addition? Students cannot expect a repeat of how to do addition when they are learning multiplication. Reading mathematics texts involves slow, careful reading of details, or important procedures might be missed as students attempt to work out proofs, derivations, and sample problems. It also requires a working knowledge of mathematical language, or a mathematical symbol system, that is quite different from our alphabet system. Further dissimilarities between social studies and mathematics include student purposes for exploring multiple texts in these fields. In mathematics, multiple texts might provide students with alternative ways to solve a problem or greater clarification of a mathematical principle or formula, whereas in social studies, students might use a variety of texts to identify multiple perspectives on a given topic. In addition, students might be able to skim a social studies text to get the "gist" of something; such an approach would not work well for mathematics, where more detailed reading is necessary. Finally, social studies texts often include visual material, such as photographs, maps, charts, and graphs, that might clarify a point or add interest; it is possible that some of these materials can be skipped without losing critical information. Such is not the case with mathematics, where every symbol, visual aid, or example is a key to comprehension.

Yet mathematics and social studies, as well as other subject areas, share the need for many skills that are familiar to literacy development practices. For instance, in math, as well as in social sciences such as history, students need to have strategies for classifying, organizing, imagining, predicting, inferring, generating questions, problem solving, restating, and illustrating and recognizing patterns. The National Council of Teachers of Mathematics (NCTM) notes in its *Expectations for Data Analysis and Probability Standard for Grades 6–8 and 9–12* (2000) that all students should be able to "formulate questions that can be addressed with data and collect, organize, and display relevant data to answer them" (pp. 248, 324). NCTM also has one entire standard for these grades on problem solving, which includes the abilities to "solve problems that arise in mathematics and in other contexts; [and] apply and adapt a variety of appropriate strategies to solve problems" (pp. 256, 334). These problems would most likely be word problems, with which even the best math students may have difficulty. Myriad thinking processes are needed to solve a word problem, including determining relevant–irrelevant information and following multiple-step procedures. Students also have to wade through the language of the problem to determine (1) what it is they are to solve, and (2) how to set up the problem to solve it. If the language skills are not there, including skills that require manipulating syntax for comprehension, making inferences, and knowing content-specific vocabulary, students cannot accurately solve the problem.

Reading and Thinking about the Sciences

Throughout their middle and high school careers, students take science courses. Some of these, such as chemistry, are very hands-on courses. Others, such as environmental science or geology, may be less so. The National Academy of Sciences published science standards in 1997. As with social studies and mathematics, *informed decision making* is central to the science standards. Describing science learning as an active process, the teaching standards for science note that, in science,

> students formulate questions and devise ways to answer them, they collect data and decide how to represent it, they organize data to generate knowledge, and they test the reliability of the knowledge they have generated.... They evaluate the data they have collected, re-examining or collecting more if necessary, and making statements about the generalizability of their findings. (National Academy of Sciences, Chapter 3, p. 5)

Also, as with mathematics and social studies, science standards emphasize that it is important for students to "establish connections between their current knowledge of science and the scientific knowledge found in many sources; they apply science content to new questions; they engage in problem solving, planning, decision making, and group discussions; and they experience assessments that are consistent with an active approach to learning" (National Committee on Science Education Standards and Assessment, National Research Council, 1996, p. 20).

Yet, there are aspects of learning science that are unique to this discipline and that depend upon literacy practices for which students may need explicit instruction in the science classroom. For instance, adolescents in science classes are expected to draw generalizations from observations of natural phenomena, to offer scientific explanations for natural events, to use mathematical formulas to analyze data. There is an exactness required for conducting experiments, and a reliance on historical and current scientific knowledge to verify conclusions. Literacy practices in other classrooms can also reinforce the critical thinking and problem solving skills needed for achieving these science standards.

Reading and Thinking about Texts in English Language Arts

In 1996, the International Reading Association (IRA) and National Council of Teachers of English (NCTE) collaborated to produce standards for the English Language Arts. As with the standards developed by other professional groups, the influence of this document is reflected in state-developed standards in terms of both rigor and content. Echoing the goals of the standards of other professional groups, NCTE and IRA report that the primary purpose of the standards is to

> ensure that all students are knowledgeable and proficient users of language so that they may succeed in school, participate in our democracy as informed citizens, find challenging and rewarding work, appreciate and contribute to our culture, and pursue their own goals and interests as independent learners throughout their lives. (p. v)

Six broad aspects of literacy were explored: reading, writing, listening, speaking, viewing, and visually representing. Standards were set for these for different grade ranges. They called for use of print and nonprint texts, and for narrative as well as expository material. Without commenting here on each individual standard, it should be noted that they include the need for students to be able "to apply a wide range of strategies to comprehend, interpret, evaluate, and appreciate texts" (NCTE/IRA, 1996, p. 3). Students are also expected to understand texts by using "prior experience, interactions with other readers and writers, their knowledge of word meaning and of other texts" (p. 3). The standards included calls for research and technological literacy, as well as cultural awareness. Thus, once again, comprehension, interpretation, evaluation, and citizenship are central themes in the standards. As we know from our own school experiences, the English Language Arts classroom is also distinct from other subject-matter classes. It utilizes more narrative texts, more analysis of structure of literature, and, in some instances, a greater variety of genres. There is direct instruction on narrative and expository writing; spoken and written grammar; and, sometimes, study skills and comprehension strategies. But underlying

English Language Arts curricula are standards with themes that are critically important to multiple content fields.

Bearing in mind these similarities and differences across standards for various content-area fields, we now look at how Tanya Reader conducts her Reading Intervention class, with the goal of helping students reach success in all their subjects.

The Teacher's Voice: Adolescents and Academic Text in a Reading Intervention Class

As I (Reader) entertain thoughts of the coming school year, I am reminded of the past 11 years' vicissitudes. I always begin each year nervous, yet excited: nervous because I don't know the personalities with whom I'll be spending the next year, and excited about the things I hope to teach my students and anticipating what they will, no doubt, teach me. Five periods each day I interact with students whose abilities run the gamut. There are those who adore reading and view their textbooks and other reading materials as tools that are helpful, familiar, and sources of (mostly) new and exciting information.

One period a day, I teach a Reading Intervention class that comprises 15 students placed in my class on the basis of their content teachers' observations or their performance on standardizes tests. These students for whom school is often a place of frustration and confusion are my greatest concern. They may be in the same classes as the students who do not struggle, but they often experience school in a much different way. These students do not have the skills to interact with academic text in a way that allows them to add to their stores of conceptual knowledge. In fact, they may have background knowledge on a given topic, but their lack of facility with the "language of school" (Pilgreen, 2007) impedes their ability to be successful. My goal is to help raise student achievement through development of literacy skills that are necessary for academic success.

My Reading Intervention students usually are not happy about having to give up their elective to be in a reading class. Although many of them do have excellent decoding skills, it is comprehension, or even just understanding what it is they are being asked to do in content-area classes, that causes them to struggle. I am well aware that their difficulties will increase as they progress through middle and secondary grades, unless I can provide them with meaningful assistance. I am aware that student literacy is key to their meeting many of the standards in all content-area subjects.

Meeting Content Standards
through Literacy Activities

At the beginning of the year, all students in my (Reader's) classes complete a Reader's Survey (Robb, 2000, p. 285). I use this as an opener to learn student attitudes about reading and their views of themselves as readers. This survey also helps me determine what types of books students like to read, so I can ensure that my classroom library correlates with their interests. Students also complete a Strategy Checklist that is repeated at the midpoint and the end of the year (Robb, 2000, p. 102), and that identifies their beliefs about the strategies they use before, during, and after reading. Once I know some of their thoughts on strategies and views of reading, we can begin the journey to make sense of all texts and to become active and automatic users of strategies.

Tapping Prior Knowledge

When struggling students read academic text, the density of the concepts often overwhelms them. This is not surprising. If students see each idea they encounter in text as unique, then they might never make sense of all they read. One way that good readers make sense of new information is to call on their background knowledge to help them purposefully integrate new ideas with what they already know. The importance of background knowledge in making sense of text cannot be overstated (Alvermann & Phelps, 2005; Burke, 2000; Tovani, 2000; Vacca & Vacca, 2005). Using prior knowledge is identified in both the Math and the Language Arts Literacy standards as an important goal for students to achieve.

Ideally, students will attempt to hook any new knowledge to what they already know, but this is not always an automatic process, especially for students who struggle with academic text. Thus, teachers need to find out whether students already possess knowledge about new topics and to activate this before asking students to meet the challenges of the new material. Such instruction at the beginning of a unit is worth the time; it will pay enormous dividends in student engagement and comprehension.

One of the easiest ways to find out what students know about a topic is simply to ask them: Adolescents are usually not too shy to tell you! I often open a unit by asking students what they have heard or read about a subject, then writing their responses on the whiteboard. Sometimes students know more than they think they do. Once they hear what their peers have to say, there is often the "aha moment," when students realize that they know at least *something* about the topic at hand. It is helpful to have some parameters in the gathering of students' knowledge. Also, there are some specific activities that activate students' background on a topic, and that students will be able to use independently to comprehend academic texts.

LIST–GROUP–LABEL

By classifying or categorizing new concepts and connecting them to prior knowledge students build connections, establish relationships, and are better able to retain ideas. As Vacca and Vacca (2005) assert, "We invent categories (or form concepts) to reduce the complexity of our environment and the necessity for constant learning" (p. 267). One strategy that requires little preparation but is quite effective in activating background knowledge for nonfiction topics and texts, and inventing the categories to reduce complexity is list–group–label (Taba, 1967). For this strategy to be most effective, students should have at least a little knowledge of the topic.

To begin list–group–label, I give students a cue word for the topic about which they are reading. For example; in sixth-grade social studies, the focus is ancient civilizations. For the unit on ancient Egypt and the chapter entitled "Land of the Pharaohs" (Banks et al., 2000), I start with the simple cue word *Egypt*, writing it on the whiteboard. Next, for 3 minutes, students jot down everything they know related to the word. Before they start, I tell them that they should write down anything that comes to mind and, if possible, whether they know where and when they learned of it. After the 3 minutes have elapsed, I call on volunteers to share their ideas, and I write the words, so that they surround the key word. I generally ask for a brief explanation of why the student believes his or her word relates to the topic. Sometimes a student includes a seemingly unrelated word that is actually appropriate, and I am able to acknowledge that the student has made a connection that I had not considered.

After we compile an adequate list, at least 10 words, I guide students as they group these by commonalities. For example, for the cue word *Egypt*, students might think of words such as *pharaoh, Nile River, delta, hieroglyphics, papyrus, King Tut, desert, hot, afterlife, pyramids, scribes,* and *Valley of the Kings*. To prepare for grouping these words, I first write them on large sticky notes, enabling us to move items around without constantly having to erase and rewrite on the whiteboard. I ask students to place the words into lists that seem to have something in common. The resultant groupings for our words might look like those on the original grouping for list–group–label in Figure 5.1. After putting items into logical groups—and there may be some items that do not fit with

1	2	3	4
Nile River	pharaoh	papyrus	afterlife
delta	King Tut	scribes	pyramids
desert			hieroglyphics
Valley of the Kings			
hot			

FIGURE 5.1. Original grouping for *list–group–label*.

any others—students label them and I write these on sticky notes. The revised groupings might look like those in Figure 5.2.

As students gain facility with the strategy, I gradually release responsibility, and students are able to work with their peers to group and to label the words. Completing an activity such as list–group–label prior to introducing a text aids students tremendously, especially struggling readers. They can accommodate new knowledge by integrating it with what they already know, and continue to use classification and categorization as they encounter new concepts in the text.

Teaching Text Structure and Signal Words

Just as not all houses are built the same way, with the same layout and number of rooms, not all texts are "built" the same way. Math, science, and social studies texts look remarkably dissimilar, including how ideas are organized and the comprehension supports they provide. If students can recognize some unique features of each type of text when they approach academic reading assignments, then doing so can make an enormous difference in their comprehension. What Burke (2000) refers to as *textual intelligence* is akin to having a map when driving: You know what to look for to get you where you want to go. Considerate authors provide this map, and successful readers know how to use it.

geography	government	everyday life	religion
Nile River	pharaoh	papyrus	afterlife
delta	King Tut	scribes	pyramids
desert			hieroglyphics
Valley of the Kings			
hot			

FIGURE 5.2. Revised grouping for *list–group–label*.

They look for signal words that indicate the author is organizing the text ideas using a particular structure, such as comparing and contrasting; showing cause and effect; suggesting a sequence; or enumerating an idea, perhaps from less important to more important, or vice versa. Some signal words are obvious and show up frequently even in texts used in the earliest grades, where we often find the sequence words *first, second,* and *finally.* Others, such as *inversely* to show contrast, and *hence* to introduce an effect, appear in more sophisticated texts and are not so obvious. Giving students a list of the common signal words is helpful but certainly not sufficient to teach these important terms. I have used several approaches to teaching signal words that students have been able to apply independently with success to academic texts.

TEACHING SEQUENCE PATTERNS

To teach how authors use a sequence pattern in academic text, I usually like to start with a short example that includes signal words with which students are probably familiar, such as a recipe, then move to more complicated text. I might begin with a recipe on the overhead that a student reads aloud, while I circle the sequence signal words. While looking at the circled words, such as *first, next, then, meanwhile,* and *after,* students discuss how these words help readers accomplish each recipe step. Next, students examine a section of a content-area textbook with a partner to locate as many sequence words as they can. They are pleased to find that they can identify quite a few. As with any strategy, continued practice and identification of sequence words eventually leads to automaticity of use.

TEACHING CAUSE-AND-EFFECT PATTERNS

To teach cause-and-effect structure, I always like to start with a reminder of how cause and effect can be observed close to home. One simple example relates to school rules. For example, I might ask students what happens if they receive three tardies. They, of course, answer that they receive detention. I write *tardies* and *detention* on the whiteboard and label them *cause* and *effect,* respectively. We review a few more examples before I introduce cause-and-effect signal words in academic text, using a graphic organizer. I find graphic organizers to be extremely efficient for making sense of a given structure.

Initially, I give students a graphic organizer that corresponds to the structure of the text they will be reading. For example, if students are studying plate tectonics, they might read text such as this: "Folded mountains form when rock layers are squeezed together and pushed upward. If you take a pile of paper on a table top and push on opposite edges of the pile, you will see how a folded mountain forms" (Todd, 2001, p. 155). This short passage illustrates cause and effect well. A graphic organizer for students to complete might include the effect *folded mountains form*. Students would have to fill in the *cause*, which of course, would be "rock layers squeeze together and push upward." This process of locating causes and effects in this science chapter continues for an entire paragraph or section of the chapter. As I alternate between providing students the *effect* and the *cause*, students complete the organizer with the one I've omitted to help them become really clear about the distinction.

TEACHING COMPARE–CONTRAST PATTERNS

Comparison and contrast can be one of the more difficult text structures that students encounter in academic texts. Cognitively, the structure requires a lot for comprehension to occur. Students must identify what elements are alike or similar (comparison), as well as what elements are different (contrast) about two subjects or topics. For example, students in a mathematics class might discuss how rectangles, triangles, and squares are similar, as well as different from each other. In literature, students might compare or contrast two short stories, perhaps by the same author. In social studies, students might compare and contrast two cultures in terms of differentiation in roles of women and men. In a science class, students might notice differences and similarities in how different chemicals interact with each other. Sometimes an author discusses only a comparison or a contrast, and students need to recognize this. Furthermore, especially in expository texts, the contrast or comparison signal word may appear in the middle of a paragraph, and students might overlook it. Also contributing to the cognitive demands of this structure is that students must keep track of both the comparison and the contrast as they read. This can be a lot to remember. Signal words and phrases often found in comparisons include *similarly, in the same way*, and *likewise*; those often used to show contrast include *on the other hand, contrary to*, and *although*, to name only a few.

Students can again use a graphic organizer to illustrate comparison-and-contrast texts. One of the most useful tools for this purpose is the Venn diagram. It shows how two items, characters, events, reactions, or places are different and similar. For the diagram, three circles are drawn; the one on the left contains information about what is unique to the first character, place, event, and so forth, being compared; what is unique to the second character, place, event, and so forth, is then placed in the circle on the right; characteristics that apply to both are placed in the area where the circles overlap. Because Venn diagrams are easy to construct and adolescents have often used them in the early grades for narrative texts, they are a good way to help middle grades and high school students practice a comparison-and-contrast structure. Before beginning compare and contrast with my students, I want them to have a successful experience with it.

To connect students more easily to a new strategy, such as creating a Venn diagram, I start with an example that they know. My example changes each year, as do fads and student interests during early adolescence. Currently, I might ask students what they know about MySpace. As students provide me with information, assuming that I know nothing about this website, I write their contributions on the board. Then I ask students about Facebook. Again, I write everything they tell me about it. With my students' help, I then use a color marker to write down everything that these two websites have in common; using a different color marker, I do the same for contrasts. We complete a Venn diagram, inserting the information for each section, and discuss how the diagram might benefit newcomers to either site. Easy, right? Maybe not, when students are reading academic text that may be less familiar and comfortable than these online communication websites. Transitioning from topics of great interest to students to academic texts that may be less so can be facilitated by careful scaffolding of instruction and ongoing opportunities for students to practice what they have learned.

Comprehending Inconsiderate Text

Sometimes when students read academic text, they are simply seeing words on the page, much like a grocery list. They may be able to understand and decode all of the words, and even understand at the sentence level, but the overall idea may elude them. Why is this? Perhaps the author has not paid enough attention to the audience, the reader. Signal words and clear patterns may be unavailable, or perhaps the author has made assumptions about the reader's background. I have used several strategies to address these issues that provide students avenues for accessing inconsiderate text.

VISUALIZING ACADEMIC TEXT

Many nonfiction texts provide illustrations and other forms of visual support (Harvey & Goudvis, 2000), and students can be taught to use these to help them make sense of what they are reading. But such textual supports are not always offered, and students must have strategies for independently navigating their way in knowing how to visualize strategically while they read. As described earlier, students can use several graphics to represent patterns in texts, and this helps them follow text ideas. But there is more that teachers can do to help students with visualization of text.

Particularly with descriptive expository texts, such as those often found in science or social studies materials, or in texts with multiple sequential steps, such as directions for completing a mathematical formula or science experiment, visualization is critical to understanding. We may visualize by actually writing down what we see, but often we visualize in our heads. For example, an oceanography unit in a sixth-grade textbook includes a section called "The Benthic Environment," with a subsection entitled "Intertidal Zone" (Todd, 2001). This section has several terms that are specific to oceanography:

> The shallowest benthic zone, the *intertidal zone,* is located between the low-tide and high-tide limits. Twice a day, the intertidal zone transforms. As the tide flows in, the zone is covered with ocean water, and as the tide retreats, the intertidal zone is exposed to the air and sun. (p. 345)

Words and phrases, such as *located between the low-tide and high-tide limits, twice a day, as the tide flows in, zone is covered, tide retreats,* and *zone is exposed,* include a wealth of information in just a short segment of text. Though these words and phrases are not concepts limited to oceanography, comprehending the paragraph requires an understanding of how these ideas are related as used in this passage from text in an academic discipline. Visualization facilitates this.

To teach students how to visualize, I put text, such as this example from Todd, on the overhead. I use materials about which my students already have some background knowledge, so that we can focus on the new strategy. I first model a think-aloud for students to demonstrate how an expert reader makes sense of such dense text (Burke, 2000). Using a variety of colors to mark the text, I read the passage aloud, while circling the words and phrases that indicate an action, event, or sequence. For example, as I read the first sentence aloud, I circle the words *located between the low-tide and high-tide limits,* because this tells me the location of the intertidal zone. Moving through the passage, I next circle *twice a day,* because it indicates how often something occurs.

Visualizing requires *metacognition,* awareness of one's thought processes while reading. My procedure shows students how I am seeing the events described in the passage, and how one event links to the next. After completing these steps for the passage, I write on the overhead what I am visualizing as I read (see Figure 5.3).

The shallowest benthic zone, the *intertidal zone,* is located between the low-tide and high-tide limits. Twice a day, the intertidal zone transforms. As the tide flows in, the zone is covered with ocean water, and as the tide retreats, the intertidal zone is exposed to the air and sun.

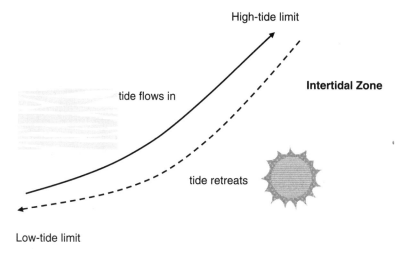

High-tide limit

tide flows in

Intertidal Zone

tide retreats

Low-tide limit

FIGURE 5.3. Visualizing. Passage from Todd (2001, p. 345).

Through the process of visualizing, students are able to identify the essential components of academic text and make the information accessible. They feel more confident about their ability to handle academic texts and are willing to take more risks with comprehension.

QUESTIONING THE AUTHOR

An excellent strategy that increases students' awareness of inconsiderate or incomplete texts, Questioning the Author, or QtA, was developed in 1996 by Beck, McKeown, Sandora, Kucan, and Worthy. It is one of the easiest strategies to teach and to use, and it is effective with both narrative and nonfiction texts. QtA allows students to see that the author is fallible and that if the student is having difficulty understanding the text, it may be because it is poorly, or inconsiderately, written. This is often a revelation to students, and it can induce feelings of efficacy and power. Five questions are included in this strategy:

1. What is the author trying to tell you?
2. Why is the author telling you that?
3. Does the author say it clearly?
4. How could the author have said things more clearly?
5. What would you say instead?

I often introduce QtA with a piece of text that students know: Signage is easy—text that students likely see on a daily basis and probably do not think about very much. In my class, I begin teaching QtA by showing students a sign they often see in restrooms: ALL EMPLOYEES MUST WASH THEIR HANDS. I put this sign on an overhead, and we discuss the five QtA questions, while I write the collective answers on the overhead. When we arrive at the final question, we determine whether we (or the author) could have written the text more clearly. For this particular piece of text, students' suggestions include adding the words, *before starting work, before leaving this room,* and *for health reasons.* Students generally agree that this is a clear sign with a clear purpose, and that it is usually seen only in a particular place, that is, a restroom of a restaurant.

As with this example, it is best to use clearly written text, with few or no changes. As students gain facility with the strategy, teachers will want to incorporate increasingly less considerate text. Newspaper or magazine articles are great sources for QtA, because they may discuss unfamiliar topics. Through QtA, students are encouraged to question their own reading, along with the author's presentation. Working in tandem with these considerations, students begin to recognize sections that may require rereading or need further explanation from the author, so these sections are ideal for practice reading of informational text with this strategy.

Developing a Questioning Attitude about Content Texts

Asking questions and seeking answers is the foundation for learning. In school settings, the questions that students are required to answer are usually not their own: Either the teacher determines them or the author has included questions at the end of a chapter. But when students do have opportunities to generate their own questions, they become more connected with the text and more focused. For struggling students, generating questions may prove difficult. In some ways it is a catch-22. Even though creating their own questions would lead to deeper understanding, these students hesitate to do so, because they already have enough difficulty with the ones they have been given! As

Tovani (2000) attests, we should teach questioning because it motivates students to read to answer their questions, helps them to interact with the text, and helps them to clarify and infer (p. 86). Direct instruction in generating questions can benefit all students, guiding them from very literal question-crafting to creation of questions that require critical thinking. As seen from earlier examples of the content standards, every content area emphasizes the importance of critical thinking to success in that discipline. I share here two strategies I have found particularly helpful for guiding students' development in generating thoughtful questions.

ANNOTATION

This is a strategy for marking text with reader responses to it (Burke, 2000; Tovani, 2000). It is enormously successful with students, as well as easy and fun to teach. I begin teaching this strategy early in the school year, because it provides a foundation for students to interact with text, to value their ideas, and to understand that individuals respond differently to the same texts. Using a think-aloud, I model this strategy for students. With the text to be read on the overhead, I tell students what I am thinking as I read, including even the most seemingly unimportant thought. Students observe how I write on sticky notes what comes to my mind, while I read and think about the text. Writing as I read, I explain to students that slowing down to think about the text can really increase my comprehension. My annotations include questions, comments, text-to-text–text-to-world–text-to-self observations, and notes on information that seem confusing or surprising, or just about anything else that provokes a reader response. I code my annotations so I can easily distinguish between the kinds of comments or questions I write. Sometimes, when I write a question that is answered as I continue to read, I make note of that, too. While I read a passage from *Always Running* (Rodgriguez, 1993), for instance, I wrote the annotations in Figure 5.4.

After I model, students practice the annotation strategy on their own, using a short passage. I usually use a selection about something controversial that lends itself to higher-order thinking and questioning, and interests students. This might be a piece on topics such as government wiretapping, doctor–patient privilege, or students' cell phones in school. Once they have made annotations and created questions on their own, I have students share their codes and notes with a partner. Often we find that we were all confused or questioned the same part, and we discuss how the author could have added clarification.

! = something new
* = probably important
? = what does this mean
✓ = know something about this
!* = wow

California ✓   year sister born

The Watts Rebellion of 1965 changed forever the civil rights struggle in this country. The fires that swept through my old neighborhood that summer swept through me, cutting deep lines, as it swept through America, turning it toward its greatest fears and hardest questions; demarcating the long-glossed-over class and national differences which have historically divided the country.

What does he mean?

A trajectory from Watts converged with the more-than-century-old fight of the Mexican people for their own freedoms to ripen into the Chicano Movement as manifested in East L.A.

? Don't know much about this

And what a time it was to be in East L.A.!

Hard to imagine junior high students doing this

✗! In 1968 several thousand junior and high school students walked out of the Mexican east side schools to demand quality and accountable education. Students in schools throughout Los Angeles followed suit—in South Central, the Harbor, the West Side and San Fernando Valley.

A handful of us at Garvey School joined with the East L.A. school "Blowouts," as they were called, when we walked out of the school yard. Led by a girl named Norma and myself, our walkout turned out as a solidarity gesture. *?* The students didn't have enough cognizance of the issues to carry it to the heights taken by those to the west of us. Still it became my first conscious political act—I was 13 years old—for which I received a day's suspension from school.

FIGURE 5.4. Annotations chart based on *Always Running* (Rodriguez, 1993, pp. 164–165).

QUESTION–ANSWER RELATIONSHIPS

I also teach this strategy at the beginning of the year because it is so useful and can be applied all year to all subjects. Students may understand what they have read but not be able to answer questions posed by teachers or text because they do not understand the relationship between a question and its answer. The Question–Answer Relationship (QAR) strategy (Raphael, 1982) teaches these relationships and helps students see, not *what* the answer is, but *how* to find it.

In this strategy, four QARs are explicitly taught. Two strategies, *Right There (RT)* and *Think and Search (TS)*, are considered to be in the text, because the reader can find the answer in the text. The remaining two, *Author and Me (AM)* and *On My Own (OMO)*, are referred to as being in the reader's head, because these QARs require the reader to synthesize information from the text, or author, with their own experiences, and these questions' answers are essentially the opinion of the reader. I give my students examples of each type of QAR. To provide students with effective practice, though, I introduce QARs by reading a story aloud, giving students a chart with the short name and brief description of each QAR, so they can record their answers.

Students are familiar with think-alouds, and even if the teacher has never done a think-aloud, QAR is an excellent place to start. Think-alouds can be a vehicle for modeling the process of interacting with text and practicing the development of QARs while reading. I tell students that I am going to read a story aloud and when I have questions, I am going to write them on sticky notes. It is best to have questions in mind before modeling the process for students, and much more authentic to write the questions as they occur as opposed to having prewritten questions. It is important for students to see the process of questioning as the teacher reads, and see that even seemingly insignificant questions can lead to deeper understanding of a text.

As I read the story aloud, I write my questions on sticky notes. I do not attempt to answer the questions right then, though. When the story is completed, I review the four types of QARs and tell students that each question I asked belongs in one of the categories, and that together we are going to put the questions in the proper categories. I then read aloud my first question from the sticky note to the class. This is, of course, the second time they have heard the question, but now we try to determine where to place the question on the chart. As we code each question, we also discuss the answer. Doing this helps students to see how the question and answer relate to each other. Sometimes, when we will look in the text, the answer is found in one place (e.g., Question: What is the name of the building where *The Westing Game* [Raskin, 1978] took place? Answer: Sunset Towers. This is an *RT* QAR).

Although I introduce and model all four types of QAR, we spend quite a lot of time practicing RT QARs, because they are generally easy and students feel successful right away. I then progress to OMO, TS, and AM relationships, respectively. I find AM to be the most difficult, because this QAR requires students to infer. In other words, the answer is not directly stated but merely implied. When explaining the difference between *infer* and *imply* to students, I use an example that probably has occurred in students' lives. For instance, if I ask a friend whether she wants to come to the mall with me on Saturday and she makes no comment, what do her actions imply or suggest? When students answer that maybe she doesn't want to go with me, I tell them that they have just made an inference. My friend did not say anything directly, but students used their observations to come to a conclusion about the meaning of their observations. Though it takes a significant time commitment to teach QAR, it is time well spent. When students realize that they have a strategy for answering questions, and that not all questions are approached the same way, they feel capable and willing to do the difficult work of comprehending academic texts.

Recognizing Perspective in Texts

As we have seen, when young adolescents open a textbook, they are not usually aware that while they are reading facts or ideas, as the author understands them, they are also reading through a particular lens that varies according to the discipline, the writer, and their own perspectives. To encourage students to examine texts more closely for the author's stance, teachers must provide explicit instruction. All of the standards documents discussed earlier in this chapter note how important it is for students to understand perspective, those of the text authors, as well as their own. Here I introduce a variety of activities I have used to help students meet this standard in their content class.

POINT-OF-VIEW ACTIVITY

Tovani (2000) notes that in addition recognizing alternative authors' points of view, the point of view of the reader impacts interpretation of text; that is, alternative perspectives are also available to the reader. In my class, I use a real estate ad, such as the following one that advertises a home for sale:

> Owners moved! Move-in ready. Beautifully landscaped 3 BR ranch on 1 acre. Immediately available. Will hold mortgage.

I ask students to read this short text and give them their purpose for reading: The first time they read the ad, I ask that students approach it as if they are prospective home buyers, and highlight what they think is important to note. The second time students read it, they highlight in a different color what would be important for someone to note if he or she were going to rob the home. The third time they read it, students look for what would be important to note by teens who wanted to be alone in a house without parents. All students are given the photocopied text and three highlighters of different colors to identify each of the three perspectives. It is a powerful exercise to show that text is not static, with one meaning that only the author knows, one that they as the readers are to discover. It helps students realize that there are various ways readers can approach text depending on their point of view. Such understanding can make a positive difference in students' comprehension.

EXPLICIT TEACHING OF MULTIPLE PERSPECTIVES

Before students are able to embark on their own to recognize multiple perspectives in academic text, is helpful to share with them some multiple texts on one topic, so that they may see how perspectives and the retelling of events can vary so widely. As students read the multiple texts, they can keep track of the information, including *text, author, audience, and conclusions,* in just a few words. Creating a chart for writing the details can be helpful, because it requires students to focus on what they think is most important. This graphic organizer can also be used, with the teacher filling in parts and having students complete the rest, or having students be prepared to justify their thinking (e.g., How do they know who the audience is? What in the text leads them to the conclusions they drew?).

For example, we might examine a chapter in their textbook on the events precipitating World War II, as well as book excerpts and newspaper articles published at the time. This multiple-perspective approach not only widens their viewpoint of the topic but also helps drive the point home that there is not a single, right way to read their social studies text, other than to acknowledge that it *can* be read multiple ways.

Keeping track of the different readings on the same topic allows students to compare and contrast the information they have read, and to see the multiple perspectives that may exist. Primary and secondary sources should be used, because they may be significant as students consider reliability and perspective.

Students can use the chart information in several ways. Class discussions can examine the differing perspectives and the possible reasons for them. Students may also choose a stance supporting or opposing readings, using the text as support. The fact that perspectives differ is probably not news to most adolescents, but that this is true of texts may be, because students tend to think that if something is in print, it must be true!

Conducting Research in Content Classes

Teachers have especially rewarding moments when students express interest in conducting further research on a topic that the class has been studying. And research projects are perfect opportunities for addressing many of the benchmarks for the standards included in each of the content standards we reviewed earlier in this chapter.

Because adolescents may have only minimal experience with research projects, scaffolding the steps of the research cycle is necessary. The research cycle comprises (1) defining the problem, developing a research question and statement of purpose; (2) developing a research plan; (3) collecting data; (4) sorting and analyzing data; (5) synthesizing data; (6) evaluating; and (7) presenting (McKenzie, 2000). Students should realize that a research project is cyclical, and that they will not go through the steps in a lockstep manner, but may instead cycle back to earlier steps to find additional information, rethink their original questions, verify data, and so on. Students can be guided carefully through these steps to ensure success (Lewis, 2004).

Questions that students have previously generated is a great starting place for the first and often the most difficult step for students. For example, students may have kept double-entry journals, learning logs, or response logs when reading about the ancient Romans, and they may have asked questions about Roman social hierarchy or the daily life of a typical citizen. Perhaps students in small groups can jot down some of their questions, prioritize them, and decide on one research question that they will investigate further, either as a group or individually. Once they have the question, students should also write a statement of purpose, which helps them focus on why their question is important enough to research and what their group hopes to learn. These steps help to build and activate background knowledge, because students can see they already have some familiarity with the topic that they can extend upon with the research project. In addition, this step can help to generate an authentic purpose for reading about a topic.

Once the teacher has approved the question and statement of purpose, students need to create a plan for conducting their research that includes a list of possible sources to consult, a time line for acquiring sources, and a division of labor if they are working in groups. Included in the search for sources should be instruction on finding valid and reliable sources. A guideline to keep in mind is when the research took place, because the information may no longer be relevant. If students are looking on the Internet for information, they must be careful that sites are reliable. One way to do so is to use sites whose URL ends in *.org*, *.edu*, or *.gov*. Students should be mindful that the first two types of sites may have biases. Sites ending in *.gov* are government sites, and are useful for getting statistics and objective reports. Another thing to keep in mind is to use sites that list an author, because students can also research the credentials of the author. Nearly anything may be posted on the Internet, but that does not ensure that the poster is writing knowledgeably about the topic. Ultimately, students should be aware that they do need to look for information with a critical eye. Furthermore, students must know from the outset that they may have to refine their research question as they gather data and learn more about their topic.

Once they have their information, students should synthesize the data they have collected. Questions to keep in mind as they do this are as follows: Do the data answer the research question? What insights do the data provide? Of the information collected, what is useful and what is not helpful? How can we communicate our results? After consideration of these questions, students next evaluate the data they have collected.

When evaluating data, students examine whether their research questions have led to a reasonable conclusion. They also evaluate whether they have enough data to support their conclusions persuasively. Because this process is recursive, students may revisit earlier steps, as needed, such as when they find that their analysis of the data is not clear enough to support their conclusions, and they have to go back to an earlier step and reanalyze their data.

After the research is complete, students may present it in many ways. They may write individual essays, using a common thesis statement and introduction; use PowerPoint to present their major findings; create posters; or give oral presentations, with different group members responsible for presenting different sections. There are many ways to present results in an engaging manner.

Research projects provide students with opportunities to gather data and use it in a meaningful way, while also providing experience in working efficiently and effectively with their peers, a skill that benefits us all as people learn to listen, compromise, and divide labor equitably. Additionally, the practice that students gain in searching for, analyzing, and using data is critical in our increasingly technology-dependent society, and something that all content-area fields address in their standards.

Concluding Thoughts

As Gordon Dryden (2000) notes, "The main aim of the school is to prepare its students to become self-acting, self-learning, self-motivated 'inventors of their own future,' global citizens competent and confident to analyze any problem based on the past, the present, the likely alternative options for the future. And, more importantly, to then reinvent an even better future." We could not agree more. Today's adolescents can have promising futures, drawing upon the multiple literacies in their own lives. Although many adolescents have literacy that is appropriate and successful in their out-of-school communities, many struggle within academic contexts. Thus, the teacher's role is key in that setting, in helping students to develop maximum personal resources and become "inventors of their own futures" that are positive and joyful.

Our chapter has offered ways we can accomplish this. And although some may view what we have presented as skills that adolescents should *already* possess when they reach middle grades and high school, we know there are numerous and complex reasons why this is not so, including maturing cognitive and social abilities of students, increasingly demanding texts, and inadequate teacher preparation for content teachers who might want to develop these skills.

Providing students with the tools that literally can help them get anywhere their imaginations can take them is a challenge for teachers, but it is one they welcome.

Questions for Reflection

1. How necessary is it for you to address background knowledge when introducing a unit? Is it possible to teach concepts in your field without addressing this? Explain.

2. Look at your state's standards for your content field. What literacy skills, in addition to those discussed in this chapter, do students need to meet these standards?

3. What do you think is the most challenging aspect of teaching students how to conduct research? What is the easiest aspect of it? How would you want students to present their work?

References

Achieve. (2008, February). *2008: Closing the expectations gap: An annual 50-state progress report on the alignment of high school policies with the demands of college and careers.* Prepublication copy retrieved from *www.achieve.org/files/50-state-2008-prepub.pdf.*

ACT, Inc. (2004). *Ready for college and ready for work: Same or different?* Iowa City: Author. Retrieved June 5, 2007, from *www.act.org/path/policy/pdf/readiness-brief.pdf.*

ACT, Inc. (2006). *Reading between the lines: What ACT reveals about college readiness and reading.* Iowa City: Author. Retrieved May 31, 2007, from *www.act.org/path/policy/pdf/reading_report.pdf.*

Alexander, P., & Jetton, T. (2000). Learning from text: A multidimensional and developmental perspective. In M. Kamil, P. Mosenthal, P. D. Pearson, & R. Barr (Eds.), *Handbook of reading research* (Vol. III, pp. 285–310). Mahwah, NJ: Erlbaum.

Alvermann, D. E., & Phelps, S. F. (2005). *Content reading and literacy: Succeeding in today's diverse classrooms* (4th ed.). Boston: Allyn & Bacon.

American Diploma Project. (2004). *Ready or not: Creating a high school diploma that counts.* Washington, DC: Achieve.

Banks, J. A., Beyer, B. K., Contreras, G., Craven, J., Ladson-Billings, G., McFarland, M. A., et al. (2000). *Ancient world: Adventures in time and place.* New York: McGraw-Hill.

Beck, I. L., McKeown, M. G., Sandora, C., Kucan, L., & Worthy, J. (1996). Questioning the author: A yearlong classroom implementation to engage students with text. *Elementary School Journal, 96*(4), 385–414.

Bourdieu, P. (1977a). Cultural reproduction and social reproduction. In J. Karabel & A. H. Halsey (Eds.), *Power and ideology in education* (pp. 487–511). New York: Oxford University Press.

Bourdieu, P. (1977b). *Outline of a theory of practice* (R. Nice, Trans.). Cambridge, UK: Cambridge University Press.

Burke, J. (2000). *Reading reminders: Tools, tips, and techniques.* Portsmouth, NH: Boynton/Cook.

Dryden, G. (2000). *Nine steps to transform education.* New Horizons for Learning. Retrieved July 7, 2008, from *www.newhorizons.org/trans/international/dryden.htm.*

Gee, J. P. (1996). *Social linguistics and literacies: Ideology in discourses.* New York: Routledge.

Harvey, S., & Goudvis, A. (2000). *Strategies that work.* York, ME: Stenhouse.

Heller, R., & Greenleaf, C. (2007). *Literacy instruction in the content areas: Getting to the core of middle and high school improvement* [Report]. Washington, DC: Alliance for Excellent Education.

International Reading Association. (2003). *Prepared to make a difference.* Newark, DE: Author. Retrieved December 11, 2007, from *www.reading.org/downloads/resources/1061teacher_ed_com_summary.pdf.*

Kern, R., & Schultz, J. M. (2005). Beyond orality: Investigating literacy and the literary in second and foreign language instruction. *Modern Language Journal, 89*, 381–392.

Lewis, J. (Ed.). (2004). *Learning through projects* (Module 2, Secondary Education Activity SEA Project). Newark, DE: International Reading Association/USAID.

Lewis, J. (2007a). Academic literacy: Principles and strategies for adolescent readers. In J. Lewis & G. Moorman (Eds.), *Adolescent literacy: Policies, programs and promising classroom practices* (pp. 143–166). Newark, DE: International Reading Association.

Lewis, J. (2007b). *Academic literacy: Readings and strategies* (4th ed.). Boston: Houghton Mifflin.

Marzano, R. (2004). *Building background knowledge for academic achievement.* Alexandria, VA: Association for Supervision and Curriculum Development.

McKenzie, J. (2000). *Beyond technology: Questioning, research and the information literate school.* Columbus, OH: Linworth.

National Academy of Sciences. (1997, October). *National science education standards.* Retrieved June 12, 2008, from *www.nap.edu/readingroom/books/nses/html.*

National Assessment of Educational Progress. (2005). *The nation's report card: Executive summary: Reading results for grade 12.* Retrieved January 6, 2007, from *nationsreportcard.gov/reading_math_grade12_2005/s0201.asp.*

National Assessment of Educational Progress. (2007). *The nation's report card: Reading 2007.* Washington, DC: National Center for Education Statistics. Retrieved August 2, 2007, from *nces.ed.gov/nationsreportcard/pdjl-main2007/2007496_3.pdf.*

National Committee on Science Education Standards and Assessment, National Research Council. (1996). *National science education standards.* Washington, DC: National Academy Press.

National Council for the Social Studies. (1994). *Expectations of excellence: Curriculum standards for social studies—Executive Summary.* Retrieved June 12, 2008, from *web.archive.org/web/20041016114251/www.socialstudies.org/standards/execsummary.*

National Council of Teachers of English and International Reading Association. (1996). *Standards for the English Language Arts.* Urbana, IL: National Council of Teachers of English.

National Council of Teachers of Mathematics. (2000). *Principles and standards for school mathematics.* Reston, VA. Retrieved December 12, 2007, from *standardstrial.nctm.org/document.*

Organisation for Economic Co-operation and Development. (2001). *Knowledge and skills for life: First results from PISA 2000.* Paris: Author. Retrieved September, 2007, from *www.pisa.oecd.org/knowledge/download.htm.*

Pilgreen, J. (2007). Teaching the language of school to secondary English learners. In J. Lewis & G. Moorman (Eds.), *Adolescent literacy instruction: Policies and promising practices* (pp. 238–262). Newark, DE: International Reading Association.

Raphael, T. E. (1982). Question–answer strategies for children. *Reading Teacher, 36,* 186–190.

Raskin, E. (1978). *The westing game.* New York: Penguin Books.

Robb, L. (2000). *Teaching reading in middle school.* New York: Scholastic.

Rodriguez, L. J. (1993). *Always running,* la vida loca: *Gang days in L.A.* New York: Simon & Schuster.

Taba, H. (1967). *Teacher's handbook for elementary social studies.* Reading, MA: Addison-Wesley.

Todd, R. W. (Ed.). (2001). *Earth science* (California ed.). Austin, TX: Holt, Rinehart & Winston.

Tovani, C. (2000). *I read it, but I don't get it.* Portland, ME: Stenhouse.

Tyson, H., & Woodward, A. (1989). Why students aren't learning very much from textbooks. *Educational Leadership, 49*(3), 4–17.

U.S. Department of Education, Institute of Education Sciences, National Center for Education Statistics, National Assessment of Educational Progress. (2007). *The nation's report card: Reading 2007* (NCES 2007-496). Retrieved January 6, 2007, from *nces.ed.gov/nationsreportcard/pdf/main2007/2007496_1.pdf.*

Vacca, R. T., & Vacca, J. A. L. (2005). *Content area reading: Literacy and learning across the curriculum* (8th ed.). Boston: Allyn & Bacon.

Whetton, C., & Twist, L. (2003, October). *What determines the range of reading attainment in a country?* Paper presented at the 29th International Association for Educational Assessment Conference, Manchester, UK, National Foundation for Educational Research. Retrieved June 2, 2008, from *www.nfer.ac.uk/publications/other-publications/conference-papers/pdf_docs/whatdeterminesrange.pdf.*

CHAPTER 6

How Can Teachers Help
Adolescent English Language Learners
Attain Academic Literacy?

FABIOLA P. EHLERS-ZAVALA
LAURA AZCOITIA

CLASSROOM PORTRAIT

Ana is a 16-year-old student in Ms. Zamora's prealgebra class. This class is very difficult for Ana. She has been in the United States for just 3 years, arriving from Russia with her two younger brothers and parents. She is unable to understand the language of story problems in her math books that translate into the mathematical equations. Ana's class participation is almost nonexistent; she never asks questions and seldom volunteers any answers. Furthermore, Ana appears to isolate herself from the other students, perhaps because she is afraid of being ridiculed about her limited English or of making mistakes in a language she is learning. This means Ana has few opportunities to develop even rudimentary social language, let alone the academic English she needs for her schoolwork.

Ana does receive tutoring during her free blocks at school, and she sometimes stays after school to receive extra support. But the help of a well-intentioned tutor does not seem to help. In spite of mathematics sometimes being called a universal language, the math class poses to Ana as many challenges as the language arts class does, where only English is spoken. As Ms. Zamora observes Ana, it becomes clearer to her that exercises in math are for Ana also exercises in the language of math and the English language. So she wonders how, as a content-area teacher, she can assist Ana in learning both math and English.

Ana's story is true. It describes an adolescent English language learner (ELL) enrolled in a secondary school in the United States, who lives on the margins of academic literacy development and is struggling to succeed. Ana's story is not unlike the story of millions of adolescent ELLs enrolled in schools across the United States and in many countries around the world. It is also the story of Ms. Zamora, Ana's teacher. As in the countless, daily stories of millions of teachers around the globe, Ms. Zamora struggles to answer the question of how to meet the needs of adolescent ELLs in her classroom effectively. Teachers know that answering this question will enable them to initiate learners like Ana more effectively into the academic discourse of secondary schools, and to offer them sustained support. But what can we, ELL experts, offer so that classroom teachers are better able to assist ELLs in the development of their academic literacy in English? What do content-area teachers need to know about ELLs and their process of becoming successful in U.S. schools?

The successful academic literacy development of ELLs in secondary schools is affected by multiple factors, variables, and/or forces. Some of them are internal to the school system (e.g., the nature of the learners; teacher quality, programmatic alternatives for ELLs, school administrators). Others are external (e.g., community support, state and federal legislation, family literacy). Teachers influence some of these forces directly and/or indirectly. In this chapter, we concentrate on one of these variables: expertise and instructional practices of teachers of ELLs. Though from different countries (Laura Azcoitia from Mexico; Fabiola Ehlers-Zavala from Chile), we are both native speakers of Spanish and have personal insights into what it means to acquire English as a second/foreign language. We both underwent the experience of attaining academic literacy in English, after having attained it in Spanish. We now collaborate to assist ELLs and teachers of ELLs in public schools in the United States and abroad.

We have organized this chapter around two integrated themes. The first component offers a theoretically driven discussion of the academic and cultural components that, in our view and also according to professional standards, constitute the core knowledge that teachers of ELLs should develop. We address issues related to language, culture, second-language acquisition, instruction, and assessment. Our second theme suggests practical procedures for ways to apply these theoretical components in middle grades and in high school classrooms.

Preparing to Work with ELLs
in the Academic Context

As a result of our work for many years with both preservice and inservice teachers, we have observed the tendency of teachers to want to learn a set of strategies that can accelerate their ELL students' development of academic literacy. Without enough attention to what we consider the fundamentals in second-language teaching and learning, this task may prove to be extremely daunting. This tendency often results from teachers' eagerness to get to the core of effective practices with ELLs before they necessarily realize the importance of first developing an understanding of what constitutes an effective ELL teacher.

With the increasing numbers of ELLs in U.S. classrooms, teachers find themselves working toward (1) gaining a better understanding of how learners use language in a variety of contexts; (2) acquiring knowledge of how to help ELLs develop in the four language domains: listening, speaking, reading, and writing, both socially and academically; (3) knowing what it means to speak a different language; and (4) knowing how the native language of ELLs likely influences the acquisition of English for both social and academic purposes. All of this has to be accomplished within the context of also developing a more accurate understanding of the term *culture*. Furthermore, teachers of ELLs need to develop expertise in effective instructional and assessment practices that can assist them in making meaningful instructional decisions. Although most classroom teachers may not be seeking English as a second language (ESL) or bilingual certification, and their certification programs do not use these standards, a brief review of core ESL understandings for those teachers may illuminate the complexities of working with ELL learners.

Language and Culture:
Fundamentals in Working with ELLs

A foundation in the study of language, interrelated with the study of culture, assists teachers of ELLs in understanding the intricacies and complexities of second-language teaching and learning, as well as the many factors that influence this process. Initially, general knowledge of the concepts of language and culture help teachers in the process of articulating their own professional views on the following:

1. What language is, or is thought to be, and how it relates to the culture of its users.
2. What language does, and how it does it, in a multiplicity of cul-

tural contexts, with special attention to the academic context—
a cultural space in its own right.

3. The complexities involved in second-language acquisition and learning, with a focus on conditions that may improve or deter such development.

4. The vastly diverse nature of the ELLs themselves as speakers of other languages and culture bearers.

5. How the cultures that ELLs bring into the learning process shape this experience.

Understanding What Language Is

Understanding language calls for the study of topics such as language as a system that comprises interrelated subsystems (e.g., morphosyntaxis, phonetics–phonology, semantics, pragmatics); first- and second-language acquisition/development; and language variation and change. These fundamental areas of linguistics can significantly contribute to language teacher expertise. At first, all of these areas may seem to be highly theoretical. Interestingly, all speakers already possess this information. For example, when we speak our native language and are able to communicate effectively with those around us, we do so because we have a great deal of implicit knowledge about our native language. This knowledge for native speakers of English (or any language) is often the result of having been socialized into a community that uses that language. It is also the result of formal language instruction in the schools. For most educated and successful speakers of any language, being proficient in the use of a native language is the result of implicit and explicit language instruction. However, whether we are able to recall the instances in which we learned something explicitly or not, in many cases we are able to use our native language without having explicit knowledge of its grammar. For example, some native speakers of English may not be able to distinguish or to describe the variety of *if* clauses in English, or to discuss how tense and aspect combine to yield the different tenses that allow English speakers to communicate. Yet they can still communicate with others. Teachers of ELLs, however, do need this type of explicit knowledge, because they may find themselves having to guide ELLs explicitly in how to use English effectively. This pedagogical intervention is particularly necessary when helping ELLs acquire and develop academic literacy across the content areas.

Researchers have pointed out the kinds of language across disciplines and subject areas that teachers need to assist ELLs (Brisk & Harrington, 2007; Fillmore, 2005; Schleppegrell, Achugar, & Oteíza, 2004). In the content areas, there is a very specific form of English that

ELLs need to acquire and to develop: academic English. ELLs need very specific language for each content area. If you are uncertain of this, simply examine the glossaries of content-area books and compare the language used across disciplines. There you will see that ELLs are likely to encounter many specialized terms only in the school, not on the playground or at home in conversation with family members. For instance, adolescent ELLs need to acquire the languages of math, science, and history. Vocabulary is only an aspect of what must be learned. For instance, ELLs need to understand how writing a lab report for chemistry class differs from writing a persuasive essay for English/language arts. ELLs' success with academic literacy tasks rests on their acquisition of academic languages and understanding variations in how language is used across disciplines or subject areas. These aspects of language learning require explicit instruction and specialized teacher preparation to ensure success.

The concept of academic language dates back to Cummins (1979), who distinguished between social language (BICS, basic interpersonal communication skill) and academic language (CALP, cognitive academic language proficiency). Three decades later, such distinctions seem to be of considerable practical value and are still acknowledged. Brisk and Harrington (2007), for example, refer to this distinction using the following terms: primary and secondary discourse. *Primary discourse* corresponds to the language used at home with relatives or community members (i.e., BICS). *Secondary discourse*, they explain, corresponds to the kind of discourse used in "institutions such as schools, stores, workplaces, government offices, churches, and business" (Brisk & Harrington, 2007, p. 2; i.e., CALP).

Teachers must also bear in mind that "much goes into using a language besides knowing it and being able to produce and recognize sentences in it" (Akmajian, Demers, Farmer, & Harnish, 2001, p. 363). Being able to function in a language, as is the case for English-speaking teachers, is a necessary but not sufficient condition to teach that language. As Canagarajah (2002) notes: "Apart from the larger differences in beliefs and practices, there can be more specific differences related to literacy. The genres and styles of communication, the practices and uses of literacy, and the attitudes and processes in composing can be different" (p. 10). Understanding how the languages and the cultures of the world differ can empower teachers to move beyond stereotypes and meaningless generalizations, and to make appropriate instructional, pedagogically sound decisions allowing teachers to empower students and to validate what they bring into the process. Teachers can become culturally responsive.

Language in Cultural Contexts

Teaching in culturally sensitive ways begins with an examination of a teacher's own culture, and an understanding of the cultural background of his or her students through reflective practices. In some instances, it may also require that a teacher challenge some notions of culture that have prevailed in educational settings and are geared toward mainstream students. A teacher may need to realize that a universal way of viewing the world may be the result of false cultural assumptions. A person's worldview is influenced by all previous life experiences, as defined in relation to the various multicultural aspects of diversity (age, ethnicity, religion, gender, socioeconomic status, possible special needs, etc.). When these experiences differ from those of mainstream groups, the resulting worldview, including values, motivations, and interests, may also be different. Different is not the same as wrong. Difference, as Canagarajah (2002) pointed out, should be approached from a resources perspective instead of a deficit perspective. In describing multilingual learners as writers for academic purposes, he notes:

> Multilingual students do—and can—use their background as a stepping-stone to master academic discourses. Their values can function as a source of strength in their writing experience in English, enabling them to transfer many skills from their traditions of vernacular communication. Even in cases where the connection is not clear, it is important for teachers to consider how the vernacular influence can be made beneficial for their writing experience rather than functioning in negative, unpleasant, or conflictual ways. Such an attitude will involve teachers orientating to their students differently. We should respect and value the linguistic and cultural peculiarities our students may display, rather than suppressing them. We should strive to understand their values and interests and discover ways of engaging those in the writing process.... Academic literacy should adopt a bilateral process—in other words, not only should students be made to appreciate academic discourses but the academic community should accommodate alternate discourses. (pp. 13–14)

Villegas and Lucas (2002) formulated an approach to educate culturally responsive teachers. In their approach, they argue that teachers who engage in culturally sensitive practices:

- have socio-cultural consciousness; that is ... they recognize that the ways people perceive the world, interact with one another, and approach learning, are deeply influenced by such factors as race/ethnicity, social class, and language. This understanding enables teachers to cross the cultural boundaries that may separate them from their students.
- have affirming views of students from diverse backgrounds, seeing

resources for learning in all students rather than viewing differences as problems to be solved.

- have a sense that they are both responsible for and capable of bringing about educational change that will make schooling more responsive to students from diverse backgrounds.
- embrace constructivists' views of teaching and learning. That is, they see learning as an active process by which learners give meaning to new information ideas, principles and other stimuli; and they see teaching largely as a process of inducing change in students' knowledge and belief systems.
- are familiar with their students' prior knowledge and beliefs, derived from both personal and cultural experiences.
- design instruction that builds on what students already know while stretching them beyond the familiar. (p. xiv)

On Second-Language Acquisition

Teachers sometimes carry strong and deeply held beliefs about the best time to learn languages. These beliefs may also extend to the role of the native language or (even) the culture of ELLs in their acquisition of English. Teachers can either facilitate or interfere with teaching and learning in culturally and linguistically diverse classrooms. In our experience, teachers' belief systems regarding the concepts of language and culture often form part of long-standing myths that interfere with putting best schooling practices in place to ensure the academic success of ELLs. McLaughlin (1992) highlighted these myths concerning second-language (L2) learning:

- "Children learn second languages quickly and easily"
- "The younger the child, the more skilled in acquiring an L2"
- "The more time students spend in a second language context, the quicker they learn the language"
- "Children have acquired an L2 once they can speak it"
- "All children learn an L2 in the same way." (pp. 2–6)

If all teachers adhered to this belief system, then students like Ana would not have a reasonable chance of making meaningful progress in American public schools. After all, Ana is an adolescent, not a young child.

Having some knowledge about second-language acquisition (SLA) theories, or theories of language as discourse, with its implications for L2 teaching and learning, can assist teachers in answering the following questions (Peregoy & Boyle, 2005): What does it mean to know a language? What theories have contributed to explain this process? What influences the process of second language acquisition?

Traditionally, SLA theories have been primarily sustained on cognitive models that emerged in reaction to the existing behaviorist models. These cognitive models treated language learners as individuals whose task in the process of acquiring language was to decode meaning. These theories ignored the context of the speaker, and there was a marked emphasis on identifying teaching methods that would work, without consideration for the uniqueness of each learner. The classroom was viewed as a neutral environment, an orientation in which the learner is viewed as someone who has yet to learn to communicate effectively in neutral contexts.

In recent years, however, there appears to be a growing shift toward adopting a sociocultural perspective of L2 learning. This means that many of today's experts on ELLs may prefer to talk about theories of discourse rather than SLA theories. Theories of discourse are highly contextualized. They view language learning as highly interactive. Learners' social identity is respected and taken into account in the process of language acquisition.

Furthermore, there is a growing consensus that teachers need to adopt a sociocultural perspective on language teaching and learning. From this perspective, as Hawkins (2004, p. 3), drawing heavily on the work of Vygotsky, suggests, "Each language is composed of many different 'social languages,' that is, different styles of languages that communicate different socially-situated identities (who is acting) and socially-situated identities that are integrally connected to social groups, cultures, and historical formations." Gee (2004) explained: Each social language offers speakers or writers distinctive grammatical resources with which they can "design" their oral or written "utterances" to accomplish two interrelated things:

(1) to get recognized by others (and themselves) as enacting a specific socially-situated identity (that is, to "come off" as a particular "kind of person") and
(2) to get recognized by others (and themselves) as engaged in a specific socially-situated activity. (p. 13)

Thus, in the case of ELLs in secondary schools, an academic language may be understood as an instance of language (i.e., English) that grants them access to a specific group of language users with specific social practices: the academic group.

From a sociocultural perspective, as teachers get to know their students, they may begin to understand more precisely what kinds of linguistic resources their ELLs may bring into the process. It is often the case that language learners make use of all their linguistic resources to communicate, including those acquired for communication in their first language. For instance, the way ELLs construct sentences, paragraphs, and larger texts in English may be heavily influenced by their own literacy practices in their native or dominant languages. This learner knowledge, as Genesee (2005) notes, is what makes a critical difference between literacy development and practices among monolingual speakers of a language, and those observed among bilingual learners. Bilingual learners are likely to use all of their linguistic resources, skills, knowledge, and experiences as they develop literacy in a language that is not their native or strongest language. These resources include those they have acquired as a result of functioning in languages other than English. Consequently, understanding both language and culture, as well as language acquisition/development in all of its dimensions, is key for beginning to understand how language can be effectively developed or acquired on the part of learners.

On the Diverse Nature of ELLs

Knowledge about language, culture, and SLA theories can assist teachers in understanding what resources ELLs bring, or do not bring, into the process of acquiring academic literacy in English. It also contributes to recognizing the challenges facing ELLs who must acquire English as an academic language. But most importantly, it allows teachers to get to know the nature of their ELLs. ELLs arrive in the United States with "a kaleidoscope of varying abilities in academics, and language proficiency" (Ariza, 2006, p. 109), as well as differences in cognitive abilities, sociocultural factors, family and community literacy experiences, and previous educational experiences (Genesee, 2005). Furthermore, whether born in the United States or abroad, all ELLs are culturally and linguistically diverse, and their levels of literacy in their native or dominant language can be extremely varied compared to that of their monolingual peers developing literacy in English. For instance, for some ELLs, oral skills in their dominant language, such as Spanish, may be developed, but they may lack writing proficiency. For others, both oral and written communication may be developed for social purposes but not for academics. Some ELLs, particularly those who have been exposed to English in schools abroad, may know how to read and write in English but not be able to speak a word of it. Clearly, there are multiple combinations one may anticipate in diverse classrooms, as a result of the interplay of language proficiency and academic development, for not just one language but for two or more.

On Instructional and Assessment Practices

ELL assessment is an integral part of effective pedagogical practices. It corresponds to "the process of collecting and documenting evidence of student learning and progress to make informed instructional, place-ment, programmatic, and/or evaluative decisions to enhance student learning, as is the case of assessment of the monolingual or mainstream learner" (Ehlers-Zavala, 2002, pp. 8–9). In public schools, ELL assess-ment must be connected with both language and content instruction, as a result of instruction that is meaningfully planned and carried out. Teachers' assessment decisions, including what and when to assess, are also informed by what teachers know about their ELLs and their literacy practices.

Knowledgeable teachers of ELLs design instruction in a way that allows adolescent learners to become proficient in the four language domains of English—speaking, listening, reading, and writing in the various content areas—and integrating these four domains through-out the curriculum. Such instruction is also meaningful and compre-hensible to learners, as well as developmentally appropriate. Effective assessment enables teachers to determine whether their instruction adequately addressed these important instructional elements.

To comply with Title III of the No Child Left Behind (NCLB) leg-islation, public school teachers are expected to plan standards-based instruction and assessment, with consideration of both specific content knowledge and students' English language needs, and these must be aligned with local and state standards for both content and language. As Ariza (2006) suggests, such efforts are mandatory: "Research and recent legislative mandates dictate that students need to learn English through content areas" (p. 108).

In the next section we look at instructional practices that are effec-tive with adolescent ELLs and that, combined with the suggestions we have made thus far for working with this population, raise their lan-guage proficiency and literacy achievements.

Instructional Practices:
Sheltering Instruction for ELLs with the SIOP Model

Now we turn our attention to the second theme of this chapter. Here we introduce a model for planning and delivering instruction to adolescent ELLs that can assist with their development of academic literacy, the sheltered instruction observation protocol (SIOP), a model developed by Echevarria, Vogt, and Short (2008), and illustrate how it is implemented in classrooms. The model incorporates the principles for effective instruction that we outlined in the first section of this chapter.

One of the most promising field-tested models for helping ELLs in middle and high school acquire language and content, SIOP is a research-based model for sheltered instruction. It has shown empirically that teachers who are properly trained in this model can make a significant difference in the academic achievement of ELLs. Echevarria and Graves (2003) defined sheltered instruction as follows:

> Sheltered instruction is a means for making grade-level content, such as science, social studies, and math, more accessible for English language learners (ELLs) while also promoting English development. Sheltered instruction is said to be the most influential instructional innovation since the 1970s, particularly because it addresses the needs of secondary students.... The approach was first introduced in the early 1980s by Stephen Krashen as a way to use second-language acquisitions strategies while teaching content area instruction. The approach teaches academic subject matter and its associated vocabulary, concepts, and skills by using language and context to make the information comprehensible. (p. 53)

The SIOP model was developed to bring about cohesiveness in the practice of sheltering instruction and ensuring ELLs' success in academic achievement when implemented properly. It comprises eight components: (1) lesson preparation, (2) building background, (3) comprehensible input, (4) strategies, (5) interaction, (6) practice/application, (7) lesson delivery, and (8) review/assessment (Echevarria et al., 2008). SIOP offers teachers the opportunity to plan and deliver instruction for ELLs that is grade-appropriate, with a curriculum that challenges students to their fullest potential. In this section, we discuss how each of the eight components may be realized in adolescent ELLs' content classes in ways that promote both content knowledge and language.

Lesson Preparation: Content and Language Objectives

During lesson preparation, when SIOP-trained teachers prepare to deliver sheltered instruction, they must formulate both language and content objectives for each lesson to support ELLs' language development. These objectives need to be clearly defined and aligned with adopted state standards for both content and language. To illustrate this, let us return to Ana, introduced in the Classroom Portrait at the opening of this chapter. Recall that Ms. Zamora worries about Ana's ability to solve story problems in math. Suppose that Ms. Zamora gives Ana the following math problem:

Veronica recycles 10 bottles of soda each week. How many bottles of soda does Veronica recycle in 6 months?

At first, this story problem may seem very simple—one that may be solved easily by means of a mathematical equation. However, Ana requires more knowledge of the language to be able to determine the elements of the equation. She must possess the following types of linguistic knowledge:

1. Morphological—knowledge of words and lexicon, including the role of each word as far as parts of speech are concerned (nouns, adjectives, adverbs, etc.).
2. Syntactic—knowledge of how words combine in a language to be able to understand and identify important grammatical information that will allow Ana to determine the elements of her equation in the right order.
3. Phonological/phonetics—knowledge of how words are pronounced, if we expect Ana to be able to orally communicate her answer to the rest of the class.
4. Semantic—knowledge of the meaning of words.

Thus, solving the problem requires Ana to understand that the question is stated in the simple present tense, to recognize the information contained in the verb phrase (recycles) in the predicate of the sentence, and to understand the use of the auxiliary in the direct question (does). Being able to recognize these important morphosyntactic features clues students in on the realization that an expected answer likely involves the use of similar structures. Consequently, the following answers would not be expected from students who master the English language:

1. Recycled 240 bottles*
2. Veronica recycled 240 bottles. (simple past tense)
3. Veronica will recycle 240 bottles. (simple future tense)
4. Veronica had recycled 240 bottles. (past perfect tense)

Note that we have marked the first hypothetical answer with an asterisk, because it is not grammatically correct; it is an incomplete sentence that is missing a subject. Some language learners may not insert a subject because such an omission is grammatically correct and appropriate in their native language, as is the case of learners whose native language is Spanish. However, in declarative statements in English, such omission results in a sentence that is ill-formed or ungrammatical.

The remaining three responses, although grammatically correct in terms of sentence formation, do not constitute appropriate answers because the statements are in tenses, shown in parentheses, that do not correlate with the intended nature (tense–aspect) of the original question. Once again, we are able to recognize the tense and aspect of all these sentences by examining the information in the verb phrase (as verbs are conjugated). Example 2 shows that the thought is expressed in simple past tense, which is marked by the inflection -ed at the end of the verb (*recycled*). Example 3 is expressed in the simple future tense, marked by the modal auxiliary (*will*) followed by the base form of the main verb (*recycle*). Example 4 is expressed in past perfect tense, marked by the presence of the verb *to have* in its past form (*had*), followed by the past participle form of the main verb (*recycled*). The original question was expressed in simple present tense, because it is asking for information that is a regular occurrence in the present time.

Thus, a math class that would support Ana's academic literacy development would require that the teacher include during lesson preparation the following objectives to support both content and language development:

> Content objective: *By the end of today's math lesson, students will learn to solve story problems using simple equations.*
>
> Language objective: *By the end of today's lesson, students will be able to answer orally the questions related to story problems formulated in simple present tense.*

This practice of explicitly including these two types of objectives in lesson plans ensures that teachers are providing the kinds of support Ana needs. This written record would also serve to set expectations for what reasonably to expect of ELLs in time. If Ana were to give any of the possible answers we offered as examples of what we would not expect from students with a strong command of English, her answer should not merely be considered incorrect. By scaffolding instruction in English and modeling, the language objective may be achieved.

Next, let us briefly consider the following example of language and content objectives for Mr. Turner's 10th-grade science lesson dealing with energy and matter conservation:

> Content objective: *By the end of today's lesson, students will learn what materials are biodegradable.*
>
> Language objective: *By the end of today's lesson, students will be able to*

compare orally the results of experiments on different types of biodegradable materials, as reported in selected readings.

Students in this class are expected to learn about biodegradable materials. But this is not all. To demonstrate that they have learned this content, ELLs have to communicate their learning orally; that is, they need to master the academic language that allows them to compare results orally. Thus, to prepare his lesson, Mr. Turner has asked himself: "What kinds of language will my students need to express orally themselves to accomplish the language goal of the lesson? What specific vocabulary do I need to ensure that they know? What grammatical structures, notions, and/or functions will they need? What grammatical tenses and aspects will they need to express complete sentences that accurately portray the information they wish to communicate?" As he goes through this analysis, Mr. Turner realizes that learners will need to have mastered the linguistic expressions that allow them to compare information. Phrases such as *in comparison, similarly, likewise,* and *in the same way* constitute examples of the metalanguage that students need to learn to "communicate information, ideas, and concepts for academic success in the area of science" (Teachers of English to Speakers of Other Languages [TESOL], 2006). This metalanguage is part of what we understand as academic language, a necessary ingredient for academic literacy. It is highly unlikely that ELLs will acquire this metalanguage anyplace other than the classroom. Mr. Turner realizes that providing access to content is a necessary but not a sufficient condition for his learners to demonstrate success in this science classroom, or any other content-area classroom.

To plan language objectives, both Mr. Turner and Ms. Zamora seek answers to questions such as the following:

- "Where are my ELLs from? How long has each been in the country?"
- "What languages do they speak at home?"
- "Are my students literate in their first language?"
- "Are there any records of their previous schooling available? What do I know about their previous schooling experiences in this subject?"
- "Can my students solve problems in this subject in their native languages?"
- "Can my students understand the language of this subject beyond memorization of facts?"
- "What are my students' communication skills in other subject areas, and outside the classroom?"

- "Can they ask questions in English?"
- "Can they provide answers?"
- "Can they communicate with their peers?"
- "How do my ELLs perform in group activities? What roles do they assume in relation to the rest of the team members?"
- "What kind of tutoring are they receiving? By whom? What kind of English as a second language/bilingual support, if any, are they receiving?"

Building Background

Students' background knowledge constitutes another pivotal component of sheltered instruction for ELLs within the SIOP framework. The practice of building background is also consistent with Cummins's (1996) framework for academic language learning, discussed earlier in this chapter. Cummins underscored the need for activating and building students' background knowledge. He stated that this practice achieves the following:

- Increases cognitive engagement and makes language and concepts more meaningful to students by enabling them to interpret new information in relation to what they already know;
- Enables teachers to get to know their students better as individuals with unique personal histories; in turn, this permits teachers to tune their instruction to the needs and interests of individual students; creates a context in the classroom where students' cultural knowledge is expressed, shared, affirmed, thereby motivating students to invest themselves more fully in the learning process. (p. 130)

Science teachers, for example, have a variety of options from which to choose for activating background knowledge of their ELLs. These activities range from simple questions that ask students to look back into their personal experiences, to students' previous learning. For a unit on biodegradable materials, a teacher could bring a photo or illustration of the often used symbol that indicates that the object, or material, is biodegradable. By pointing at the symbol, the teacher may ask questions such as the following:

"Has anybody ever seen this symbol before?"
"Does anybody recognize it?"
"Can anyone give me one example?"

Then, teachers can scaffold student responses to yield more information, first giving students a chance to brainstorm in writing the different products they have seen carrying such symbol, then having students share their lists with their peers and, finally, with the whole class. Thus, native and non-native speakers of English can learn about different environmental concerns and responses around the world. ELLs will have had a chance to fulfill the task either on their own or with the assistance of their peers or teachers, and they should be able to contribute to the classroom discussion.

Comprehensible Input: A Necessary Ingredient of SIOP

Among the essential features of sheltered instruction, comprehensible input plays a unique and special role. Providing *comprehensible input* to ELLs, according to SIOP, means that (1) teachers pay special attention to their own speech (not too slow; not too fast) depending on the ELLs' various levels of language proficiency; (2) teachers strengthen their ability to offer clear explanations of academic tasks; and (3) they implement a variety of techniques to help ELLs to understand what is expected of them (Echevarria et al., 2008). Of all these features, teachers' speech is key for ELLs. This particular feature requires that teachers enunciate clearly and speak at a rate that students can effectively comprehend (Echevarria & Graves, 2003). It is also probably one of the most challenging features of SIOP, to monitor, because it is connected to teachers' self-perceptions of their own speech, which may differ radically from ELLs' perceptions. Some teachers may think that they are speaking at the level of linguistic proficiency that ELLs can follow, when in fact they are not. Increasing experience, careful observation, and adequate assessments should help teachers make a more accurate judgment of whether they are providing comprehensible input.

In the case of the two teachers we have introduced, we suggest that Ms. Zamora do the following:

- Continue to be enthusiastic and friendly as she interacts with struggling students in particular.
- Use visuals with the presentation of the math problem.
- Demonstrate how to solve the problem in visual/tangible ways.
- Repeat and review vocabulary, inviting students to use their previous knowledge as a resource.
- Keep the linguistic load of problems and explanations relatively simple and easy to understand.
- Offer options of math problems from which learners can choose to give them opportunities to show their strengths.
- Assess students' self-perceptions of the difficulties of various problems by means of a rating scale that students can easily complete.

In the science class, we would recommend that Mr. Turner provide the following additional supports:

- Model a similar experiment step by step, with students completing each step after you.
- Use longer pauses to ensure that no student is left behind in the process.
- Have students practice giving directions and following steps.
- Use visuals that students can review at any time to help them retain and recall information.

These approaches ensure the comprehensible input that ELLs need to participate fully in content classes.

Strategies

Strategies may be the most familiar SIOP component to literacy specialists given that a lot of their work centers around strategic instruction. Strategies have also been the focus of extensive research of many TESOL specialists. SIOP specifically calls for teachers to provide learners with (1) ample opportunities to use learning strategies; (2) scaffolded instruction; and (3) questions that call for higher-order thinking, also termed *referential questions* (Brown, 2007), which are questions that may be open to interpretation and may or may not have correct or discrete answers. Lewis and Reader (Chapter 5, this volume) and Falk-Ross and Hurst (Chapter 7, this volume) offer many suggestions for promoting this kind of thinking in adolescents' classrooms.

Lenski and Ehlers-Zavala (2004) offer additional suggestions for reading instruction that are also applicable to the four language domains in a variety of academic contexts or subject areas, including formally and informally assessing students' prior literacy experiences, ranging from concepts about print, text types, and topics to family literacy practices; formally introducing the various strategies they want students to implement, using a variety of reading materials/topics; modeling strategy use in diverse reading contexts, so that students observe how these can be applied in different learning situations; and providing ample opportunities and appropriate pacing for students to use the strategies in the classroom independently and as part of collaborative and cooperative practices with peers (p. 6).

Even in areas in which teachers intuitively may think that learners can easily transfer their literacy abilities from the first language to the second language, explicit teaching matters considerably, as in the case of Ana, who struggles with both mathematical concepts and the language of math. In interactions with teachers, Robison (2006) found that there is a pervasive belief that mathematics "should be easy for English learners because the concepts translate across languages," adding that "this idea appears to make sense because many ELLs do well in math, especially when they are functioning at a rudimentary level of language proficiency. However, language misunderstandings eventually emerge since mathematics is a subject that has its own vocabulary, double meanings, and idiosyncrasies seen nowhere else" (p. 127). For example, consider the vocabulary found in math and science texts. Some terms have a multiplicity of meanings, such as the word *table*. This word may refer to the physical object we use as a piece of furniture, a multiplication table, the periodic table in a science class or a book's table of contents, or a type of chart that shows data (e.g., a table of results). Consequently, it is vitally important that content teachers provide content-specific word meanings, teach them explicitly, and use strategies such as those suggested by Nichols, Rupley, and Kiser (Chapter 8, this volume).

Student Interactions in the Classroom

This aspect of instruction makes a positive difference for language learners. As SIOP emphasizes, teachers should avoid dominating classroom discourse, so that ELLs can have as many meaningful opportunities for interaction as possible. Teachers should also refrain from providing answers on behalf of ELLs, or completing their thoughts. Instead, they need to extend the amount of time ELLs are given to respond to questions posed by the teacher or other students. Teachers can accomplish this by using the type of think–pair–share activity students used to brainstorm their familiarity with the sign that designated a product was biodegradable. Teachers can also offer different approaches for sharing responses with the rest of the class. Learners, for instance, may write their answers on a chart or overhead. If they are not comfortable speaking English in front of the class, they may be allowed to read their answers. Students could illustrate their ideas and let the class or a small group discuss what they see represented in the drawing.

To promote a variety of interactions between and among ELLs, teachers also need to plan grouping configurations that ensure the participation of all learners. Depending on the nature of the task or goal to be accomplished, ELLs may need to be grouped according to similar proficiency levels; at other times, they may benefit more from linguistically heterogeneous groups. Some grouping configurations may be random; at other times, this would be less appropriate for the task. To create random groupings, teachers may want to develop a repertoire of techniques to use as the need arises. For instance, they can have on hand different colored or shaped paper strips or objects that students can draw from a box or envelope to find their teammates.

Cultural considerations should also play a role in grouping decisions. For some ELLs, working in groups may seem natural; for others it may not. Some ELLs may have experienced very traditional schooling in their native countries that is less conducive to interactions or group work. Keeping this in mind, teachers want to introduce these ELLs gradually to grouping practices, realizing that the more students get to interact with others, the greater their progress in L2 development for academic and social purposes.

Finally, depending on the classroom composition and resources, teachers may want to consider providing ELLs with support in their dominant language. This practice historically has not been recommended in highly linguistically diverse classrooms of ELLs, so as not to show favoritism to any one group of students or individual learners. However, there may be scenarios in which this type of support is absolutely necessary and should be offered, if available, as in the case of a newcomer who has just joined the class and has little or no English. The ideal situation would be to have a paraprofessional available for such students, but this is not always possible. Some students who are native speakers are eager to help those in greater need, and they should not be deterred as long as doing so does not affect their own performance.

Classroom Practice and Lesson Delivery

Classroom practice that offers students the opportunity to apply newly constructed knowledge to real situations, and lesson delivery that encourages maximum student involvement are two closely related SIOP components.

In our introduction to the SIOP components, we discussed the need for teachers to formulate both language and content objectives. Although this is initially a challenging task for teachers, the greater challenge comes during classroom practice and lesson delivery. This is when the teacher's plan comes to life, and there must be clear alignment between classroom activities and the teacher's content and language objectives.

In Ana's case, for example, given that she faces difficulty with math story problems, it is important that she practice the language associated with the problems. Teachers do not want to overload students like Ana linguistically with very complex syntactic structures. They may need to adjust the language used in math story problems, and gradually advance Ana in the language continuum. Ana may start solving math problems in the simple present tense, as presented in our earlier examples, before moving to statements/questions with more complex grammar. For instance, a problem that reads "How many bottles will she have saved in 10 years?", may be more challenging to comprehend at first than the sentence in the simple present tense we offered as an example. Yet the mathematical equation that is needed to solve the problem is the same. Teachers may also help students like Ana write simple equations, using the simple present tense to understand sentence/question construction, then move to writing more complex structures. This activity includes reading and writing; the remaining two domains, speaking and listening, can be addressed as students solve problems together.

Teachers can implement numerous classroom-based activities to learn more about their students. Peregoy and Boyle (2005) suggest having students create illustrated autobiographies or dialogue journals. Students might organize a scrapbook with family pictures or other illustrations that visually tell their own stories. Activities like these do not require that students be proficient in English, but they do require that teachers communicate in a way that allows learners to understand the nature of the task. Activities can be adjusted according to the language proficiency level of students or literacy practices. Some students, for example, may have developed oral English but may not have written literacy skills. Students may still initially engage in oral accounts of their personal histories and offer vibrant accounts. These student oral narratives may also be represented pictorially, then, with the assistance of other learners who are proficient in English, be translated into the target written language.

Giving students opportunities to communicate information about their own selves, which reassures and validates their identities, is at the core of the academic success of ELLs (Cummins, 1996; Lewis & Jones, Chapter 1, this volume). In carrying out these activities, teachers communicate to students that they are interested in them, that their past histories are important, and that they are welcome in this country. It also offers teachers a world of information in regard to learners' implicit knowledge of literacy practices. By analyzing learners' narrative accounts, as McCabe and Bliss (2003) explain, teachers can begin to determine whether learners are able to (1) maintain a topic; (2) present ideas in a sequence; (3) inform and elaborate on information; and (4) engage in referencing, assessing the varying degrees of success—all of which helps teachers prepare to work with ELLs.

Review and Assessment

Lessons for ELLs are not successful without review and assessment. These two SIOP components ought to guide future planning and implementation of instruction for ELLs. When it comes to assessment practices for ELLs, current and desirable practices do not differ much from the ones teachers implement among monolingual learners. Essentially, teachers of ELLs should review and assess students using authentic tools, such as those described by Gillis, Haltiwanger, Ficklin, Dillingham, and Davis (Chapter 12, this volume). These can truly offer ELLs the opportunity to demonstrate learning of new concepts and new vocabulary, as well as to attain both language and content objectives. The primary difference between assessment of monolingual learners and assessment practices of ELLs is that, in the case of ELLs, teachers want to be guided by the fuller picture of what their ELLs are able to do by asking questions, such as those we posed earlier in this chapter. Whenever possible, teachers or literacy experts who assess ELLs should also consider involving bilingual or multilingual specialists to assist with assessment.

For effective assessment practices of ELLs in reading, Lenski, Ehlers-Zavala, Daniel, and Sun-Irminger (2006) also recommend that teachers modify traditional assessments, which includes the following:

- Permit students to answer orally rather than in writing.
- Allow a qualified bilingual professional to assist in the assessment.
- Consider offering ELLs the opportunity to demonstrate reading progress and growth through group assessments.
- Allow students to provide responses in multiple formats.
- Accept responses in students' native language, if translation support systems exist in the school or community (e.g., paraprofessionals or teachers-in-training from nearby universities, who can come into the classroom or serve as e-buddies online to offer additional support).

Feedback during these assessments is extremely important for ELLs. Rubrics, such as those suggested by Birdyshaw and Hoffman (Chapter 11, this volume), provide clear guidelines for students, but even more information is needed that lets ELLs know how they are doing with regard to their development of both content knowledge and language learning.

ELLs also need many opportunities for self-assessment, using approaches such as those described by Lewis and Jones (Chapter 1, this volume). By guiding ELLs in the process of engaging in self-assessments, teachers also empower ELLs to become active agents, who are responsible for their own learning. When ELLs become empowered, they are more likely to become independent learners. Through self-assessments, ELLs also learn to distinguish between what works for them and what does not, and they develop the ability to gain insights into their own learning strategies. Finally, ELLs' ability to engage in self-assessments provides for teachers a critical and direct perspective into what they can offer to help their ELLs reach academic success.

Concluding Thoughts

Our chapter opened with the story of Ana, an adolescent ELL enrolled in a secondary school in the United States. Her story represents the challenges faced by many ELLs who struggle in their classes because they have not fully developed the necessary proficiency in English to experience academic success. In Ana's story, we also underscored the difficulties that teachers of adolescents face as they work with ELLs like Ana, who lack academic English, and offered a research-based discussion on the fundamentals of L2 teaching that shape the process of acquiring academic language. We realize that some of these basics are not always fully developed in teacher training preparation programs that are traditionally oriented toward learners whose native language is English, not their L2, as in Ana's case. To help teachers more effectively meet the academic needs of ELLs in their classrooms, we have also shared our thoughts and experiences on these topics, including fundamentals of language/SLA, culture, instruction, and assessment.

In examining the most current trends in L2 teaching and learning, we also provided middle and high school teachers practical suggestions for incorporating in their classrooms the SIOP model for sheltered instruction. We believe this model will make a positive difference. It guides teachers in how to support and foster L2 development, while giving learners access to content.

As readers may have already discovered, the question of how to develop academic literacy among adolescent ELLs may not have a simple answer, but all teachers who possess adequate understanding of what constitutes effective instruction for ELLs, and who have the desire to accomplish the goal of meeting the needs of all learners, can successfully address it.

Questions for Reflection

1. What language objectives would you formulate for a lesson in your content field? Give an example of how you would proceed in your lesson to ensure that students such as Ana reach those language objectives.

2. ELLs sometimes find it difficult to integrate classroom dynamics into the new/foreign context for fear of being ridiculed. What kinds of collaborative activities would you implement to encourage positive interactions to support and foster the academic language development of ELLs in your classes?

3. Observe several classrooms in which you find ELLs. Take notes on what you observe to answer the following questions: How do teachers seem to address the needs of ELLs? Provide specific examples of any adaptations the teachers make. Are your observations consistent with what we have recommended in this chapter? If not, in what ways does the observed teaching differ?

References

Akmajian, A., Demers, R. A., Farmer, A. K., & Harnish, R. M. (2001). *Linguistics: An introduction to language and communication* (2nd ed.). Cambridge, MA: MIT Press.

Ariza, E. N. (2006). *Not for ESOL teachers: What every classroom teacher needs to know about the linguistically, culturally, and ethnically diverse student.* Boston: Pearson/Allyn & Bacon.

Brisk, M. E., & Harrington, M. M. (2007). *Literacy and bilingualism* (2nd ed.). Mahwah, NJ: Erlbaum.

Brown, H. D. (2007). *Teaching by principles: An interactive approach to language pedagogy* (3rd ed.). White Plains, NY: Longman.

Canagarajah, S. A. (2002). *Critical academic writing and multilingual students.* Ann Arbor: University of Michigan Press.

Cummins, J. (1979). Cognitive/academic language proficiency, linguistic interdependence, the optimum age question and some other matters. *Working Papers on Bilingualism, 19,* 121–129.

Cummins, J. (1996). *Negotiating identities: Educating for empowerment in a diverse society* (2nd ed.). Los Angeles: California Association for Bilingual Education.

Echevarria, J., & Graves, A. (2003). *Sheltered content instruction: Teaching English-language learners with diverse abilities* (2nd ed.). Boston: Pearson Education.

Echevarria, J., Vogt, M. E., & Short, D. (2008). *Making content comprehensible for English learners: The SIOP model* (3rd ed.). Boston: Pearson Education.

Ehlers-Zavala, F. P. (2002). *Assessment of the English language learner.* Chicago: Chicago Public Schools.

Fillmore, L. W. (2005, January). *Changing times, changing schools: Articulating leadership choices in educating bilingual students.* Paper presented at the annual meeting of the National Association for Bilingual Education, San Antonio, TX.

Gee, P. (2004). Learning language as a matter of learning social languages within discourses. In M. R. Hawkins (Ed.), *Language learning and teacher education* (pp. 13–31). Buffalo, NY: Multilingual Matters.

Genesee, F. (2005, January). *Literacy development in ELLs: What does the research say?* Paper presented at the annual meeting of the National Association for Bilingual Education, San Antonio, TX.

Hawkins, M. R. (Ed.). (2004). *Language learning and teacher education.* Buffalo, NY: Multilingual Matters.

Lenski, S. D., & Ehlers-Zavala, F. (2004). *Reading strategies for Spanish speakers.* Dubuque, IA: Kendall/Hunt.

Lenski, S. D., Ehlers-Zavala, F. E., Daniel, M. C., & Sun-Irminger, X. (2006). Assessing English-language learners in mainstream classrooms. *Reading Teacher, 60*(1), 24–34.

McCabe, A., & Bliss, L. (2003). *Patterns of narrative discourse: A multicultural, life span approach.* New York: Allyn & Bacon.

McLaughlin, B. (1992). *Myths and misconceptions about second language learning* (Report No. 5). Retrieved December 15, 2008, from National Center for Research on Cultural Diversity and Second Language Learning at *www. ncela.gwu.edu/pubs/ncrcdsll/epr5.htm.*

Peregoy, S. F., & Boyle, O. F. (2005). *Reading, writing, and learning in ESL: A resource for K–12 teachers* (4th ed.). New York: Pearson Education.

Robison, S. (2006). Teaching math to English learners—Myths and methods. In E. N. Ariza (Ed.), *Not for ESOL teachers: What every classroom teacher needs to know about the linguistically, culturally, and ethnically diverse student* (pp. 127–139). Boston: Pearson/Allyn & Bacon.

Schleppegrell, M., Achugar, M., & Oteíza, T. (2004). The grammar of history: Enhancing content-based instruction through a functional focus on language. *TESOL Quarterly, 38*(1), 67–93.

Teachers of English to Speakers of Other Languages. (2006). *Pre-K–12 English language proficiency standards.* Alexandria, VA: Author.

Villegas, A. M., & Lucas, T. (2002). *Educating culturally responsive teachers.* New York: State University of New York Press.

CHAPTER 7

How Can We Use Adolescents' Language and Classroom Discourse to Enhance Critical Thinking Practices?

FRANCINE FALK-ROSS
SHANNON HURST

CLASSROOM PORTRAIT

Maria, a seventh-grade bilingual student, sat as she usually did in this science class: near the back of the classroom. She expected that once again she would become confused by the unfamiliar science terminology the teacher usually used at the start of class, then she'd tune out, barely listening or participating in classroom discussion during the last 20 minutes. Her teacher, Ms. Cali, was aware of this behavior and thought that maybe today she could engage Maria, at least a little, in what was happening by helping Maria with the vocabulary needed to comprehend this geology unit.

Ms. Cali: From our assigned reading we know that minerals are materials taken from rocks and earth to provide us with products we need in our everyday lives. Which of the minerals listed in our text do you recognize that we need each day?

Ken: I think we use coal and oil. We use them all the time for heat. My grandfather told me about using coal in trains.

Ms. Cali: Yes, and coal and oil are called fossil fuels. Maria, what problem has been in the news recently about fossil fuels? Why do we need to be more responsible about using these products?

Maria: I don't know. I don't know what a fossil is.

Ms. Cali: Let me help you then. Fossils are hardened leftovers of animals and plants that once lived in the earth. There are many fossils left in the volcanic ashes in Mexico, near where you lived. Oil and gas come from

---

these leftover materials. What have you heard your parents saying about oil and gas?

MARIA: I guess that we need more.

MS. CALI: Exactly. This article was written by a scientist. How might the content be different if it had been written by an environmentalist? What about an oil producer?

The conversation continued as students considered these perspectives, as well as their own. Ms. Cali was pleased that at least Maria participated a little and thought that Maria might even sense that her teacher was there to help. But then Ms. Cali's thoughts turned to George, another student of hers in the next class, with different literacy problems. Ms. Cali knew from conversations that George didn't think he would ever become a science major if he went to college, and he had no interest in volcanic ash or landforms. He was mostly interested in sports activities with his friends, in and out of school, and he had frequent conversations with his friends about travel to other cities with the teams. Ms. Cali realized that to get students like George to attend to learning in her class, she would need to engage them in thinking about connections between the science topics and their lives. This might be difficult for today's topic, but Ms. Cali thought she'd give it her best effort as George's class began.

MS. CALI: Volcanoes occur when there are shifts in the earth's core. The great pressure causes the explosions. There are volcanoes still erupting in the United States. Who knows where?

GORDON: I heard of Mt. St. Helens in Washington. That was awful. People had to get out of the way of the ash and animals were hurt.

GEORGE: That's an important city. The Seattle Mariners play there. I've been there with my family. How often does it explode?

MS. CALI: Not very often. The last big eruption of Mt. St. Helens was in 1980 but there has been some minor activity in the last few years. How do you think this volcano and others affects the lives of the people who live near them? How does geology affect the way we live?

GEORGE: Well, we need to protect ourselves but no one wants to move from their homes. Did the government help the people? What do you do when that happens?

SONDRA: Can people tell when it's going to blow?

MS. CALI: We can look online to learn more about the effects. Those are good questions that we need to discuss. Let's see if we can find ideas on this from people who live close to volcanoes, as well as from groups such as geologists around the world.

Maria and George were both seventh-grade science students, but they struggled with connecting to the content-area material in very different ways. Maria was not familiar with the multiple meanings and technical connotations of many of the words used in the varied reading materials for which she was responsible. She tried to look up the words in the classroom dictionary; however, these definitions were still unclear, and she was embarrassed to ask Ms. Cali for help. George was able to read the material, but he was not convinced of the importance that the scientific knowledge had in his life as a young teenager. He had interests far removed from the course content and did not independently explore topics in science.

The difficulties that George and Maria had with content-area reading in both vocabulary and connections are representative of many students we have observed in other classrooms throughout this school (and others similar to it). But as the Classroom Portrait illustrates, middle and secondary classroom teachers want their students to demonstrate a clear understanding of concepts that are taught and will do whatever they can to help students accomplish this. They want their students to think deeply about new content material and to realize the importance of students' comprehension of new material beyond the surface structure and facts. Instruction is often followed by assessment of what students have learned, often through written summaries, end-of-chapter tests, or class presentations. Unfortunately, many teachers find the results lacking in deep, practical, critical thinking and are dismayed by their students' unquestioning acceptance of facts and generalizations portrayed in text, whether in print or in media/nonprint formats.

Teachers also search for ways to integrate theory and real-life applications of new knowledge for all students (National Middle School Association, 2003). They want students to engage in critical literacy by thinking about how texts are shaped by perspective, the perspective of the reader, as well as that of the writer. Critical literacy theory derives from the work of Paulo Freire (1970), who described the importance of "reading the world." His influence affected the way we consider the perspectives of authors of text in literature and content-area reading.

We propose that allowing more time for discussion about the cultural, historical, and social significance of this information, as well as authors' particular and diverse perspectives, will improve student practices for thinking about texts. We also believe that teachers can trigger this kind of reflection through the questions they pose during instruction. Research investigations in the area of critical literacy are generally focused on four main applications that impact deeper thinking and energize adolescents' conversations. Lewison, Flint, and Van Sluys (2002) very clearly describe these as disruption of a common understanding to gain perspective; examination of multiple viewpoints, such as different characters and different interest groups; consideration of power relationships between people, such as who stands to gain from this viewpoint between people; and promotion of social justice through reflection and action to change an inappropriate action or relationship.

This chapter focuses specifically on the promise and the challenge that teachers may face as they use open questioning and thoughtful comments during interactions in content-area classes. We look at ways to provide middle and high school students with (1) models of *critical thinking*, which refers to reflective considerations about topics with connections to students' own self, world, and other texts, and (2) models of *critical literacy*, which refers to analyzing wording and the author's stance toward a topic, and understanding how perspective shapes communication and reflects power structures. To respond to this chapter's question (How can we use language and classroom discourse to enhance adolescent literacy?), we develop three themes through the eyes of a literacy specialist and a classroom teacher. First, we examine the central role of language in adolescents' literacy learning. Second, we discuss the nature of language interaction in the classroom. Our third theme offers possibilities for infusing critical thinking and critical literacy into our curricula. Francine Falk-Ross, a teacher-educator who provides professional opportunities to teachers and acts as a second pair of eyes for research in middle grade classrooms, has taught preservice and practicing teachers about the importance of discussions to spark interest, personal connections, and critical thinking for young adolescents. Shannon Hurst, a science teacher-researcher who teaches a diverse set of students in a semiurban community, routinely connects the facts of science with everyday applications for students as she brings alive the important purposes of scientific knowledge.

The Central Role of Language
in Young Adolescents' Literacy Learning

As student populations within schools become increasingly more diverse, in general, literacy instruction requires creative and substantive approaches to teaching, especially for middle and secondary students who struggle with comprehension of complex ideas in content-area texts. Effective use of classroom talk can play a foundational role in supporting students' inquiry and literacy achievement. Yet it is often not given the attention it deserves (Nystrand, 2006), and talking is not always a part of reading and learning activities (Alvermann, 1995). Talking is such a natural part of what we do that we may overlook the reality that we communicate, teach, evaluate, and socialize in the classroom through language (Cazden, 2001). Furthermore, we know that middle and secondary students with language difficulties or language differences are at a disadvantage in classrooms where language participation is not valued (Lipsky & Gartner, 1997). It is also the case that because many students may be marginalized in their classrooms by language differences and limited vocabulary (Delpit, 2006), they are unable to participate fully in class routines.

So it is clear that attention to classroom dialogue to promote comprehension can increase achievement for all students, especially for those with language differences and difficulties. Teachers need to be highly skilled communicators who understand the contribution that classroom conversation makes to language development. To address this need, more effective ways for teachers and students to question and talk in class have recently gained attention (Falk-Ross, 2002; McCormick, Loeb, & Schiefelbusch, 1997). In the next section, we look at the nature of language interaction in classrooms; this is followed by suggestions for promoting critical literacy and critical thinking about texts through effective classroom talk.

The Nature of Language Interaction in the Classroom

Language is considered the primary cognitive, or thinking, tool through which we learn (Vygotsky, 1978). For teachers and students, the need for more talk, the vocabulary for talking, and the nature of language interaction in the classroom require careful attention to address critical questions and issues that extend young adolescents' thinking (Santman, 2005). In fact, classroom talk is often equated with education as the medium of learning (e.g., Lemke, 1989), and classroom discourse is worthy of analysis.

Consider your own experiences with teacher talk in classrooms. Can you identify recurring conversation routines? Teacher–student talk in most classrooms can be characterized by particular patterns, and in many ways students' learning in the classroom is tied to instructional language routines set by the teacher and used by peers to question and respond to new information. These routines provide a context that influences learning and literacy development (Gutiérrez, 1995; Nystrand, 2006).

Familiar routines include the questions that teachers initiate (e.g., "What is a fact that you remember about protists that you read about for today?"), the responses that teachers expect from students (e.g., "They can be unicellular or multicellular."), and the evaluative comments that teachers use to complete the "turn" (e.g., "OK. This is true. You understood those characteristics."). This format for discussion, initiation–response–evaluation, is often referred to as an IRE pattern. Teachers generally use this set of interactional language patterns to question and comment during lessons (Cazden, 2001) to scaffold, guide, or control students' learning (Bernstein, 1990; Wilkinson & Silliman, 2000). On further analysis, we see that teacher initiations, typically in the form of questions, are skewed in favor of a high percentage of teacher talk (Nystrand, Gamoran, Kachur, & Prendergast, 1997). By the time students reach middle grades and high school, they and their teachers understand, and perhaps even expect, this flow of discourse. But adolescents who tend to be resistant to compliance with structured routines, and who also may be from cultures where other classroom routines are more prevalent, may not be well suited to this form of interaction.

Teachers can change these routines and open conversation simply by modifying their form of comments and questions (Just & Carpenter, 1987) to include more expansive forms of turn taking, giving students a greater role in the conversation. Student-centered language motivates students to voice personal connections. It can draw students into literacy discussions with their class members and the teacher through co-construction of knowledge (Falk-Ross, 2001; Nystrand, Wu, Gamoran, Zeiser, & Long, 2003). Teachers who use more supportive language can encourage deep conversation, promote critical literacy, and boost students' confidence about the significance of their own experiences (Johnston, 2004).

Several researchers have contributed to how we characterize the more open and expanded versions of classroom discourse that facilitate adolescent learning. Such discourse includes more turns between speakers before moving on to another; more depth or explanation of responses; and consideration of students' voice in developing answers, including interactive opportunities, question uptake, curricular connections, extended individual exchanges, and higher-level evaluation, among others. These elements may be explained, as they are below, in terms of classroom interactions.

Definitions of Expanded Language Elements

• *Interactive opportunities* (Nystrand et al., 1997). Teachers provide ample time for student-initiated questions, comments, and discussion within all classroom activities.

• *Question uptake* (Collins, 1995). Teachers and students pose questions that do not have prespecified answers but, depend instead on the responses that precede them. They allow students' observations to create changes in the discussion in substantive ways.

• *Dialogic conversations* (Bakhtin, 1986). Teachers encourage students to interact with the text and the ongoing responses of their peers and the teacher's comments. In the classroom this occurs through curricular connections, such as connecting language contributions to previous discussions and continuing constructions.

• *Individual language exchanges* Teachers use individual conferencing and interactive journaling to model and develop learning within students' zone of proximal development (Vygotsky, 1978) or their instructional levels of learning.

• *High-level evaluation* (Nystrand et al., 1997). Teachers elicit responses that involve analysis of material, synthesis of ideas, and personal connections with text through language. Teachers ask for the student's interpretation of a concept rather than the listed or given definition from workbooks or guides.

• *Scaffolded instruction* (Wilkinson & Silliman, 2000). Teachers use reciprocal teaching methods to guide students through development of new strategies toward independent learning.

• *Negotiated meanings* (Wells, 1999). Teachers respond with observations and added information rather than objective evaluation (i.e., use language that is collaborative to reach shared understandings of concepts and vocabulary).

Useful examples of these expanded forms include higher-level questioning strategies, such as associations between content in different texts or readings, and text-to-world connections (Keene & Zimmerman, 1997). Another effective expansion is the use of open questions for which several responses would be appropriate to guide and to scaffold instruction for young adolescents (Wilkinson & Silliman, 2000). One more approach is to use negotiated meanings, such as a compilation of students' suggestions or interpretations of meaning, rather than the dictionary or teacher-constructed definitions. Each of these strategies provides for an increased level of student ownership of classroom talk that feeds into young adolescent learners' burgeoning sense of self. Teachers, however, may not be capitalizing on the necessary specifics of communication competence (or academic language) to engage in discussion during teaching and learning events (Collins, 1995).

Literacy competencies and comprehension change within and between middle-grade students as their abstract thinking matures during the early adolescent years (see Lewis & Jones, Chapter 1, this volume). Thus, it makes sense that research findings support a view that students in content-area courses benefit more from higher-order problem solving and reasoning activities than from activities developed solely to build declarative knowledge (Baker & Piburn, 1990). Educators can support this maturation in thinking process by using classroom discourse to scaffold students' questions and model new strategy development (Falk-Ross, 2002; Wilkinson & Silliman, 2000).

Using Language to Develop Critical Thinking, Vocabulary Development, and Critical Literacy in Content Classes

Knowledge about the value and types of classroom talk that can promote literacy achievement in adolescents now allows us to consider practical classroom applications. In this section, we offer examples of dialogue between teachers and students that generate more mature thinking and conceptual understanding.

Classroom Talk That Encourages Critical Literacy

Immersing students in discussions about how context affects perceptions is an important step toward promoting critical literacy. Dozier, Johnston, and Rogers (2006) discuss how context colors life, and how students need opportunities to consider multiple contexts, including society, family, friends, or a context created by their own ideas and experiences. Context provides a glimpse into different places from which we can view the world. These authors also discuss the importance of developing with students the concept of "power," and of how texts evidence power relationships in their choice of content and depiction of facts. Students' differing interpretations of meanings of texts also need to be examined during instruction.

To accomplish such dialogue, students need models and support guided by teachers (Dozier et al., 2006; McLaughlin & DeVoogd, 2004), including teachers' scaffolding as students construct and reconstruct ideas. Used effectively, classroom discourse can mediate this process (Ash, 2008). Both teachers and students can discuss the situated context of the text, including the history of the text, the nature of the language and the message, and the power "moves" that underlie the text (Freire, 1970; Gee, 2001; Luke, 2000). Here we illustrate how content-area talk concerning social issues that affect adolescents provides ample opportunity for such conversations:

- *Social studies talk.* "When we read in our textbook that there are certain 'duties and responsibilities as a citizen of the United States,' to what do you think those duties and responsibilities refer? Who decides fairly what those duties and responsibilities will be? What challenges can you think of that affect these duties and responsibilities?"

- *Reading/language arts talk.* "In the trade book *Stargirl* (Spinelli, 2000), why did the students make fun of the main character? Why are some people considered different than others? What would have happened if Leo had sided against his friends and gone to the dance with Stargirl?"

- *Science talk.* "In our readings about drugs and physical addictions, do you recognize cigarette smoking as one of those drugs? Do you think teenagers are aware of this information? Why do you think teenagers begin and continue to smoke? How might each of these groups feel about teen smoking: doctors, drug companies, tobacco companies, parents of teens?"

Classroom Talk that Promotes Vocabulary Development

Earlier in this chapter we established the need to use classroom talk for expanding students' vocabulary. This can be accomplished in all content areas, and here we provide a few examples. Teachers can facilitate vocabulary development by activating prior knowledge and word associations, discussing word connotations and personal meanings, and sharing applications of new vocabulary to what students bring from family or community experiences. Some examples of questions to stimulate discussions of vocabulary in the content areas include the following:

- *Science talk.* "In your own words, how would you describe the meaning of the term *chlorophyll?* What else do you know about that term? How do you know that? Would someone else please add more information? So, let's sum up. Do we agree that the term refers to _____? How will this term apply to what we and our families know?" [negotiated meaning, uptake]

- *Reading/language arts talk.* "We know to use context to help us figure out words that are long or difficult. Tell us what phrases or sentences before or after this word help you to identify it? Where have you heard this word before?" [scaffolding]

- *Social studies talk.* "We differentiate the organization of some governments as being a democracy or a republic. What are some of the words you have heard in past classes that we use to describe a democracy and republic? What countries would we list under each category? Talk together in pairs to complete the lists. How do people participate in the governing process in each type of government? Which would be more appealing to you, and why?" [negotiated meaning, higher-order evaluation, dialogic conversations]

Classroom Talk That Increases Critical Thinking

Problem solving and decision making can also be encouraged through use of questions that ask students to identify background knowledge and select processes for making decisions. Classroom talk can be extended as students share critiques of texts, debate issues, and defend opinions, Examples include the following:

- *Math talk.* "What steps did you follow to determine that result? How else could you have come to that decision? What information that you knew before helped lead you through that thinking process? How is this similar to the way you solve other problems? What outcome will your decision have on other people?" [higher-level responses, personal analysis]
- *Reading/language arts talk.* "What do you think the author was trying to tell us in that passage? Do you agree or disagree with the message? What do you think the different characters are thinking. What about their perspectives, or previous experiences, might cause them to think this way? What information in the text supports/substantiates your answer? Anyone else have an idea to add to that response? What if I told you that _____?" [question uptake, negotiated meaning, additional information]
- *Social studies talk.* "What do you think were the motivations of the different groups of people involved in the unfolding of this historical event? How can we connect their concerns to our own experiences? Who agrees or wants to add to that answer?" [question uptake, negotiated meaning, higher-level response] and "As we know, Native Americans had lived on this land for many years and spoke another language, different from the colonists. How did the westward movement, as described in our reading, affect Native Americans? What other groups were affected? To what other events in history can you compare that event? Would it be possible for such a movement to occur in the United States today? What about in other parts of the world? What are the necessary conditions for a similar event to happen?" [scaffolding, connections]

There are also some large-scale instructional approaches that encourage expanded language routines and extended periods of class time for conversation, such as the classroom organization offered through Reading/Writing Workshop (Atwell, 1998). Workshops include initial instruction through minilessons on some aspect of reading or writing, followed by a block of time during which there are paired interactions or conference opportunities for conversation between class members.

Small-group literature and inquiry circles are also effective strategies, because they provide more manageable opportunities for classroom talk and can promote critical thinking and critical literacy, along with vocabulary development, especially if questions focus on purposes and perspectives underlying text. For middle- and secondary-level students, small groups provide safe outlets to experiment with new ideas. Additional benefits accrue to second-language learners and struggling readers, since these small groups provide them with longer time periods to voice their opinions and perspectives and also may develop more background knowledge needed for content-area learning.

The Teacher's Voice: Classroom Research on Language in the Classroom

In this section on language development during classroom discussion in content-area classes, Shannon shares her experiences with marginalized students in a middle school science class in the Midwest. Her school is an urban-like suburb that borders Chicago on its northern and eastern fronts. In recent years, the spillover effect, following a conventional pattern of concentric migration, has greatly increased the number of limited-English-proficient (LEP) students within this school district, particularly students of Hispanic descent. According to the district's Report Card, the percentage of Hispanic students enrolled in the district is 94% of the population of over 13,500 students. The current percentage of LEP students enrolled in the district is almost 47%, nearly 6,000 students. The low-income rate is 76%, double that of the state figure of 34.9%. Students tested in the Illinois Standards Assessment Test (ISAT) scored below 50% in reading and math.

The classroom that Shannon discusses here comprised 27 students in a seventh-grade, inner-city urban junior high school. This particular group of students had limited English skills, low levels of grade-appropriate literacy, and various Hispanic backgrounds. The class was 45 minutes in length, and it was the last period of the day. As Shannon worked with these students, one of her underlying premises was that because students at the middle level are immersed in mostly content-area classes with expectations for considerable reading responsibilities, often about populations or topics that are open to scrutiny for the nature of their assumptions, students with language differences are at a distinct disadvantage.

Instructional Goals in Shannon's Class

The primary goal in my seventh-grade science class was to help students understand a scientific idea, explain and interpret it, connect it, and use critical thinking through a process of dialogic reading, wherein students are encouraged to participate in the interpretation through think-alouds and self-questioning, and peer conversations to problem solve. I also wanted students to understand the importance of scientific knowledge and to realize that they, too, can discover and manipulate scientific truths.

I believe in establishing a community of inquirers and scaffolding their learning as needed. My plan was for students to learn science content through four instructional approaches that also incorporated balanced literacy instruction, integrating language arts (i.e., listening and speaking, spelling, vocabulary, reading to and with students, comprehension, and writing). The four approaches were (1) cooperative structures, such as working with students to create shared knowledge in mutually supportive environments; (2) scaffolding instruction and learning by providing boundaries or guided feedback to support success; (3) classroom interaction and encouragement of participation in questioning activities; and (4) authentic experiences, such as providing meaningful activities with everyday applications.

I undertook classroom research to learn how to address the needs of these students with limited proficiency in language and literacy, and to help them form critical connections to science and the natural world around them. I felt the challenge would be to use discourse opportunities to scaffold the connections students could make between the science content in their texts, and to form a deeper understanding of the science curriculum, while also developing their proficiency in seventh-grade-level reading, writing, and vocabulary. I wanted to increase students' success and motivation, while they had fun in the classroom. My language goals for students included developing academic English proficiency in science content, while also meeting district and state science goals. Simultaneously, I hoped to achieve cultural goals with my students by integrating science and American culture, so that students could understand how science applies to their lives.

A Representative Interaction about an Assigned Reading

The lesson I describe here, and that I used for my research, allowed for my success in selected approaches to work and for achievement of my goals. The lesson was loosely aligned with the four elements for critical thinking noted by Lewison and colleagues (2002) and described previously, and the connections with text as readings are considered to be situated language interactions with the reader (Gee, 2001; Luke, 2000). I intended my instruction to stimulate the thinking of predominantly Mexican students about the applications of this new scientific knowledge. As I discuss the lesson procedures, results, and observations of the study, I want to emphasize my view that no single method of teaching science is best for all teachers, all students, all the time, and under all circumstances. The importance of knowing our own students, and finding the language and discussion points that interest and motivate them, is key to infusing effective instruction. Integrating language arts skills development, along with teaching content, places considerable responsibility on content-area teachers but allows for greater realization of those social aspects of learning that are reached through discussion, as opposed to instruction from the text alone, or from solely direct instruction from the teacher.

Because this particular group of seventh graders was approximately 2 years below grade level in reading comprehension, I decided first to connect some features of pop culture to this text, then to discuss how these features were affecting students' interpretation of the content material. I wanted students to form opinions and generate questions, and I hoped my teaching would promote understanding of scientific reading material and generate interest. I know that setting high academic expectations for their success early in the lesson set a positive tone for students and generated an internal appropriation of responsibility for meeting those expectations. By using the selected material, I let the students know that I had confidence in their ability to understand scientific articles and to read critically.

I began by providing students with a scientific article (2007) about how a chemist named Mark Zoller altered tastes in food ("What's the Big Idea?"). The author discusses how Zoller, a chemist, is devising synthetic taste chemicals to make people enjoy the taste of healthier foods. He then describes the scientific mechanisms of taste buds and receptors. The article was difficult for many students to read, because the text was in their second language and also written at grade level, a higher level than the one they are accustomed to reading. However, I felt that through my scaffolding, the students could learn the content. I provided students with 10 minutes of uninterrupted reading time for the four-page article and let them know we would be discussing the material afterwards. I felt that the article would have high interest, because one-half of class members were seriously overweight for their age group. To create a successful learning environment, I planned to include verbal prompting, asking questions, and elaborating on student responses, starting with a discussion on the overlap of the topics of obesity and students' eating habits. This transcript illustrates how the dialogue that followed the reading facilitated students' understanding of the impact of science on their lives.

SHANNON: Now that you have finished reading this article, let's talk about it. First, I am going to ask you a few questions about this reading. Think about this and give the best answer you can, OK? I want to have a discussion about this ... about what you think about this. What do you think about how Mike Zoller is fixing the food?

STUDENT 1: Kids who don't want to eat their vegetables are not eating good and this is an easier way to get them to eat right.

STUDENT 2: They are doing this with chemicals and the spray on the food.

STUDENT 3: I think it's wrong even though people are not eating the right foods and are not healthy.

STUDENT 4: If they do this, will it [the foods] still have the same nutrients?

SHANNON: Does it say that in the article?

STUDENT 5: No, it just says that it will change the taste. It will change the taste of carrots and vegetables. It doesn't say why.

STUDENT 3: Kids'll eat their vegetables.

SHANNON: Think about this when you answer. There is an epidemic in America and obesity is affecting your age group the hardest. There are already additives in foods like chips that make it taste good to students, but these additives are things like extra salt and fat, and sometimes sugar. (*Students are silent but paying attention.*)

STUDENT 6: Then with the new tastes, eating healthy foods, there'll be less obesity.

STUDENT 2: There'll be less health problems.

STUDENT 7: And there will be less diabetes, maybe.

STUDENT 1: I think there might be no high blood pressure.

SHANNON: What do you think of the future of this type of science ... of adding this. Let's think about it. What if they do this to all kinds of food?

STUDENT 8: I wouldn't like it.

STUDENT 4: It would be hard to get used to it. It would taste different and I wouldn't be used to it.

STUDENT 9: Yeah ... because this would be a change in the styles we eat ... and we won't even eat the same any more.

STUDENT 8: I think we would not eat so much fast food.

STUDENT 4: If you change the way it tastes, then you might adapt to it, but it might take a while ... to get all people to do it.

SHANNON: What does this mean for you as scientists ... in becoming scientists?

STUDENT 10: We could be food scientists ... or health conservationists.

STUDENT 3: It could be good and bad. If nothing were to change how it tastes, then people could eat it and be healthier, and they wouldn't know it. But some people won't eat it, and then it's a waste of food.

STUDENT 4: Maybe people may take [eat] things and get sick and then not know what the real food is or why they got sick.

STUDENT 10: It's like with animals.... They don't know it and the food is better for them.

SHANNON: Good point. Like apples that have been infused with grape, and they call it *grapples*, or something like that.

STUDENT 2: Why would they put this on food that is already good for us?

STUDENT 10: It's money. I saw it used in the form of like a gum pill ... for medication.

SHANNON: Can you think of any groups that might oppose this kind of science?

Many students start reacting to this question and share their ideas with peers. This continues for a few minutes, then I introduce them to a Discussion Web activity (Alvermann, 1991) in which small groups discuss the pros and cons of the question "Should the federal government fund this kind of research?"

Results/Observations

This conversation demonstrates how students can be encouraged, through class talk, to consider how what they are reading in science lessons links to their everyday lives and to make connections. My intention to make the lesson meaningful was achieved, and students were motivated to read text written at a higher level than what they typically experienced; they were also able to see how science can affect their lives. My high expectations allowed students to take on, and to meet, a challenge that in turn improved their abilities to analyze, summarize, discuss, and take positions on ideas they saw and heard. In a discussion of this sort, students can learn that there is a practical application to everyday life science, and that they can change outcomes in their own lives. The discussion and Discussion Web helped me assess their ability to interact with peers in an academic setting. The discussions also reinforced word and concept knowledge.

Concluding Thoughts

Our goals in this chapter were to consider the promise and the challenges of open questioning and thoughtful comments in content-area reading activities designed to promote high-level classroom discourse. We asked educators to consider the integral role of language in learning for adolescents, and to modify classroom talk, so that it is less teacher-centered and allows for expanding question formats beyond the traditional one-word response and IRE routines. Educators who are aware of increasing diversity in student populations realize the need to clarify the deeper and multiple meanings of vocabulary in print and nonprint resources. As adolescents are exposed to a burgeoning amount of information from the now ever-increasing information networks available to them, educators can use questions in discussions to clarify meanings, introduce multiple interpretations of texts, and develop students' thought processes.

The most important theme woven through the examples of interactions in this chapter is that questions, comments, and discussions are most effective when they are authentic, referring to real, everyday activities; personal, referring to students' needs and interests; and contextually specific, referring to the specific content area being discussed. As we have seen, these conversations can develop naturally as students share ideas they obtain from classroom readings and other texts. By embedding these conversations into content-area classes, students learn models and develop appropriate lines of thinking to emulate as they read independently.

Finding time for discussion may seem difficult for many teachers, because it seems to slow down the pace, and the practice may change the nature of their classroom routines. Although this is a legitimate concern, adolescents learn best when they have a "guide on the side" rather than a "sage on the stage." We encourage you as teachers to build in the necessary time for extended discourse for learning, making it a habit of your teaching routine.

Questions for Reflection

1. Consider the last fiction and nonfiction books that you read either to students or on your own. What social issues were evident that might present opportunities for deeper discussion? What questions would you ask to initiate discussion of these topics in a fair and unbiased way?

2. Think aloud as you comprehend text from a content area. What have you learned about yourself as a reader from this process? How might you use this information about your reading behavior with your students?

3. Observe a middle grade or high school content-area classroom. Is the IRE discussion pattern evident? What does the teacher do to extend discussion? How might you modify this lesson to promote critical thinking and critical literacy?

References

Alvermann, D. E. (1991). The Discussion Web: A graphic aid for learning across the curriculum. *The Reading Teacher, 45,* 92–99.

Alvermann, D. E. (1995, April). *Talking is something we're pretty deprived of at school: Middle school students speak out.* Paper presented at the annual conference of the American Educational Research Association, San Francisco.

Ash, D. (2008, January). Thematic continuities: Talking and thinking about adaptation in a socially complex classroom. *Journal of Research in Science Teaching, 45*(1), 1–30.

Atwell, N. (1998). *In the middle: New understandings about writing, reading, and learning.* Portsmouth, NH: Heinemann.

Baker, D. R., & Piburn, M. D. (1990). Teachers' perceptions of the effects of a scientific literary course on subsequent learning in biology. *Journal of Research in Science Teaching, 27*(5), 477–491.

Bakhtin, M. M. (1986). *Speech genres and other late essays.* Austin: University of Texas Press.

Bernstein, B. (1990). *The structuring of pedagogic discourse: Vol. IV. Class codes and control.* London: Routledge & Kegan Paul.

Cazden, C. (2001). *Classroom discourse* (2nd ed.). Portsmouth, NH: Heinemann.

Collins, J. (1995, April). *Discourse and resistance in urban elementary classrooms: A poststructuralist perspective.* Paper presented at the annual conference of the American Educational Research Association, San Francisco.

Delpit, L. (2006). *Other people's children: Cultural conflict in the classroom* (updated ed.). New York: Norton.

Dozier, C., Johnston, P., & Rogers, R. (2006). *Critical literacy, critical teaching: Tools for preparing responsive teachers.* New York: Teachers College Press.

Falk-Ross, F. C. (2001). Classroom discourse routines: Changing the rules. In G. B. Moorman & W. R. Trathen (Eds.), *Multiple perspectives in the millenium: The twenty-first yearbook of the American Reading Forum* (pp. 243–253). Boone, NC: Appalacian State University, American Reading Forum.

Falk-Ross, F. C. (2002). *Classroom-based language and literacy intervention: A case studies approach.* Boston: Allyn & Bacon.

Freire, P. (1970). *Pedagogy of the oppressed.* New York: Continuum.

Gee, J. (2001). Reading as situated language: A sociocognitive perspective. *Journal of Adolescent and Adult Literacy, 44,* 714–725.

Gutiérrez, K. (1995). Unpackaging academic discourse. *Discourse Processes, 19*(1), 21–37.

Johnston, P. (2004). *Choice words: How our language affects children's learning.* Portland, ME: Stenhouse.

Just, M., & Carpenter, P. (1987). *The psychology of reading and language comprehension.* Boston: Allyn & Bacon.

Keene, E. O., & Zimmerman, S. (1997). *Mosaic of thought: Teaching comprehension in a reader's workshop.* Portsmouth, NH: Heinemann.

Lemke, J. (1989). *Using language in the classroom.* New York: Oxford University Press.

Lewison, M., Flint, A. S., & Van Sluys, K. (2002). Taking on critical literacy: The journey of newcomers and novices. *Language Arts, 79,* 382–392.

Lipsky, D. K., & Gartner, A. (1997). Inclusion, school restructuring, and the remaking of American society. *Harvard Educational Review, 66,* 762–796.

Luke, A. (2000). Critical literacy in Australia. *Journal of Adolescent and Adult Literacy, 43,* 448–461.

McLaughlin, M., & DeVoogd, G. L. (2004). *Critical literacy: Enhancing students' comprehension of text.* New York: Scholastic.

National Middle School Association. (2003). *This we believe: Developmentally responsive middle level schools.* Westerville, OH: Author.

Nystrand, M. (2006). Research on the role of classroom discourse as it affects reading comprehension. *Research in the Teaching of English, 40*(4), 392–412.

Nystrand, M., Gamoran, A., Kachur, R., & Prendergast, C. (1997). *Opening dialogue: Understanding the dynamics of language and learning in the classroom.* New York: Teachers College Press.

Nystrand, M., Wu, L. L., Gamoran, A., Zeiser, S., & Long, D. A. (2003). Questions in time: Investigating the structure and dynamics of unfolding classroom discourse. *Discourse Processes, 35*(2), 135–198.

Santman, D. (2005). *Shades of meaning: Comprehension and interpretation in middle school.* Portsmouth, NH: Heinemann.

Spinelli, J. (2000). *Stargirl.* New York: Random House.

Vygotsky, L. (1978). *Mind in society: The development of higher psychological processes.* Cambridge, MA: Harvard University Press.

Wells, G. (1999). *Dialogic inquiry: Towards a sociological practice and theory of education.* Cambridge, UK: Cambridge University Press.

What's the big idea? (2007). *Popular Science, 270*(5), 41–43.

Wilkinson, E. R., & Silliman, L. C. (2000). Classroom language and literacy learning. In M. Kamil, P. D. Pearson, & R. Barr (Eds.), *Handbook of reading research* (Vol. III, pp. 337–360). Mahwah, NJ: Erlbaum.

CHAPTER 8

■ ■ ■

How Can Vocabulary Instruction Be Made an Integral Part of Learning in Middle and High School Classrooms?

WILLIAM DEE NICHOLS
WILLIAM H. RUPLEY
KENDALL KISER

CLASSROOM PORTRAIT

It is Monday, the period right after lunch, when Mr. Delaney, a veteran eighth-grade teacher, addresses his North Carolina History class of 28 eighth-grade students:

> "Students, students, may I please have your attention. Mark, (*more force-fully*) Mark! We are waiting. . . . Now, as all of you know, we just completed our unit on the Antebellum Period in North Carolina (*audible groans from the class*), and from your grades on the exam (*more groans*) and from the sounds I am now hearing, I have concluded that you are going to need to spend more time preparing for our present unit on North Carolina in war and reconstruction. Now, as you are all well accustomed, here is your list of vocabulary terms for this unit (*groans continue*). Please get out your North Carolina History books (*more groans*) and copy the definitions from your glossary."

Mr. Delaney is very concerned about his students' learning and overall attitude toward North Carolina history. He remembers when he first started teaching North Carolina History and how he thought the kids would love the curriculum and find this history course to be one of the most exciting ones they would encounter. Now, in his 10th year of teaching, he wonders what went wrong. The grades in his North Carolina History class are abysmal and he is frustrated by the fact that the text appears to be too difficult for his students. To make matters worse, the students appear to be disengaged, unmotivated, and even hostile toward the subject matter. Mr. Delaney blames a lot of his frustrations on the difficulty and complexity of the vocabulary words, and he truly believes that if students had a better understanding of the vocabulary, then their overall comprehension and performance on the tests would improve. How are the kids supposed to remember all of the key vocabulary and concepts for this unit? After examining the list of words that includes *compromise, abolitionism, underground railroad, annex, Wilmot Proviso, secede, popular sovereignty, extremist, emancipation proclamation, blockade, ironclad, Conscription Act,* and *writ of habeas corpus,* he sighs audibly and asks no one in particular, "How can vocabulary instruction become an integral part of learning in my classroom? How can I help my students gain a better understanding of these key concepts and vocabulary terms?"

Our conversations with middle grade teachers over the years have suggested that vocabulary instruction revolves around both definitional and contextual approaches that have restricted capabilities for increasing the students' vocabulary. A preponderance of vocabulary instruction has students either copy definitions from a glossary or expects them to acquire vocabulary through free-reading experiences. Although it is disheartening that so many content-area teachers do not teach vocabulary, some teachers, such as Kiser, a coauthor of this chapter, report using broad-based strategies for vocabulary instruction that are reflective of students' needs and build on students' existing capabilities.

The prevailing vocabulary instructional practices are woefully inadequate in most instances and emphasize the importance of seeking answers to the following questions:

1. How can teachers better teach students how to learn the large number of academic vocabulary words they encounter in informational texts, so that they better comprehend the information found in them?
2. How can research-based instruction in vocabulary become an integral part of content-area instruction?

This chapter focuses on these questions specifically with regard to adolescent learners in the classroom and shares principles that foster active vocabulary learning. William Dee Nichols and William Rupley first provide a rationale for the principles of active vocabulary instruction, then Kendall Kiser shares her experiences as a teacher and literacy coach to illustrate how she address each principle through her instruction.

William Nichols has taught at both the elementary and middle grade levels, and for the past 13 years has been teaching graduate and undergraduate courses in the areas of literacy development, literacy teaching methods and strategies, reading diagnosis, and young adult literature at Cumberland College, the University of North Carolina at Charlotte, Virginia Tech, and currently at Western Carolina University, where he is a Head of the Department of Elementary and Middle Grades Education. His research and service interests include vocabulary instruction and reading comprehension, as well as the early stages of reading development.

William H. Rupley taught elementary school at the fourth- and sixth-grade levels. He is professor, Regent Scholar, and Distinguished Research Fellow at Texas A&M University, where he teaches both graduate and undergraduate reading courses in the Department of Teaching, Learning, and Culture. His research interests include reading acquisition, reading assessment, teacher effectiveness, and reading vocabulary.

Kendall Kiser, currently a literacy coach at an urban middle school in Union County, North Carolina, works with a diverse student population that includes a significant number of English language learners and students who typically have academic struggles. She explains, "As a literacy coach, I am afforded the opportunity to work across grade levels and content areas to improve and advance academic literacy. I support teachers formally, by modeling and coteaching lessons, and informally through professional development and study groups." She is also a doctoral candidate in the Curriculum and Instruction Program at the University of North Carolina at Charlotte, and her research is focused on empowering black adolescent males in literacy development and advancing all students' multiple literacies in schools: academic, social, cultural, and emotional. She notes:

> "When I first started teaching, one of my greatest challenges as a classroom teacher was to offer quality vocabulary instruction for my struggling students. I quickly realized that vocabulary knowledge was the key to enabling my students to communicate and achieve effectively with their peers, which would in turn provide them greater access to education and lifelong aspirations. Through my research and practice, I soon understood that to sustain vocabulary growth, students and teachers need multiple opportunities to work with the words before, during, and after their reading. Students also need time to discuss the words with their peers. To learn a word and be able to use it, students need a variety of strategic processes to ensure vocabulary development."

A Need for Vocabulary Instruction

National Assessment of Educational Progress (NAEP) data (Lee, Grigg, & Donahue, 2007), present a sobering state of affairs: Almost two-thirds of fourth-grade students cannot read with understanding in fourth-grade-level content-area materials. Many students who are reading on grade level in third grade begin to fall behind and experience difficulty reading their content textbooks in fourth grade and beyond; this downturn in performance, often referred to as the "fourth-grade slump," may be the result of many factors; however, there is general agreement that reading for comprehension and learning from content textbooks goes far beyond just pronouncing the words (Chall & Jacobs, 2003). Necessary for understanding informational texts are prior knowledge, to connect with what is read and learned; vocabulary knowledge, to understand the concept-laden words that are esoteric to the subject; and metacognitive skills, to monitor learning (Baumann, Kame'enui, & Ash, 2003; Gardner, 2007; Nagy, 2005).

Other NAEP assessments have exposed deficiencies in the instruction of students in reading and thinking strategies, and reveal that only 29% of eighth graders are able to meet the standard for proficiency in reading (Donahue, Daane, & Jin, 2005). The main concern relative to these disheartening results is that adolescent learners who typically begin to fall behind in content-area reading in fourth grade often do not catch up with their more successful peers, they show lower self-esteem, they display less motivation for participating in reading and subject-matter instruction, and the end result is that they fall off of the eighth-grade cliff.

Developmentally, by the end of the fourth grade, most readers have just accomplished the task of *learning-to-read* just when the school curriculum and content-area assignments require proficiency at *reading-to-learn*, using more varied forms of expository text. To complicate matters, the switch from learning-to-read to reading-to-learn also requires that learners use strategies that previously were not emphasized during the learning-to-read stages (Chall, 1996). Many students have not received sufficient instruction for understanding the vocabulary encountered in expository text to comprehend adequately this type of reading (Freebody & Anderson, 1983; RAND Reading Study Group, 2002). As Bromley (2007) notes, vocabulary development is a principal contributor to reading comprehension and one of the best predictors of reading achievement, and the National Institute of Child Health and Human Development (2000) has also acknowledged the importance of vocabulary development and instruction.

The Role of Vocabulary in Content-Area Learning

A common source of difficulty for middle and secondary school learners is their lack of an academic vocabulary. As students progress through the adolescent years, the academic vocabulary demands they encounter increase in staggering proportion to their everyday conversational vocabulary. By the time students make it to secondary classrooms, their everyday conversational vocabulary comprises 5,000–7,000 words (Klein, 1988), whereas the academic vocabulary they encounter throughout the content areas can reach up to 88,000 words (Nagy & Anderson, 1984). This large gap between conversational and academic vocabulary only adds to the intrinsic importance of vocabulary instruction in all content areas, and highlights how critical vocabulary knowledge is to students' comprehension of text (Fisher & Frey, 2004). For example, as noted by Rupley and Slough (2008):

> Vocabularies used in science, time and again denote meanings unlike the general everyday use of a particular word. The meanings are more restrictive and carry the concepts represented in the text. For example, *parent* in everyday general language use refers to somebody's mother, father, or legal guardian. However, in the science text of chemical reactions, *parent* is the starting component in a chemical reaction—the *parent* molecules. In the science context of biology, *parent* is any organism that produces or generates another—including asexual reproduction. And finally, in the physics context, *parent* refers to the first nuclide in a radioactive series. (p. 3)

Research indicates that vocabulary levels of 18-year-olds bound for college have dropped sharply in recent years (Manzo, Manzo, & Thomas, 2006). According to Nagy and Anderson (1995) college-bound 18-year-olds during the 1940s knew the meanings of 80% of the words they encountered on standardized tests, but by the mid-1990s, the rate of words students knew on standardized tests had dropped to 30%. Although various factors might contribute to this decline of vocabulary knowledge, it is clear that adolescent learners would be better served by increased vocabulary instruction and enrichment (Manzo et al., 2006).

Vocabulary and reading comprehension have a reciprocal relationship (Rupley, Logan, & Nichols, 1998/1999). The more developed and rich the learner's vocabulary, the better he or she is able to analyze and comprehend text. The better a learner is able to understand what he or she is reading, the more likely the learner can continue reading, thus increasing his or her exposure to new and enriched vocabulary.

Vocabulary instruction is an integral component of teaching students how to read both narrative and expository text, and even students who successfully decode words may struggle with comprehension if they encounter too many words for which they have limited or no meaning. Extant research documents that the relation of students' background knowledge and comprehension increases with age (Evans, Floyd, McGrew, & Leforgee, 2002), and notes that increased vocabulary and background knowledge are potentially two of the more powerful means of improving learning and comprehension of adolescent readers (Cromley & Azevedo, 2007). Many impoverished students, students who struggle with reading, and English language learners (ELLs) begin school with vocabularies half the size or less of those of their middle-class classmates (Graves, 2006). Not having access to the meaning of words that are representative of the concepts and content found in texts causes difficulty in learners' comprehension, limits students' ability to make a connection with their existing background knowledge, inhibits their capacity to make coherent inferences, and impacts their ability to reason (Nichols & Rupley, 2004). These limitations are even more apparent in struggling adolescent readers, who often experience a mismatch between their background experiences and requisite prior knowledge for learning. This mismatch often influences motivation and interferes with students' comprehension during learning tasks.

Continuous development of students' language ability provides the foundation for vocabulary growth. Students often share meanings of words orally through their direct experiences with the people, places, objects, and events they encounter in their lives. Students also gain vocabulary concepts through vicarious experiences, including interactive technology, virtual tours, pictures, movies, reading, and writing (Nichols, Rupley, Blair, & Wood, 2008). Students' knowledge of vocabulary closely reflects the breadth of their real-world and vicarious experiences (Heilman, Blair, & Rupley, 2002). Because learners' vocabulary knowledge is dependent on their experiences, it is best that the content of the curriculum reflect these experiences (Rupley & Nichols, 2005). But as educators know, variations in students' life experiences are often a mismatch with the school curriculum (Au, 1993) and, as previously noted, the difference between the number of words that students use and encounter in conversational vocabulary is vastly out of proportion to the academic vocabulary required to comprehend content-area texts.

In addition, the adolescent learner's knowledge of word meanings can range along a continuum from simple to complex. One form of simple knowledge is *definitional*, that is, word knowledge based on a definition from a dictionary, thesaurus, glossary, word bank, or other individuals, such as the teacher. But when students encounter an unfamiliar word during reading, they often fail to make the connection between such definitions and the meaning in the text. This inability interferes with comprehension. To comprehend, a reader needs some idea of not only the word's meaning but also the ways the meaning contributes to the cohesiveness of the ideas presented in the text (Rupley et al., 1998/1999).

Another type of word knowledge is *contextual knowledge*, or word meaning derived from context, which can include a sentence, a passage, a discussion, or a picture. Anderson and Nagy (1991) emphasized the difficulty of learning new vocabulary and estimated that students reading on grade level learn between 2,000 and 3,000 new words a year; they concluded, therefore, that most words must be learned through context. Although we agree that contextual knowledge often has a stronger connection to the text than does definitional knowledge, the contextual clues are still insufficient and limited to deriving the meaning of content vocabulary that is central to key concepts. For example, in Mr. Delaney's North Carolina History class, the students encountered the following sentences:

> During the *antebellum* period, North Carolina at last awoke from its Rip Van Winkle sleep. Political reform had created the conditions for economic and social progress.

From the context of these sentences, it is difficult to derive the meaning of the word *antebellum*. However, if students had had knowledge of the Latin prefix *ante* (before, prior) and the Latin root *bellum* (war), then they would have understood that the word *antebellum*, in the context of North Carolina History, refers to the time prior to the Civil War (1812–1860). To derive the contribution of contextual clues associated with word meanings to the comprehension of text requires knowledge of the content and how the combined word meanings facilitate communication of the content through author and reader interaction (Rupley et al., 1998/1999).

Knowing a word in the fullest sense, especially a low- or medium-frequency word encountered often in content-area reading, goes beyond simply being able to define it or to get some basic meaning of the word from context; instead, it means being able to discuss, elaborate, and demonstrate the meaning of the word in multiple contexts in which the word occurs. According to Nagy (1988), traditional definitional and contextual approaches to teaching vocabulary are not especially effective ways to learn vocabulary or improve comprehension.

Principles of Vocabulary Instruction

To help learners acquire a true account of the new vocabulary word's meaning, we believe that teachers should conscientiously apply principles of vocabulary instruction. In this section we elaborate on each principle and Kendall describes how she applies them in her teaching.

> *Principle 1: Vocabulary instruction is more meaningful when the newly introduced vocabulary words are included in authentic texts, and when instructional activities are used throughout the unit.*

It is our belief that students should be engaged in learning new words and expanding their understanding of words through instruction based on active processing. Such instruction goes beyond having students just memorize word definitions. It also provides guidance and opportunities to integrate word meanings with students' existing knowledge, building a conceptual representation of the word that enables students to use and understand it in multiple contextual situations. Instruction for active processing immerses students in language-rich activities that teach words as part of meaningful, authentic reading experiences.

Research has indicated that students learn words through immersion in a vocabulary-rich environment that includes reading books independently and reading books aloud (Anderson, Wilson, & Fielding, 1988; Baumann, Ware, & Edwards, 2007). Therefore, vocabulary instruction should revolve around words that readers will encounter in their various content texts. Vocabulary instruction is often criticized when it is taught in isolation from text and is limited to a dictionary activity. Vocabulary instruction that has students just copy definitions of words from a dictionary, then write a sentence using these words, never allows students the opportunity to fully own these words, and it misses out on authentic vocabulary learning. In essence there is no active engagement and, in most cases, no actual learning of the new concept associated with the word. Vocabulary instruction, whether focused on narrative or informational text, is most effective when it relates new words or derivations of words to existing vocabulary and background knowledge, and includes words that the reader encounters in authentic reading experiences.

Using a formative experimental research framework, Baumann and colleagues (2007) demonstrated that students' vocabulary improved, along with their attitudes toward vocabulary instruction, when they encountered vocabulary words in authentic reading activities. Using student-selected books and literature circle activities, Daniels (2002) had students keep records of new and interesting words they encountered while reading, which then led to thoughtful discussions in a variety of formats, including dialogue journals. As a result of immersing learners into a world of rich reading opportunities and selecting words from the books they were reading, students demonstrated vocabulary growth.

The Teacher's Voice: Encountering Vocabulary in Assigned Readings

A key component to my vocabulary instruction is based on the belief that it is important to teach and to model effective vocabulary instructional strategies for my students, and to provide students with multiple opportunities to practice working with the new terms. I often begin by choosing a list of less than eight words that Beck, McKeown, and Kucan (2002) defined as Tier 2 words. These words represent the more sophisticated vocabulary of written texts. To model, I pronounce the words for the students, then we repeat these as a class. We also find the key word within the context of our reading material, which offers additional support toward understanding. Then I provide the "book definition" of the word and a visual to help students create a mental file folder in their minds. As a class, students create "student-friendly" definitions to completely understand the words. Students then practice working with the new words by creating their own visuals for certain words. Recently, I taught a lesson in which *interaction* and *economy* were two of our Tier 2 words. One student drew two girls interacting on their cell phones to represent the word *interaction*. Another student drew several $100 bills to represent the word *economy*. Upon completion of the individual activity, students then work in small groups to share their visuals and create a group chart, with the new terms "student definitions" and their visuals. I believe the following when it comes to vocabulary instruction for difficult concepts and Tier 2 words:

- Vocabulary instruction should not be limited to a once-a-week activity; rather, students need to practice and work with key vocabulary multiple times per week.
- Explicit teaching of critical vocabulary and instructional strategies (e.g., syntactic, contextual, morphemic) should be an integral part of vocabulary instruction.
- Word meanings that are critical to understanding core concepts should be taught explicitly and deeply.
- Activity-based instruction that involves students working in groups on activities related to vocabulary enhances discussion

and helps students collectively increase their experiences related to new concepts and vocabulary.

Another key aspect of my vocabulary instructional beliefs is that a sustained amount of time devoted to reading enhances vocabulary learning. By doing read-alouds twice each week, I provide students the opportunity to listen to key vocabulary that will be reiterated throughout the unit. For example, as an introduction to the unit on the Civil War, I use the picture book *Pink and Say* by Patricia Polacco (1994). This picture book aids students' vocabulary development and also gives them a visual for many of the key terms that they will see throughout the unit. Before beginning the read-aloud, I introduce key words that are central to the comprehension of the story, as well as the entire unit of study, such as *Confederate, union, brow, slaughter,* and *starvation.* To ensure that students have a clear understanding of the words, I provide an instructional context, in which we have a discussion about the possible meanings of the words and create student-friendly definitions. For the word *Confederate,* for instance, I used the following sentences:

Confederate leaders urged the other Southern states to join them.

The Confederate states separated themselves from the United States of America to form their own nation.

As a class, we then discussed possible meanings of the word *Confederate* and created a class definition that would support comprehension of the book and our unit of study: "Southern states that broke away from the United States." Students then recorded the student-friendly definitions in their notebook to use as a reference throughout the unit.

Following the discussion, I read the book aloud, encouraging students to become "word detectives" by listening for our key vocabulary words and alerting me when they heard such a word. We then talked about how our class definitions fit into the meaning of the context of the word. This reinforcement ensured that students had a clear understanding of essential vocabulary for the entire unit of study.

> *Principle 2: Vocabulary knowledge is increased when students study word structure, including looking for recognizable parts, prefixes, suffixes, affixes and other morphemic information, to understand word origin and to assess familiarity with the new vocabulary.*

Learning new vocabulary in content-area classes presents many unique challenges for adolescents. One challenge is that most students encounter new vocabulary daily in many subjects, such as science, mathematics, health, art, and music. These new concepts are often low- to medium-frequency words that seldom appear in other contexts. To complicate matters and present yet another challenge, these words may take on different meanings depending on the subject in which they are encountered (Bromley, 2007). For example, the word *impregnable* in social studies takes on a very different meaning when it is encountered in biology or health. Having knowledge of the structure and origin of the word would help students decipher the meaning in a variety of contexts. Teaching students about word structure can be a very powerful instructional strategy to increase students' understanding and acquisition of academic vocabulary (Baumann, Edwards, Boland, Olejnik, & Kame'enui, 2003; Kieffer & Lesaux, 2007).

Teaching about Morphemes

Morphology in language and reading refers to the study of how words are structured and the most basic meanings of words (Baumann et al., 2002; Kieffer & Lesaux, 2007; Nagy & Anderson, 1984). Morphemes can generally be broken down into categories of bound and free morphemes. *Bound* morphemes include prefixes, suffixes, and inflectional endings that cannot stand alone, such as *im-* and *-ous*, whereas *free* (unbound) morphemes are roots within more complex words that can stand alone, such as *possess* (Kieffer & Lesaux, 2007).

Morphemes are essential for understanding text and conceptualizing informational content. Knowledge of common prefixes and suffixes (*affixes*), base words, and root words can help students learn the meanings of many words they encounter in content areas. For example, if students learn just the four most common prefixes in English (*un-*, *re-*, *in-*, *dis-*), then they have important clues about the meaning of about two-thirds of all English words that have prefixes (Armbruster, Lehr, & Osborn, 2001). The following word problem encountered in a math text emphasizes the importance of teaching morphemes. In this example, there are 123 free and 25 bound morphemes, totaling 148 meaning units. The bound morphemes appear in *italics*:

> The weather *re*port *pre*dict*ed* a bad storm. Bob'*s* plan was to tie down lawn chair*s*, move hang*ing* plant*s* inside, and cover the car with blanket*s* so the hail would not put dent*s* in it. He had 5 rope*s* of var*ious* length*s*. He ti*ed* down 8 lawn chair*s* with the long*est* rope, but forgot that he had five chairs on the front porch so he had to *re*tie the chairs us*ing* a total of 3 rope*s*. He *re*mov*ed* 11 hang*ing* plant*s* and put them inside the house. He found three large blanket*s* roll*ed* up in the attic and *un*roll*ed* two of them to cover his

car. How many rope*s* and blanket*s* were remain*ing* for Bob to loan to his neighbor?

Research has indicated that students' knowledge of morphemes is related to reading comprehension and vocabulary development (Kieffer & Lesaux, 2007). For example, students who are taught commonly occurring Latin and Greek roots prior to reading, and are shown how these morphemes connect to their English equivalents, have a higher likelihood of learning the new vocabulary and comprehending the text in which the word is encountered (Baumann et al., 2002). The information in Figure 8.1 illustrates the benefit of teaching a few of these Latin and Greek roots, and how students' knowledge of these may assist their understanding of many new concepts encountered in content texts.

Prior to reading a text that includes key, low-frequency vocabulary words, teachers should ask students to think of words containing particular Latin or Greek morphemes that have been preselected because they appear in the reading selection. To facilitate discussion, another important aspect of vocabulary instruction, teachers can place students into heterogeneous groups to brainstorm words they already know based on the selected roots. At the end of the small-group session, the lists produced by each group may be compiled into a class list. As the meanings of the generated words are discussed, students can better understand each morpheme on the prereading list. Then, as they begin to read their assigned texts, students should be encouraged to pay particular attention to these morphemes in context.

When teachers activate students' background knowledge of these morphemes and preteach concepts that they will later encounter in

appareo	=	visible	=	apparent, apparently, appear
audi	=	hear	=	audience, auditorium, audible
auto	=	self	=	automobile, automatic, autograph
cred	=	believe	=	credible, credit, discredit
hydro	=	water	=	dehydrate, hydrant
mens, mentis	=	mind	=	mental, demented, dementia
ology	=	study of	=	geology, biology, archeology
pes, pedis	=	foot	=	centipede, expedite, pedestrian
photo	=	light	=	photocopy, photosynthesis
port	=	carry	=	portable, important
scop	=	see	=	microscope, periscope, stethoscope

FIGURE 8.1. Latin and Greek roots. Based on Bromley (2007); Kieffer and Lesaux (2007); and Nilsen and Nilsen (2006).

their reading of the text, students are better equipped to recognize the morphemes in context and can attempt to decipher the meanings of content-related words that they otherwise might have skipped. Common prefixes and suffixes, as well as both common and complex root words, can be pretaught in a similar manner (Kieffer & Lesaux, 2007; Nilsen & Nilsen, 2006).

Determining Vocabulary Familiarity

Teaching morpheme analysis to students provides access to a wide range of vocabulary, but not all words can be analyzed by students and broken into root words, prefixes, and suffixes (Mraz, Taylor, Nichols, Rickelman, & Wood, in press), and even words that do contain common morphemes may still remain unfamiliar to learners. One approach that helps students analyze and self-assess their familiarity and knowledge of new vocabulary is the *Assessment of Word Knowledge Scale* (Blachowicz, 1986; Dale & O'Rourke, 1986). For example in an eighth-grade science unit on adaptation and behavior, students may encounter the words *geotropism* and *phototropism*. Whereas these two words contain common root words that students may recognize, students usually are still unfamiliar with the vocabulary words and unsure of their meaning.

Using an Assessment of Word Knowledge Scale similar to the one in Figure 8.2, the teacher provides vocabulary terms that students encounter in their reading or in a unit of study. Using the previous example of the science unit on adaptation and behavior, the teacher presents the following vocabulary terms: *mutation, natural selection, camouflage, mimicry, tannin, tropisms, geotropism, phototropism, innate, reflexes, imprinting* and *territoriality*.

1. The teacher asks students to assess their familiarity and understanding of vocabulary words by ranking each word on the Assessment of Word Knowledge Scale.
2. The teacher allows students to discuss the words in small groups prior to reading the text, and encourages them to share what they know about the words and to elaborate on other contexts in which they may have seen or used these words.

As students read the chapter and encounter the new vocabulary terms in context, they refer back to their initial Assessment of Word Knowledge Scale and reflect on how encountering the word within the context of the chapter has increased their overall understanding of the word's definition. The teacher also encourages students to consider how this process affects their overall comprehension.

	I know the meaning of . . .			
Vocabulary terms	Very well	Somewhat	Have seen/ heard	Not at all
mutation				
natural selection				
camouflage				
mimicry				
tannin				
tropism				
geotropism				
phototropism				
innate				
reflexes				
imprinting				
territoriality				

FIGURE 8.2. Assessment of Word Knowledge Scale (unit on adaptation and behavior).

The Teacher's Voice: Assessment of Word Knowledge

To address morphemes with my students, I use a summarization or review activity in which I have students play a word game using chosen morphemes that we have worked with during class. For example, I recently asked students to write, in less than 1 minute, as many words as they could think of with the suffix -*ology*. When time was up, students shared how many words they had each written. One student was able to write eight words: *anthropology, technology, ecology, biology, sociology, astrology, psychology,* and *paleontology.* As an extension, she defined all the words that she had written. With some assistance from her classmates, she was able to accomplish this successfully, which also supported all students' knowledge of the suffix -*ology.*

As a classroom teacher, I often use the Assessment of Word Knowledge Scale, shown in Figure 8.2, but I've modified the five columns to read, from left to right, in the following order: *Key Vocabulary, Know It Well, Have Heard/Seen It, No Clue,* and *Definition.* Initially, students individually place an *X* under the appropriate column next to the word.

Students who place an *X* in the *Know It Well* column try to write a definition for the word.

Recently, I introduced a new social studies unit of study that focused on the Underground Railroad. Prior to the unit, I preselected six words that I felt were critical to the students' comprehension of the unit: *Underground Railroad, Harriet Tubman, conductor, abolitionist, slavery,* and *freedom.* After I introduced each term students were provided with the Assessment of Word Knowledge Scale handout for the new terms. Without conveying the topic of study, students rated their knowledge of each term. One student marked an *X* under the *Know It Well* column for the term *slavery.* He then proceeded to write his definition for slavery: "Slavery is like when blacks were forced to work for white people."

After they completed the Assessment of Word Knowledge Scale, I divided students into mixed-ability groups of three or four students from ethnically diverse backgrounds; this grouping increased the richness of discussion. Within the groups, students spent time discussing each of the vocabulary words and modifying their Assessment of Word Knowledge Scale to reflect their new understandings. They reached consensus about the meaning of the words they knew well and began to make predictions about the topic of study. Students then read the selected text and confirmed or changed their definitions of the vocabulary words. As a whole class, we spent time discussing each word to elicit information about the key words and to clarify any misunderstandings. We created a class Assessment of Word Knowledge Scale that remained as a visual for students throughout the unit of study. At the end of the unit, students had to prove they learned the new word by again rating each vocabulary word individually. This provided the needed feedback to support my future instruction.

One eighth grader who often struggled with new vocabulary needed frequent interaction opportunities with her peers to support vocabulary development. By participating in groups to complete the Assessment of Word Knowledge Scale, she was able to hear her fellow classmates use the think-aloud process of attacking vocabulary words. Through appropriate grouping practices and opportunities for pre-, during-, and postreading discussion, other struggling students were able to benefit from their peers.

Another great instructional organizer that I have used over the years for assessing students' familiarity with new vocabulary words is the dump and clump strategy, which helps students sort and organize their knowledge of the terms. Students are given a list of already-labeled words in the "dump" box, then they try to "clump" the words into specific categories. Students must sort words into specific categories by finding commonalities among the words. Students then assign labels for each category and create a summary sentence for each category of words. Using grouping practices similar to those described when using the Assessment of Word Knowledge Scale, students have meaningful discussions regarding their familiarity with the words and their rationale for sorting the words into categories.

Principle 3: Vocabulary development is enriched when students make connections between the new vocabulary word and their prior experiences with and initial concepts of the words.

Although students learn many vocabulary words incidentally through wide reading, it is also important for teachers to address vocabulary learning through more explicit instruction to support student learning of new concepts, especially in content-area classes (Baumann, Kame'enui, & Ash, 2003). One key step in providing explicit instruction in learning vocabulary is to activate and build on students' existing prior knowledge. Relating new words to previously learned concepts, before students encounter these words in reading, has been identified as an important first step in creating elaborated representation of knowledge and links between concepts that will be presented in the text (Anderson & Nagy, 1991; Blachowicz & Obrochta, 2005). Good teachers understand the importance of making content-area materials relevant to readers, thus providing opportunities for learning that endure (Blacowicz & Obrochta, 2005; Ivey & Fisher, 2005).

The learner relies on background experiences to develop, expand, and refine concepts represented by words encountered in speech and print. Because our individual backgrounds are in continuous development throughout our lives, word meanings are also in an endless state of flux (Readence, Bean, & Baldwin, 1998). Meanings for words are constantly modified as new information is associated with existing representations for the word, or as the new experience with the word causes the learner to accommodate an adjustment or modification of the represented meaning. Robustness for a word's meaning is dependent on the richness of the learner's experiences and associations with that word. Lack of fully developed experiences for the content being learned in schools plays a critical role in many struggling readers' vocabulary development and comprehension of text.

The Teacher's Voice: Connecting Vocabulary to Prior Experiences

During my first year teaching at an urban middle school, I often taught in a classroom with a high-percentage of ELL students. As a new teacher,

I taught vocabulary in the traditional assigning-and-telling manner illustrated by Vacca and Vacca (1999, p. 316). I gave students new vocabulary words on Monday and directed them to look up the definitions; on Tuesday, students would create sentences with the words; on Wednesday and Thursday, students would create of some type of illustration or work on a crossword puzzle that used the words; on Friday, students would have a quiz on the words, after which they would rarely see or use the vocabulary words again.

"Ms. Kiser, what does *melancholy* mean?" I heard this and similar queries repeatedly, even after we studied new vocabulary words during our weekly sessions of copying definitions from the glossary. I would get frustrated, because students could work with the vocabulary during our focused study, but they were not able to use it over the long term or connect the definitional knowledge of words to authentic context. Quickly, I began to realize that students were not developing their word knowledge. I had to dig a little deeper to truly understand that my students needed a context for developing their vocabulary knowledge, and it was my job to facilitate and lead them to work with the words before, during, and after reading. This is often a struggle for ELLs, so I needed to build explicitly the background for my students and scaffold their vocabulary acquisition.

One of my limited-English-proficient students lacked the necessary background knowledge to understand many content-related vocabulary words. To maximize Ramiro's learning, I quickly realized that the key to his growth was to link new vocabulary words to things he already knew and had experienced. As I began to introduce a science unit on types of pollutants, I knew that he, as well as many other students, lacked a clear and precise understanding of the new words. Based on my reading and research pertaining to ELL students, I knew that I needed to build Ramiro's prior knowledge of the topic. One way that I did this was to link new vocabulary to his background and experiences. I knew that he saw examples of the vocabulary words associated with pollutants each day as he walked to and from school. I took photos of our campus and the surrounding community to show concrete examples of the words *pollution, pollutants, hazardous wastes, renewable resources,* and *nonrenewable resources.* I introduced key vocabulary words by pronouncing each word, then providing visual images. Thus, Ramiro's first experiences with the words enabled him to make the connections between his background experiences and new concepts.

A vital component in using the visuals was the fact that they related to Ramiro's everyday experiences. But visual representations were not enough to ensure deep understanding. I also partnered him with a classmate, so that they could work on modified cloze sentences to reinforce the new vocabulary words. This type of partner work allowed the students to discuss and to apply new information in a meaningful way. Each pair read a sentence that had strong contextual support for the vocabulary word that had been omitted from the sentence, then tried to insert the correct word in the blank space. For example, _ is when water, air, or land is damaged (Pollution). The modified cloze activity provided an opportunity for Ramiro and other students to increase their vocabulary knowledge, as well as review vocabulary in context.

> **Principle 4: Vocabulary learning is enhanced with visual connections and graphic organizers that display the relationships among words and how the new words fit with existing prior knowledge or concepts of the words.**

As Kendall demonstrated in her description of enhancing Ramiro's vocabulary knowledge on pollutants, instructional activities that visually display new words, while providing students with the opportunity to compare and contrast these new words and already learned words, can increase students' vocabulary knowledge. Visualization has been identified as an important activity for active engagement in not only vocabulary learning but also learning in general. Connecting new words to existing images already associated with the learner's background knowledge is beneficial to learning new concepts and helps learners connect abstract concepts to concrete experiences, and provides alternative codes for understanding and retention (Blachowicz & Obrochta, 2005; Sadoski, Goetz, Kealy, & Paivio, 1997).

When a teacher combines elements of thoughtful discussion with visual display, students begin to connect the new vocabulary terms to previously encountered words, and they recognize relationship among the words. For example, demonstrating visually the connection between *hydrodynamic* and *hydrant*, then having a thoughtful discussion about how these two terms share a common Greek root, *hydro*, emphasizes the relationship between the words, taking an abstract term and providing a concrete visual example (Pressley, Levin, & MacDaniel, 1987).

Another type of visual image that assists learners in creating mental images and connections of concepts is the graphic organizer, which helps students explicitly visualize connections between newly encountered vocabulary and the key concepts presented. Graphic organizers are useful visual tools that support students in building both knowledge of concepts and understanding of the relationship of these concepts to each other, and that help learners recognize common features, objects, symbols, ideas, processes, or events (Vacca & Vacca, 1999). Although graphic organizers can vary in format, their use can provide readers, particularly struggling readers, with the structure and organization necessary to make difficult and complex concepts more comprehensible.

For vocabulary learning, instructional strategies that include graphic organizers, such as concept wheels, semantic word maps, webbing, and semantic feature analyses, to name just a few, help to support student learning of new vocabulary, as well as reinforce the relationships among words (Fisher & Frey, 2004; Nichols & Rupley, 2004). When teachers provide graphic organizers for new vocabulary, students are able to create brief statements that express relationships between the new words and summarize main points, and to see the flow of ideas from main points to lesser details. Graphic organizers are effective tools that incorporate many of the guidelines for the active processing of vocabulary and ultimately lead to improved comprehension of text.

Teachers who match graphic organizers and visual displays with the appropriate instructional design (i.e., whole class, grouping practices, independent work) help to engage learners in vocabulary acquisition before, during, and after reading activities (Nichols & Rupley, 2004).

The Teacher's Voice: Using Graphic Organizers and Other Visual Displays

All students benefit from using a graphic organizers as a visual, working document to increase understanding of vocabulary words. One strategy that I (Kiser) have been able to use across all content areas is the KIM strategy, in which *K* represents the *key* vocabulary word, *I* stands for *information*, and *M* represents a *memory* clue. The KIM strategy lends itself to opportunities for multiple group settings and allows students to work with words before, during, and after instruction.

For example, to prepare for a short reading selection entitled "At Home in My World," by Alicia Zadrozny (2008), I identified eight key vocabulary words that were integral to understanding the selection: *culture clash, gentrification, identity, resurgence, minority, cuisine, bodegas*, and *corridor*. Students used the KIM organizer throughout their individual, small-group, and whole-class discussion of the story. To begin instruction I pronounced and read the sentence in which each word was found in the selection. I first modeled my thought process by using the context clues that would help me develop meanings of the words. Next, I modeled how I used clues and graphics found within the text to create an image for the *M* column. For instance, the memory clue that represented *bodegas* for me comprised the Food Lion symbol used by a popular grocery chain in our state. Students then recorded information about each word under the *I* column, but in their own words. Under the

M column, students then sketched something to help them remember the key word, which helped them synthesize the vocabulary words. For instance, to represent the word *minority,* one student drew a picture of one white girl surrounded by several Hispanic and African American children. Another child illustrated the word *cuisine* by drawing a plate of tamales with green salsa on top.

When I want students to compare and contrast certain words across a common set of features, I use the *semantic feature analysis* strategy (Johnson & Pearson, 1984). The analysis comprises a vertical grid that lists essential vocabulary words, and a horizontal grid that lists common features. To expand students' vocabulary understanding I have them complete the feature analysis before and after their reading of a text.

Recently, I taught a language arts lesson that focused on common prefixes and suffixes using semantic feature analysis. For this lesson, I created a grid that listed essential prefixes and suffixes vertically and features and/or ideas, horizontally. Common features included prefix, suffix, multiple meaning, and the specific meanings. For instance, when students worked with the prefix *en-,* they placed a + under the prefix column and a + under the meaning column of *not.* Initially, students completed the grid based on their prior knowledge of the prefixes by indicating with a plus or minus sign whether each word possessed the stated features or was related to the ideas. After students read the text with a partner, they reviewed their semantic feature analysis grids again to confirm or to change their initial decisions. Providing the students opportunities to work in pairs allowed each individual to strengthen and/or refine his or her vocabulary knowledge.

I also taught a seventh-grade math lesson that focused on polygons. I created a grid in which two-dimensional shapes were listed horizontally and characteristics of polygons were listed vertically. Like the previous example on common affixes, students completed the grid based on their prior knowledge of the terms by indicating with a plus or minus sign whether each math term possessed the stated features. For instance, when students worked with the math term *square,* they placed a + under the following columns: polygon, at least two pairs of opposite sides are parallel, figure forms four right angles, all sides have equal lengths, and sum of interior angles equals 360 degrees. Students worked in pairs, facilitating discussion and enabling students to access and build their background knowledge about polygons. As the students learned more about polygons through the completion of the unit, they continued to add to and refine their semantic feature analysis, as illustrated in Figure 8.3.

	Is a polygon (a closed plane figure having three or more sides)	At least two pairs of opposite sides are parallel	Only one pair of opposite sides are parallel	Figure forms four right angles	All sides have equal lengths	Sum of interior angles equals 360 degrees
Circle						+
Triangle	+				if equilateral	
Square	+	+		+	+	+
Rectangle	+	+		+		+
Trapezoid	+		+			+
Parallelogram	+	+			+	+
Rhombus	+	+			+	+
Regular pentagon	+				+	
Regular hexagon	+		+		+	
Regular heptagon	+				+	
Regular octagon	+	+			+	

FIGURE 8.3. Semantic feature analysis on pentagons.

Other Classroom Strategies for Engaging Learners in Meaningful Vocabulary Discussion

Typically, many of my students have had little experience with engaging in meaningful discussion about vocabulary words before, during, and after the lesson. To develop students' vocabulary, I endeavor to move their thinking from the abstract to concrete. To begin classroom discussion around new learning, I always begin with a class discussion to link past and new learning. For example, I began a unit of study around volcanoes by eliciting responses to the following question: "Has anyone seen a volcano before?" After learning that none had, I showed the students a picture of a volcano. I also connected this unit to our previous study of mountains to increase students' understanding. This scaffolding provided a context for student learning. Elicitation of their background knowledge increased students' interest, which in turn facilitated their learning of new ideas.

Another way that I stimulated meaningful vocabulary discussion in my classroom was by inviting students to become word detectives. After class instruction, I would encourage students to find the vocabulary words we studied outside of our direct classroom instruction. Students kept a section in their notebook to record where they saw, heard, or used the vocabulary word. During the last portion of class, students shared their entries, then created sentence strips to place on our Word Wall, using the word within context. Every time students found words and shared them with the class they earned points toward celebration days, which included uninterrupted time for independent reading.

Concluding Thoughts

Throughout this chapter we have shared several key principles of sound vocabulary instruction to assist all teachers faced with Mr. Delaney's dilemma of teaching complex and often low-frequency vocabulary concepts to adolescent learners. We have emphasized that content-area teachers must identify ways to enable students to acquire the necessary vocabulary to comprehend content-area texts (Manzo et al., 2006). Adolescent learners who acquire a rich knowledge of vocabulary are not only able to understand more of the content to which they are exposed, but they also use that understanding to acquire new knowledge, and the vocabulary that is connected to that knowledge (Spencer & Guillaume, 2006).

Recently, Flanigan and Greenwood (2007) noted that although principles of vocabulary instruction provide teachers with useful vocabulary generalizations and ideas for vocabulary instruction, they often fall short of providing a framework for actually teaching vocabulary to students. They suggest that content-area teachers need a bridge between principles and authentic classroom practices that takes into account the students, the nature of the words themselves, the purpose for teaching and selecting words, and the thoughtful identification of the instructional strategies that they employ. We could not agree more with their instructional framework that places the student in the center. As Kendall's examples illustrate, there is no single method or combination of methods to teach vocabulary for all learners. Teachers must use formative assessment to guide their instruction and thoughtful deliberation in choosing vocabulary words, know which words are critical to teach and which words are not, and select the appropriate instructional strategy to meet student needs and instructional goals.

Questions for Reflection

1. The teacher involved in writing this chapter has shared a number of classroom activities correlated with active vocabulary instruction. Which of these do you foresee implementing in your classroom? What other activities do you know that would fit into active vocabulary instruction?

2. Today's teachers who work with adolescent learners feel overburdened with dense curriculum demands and are often faced with not enough time in the day. Given this acknowledgment, how do you think teachers can find the time for effective vocabulary instruction? Or do you think teachers should continue vocabulary approaches that have students receive a list of words on Monday, copy definitions from a glossary, and take a test on Friday, because there is just not enough time to teach vocabulary as described in this chapter? Explain your viewpoint.

3. One of the principles of vocabulary instruction is based on students' ability to make a visual connection to a word. How can technology be used in making this visual connection?

References

Anderson, R. C., & Nagy, W. E. (1991). Word meanings. In R. Barr, M. L. Kamil, P. B. Mosenthal, & P. D. Pearson (Eds.), *Handbook of reading research* (Vol. 2, pp. 690–724). New York: Longman.

Anderson, R. C., Wilson, P. T., & Fielding, L. G. (1988). Growth in reading and how children spend their time outside of school. *Reading Research Quarterly, 23*, 285–303.

Armbruster, B. B., Lehr, F., & Osborn, J. (2001). *Put reading first: The research building blocks for teaching children to read.* Washington, DC: National Institute of Child Health and Human Development and U. S. Department of Education. Available online at *www.nifl.gov/nifl/publications.html.*

Au, K. H. (1993). *Literacy instruction in multicultural settings.* Orlando, FL: Harcourt Brace.

Baumann, J. F., Edwards, E. C., Boland, E. M., Olejnik, S., & Kame'enui, E. J. (2003). Vocabulary tricks: Effects of instruction in morphology and context on fifth-grade students' ability to derive and infer word meanings. *American Educational Research Journal, 40*, 447–494.

Baumann, J. F., Edwards, E. C., Font, G., Tereshinski, C., Kame'enui, E. J., & Olejnik, S. (2002). Teaching morphemic and contextual analysis to fifth-grade students. *Reading Research Quarterly, 37,* 150–173.

Baumann, J. F., Kame'enui, E. J., & Ash, G. E. (2003). Research on vocabulary instruction: Voltaire redux. In J. Flood, D. Lapp, J. R. Squire, & J. M. Jensen (Eds.), *Handbook of research on teaching the English language arts* (2nd ed., pp. 752–785). Mahwah, NJ: Erlbaum.

Baumann, J. F., Ware, D., & Edwards, E. C. (2007). "Bumping into the spicy, tasty words that catch your tongue": A formative experiment on vocabulary instruction. *Reading Teacher, 61*(2), 108–122.

Beck, I. L., McKeown, M. G., & Kucan, L. (2002). *Bringing words to life: Robust vocabulary instruction.* New York: Guilford Press.

Blachowicz, C. (1986). Making connections: Alternatives to the vocabulary notebook. *Journal of Reading, 29,* 643–649.

Blachowicz, C. L. Z., & Obrochta, C. (2005). Vocabulary visits: Virtual field trips for content vocabulary development. *Reading Teacher, 59*(3), 262–268.

Bromley, K. (2007). Nine things every teacher should know about words and vocabulary instruction. *Journal of Adolescent and Adult Literacy, 50*(7), 528–537.

Chall, J. S. (1996). *Stages of reading development.* Orlando, FL: Harcourt Brace.

Chall, J. S., & Jacobs, V. A. (2003). Poor children's fourth-grade slump. *American Educator, 2*(1), 14–15, 44.

Cromley, J. G., & Azevedo, R. (2007). Testing and refining the direct and inferential mediation model of reading comprehension. *Journal of Educational Psychology, 99,* 311–325.

Dale, E., & O'Rourke, J. (1986). *Vocabulary building: A process approach.* Columbus, OH: Zaner-Bloser.

Daniels, H. (2002). *Literature circles: Voice and choice in book clubs and reading programs* (2nd ed.). Portland, ME: Stenhouse.

Donahue, P. L., Daane, M. C., & Jin, Y. (2005). *The nation's report card: Reading 2003* (NCES 2005-453. U. S. Department of Education, Institute of Education Sciences, National Center for Education Statistics). Washington, DC: U. S. Government Printing Office. Available online at *www.edpubs.org* and *nces.ed.gov/pubsearch.*

Evans, J. J., Floyd, R. G., McGrew, K. S., & Leforgee, M. H. (2002). The relations between measures of Cattell–Horn–Carroll (CHC) cognitive abilities and reading achievement during childhood and adolescents. *School Psychology Review, 31,* 246–262.

Fisher, D., & Frey, N. (2004). *Improving adolescent literacy: Strategies at work.* Upper Saddle River, NJ: Pearson Education.

Flanigan, K., & Greenwood, S. C. (2007). Effective content vocabulary instruction in the middle: Matching students, purposes, words and strategies. *Journal of Adolescent and Adult Literacy, 51*(3), 226–238.

Freebody, P., & Anderson, R. C. (1983). Effects of vocabulary difficulty, text cohesion and schema availability on reading comprehension. *Reading Research Quarterly, 18,* 277–294.

Gardner, D. (2007). Children's immediate understanding of vocabulary: Contexts and dictionary definitions. *Reading Psychology, 28,* 331–373.

Graves, M. F. (2006). Building a comprehensive vocabulary program. *New England Reading Association Journal, 42*(2), 1–7.

Heilman, A. W., Blair, T. R., & Rupley, W. H. (2002). *Principles and practices of teaching reading* (10th ed.). Upper Saddle River, NJ: Merrill/Prentice-Hall.

Ivey, G., & Fisher, D. (2005). Learning from what doesn't work. *Educational Leadership, 63*(2), 8–15.

Johnson, D. D., & Parson, P. D. (1984). *Teaching reading vocabulary* (2nd ed.). New York: Holt, Rinehart & Winston.

Kieffer, M. J., & Lesaux, N. K. (2007). Breaking down words to build meaning: Morphology, vocabulary, and reading comprehension in the urban classroom. *Reading Teacher, 61*(2), 134–144.

Klein, M. L. (1988). *Teaching reading comprehension and vocabulary: A guide for teachers.* Upper Saddle River, NJ: Prentice-Hall.

Lee, J., Grigg, W., & Donahue, P. (2007). *The nation's report card: Reading 2007* (NCES 2007-496). Washington, DC: National Center for Education Statistics.

Manzo, A. V., Manzo, U., & Thomas, M. (2006). Rationale for systematic vocabulary development: Antidote of state mandates. *Journal of Adolescent and Adult Literacy, 49*(7), 610–618.

Mraz, M., Taylor, B., Nichols, W. D., Rickelman, R., & Wood, K. D. (in press). Explicit vocabulary instruction for the struggling reader. Themed issue for *Reading and Writing Quarterly.*

Nagy, W. E. (1988). *Teaching vocabulary to improve reading comprehension.* Newark, DE: International Reading Association.

Nagy, W. E. (2005). Why vocabulary instruction needs to be long-term and comprehensive. In E. H. Hiebert & M. L. Kamil (Eds.), *Teaching and learning vocabulary: Bringing research to practice* (pp. 27–44). Mahwah, NJ: Erlbaum.

Nagy, W. E., & Anderson, R. C. (1984). How many words are there in printed school English? *Reading Research Quarterly, 19,* 304–330.

Nagy, W. E., & Anderson, R. C. (1995). *Metalinguistic awareness and literacy acquisition in different languages.* Urbana, IL: Center for the Study of Reading. (ERIC Document Reproduction Service No. ED391147)

National Institute of Child Health and Human Development. (2000). *Report of the National Reading Panel: Teaching children to read: An evidence-based assessment of the scientific research literature on reading and its implications for reading instruction* (NIH Publication No. 004769). Washington, DC: U.S. Government Printing Office.

Nichols, W. D., & Rupley, W. H. (2004). Matching instructional design with vocabulary instruction. *Reading Horizons, 45*(1), 55–71.

Nichols, W. D., Rupley, W. H., Blair, T. R., & Wood, K. D. (2008). Vocabulary strategies for linguistically diverse learners. *Middle School Journal, 39*(3), 65–69.

Nilsen, A. P., & Nilsen, D. L. F. (2006). Latin revived: Source-based vocabulary lessons courtesy of Harry Potter. *Journal of Adolescent and Adult Literacy, 50*(2), 128–134.

Polacco, P. (1994). *Pink and Say*. New York: Philomel.

Pressley, M., Levin, J. R., & MacDaniel, M. A. (1987). Remembering versus inferring what a word means: Mnemonic and contextual approaches. In M. C. McKeown & M. E. Curtis (Eds.), *The nature of vocabulary acquisition* (pp. 107–129). Hillsdale, NJ: Erlbaum.

RAND Reading Study Group. (2002). *Reading for understanding: Toward an R&D program in reading comprehension*. Santa Monica, CA: RAND Corporation.

Readence, J. E., Bean, T. W., & Baldwin, R. S. (1998). *Content area literacy* (6th ed.). Dubuque, IA: Kendall/Hunt.

Rupley, W. H., Logan, J. W., & Nichols, W. D. (1998/1999). Vocabulary instruction in a balanced reading program. *Reading Teacher, 52*, 336–346.

Rupley, W. H., & Nichols, W. D. (2005). Vocabulary instruction for the struggling reader. *Reading and Writing Quarterly, 21*, 239–260.

Rupley, W. H., & Slough, S. S. (2008). *Building prior knowledge and vocabulary in science in the intermediate grades: Creating hooks for learning*. Unpublished manuscript, Texas A&M University, Commerce.

Sadoski, M., Goetz, E. T., Kealy, W. S., & Paivio, A. (1997). Concreteness and imagery effects in the written composition of definitions. *Journal of Educational Psychology, 89*, 518–526.

Spencer, B. H., & Guillaume, A. M. (2006). Integrating curriculum through the learning cycle: Content-based reading and vocabulary instruction. *Reading Teacher, 60*(3), 206–219.

Vacca, R. T., & Vacca, J. L. (1999). *Content area reading: Literacy and learning across the curriculum* (6th ed.). New York: Longman.

Zadrozny, A. (2008). At home in my world. *READ Magazine, 50*(12), 28–30.

CHAPTER 9

How Does Creative Content-Area Teaching Work with Adolescents?

TOM BEAN
NANCY WALKER
JENNIFER WIMMER
BENITA DILLARD

CLASSROOM PORTRAIT

We are driving west of the Strip on Sahara Avenue, one of the busiest streets in Las Vegas, dotted with aging strip malls and ad boards. As we near Cleveland Lane, we make a right turn into a quieter, older neighborhood and pull into the parking lot of Jones Charter High School, one of Clark County Nevada's public charter schools. The one-story, vanilla-colored stucco building resembles an insurance office or business center, with adequate parking and a formal reception area, similar to a doctor's office. What is most striking about this school site is the absence of hallway jostling and ambient noise that are typical of traditional, often overcrowded urban high schools.

Once inside we sign in at the reception area and Sarah, the English teacher with whom we are visiting and collaborating, greets us. We walk down quiet hallways toward the faculty office area, past small groups of students working on desktop computers in their homerooms. Sarah, an experienced high school English teacher, is completing her doctorate at the University of Nevada, Las Vegas (UNLV). Prior to taking a position at Jones High School, Sarah taught in more traditional settings in crowded California classrooms. Unlike traditional high school settings, where students are on campus daily, Jones is a virtual high school, where students take their required content-area classes online 4 days a week, with 1 day on campus to meet with their homeroom teacher, get assistance with projects, and use the school-based computers.

Jones students, an ethnically and socioeconomically diverse group, come from all walks of life. They elect to attend Jones High for a variety of reasons. Some students are homebound due to illnesses; others see this form of online curriculum as the best route to college preparation; still others are simply put off by the bullying and psychosomatic stresses of crowded urban high schools; and some students are incarcerated. Thus, because of its online curriculum, Sarah's students can take her courses in ninth-grade English from home, interacting with other students in chat forums and the on-campus homeroom each week. But Sarah's teaching goes well beyond simply transmitting English literature content in traditional form. She engages with students in nontraditional ways, using multiple resources and various pedagogical approaches to create meaningful learning opportunities.

Multimedia Teaching in Action

Although this portrait is peculiar to online teaching, this chapter examines how teacher creativity, with implications for incorporating digital literacies, can be fostered in both traditional and nontraditional high school settings. We address how Sarah is able to balance online teaching with the state's standards movement, which often is seen as narrowing curriculum rather than creating spaces for enriching students' learning (Au, 2007). In addition, we examine how Maria, an eighth-grade physics teacher in a more traditional school setting in Los Angeles, is able to incorporate multimedia elements in a roller-coaster project. Before getting into our guiding question, we want to introduce ourselves.

Tom Bean and Nancy Walker are professors working extensively in content-area literacy research and professional development projects in middle and high school settings. Over the last 6 years they have conducted a series of studies aimed at understanding how content-area teachers creatively incorporate multiple texts, and more recently, multimedia sources in economics, history, physics, English, and other disciplines (Walker & Bean, 2004, 2005). Jennifer Wimmer, a doctoral student in literacy at UNLV, conducts research in three middle schools as part of a funded project with Tom Bean. Benita Dillard, a ninth-grade English teacher and coresearcher on this project, is currently at work on her dissertation exploring African American girls' experiences with young adult literature written by African American female authors in an online environment. Throughout our visits over the past 2 years to Jones High School, Jennifer, Benita, Nancy, and Tom have interviewed Sarah about her online teaching and have observed the dynamic and engaging projects her students produce. In an early interview about online teaching, Sarah said: "So I feel like I have more freedom to teach the way I want to, but I also feel like I'm being forced to really utilize my creativity, and that's something I really didn't do in a traditional setting." This early quote and subsequent conversations with Sarah over the past 2 years stimulated our interest in the intersection of new literacies and teacher creativity. We began to look toward the relatively fledgling work on teacher creativity, with an eye toward how digital and multimedia settings in both online and traditional classrooms support this effort.

Our central question for this chapter is as follows: *How does creative content-area teaching in cyberspace and multimedia settings work with adolescents?*

Based on our observations and conversations with Sarah and other teachers, such as Maria, we offer a picture of teaching-in-action, with artifacts and lesson design features that should be helpful for teachers incorporating elements of online teaching and multimedia in a variety of middle and high school settings. Our road map for this journey is a shared effort with Tom and Nancy, leading us to look at some of the current thinking about new literacies and teacher creativity, followed by Jennifer's interviews and conversations with Sarah about the opportunities and challenges presented by full-time, online teaching. Maria's teaching in physics offers to readers who cope with more traditional classrooms environments a window on how to engage students in creative thinking aimed at problem solving in physics.

Research on New Literacies and Teacher Creativity

New literacies is a term referring to a host of literacy practices that often, but not always, involve multimedia and the Internet. However, this is a fast-shifting territory and scholars such as Lankshear and Knobel (2003, p. 31) note that "New Literacies and social practices associated with new technologies are being invented on the street." Writing blogs, creating podcasts, writing Wikipedia entries, and online zines represent the tip of the iceberg in this fast-moving medium (Bean, Readence, & Baldwin, 2008). And, in general, studies suggest that reading on the Internet is in many ways more complex than traditional, print-based formats (Coiro & Dobler, 2007). This is due to the idiosyncratic nature of hypertext, which presents the reader with a kind of "Alice and Wonderland" labyrinth of navigational choices. There is some evidence that contemporary adolescent readers can manage this ill-structured environment quite well if they have prior knowledge about the topic, knowledge of print-based text structures, informational web-based structures, and knowledge of how to use Web-based search engines effectively (Coiro & Dobler, 2007). However, for struggling readers, Web-based digital terrain, with its idiosyncratic formats, presents special challenges (Wilder & Dressman, 2007). Nevertheless, adolescents are native users of technology, and they often bring out-of-school experiences with video games and other layered forms of digitized texts with them to the classroom (O'Brien, 2007). They are often perfectly poised to capitalize on the creative potential of digitized, multiple texts.

The world of texts continues to change, expand, and shift, with a steady movement away from the use of a single, traditional textbook in many content areas (Wade & Moje, 2000). The use of multiple texts, including magazines, news articles, multimedia, and Internet texts, is an increasingly common phenomenon in many middle and high school classrooms. Indeed, students expect teachers to incorporate multiple texts and, in particular, Internet-based lessons that involve navigating an array of websites. For example, Mitty Blake, the main character in the young adult novel *Code Orange* (Cooney, 2005), nicely demonstrates the primacy of digital texts in adolescents' lives. His high school biology teacher requires a research paper that includes "four physical books" (p. 1). In the following excerpt, Mitty offers his opinion of this assignment:

> "Books?" said Mitty, stunned. He was sure this had not been mentioned before. "Mr. Lynch, nobody uses books anymore. They're useless, especially in science. Facts change too fast." (p. 2)

Although the complete demise of books may be an exaggeration, Mitty does have a point, and students with access to up-to-date, reliable scientific information certainly have an advantage. But new literacies classrooms can exist without the luxury of a completely online setting. For example, Kist (2005) visited seven school sites and classrooms in the United States and Canada where teachers were incorporating creative new literacies teaching practices.

Kist characterized new literacies classrooms as ones that featured the following:

- Daily work in multiple forms of representation.
- Explicit discussions of the merits of using certain symbol systems.
- Modeling by the teacher to demonstrate the use of varying symbols.
- Students engaged in collaborative and individual activities.
- Students who report experiencing flow states, with time passing quickly.

These important characteristics should guide our thinking about creating lessons that capitalize on adolescents' in- and out-of-school literacies. Sheridan-Thomas (2007), a teacher-educator working with preservice content-area teachers, noted that "the concept of multiple literacies is not only about multiple texts or varied text forms. It begins with the multiplicity of cultural identities that are expressed through literacies" (p. 122). Without an explicit focus on adolescents' multiple literacies, this study found that preservice teachers initially conceptualize content literacy as a simple, skills-based process. Over the span of Sheridan-Thomas's course in content-area literacy, these preservice teachers quickly expanded their views of what counts as text, embracing the multiple literacies and multiple texts that students actually use, both in and out of school. Video games, computers, magazines, newspapers, cell phones, and contemporary television dramas, such as *CSI*, became sites for curriculum development. For example, a preservice chemistry teacher planned to use selected clips of the most interesting scientific moments from a *CSI* episode and to have students pick a scientific technique that captivated their interest for further exploration. In Sheridan-Thomas's content-area literacy course, these future teachers came to understand that "adolescents' multiple literacies can provide bridges to engaging students in content learning and academic literacies. These bridges can be based on high interest topics and the engaging and accessible formats of multiple texts (p. 135).

In our ongoing studies of content-area teachers' use of multiple texts, we couldn't help noticing that the foundation for many successful teaching practices, including those using multimedia or Internet sites, rests in creativity. For example, how many times have you planned or visually projected how a lesson you have designed might play out? Undoubtedly, this planning was ongoing, fluid, and occupied your mind while you were grocery shopping, washing clothes, driving in traffic, or simply going for a walk. Going back to Sarah's comment that her high school's virtual online curriculum calls for creative use of this medium to tap students' natural interest in the Internet, we can see the connection between new literacies and teacher creativity. As we discovered, a number of prominent thinkers in the United States and abroad have been begun to look closely at teacher creativity (Craft, 2001; Runco, 2007; Sak, 2004). This body of work is important, because it suggests to us that technology, particularly the Internet, offers teachers a space to design creatively and deliver more interactive and powerful lessons.

Efforts to define *creativity* have become more refined and focused in recent years. Consistent with many views of literacy as a social practice, recent definitions of teacher and student creativity emphasize its collaborative, social nature. These newer characterizations of creativity move us beyond the myth of the rugged individual genius, sometimes referred to as *big C* creativity (Sawyer, 2006), toward *little c* creativity (Beghetto & Kaufman, 2007). For example, *big C* creativity might characterize the invention of the Apple Mac computer and its huge impact on design and graphics work. *Little c* creativity is more typical of classroom creations (e.g., zines) and projects. Both forms of creativity require depth of knowledge in a subject-area domain, as well as careful teacher scaffolding and modeling.

As we take a closer look at Sarah's lessons designed for a public charter high school, where classes are conducted totally in an online environment, and Maria's roller-coaster project in a more traditional school site, we are mindful of those elements of new literacies teaching and *little c* creativity in play. Our goal is to provide a rich, contextualized picture of accomplished teachers in action but to keep the following caveat in mind: Start small. During 2 years of developing online curricula in English literature at Jones, Sarah spent many weekends conceptualizing and envisioning how a unit and its related lessons might unfold in practice. Maria's highly creative, engaging approach to teaching science was at times out of step with more rigid content delivery approaches to teaching in her department. Nevertheless, both Sarah and Maria forged ahead, and their students benefited as a result of their risk-taking efforts to design captivating lessons. Constant reflection and revision are natural parts of this process, and we do not want to suggest that there is any magic pill for developing lessons that capitalize on teachers' creativity and induce students to stretch their thinking about literature in creative ways. What we can offer is a rich picture of new literacies and teacher creativity in action.

In our discussion, we also argue that students need to be producers of digital texts. In one of our interviews, Sarah commented that "students need to learn how to communicate in an online environment using both pictures and words." In essence, the same layout and design features that have been part and parcel of production editors' domains are now very much a part of teachers' and students' worlds. And, as producers of digital texts, adolescents become insiders in this medium, able to interpret and critique others' texts, as well as their own (Kellner, 2002). As the reader will see when we get into the actual lessons that Sarah creates, elements of visual design and composition, in addition to print-based features, drive creative thinking in this medium. Because teachers plan lessons and units "on the fly," while jogging, driving to school, or waiting in lines, we want to make the reality of teacher planning and creativity more transparent than might be the case with more disembodied views of teacher creativity.

Maria: Eighth-Grade Laws of Physics and Roller Coasters

The science classroom provides tremendous possibilities for new literacies and creativity in action. Maria, an eighth-grade physics teacher, shows us how she incorporated physics elements into a multiliteracy project. Students in Maria's physics class had the opportunity to build roller coasters that demonstrated their knowledge of gravitational energy, momentum, and potential energy. Once these were built, students wrote lab reports, calculating the speed and velocity of the marbles as they rolled on the roller coaster. The second portion of the project was to redesign a theme park in financial trouble by adding a roller coaster to attract people to their park. Students used the Internet to research information on theme parks. Once their research was completed, they used various forms of multimedia, including PowerPoint or video, to present their projects to the class. Maria was also concerned about the low test scores in writing; thus, she created opportunities to incorporate writing within her curriculum. Students' persuasive writing was geared to selling their designs to prospective theme parks, and their reading encompassed contrasting articles about roller-coaster safety issues. In one student's words: "This class is fun."

The roller-coaster project grew out of Maria's conversations with a colleague, who then gave her the website where it was described (see *www.angelfire.com/on2thrillsand chills*). The research project resulted in student-generated bibliographies and wide reading across various forms of texts. Maria had a particular interest in helping students improve their reading of expository texts. She comments:

> "I knew they needed other examples of reading. In the lower classes they are not readers, and they are not going to take the time to read the articles. I wanted them to make sure they could read and utilize different forms of text. They are learning how to read expository texts. Some kids know how to use recreational reading, but I don't think a lot of kids know how to read the newspaper."

Indeed, as "digital natives" (Alvermann, 2007), these students flourished in a constructivist science setting, where visual representations of roller coasters dominated. They are growing up in an era in which visual modes of representation have fast overtaken print-based modes.

Using the Internet, students searched key sites for information on roller coasters. Then, in teams, they designed large models of their proposed theme park ride, along with technical reports covering design factors, safety, and advertising. Team members had a specific role to play, including architect, researcher, public relations, engineer, and so on, under a company name they created. For example, one team designed a new roller coaster called SpyRoll, and their public relations ad copy on their PowerPoint presentation read:

> The brand new thrill ride, SpyRoll incorporates many new techniques never used before. This ride will be a great addition to any theme park willing to take a mob of anxious thrill seekers.

Indeed, this team developed a roller-coaster ride that departed from most common designs. This team's promotional campaign for their highly creative design advertised:

> SpyRoll features a drop that goes into a horizontal twist, a feat that has never been done before.

Once the initial planning was completed, Maria's students executed their roller-coaster designs in working models for testing. Finally, students tested their completed roller coasters.

Maria's classroom demonstrates examples of multimedia and creativity, and their possibilities. Providing students with the space to create allowed a deeper understanding of the physics concepts set by the state standards. At the same time, Maria had an opportunity to set the core text aside and visualize a hands-on project for the students with the help of the Internet.

Van Tassel-Baska (2006) discusses five ways to instill creativity in schools. Students need to feel that they have *choice* in the curriculum they study and the projects they complete. They also need large amounts of *time* to dedicate to projects. *Mentors* are necessary to guide students to high levels of learning and productivity. Having a *supportive environment* that is risk free for their work is a necessity. Finally, students need to be able to bring *creative skills* to their classroom tasks. Maria has the flexibility to pursue highly creative projects in her physics classroom despite high-stakes testing and standards that dictate the curriculum. Maria's need to be creative in her lesson and design, and to allow the freedom of creativity in her classroom, meets these criteria and ensures a high level of engagement with her students.

In fact, Maria's pedagogy is a departure from the old-style transmission of teaching science. Other content areas have also departed from the traditional style of teaching. A recent study aimed at understanding how one seventh-grade English/language arts teacher incorporated multiple texts to develop students' conceptual understanding of the 1957 integration of Central High School in Little Rock, Arkansas

(Boyd & Ikpeze, 2007), noted that multiple texts help develop students' ability to think creatively in ill-structured domains. Referred to as cognitive flexibility theory (Spiro, Coulson, Feltovich, & Anderson, 2004), this notion suggests that creative problem solving is complex, involving multiple texts, experimental trials of a design (e.g., the roller coaster), and application of knowledge. In short, "it must be learned, represented, tried out, and applied in many ways" (Boyd & Ikpeze, 2007, p. 223). Application of knowledge, and a recognition that problem solving involves multiple texts, multiple voices (e.g., the roller-coaster design teams), and a willingness to experiment, is the hallmark of a curriculum like the one in Maria's physics class. It requires a teacher disposition to go into depth with a topic rather than to survey many topics, skimming across the surface of each one. Nevertheless, this is a promising direction, exemplified by Maria's students and those in Sarah's English class.

Sarah's High School English Class in an Online Environment

Sarah teaches ninth-grade English to over 200 students at Jones Charter High School, described in the School Portrait at the opening of this chapter. Most of Sarah's students were unsuccessful in the traditional public school setting. In an online survey, several students reported peer pressure, fighting, poor school attendance, physical disability, learning disability, drug abuse, overcrowded classrooms, or problems with teachers as the reasons they were not successful in traditional public schools. However, these students, who may previously have been marginalized by traditional print-based literacies, had the potential to find a space in a new literacies environment, where multiple ideas and skills are both needed and valued (Leu, Castek, Henry, Coiro, & McMullan, 2004). In this particular school, students are required to attend school once a week for 4 hours. During this time, they attend homeroom for 1 hour, math lab for 1 hour, and applied communications for 2 hours. Beyond the 1 day a week attendance policy, students are expected to log on to the school's website and complete their assignments.

Sarah, who had also taught in traditional public schools, believed that teaching in an online environment offered more opportunities to help students achieve academic success, because of increased attention to the individual, as well as the use of technology. This type of education relies heavily on the use of technology. Perhaps the success of this model is due to the fact that students growing up in this technological age do not know a life without computers (Lewis & Fabos, 2005). In fact, students often do not feel that their use of chat rooms, instant messaging, blogging, and other computer programs is "technology"; it is a "fact of life, a way of being in the world" (p. 470). This belief holds true for the student body at Jones High School. These students attend class, work on assignments, and communicate with their peers and teachers through the use of technology.

In this learning environment, Sarah has unlimited access to multimedia resources that enable her to develop lessons that provide students with opportunities to stretch their thinking about literature in creative ways. Although Sarah adheres to specific state and national standards, she designs lessons in an effort to meet those standards and engage her students in reading, critiquing, interpreting, analyzing, and creating texts.

As an example, Sarah created a short story unit that required students to blog about specific topics. Within this unit, students read short stories such as Charlotte Perkins Gilman's "The Yellow Wallpaper," Kurt Vonnegut's "Harrison Bergeron," and Amy Tan's "Two Kinds." The theme for this short story unit was the role of women in the 19th, 20th, and 21st centuries in American society. Sarah chose these short stories so that students could understand how factors such as race, class, nationality/immigration status, and marital status have affected women's place and role.

To get students to discuss these issues, Sarah created a blog account for her English I class. Instead of just submitting five-paragraph essays and computer-graded exams, she posted several topics on the blog that required students to respond. Sarah did not grade students' comments based on grammar, sentence structure, or punctuation. Rather, she created the blog assignments as informal writing exercises, so that students could feel free to voice their opinions on assigned topics. Furthermore, Sarah used blogging as a resource to help students connect their experiences with those of peers, along with some of the issues explored in the short stories. Sarah used blogging as a means to help students in an online English class communicate their thoughts to her and to other students.

As an advocate of critical literacy, Sarah felt that it was vital for her students to begin to think beyond literal recall and to engage in critical conversations that questioned the author, society, and themselves. Because Sarah was not searching for a particular answer, the students were able to respond creatively in any manner, as long as they were able to defend their answers.

As an introduction to the unit, Sarah posted an image of an African American woman and a European American woman protesting. The European American woman faced the camera and held a sign that stated, "All we want is equal rights with equal opportunities, no discrimination." Below the image, Sarah wrote:

> In what time period do you think this protest took place? Why do you think the women in the photo participated in this protest? Give some reasons. Why do you think the one lady facing the camera is smiling? Do you think the matter of discrimination toward women has been resolved? If yes, discuss why; if no, discuss why. Post your answer in the blog.

To post a comment, students had to create a Google account. Almost half of the class created an account to post a response to this topic. A year earlier, students had to write an essay on the same topic, and less than half completed the assignment. Sarah decided to make it a blog activity that did not penalize students for misspelled words, capitalization errors, and fragment or run-on sentences. Perhaps as a result of revising the assignment in this way, more students posted responses. In fact, one female student posted:

> I think this protest took place in the 1960's. It was the third movement towards women's rights. I think the women in this photo participated because she was fighting for women's rights. She agreed that women should have equal rights and equal opportunities. I think the one lady was smiling because she was fighting for women's rights. She is proud and happy that someone is taking action and fight for women's rights. No, I do not think that the discrimination towards women has been resolved. We are still underestimated, under-looked, and under-rated because we are women. You have all these men out there saying they are better and this and that. When in reality, we as women can do the same exact things if not better than they can. We should all be treated equally. It shouldn't matter if someone was a woman or not. But it does. It matters to most if it was a woman because to most a woman is someone whom should stay at home raising the kids, coking, cleaning, and being a housewife. What about the ones that aren't housewives? What about the ones that are? What about what they wanted to do. I'm not saying they shouldn't but you can still be a housewife and stand up for your rights and stand your ground.

A male student posted:

> This photo seems to be taken during the 1960's. The women participated in this protest because they felt discriminated against unequal women's rights. I don't believe the issue regarding equal rights has been fully resolved. I support this by saying there was a study done stating that men make more money than a woman doing the same job and women always seem

to be underestimated. It is a male dominated world still, it has changed significantly but I don't believe women are given the same respect men are. The woman in this picture is smiling because effort is finally being made.

By implementing blogging in the curriculum, Sarah provided for her students the opportunity to switch from being consumers of knowledge to being producers of knowledge. Sarah stated, "Blogging is a space where they're supposed to feel free to just talk, and so I just give them that platform to just talk." The use of blogs as an outlet for discussion was one way in which Sarah hoped to tap into her students' interests. She argued, "If you don't capture their attention, then it's not that they can't do the work, it's that they won't do the work." New literacies provide teachers like Sarah the opportunity to draw on their students' interests through a medium that is both familiar and motivational.

Concluding Thoughts: What We've Learned from Observing New Literacies in Action

Both Maria and Sarah push the envelope in their teaching to tap their own and their students' creative potential in the content areas of science and English. Renowned creativity researcher, Csikszentmihalyi (1999) has noted that creativity is not simply a property of individuals but a sociocultural dimension. Indeed, Sawyer (2006, p. 119) argues that "the most important forms of creativity in our culture—movies, television shows, big science experiments, music videos, compact discs, computer software, videogames—are joint cooperative activities of complex networks of skilled individuals." As such, if we are truly interested in the development of a literate, creative citizenry, then the content-area classrooms of today and tomorrow must embrace a model of curriculum design that fosters students' creative, flexible problem solving. Maria's roller-coaster project and Sarah's online blog example offer glimpses of what is possible as we integrate content-area teaching and new literacies practices.

Questions for Reflection

1. In your view, how can teacher creativity be supported in a new literacies environment?

2. What are some key characteristics of new literacy classrooms that you are using or thinking of trying?

3. Does online teaching foster teacher and student creativity? What are your reasons for your views?

References

Alvermann, D. E. (2007). Content area literacy: The spotlight shifts to teacher educators. In M. B. Sampson, P. E. Linder, F. Falk-Ross, M. Foote, & S. Szabo (Eds.), *Multiple literacies in the 21st century: 2006 College Reading Association Yearbook* (pp. 14–19). Commerce: Texas A&M University.

Au, W. (2007). High-stakes testing and curricular control: A qualitative meta-synthesis. *Educational Researcher, 36*(5), 258–267.

Bean, T .W., Readence, J. E., & Baldwin, R. S. (2008). *Content area literacy: An integrated approach* (9th ed.). Dubuque, IA: Kendall/Hunt.

Beghetto, R. A., & Kaufman, J. C. (2007, April). *Creativity in the classroom: Between chaos and conformity.* Paper presented at the annual meeting of the American Educational Research Association, Chicago.

Boyd, F. B., & Ikpeze, C. H. (2007). Navigating a literacy landscape: Teaching conceptual understanding with multiple text types. *Reading Research and Instruction, 39*(2), 217–248.

Coiro, J., & Dobler, E. (2007). Exploring the online reading comprehension strategies used by sixth-grade skilled readers to search for and locate information on the Internet. *Reading Research Quarterly, 42*(2), 214–157.

Cooney, C. (2005). *Code orange.* New York: Delacorte Press.

Craft, A. (2001). *An analysis of research and literature on creativity education* (United Kingdom Qualifications and Curriculum Authority). Retrieved March 8, 2007, from *www.naction.org.uk.*

Csikszentmihalyi, M. (1999). Implications of a systems perspective for the study of creativity. In R. J. Sternberg (Ed.), *The handbook of creativity* (pp. 313–335). New York: Cambridge University Press.

Kellner, D. (2002). Technological revolution, multiple literacies, and the restructuring of education. In L. Synder (Ed.), *Silicon literacies: Communication, innovation, and education in the electronic age* (pp. 154–169). New York: Routledge.

Kist, W. (2005). *New literacies in action: Teaching and learning in multiple media.* New York: Teachers College Press.

Lankshear, C., & Knobel, M. (2003). *New literacies: Changing knowledge and classroom learning.* Buckingham, UK: Open University Press.

Leu, D. J., Jr., Castek, J., Henry, L. A., Coiro, J., & McMullan, M. (2004). The lessons that children teach us: Integrating children's literature and the new literacies of the Internet. *Reading Teacher, 57*(5), 496–503.

Lewis, C., & Fabos, B. (2005). Instant messaging, literacies, and social identities. *Reading Research Quarterly, 40*(4), 470–501.

O'Brien, D. (2007). "Struggling" adolescents' engagement in multimediating: Countering the institutional construction of incompetence. In D. E. Alvermann, K. A. Hinchman, D. W. Moore, S. F. Phelps, & D. R. Waff (Eds.),

Reconceptualizing the literacies in adolescents' lives (2nd ed., pp. 29–46). Mahwah, NJ: Erlbaum.

Runco, M. A. (2007). *Creativity theories and themes: Research, development, and practice.* Burlington, MA: Elsevier Academic Press.

Sak, U. (2004). About creativity, giftedness and teaching the creatively gifted in the classroom. *Roeper Review, 26,* 216–222.

Sawyer, R. K. (2006). *Explaining creativity: The science of human innovation.* New York: Oxford University Press.

Sheridan-Thomas, H. K. (2007). Making sense of multiple literacies: Exploring preservice content-area teachers' understandings and applications. *Reading Research and Instruction, 46*(2), 121–147.

Spiro, R. J., Coulson, R. L., Feltovich, P. J., & Anderson, D. K. (2004). Cognitive flexibility theory: Advanced knowledge acquisition in ill-structured domains. In R. B. Ruddell & N. J. Unrau (Eds.), *Theoretical models and processes of reading* (5th ed., pp. 640–653). Newark, DE: International Reading Association.

Van Tassel-Baska, J. (2006). Higher level thinking in gifted education. In J. C. Kaufman & J. Baer (Eds.), *Creativity and reason in cognitive development* (pp. 297–315). New York: Cambridge University Press.

Wade, S. E., & Moje, E. B. (2000). The role of text in classroom learning. In M. L. Kamil, P. B. Mosenthal, P. D. Pearson, & R. Barr (Eds.), *Handbook of reading research* (Vol. III, pp. 609–627). Mahwah, NJ: Erlbaum.

Walker, N. T., & Bean, T. W. (2004). Using multiple texts in content-area teachers' classrooms. *Journal of Content Area Reading, 3*(1), 23–35.

Walker, N. T., & Bean, T. W. (2005). Sociocultural influences in content-area teachers' selection and use of multiple texts. *Reading Research and Instruction, 44*(4), 61–77.

Wilder, P., & Dressman, M. (2007). New literacies, enduring challenges?: The influence of capital on adolescent readers' Internet practices. In D. E. Alvermann, K. A. Hinchman, D. W. Moore, S. F. Phelps, & D. R. Waff (Eds.), *Reconceptualizing the literacies in adolescents' lives* (2nd ed., pp. 205–229). Mahwah, NJ: Erlbaum.

CHAPTER 10

■ ■ ■

How Can We Help Adolescents Think about Content through Writing?

THOMAS DeVERE WOLSEY
LORI KELSEY

CLASSROOM PORTRAIT

Every time I turn in a paper, I know what the score is going to be. It's always low and always the same, but I don't know what I have to do to be a better writer.

—JULIANA, 10th grade

Juliana knows she has to write, and she wants to be better at it. Her teachers have her write frequently, because they correctly believe that students can learn to think about content, such as math, literature, or science, through writing. She especially likes her history class and actively listens to lectures. Juliana also likes sharing ideas with classmates during group assignments. When her teacher asked her to write about the financial turmoil in France during the reign of King Louis XVI, she thought she was prepared. She wrote a speech for King Louis to deliver to the people explaining why the Assembly of Notables should be given the right to vote for new taxes. Working from memory, she devised a letter of five paragraphs and turned it in.

When her paper was returned, she was sad but not surprised: another "C" on another paper. Even though she had worked hard and used a familiar format for her work, the teacher had written "elaborate" in three places on her paper and "awk" in another. Juliana thought she had elaborated; after all, wasn't that the purpose of the five paragraphs? The "awk" puzzled her, but she didn't know what to do about it. Juliana also worried about the upcoming state tests, which called for her to write responses to documents in social sciences. The tests would determine whether she would graduate from high school. If all she could muster was a "C" on papers she wrote for class, how would she ever write a paper that would earn a passing grade on the state high school exit exam?

Both new and seasoned teachers struggle with the role of writing in content classrooms. Language arts teachers completing their certification programs are often prepared to teach only the parts of the five-paragraph essay to students, and content-area teachers are usually on their own when it comes time to assign, read, respond, and grade student writing. It can be disappointing for them to read canned student responses to writing assignments, especially when the writing conveys little meaning. Many content-area teachers are lost and discouraged when providing feedback that will help student writers, but they realize that a letter grade doesn't provide enough information to help student writers like Juliana on the next assignment.

At the same time, many students dread writing assignments because they haven't learned to use writing to think through what they know already, and what they might learn through interaction with other students, and through their encounters with texts. Writing is a complex cognitive task; it is not just talk written down. In composing, students must exert control over minor details, such as word choice and punctuation, and macrochoices, such as text organization structures. Additionally, students must bring to bear a great deal of content knowledge and determine which data are useful for their purposes and which are not. Many writing tasks require students to write *to demonstrate their learning.* Here, we argue that writing *is a way of learning.* By situating writing as a way of thinking about content, teachers help young writers to learn because they compose.

If teaching writing is more than just teaching the parts of an essay and grading papers with letter grades, then what does effective writing instruction entail? Teachers assist students when expectations are clear and when classroom interactions result in meaningful topics about which students can write. Through writing, students understand and learn how to think critically about content, while applying principles of argumentation, learning the moves of academic writing, and using effective feedback.

In this chapter, through theory and demonstration, we address the question and illustrate how teachers can use writing as a tool for learning about content. Tom Wolsey is a professor of literacy and learning. Lori Kelsey is a middle school teacher at Rancho Santa Fe School in southern California. Both authors enjoy writing, teaching writing, and expanding their own knowledge of how to teach writing. They have a combined total of 30 years of teaching in sixth- through twelfth-grade classrooms.

Research on Teaching Writing as a Process

For more than 30 years, writing has been taught as a process that suggests idea generation (teachers recognize this as brainstorming or prewriting), an organization stage (outlining or mapping), a drafting stage that includes revision and proofreading, and a final copy or publishing stage. The process approach (e.g., Atwell, 1987; Day, 1947; Emig, 1971) to teaching student writers is modeled after descriptions of the approaches that writers use when writing. For example, writers may make a list, narrow it down, create an outline, and begin a draft. However, such models cannot account fully for exactly how young writers craft their work.

Teachers of content areas, such as literature, science, or social studies, can promote student learning through written tasks. For example, how might a science teacher use writing to engage students in thinking about the concept of *momentum* instead of merely to assess whether the student completed an assigned textbook reading about *momentum*? How might the social studies teacher use writing to encourage students to think about the idea of *culture*? Teachers of content areas are rightly concerned about teaching the content of their disciplines and sometimes view writing as something extra to which they must attend. This need not be the case, however. Writers must have something to write about, and in content areas, there are rich opportunities for thinking through writing. When students write, they organize information, reexamine it, reformulate understandings, and elaborate to create rich comprehension.

The biochemist James Zull (2002) suggested that learning is not just something the brain does; rather, learning actually changes the brain. His theory of the biology of learning is that data accumulated through experience are just data until the learner engages in reflection by organizing and rearranging the experiential data. Transforming experience into meaningful learning is a goal shared by math, physical education, and science teachers: Writing is an important tool in attaining that goal (Nagin & the National Writing Project, 2003).

The Teacher's Voice:
How Difficult Can It Be to Teach Writing?

While awaiting the arrival of first period, I (Kelsey) calmly began sharpening the new number two pencils that would soon be in the hands of the next great generation of writers. Little black and white composition books decorated the desks of my future Emersons and Steinbecks. The inside blank pages were begging to be saturated with outlines of the next great American novel. I envisioned myself as a retired school teacher, with my gray hair pulled softly back in a bun and an old navy blue sweater draped over my hunched shoulders, peering through cat-eye glasses as John Henry, one of my very first writing students, accepted the Nobel Prize in literature. "And finally tonight," John Henry says, "I would like to thank my seventh-grade writing teacher, Mrs. Kelsey, for refusing to believe that writing cannot be taught." I struggle to stand as the house fills with applause.... *Bzzzzz bzzzzz.* The warning bell for first period jolts me out of my reverie. Sitting at my desk, I try to get an idea of what members of my very first class look like as I discreetly peer through the venetian blinds. "Hmm," I think, "They certainly look little for seventh grade." With that, I swung open the door and greeted each student with a smile, a pencil, and a notebook.

Although that was my first year of teaching, I felt things were under control—that is, until I shut the classroom door and 20 pairs of eyes were watching me. How hard could it be to teach writing? Although I hadn't really taken a writing class per se in my methods classes, the one thing I knew was how to model. I figured that if I sat in front of the class and began to write, then they would follow my lead. So, in my naiveté, I sat down in my chair, opened my notebook, and began writing in my journal. I suggested that the students do the same.

Instantly they bombarded me with what I know now are typical questions when students write: "What do I write about?"; "How long does it have to be?"; "When is it due?" Gee, I hadn't thought about any of that. My nightmare began. Fortunately, as most teachers realize sooner or later, all school nightmares do eventually end, as did my very first year of teaching middle school language arts.

What I have learned since that first year is that teaching students to write is really teaching them how to think and to express their views formally, so that they be understood by those around them. I have also learned that before students can write anything, they first must recognize that to write means to make a point about something. Even creative writing argues some point. Before students begin to write, teachers must take advantage of precious class time for reading and discussion. My mentor-teacher many years ago gave me some wise advice. "Anything you value, do in class." I cringe when I think about how many writing pieces are just assigned as homework, with little or no classroom discussion.

Learning to teach writing should not be painful or be thought of as something insurmountable. As a seasoned teacher, I wanted to help beginning middle school language arts teachers to learn how to teach writing and make the most of their time with students. I decided that the best way to do this is to write what I know.

Research on Writing Tasks in Classrooms

More than 20 years ago, researchers (Applebee, 1984; Langer & Applebee, 1987) explored how teachers used writing tasks in their class-rooms. They found that teachers often adapted tasks to fit their teach-ing practices and used writing tasks as a means of assessment rather than as a means of learning. Students were asked to compose text for the purpose of demonstrating what they knew. Writing as an evaluation of learning is often appropriate; the essay exam is a valid summative assessment—evidence that learning has occurred. On the other hand, composing can also be a means of coming to know and to understand. Langer and Applebee (1987), in a series of studies, found that students who wrote analytically were more apt to have learned and retained their understanding than students who wrote short answers to questions, or who took notes only.

Students engage in many types of writing tasks in classrooms. Per-sonal writing (e.g., a memoir) is a useful purpose for writing, as is much creative writing done in school. Informal writing, such as free writing (Elbow, 1973), journals, and quickwrites, have important uses; these forms may be employed in the service of learning within the disciplines. The goal is generation of ideas, but these generative forms do not auto-matically promote thinking about content; indeed, by nature, journal-ing and free writing avoid the potential judgment of an audience, and the structures and conventions of standard edited English. As such, they can be helpful as students form initial thoughts. But we suggest that students who wish to understand a discipline must contend with critical audiences, as well as with conventions of English as they might appear in other written work within the discipline. Simply put, writing that shapes thinking must eventually be written in Standard English, use the vocabulary of the discipline, conventional spelling and punctua-tion, and grapple with disciplinary (subject area or content) concepts for the student's level.

Another important writing task is summarization. Some theories of learning capture ideas that effective teachers have known for some time: Learning is promoted when multiple pathways for student action, multiple means of expression in multiple formats and media, and mul-tiple means of capturing student interest are part of the instructional design (Rose & Meyer, 2002). More formal than journals and free writing, summarization affords students an opportunity to review and to clarify the text- or lecture-based information they encounter (Newell, 2006). *Summarizing* means making judgments about what is meaningful and particularly relevant (e.g., Kintsch, 1990; Moss, 2004) and has measurable effects on learning (Rinehart, Stahl, & Erickson, 1986). Teachers who wish their students to make informed arguments about content may begin by using study questions and summarization. Argumentation, an important writing tool for adolescent learners in content subjects, is discussed in the next section.

Writing as Thinking: Argumentation

When ideas are complex and sophisticated, teachers often encourage students to write in greater depth and sometimes at greater length. Analysis, evaluation, and synthesis of ideas come to the fore when students must organize and comprehend ideas in the content areas; for these purposes, we argue for argumentation (Toulmin, 2003). Some related terms, such as *informational writing* or *analytic writing* (Applebee, 1984) are helpful but less precise. *Argumentation* calls for students to conceptualize and to transform the knowledge they encounter, associating new ideas and reformulating their understanding by constructing new relations between and among concepts, and supporting underlying thinking. Reformulation of ideas for adolescents in content area courses should include, but also transcend, personal connections. Multiple expressions, scaffolded so that learning results, are built in when study questions and written summaries are familiar writing tasks, yet simply writing more often is not sufficient. Fearn and Farnan assert that instruction should "promote informed practice for every student, every day" (2007, p. 20), because uninformed practice makes poor writing habits permanent.

Arguments in school are often the sort of thing that can result in one being sent to the principal's office. But when serving as the basis for a writing task, the patterns of well-constructed arguments are very worthwhile. Toulmin (2003) identified the four main elements of argumentation: *claim* (the position), *clarification* (qualifiers limiting the claim), *evidence* (support for the claim), and *warrant* (reasoning that connects the evidence to the claim). In constructing an argument, a writer must consider and perhaps identify a problem or claim. Having identified the problem, the student must get to work identifying the limits of the argument, and proposing suitable solutions and positions. In doing so, the writer considers what others have written or said about the topic, what data may or may not be available, and what positions others have taken that may not be in agreement. Though we apply argumentation in literature study in this chapter, it also works well in exploration of science, social studies, mathematics, and other content topics.

The Teacher's Voice:
Applying the Toulmin Argumentation Model

Each year my seventh-grade class begins by reading the classic *The Outsiders* by S. E. Hinton (1967). The main character is 14-year-old Ponyboy, whose parents died in a car wreck; he lives on the far side of town with his two brothers. Throughout the novel, Ponyboy struggles with the differences between himself, a Greaser, and the others, the Socials, who represent the upper class in the small Oklahoma town. By the end of the novel, Ponyboy realizes that all people struggle, though their struggles may be different, and one can't judge an individual based on the actions of the rest of the group. Students enjoy this novel; thus, it remains as part of our district's language arts curriculum for seventh grade. But after a few years of teaching *The Outsiders*, I noticed that much of the student writing I assigned seemed circular and lacked evidence to support students' theses or claims. I also noticed that students often just repeated their claims or theses in different ways. In those early days of teaching, barely any of my middle school writers wrote about others' points of views or counterarguments.

One evening, in the midst of grading these inadequate papers after a particularly difficult day of teaching, I decided that I really needed to come down hard on the kids. After all, they were intelligent and by now should be effective writers. I was convinced that students were going to have to try harder and spend more time drafting before publishing a final copy for the grade.

The next day, armed with my red pen and a "Don't smile until Thanksgiving" face, I laid it on the line to my students. I scolded, "Well, everyone flunked the writing assignment." I tried to pretend I didn't see the disappointed faces of all of those students who had earnestly tried on the assignment. Attempting to explain why they failed, I displayed a few particularly circular pieces on the overhead and instructed, "This type of merry-go-round writing is just unacceptable. For as much as you like to argue, why can't you make a point and back it up?" I was so sure these examples would result in much better argumentation in students' essays. But looking back on that day in my teaching career still makes me sad. What was I thinking?

After class, Janie, one of my brightest and most shy students, approached me with tears in her eyes. " Mrs. Kelsey, " she said, " I don't know what you want. I don't know how to do what you are asking ."

My heart began to pound, and I felt like crying myself. "Oh, thanks. Let's go so you aren't late to next period" was all I could manage.

Recognizing that Janie couldn't be the only lost student, I decided that I was the one who had failed the writing assignment, not the students. I knew I had blamed the victims rather than think about how I had failed in my instruction. I realized that I had to think about the way I was teaching writing—or not teaching writing. I knew I needed to encourage my class of dejected students with an engaging teaching plan, one that involved much discussion, scaffolding, concrete examples, and feedback on their writing.

At our English language arts department meeting that afternoon, I broached the subject of student writing and asked teachers about the quality of writing they were collecting from their students. Joe, on the verge of retirement confessed, "I send all writing home. Hey, I have too much material to cover to be having the kids write in class."

"OK," I said, "but Joe, what do you do in class to model the home assignments? What are you showing them? What types of writing conversations are you having?"

Joe looked at me and began to laugh. "Well, nothing—these kids have been in school now for six, seven, and eight years—shouldn't they know?"

Realizing that Joe wasn't going to be able to help me, I turned to Tanya, a teacher earning her master's degree in curriculum and instruction. Tanya suggested, "You might want to look up *argumentation* and see if that gives some ideas about how to develop this form of writing. Kids are really naturals at arguing and love it, but we need to model for them how to take that dialogue and turn it into real-world writing that has a point. Think about it. When was the last time you wrote something, and what was the point of the writing?"

"Oh," I replied, "Well last week I sent an e-mail to my sister."

"OK," encouraged Tanya, "let me walk you through this a minute using what I learned about Toulmin's model of argumentation."

"Well, OK," I agreed.

"Now, what was the point of that e-mail to your sister?" Tanya asked.

"Well I was trying to convince her to postpone a visit to San Diego until the winter months."

"I see," said Tanya. "So that was your proposal or thesis, then?"

"Well, yes, I guess you could look at it that way," I agreed.

Tanya continued, "So now I would ask you, why? Why should your sister wait until the winter to visit San Diego? Under the Toulmin model, this would be considered your warrant."

"Well, why? I guess because airfare is typically cheaper in the off-season, lines to do things are shorter, like at Sea World or the zoo, for example," I said.

"OK, this is the exact type of conversation you could have with your students before they begin to write."

"I see," I said. After speaking a little more with Tanya, I realized that if I didn't start changing the way I taught writing, I would show signs of becoming a disengaged teacher, perhaps like Joe—not talking to the kids about their topics and sending all writing assignments home. I also realized that I cared too much about my young writers not to give them a fair crack at doing their best. How could I expect them, after all, to do their best if I never showed them how?

I thought it might be a good idea to read about and introduce Toulmin after my classes read the first core novel of the year, *The Outsiders* (Hinton, 1967). Instead of assigning out-of-class writing, I wanted to work with them in class to model what it means to write well about content.

After finishing *The Outsiders*, the class and I typically have a conversation about the different characteristics and challenges of social classes. Before students arrive, I write a word or phrase on index cards and tape them underneath their chairs. The students are asked to write a response in their journals to the words or phrases. Examples of words or phrases on the cards include *might drop out of high school, takes SAT prep classes, often makes dinner and does laundry while Mom is working*. After about 7 minutes, I designate three areas of the room to represent different socioeconomic groups. I then invite students to migrate to the space that matches their words or phrases. Students create group posters representing the challenges and characteristics of different socioeconomic groups. We congregate as a whole class once again and discuss how life circumstances affect personal development of individuals in different socioeconomic groups. Finally, I ask, "Is it possible for an individual to improve him- or herself despite life's circumstances? If so, how might individuals in our society do so?"

We then turn back to the novel and our main character Ponyboy. As a class, we create a graphic organizer (Figure 10.1) for Ponyboy that describes important character attributes. We use this as we work through the writing process.

Once we have completed the graphic organizer, we pose the question together: "Will Ponyboy always remain a Greaser? Why or why not?"

Character's Background	Personality
Grew up on the west side.	*Ponyboy seems serious in some ways for only 14.*
His parents are dead. He lives with his two older brothers.	*He is a deep thinker.*
Likes to read and run track.	*He is naive to think that the Greasers are the only people with problems.*
Smart—skipped a grade in school.	
Studies—gets A's and B's.	*He changes through the book and has an open mind about the Socials.*
Relationships	**Appearance**
His older brother Darry works two jobs, so the boys can stay together.	*Ponyboy has pride in his long hair.*
	The way he wears his hair shows he is a Greaser.
Ponyboy and his older brother Darry fight a lot.	*He doesn't wear madras—but T-shirts and jeans.*
Ponyboy feels bad that Darry gave up his football scholarship.	*His look is both tough and tuff.*
Darry gets mad at Ponyboy for not not using his head.	

FIGURE 10.1. Character map for Ponyboy.

Students formulate answers in their journals, then we discuss this in more detail as a class. Asking students to write in their journals before beginning a discussion encourages them to do some thinking before talking. Also, more students feel comfortable engaging in class discussion if they have taken a few minutes to gather their thoughts.

Thanks to my conversation with Tanya and subsequent investigation of Toumlin's model, I can now proceed with teaching argumentation. We first listen to student responses, then I begin to introduce the language of argumentation. As Gleason (1999) recommended, the vocabulary of argumentation must be put into terms that students are likely to understand. Thus, I provide students with a framework and provide a query that they must answer with a proposal:

> "Will Ponyboy always remain a Greaser? So, what do you think or propose? [The answer to this question will be the claim or opinion.] Why do you think this? [The answer to this question will be reasons or data.] How do you know the reasons support your thoughts? [These are the warrants—backing or support.] Are there any limitations or clarifications?"

To guide students along in the process, scaffolding must be included during explicit instruction. I have found that an argumentation map such as the one in Figure 10.2 works well with the explicit instruction of teaching argumentation; the argumentation map parallels Toulmin's model in terms familiar to students.

With a projector, I display the argumentation map and type students' responses as we discuss their arguments. I also save our class

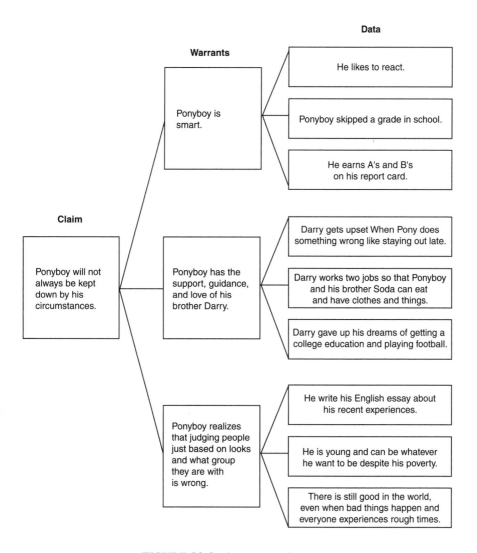

FIGURE 10.2. Argumentation map.

argumentation maps at various stages and print copies that students paste into their literature notebooks for reference when working independently. Of course, if students have their own computers, then they can type and save responses as we go along.

As a class, we fill in the claim or thesis (proposal) together. Ponyboy will not always remain a Greaser. I invite the class now to look back at the graphic organizer and find three main reasons why they think Ponyboy will move out of his Greaser social status. A student, Brittany, offers reason number one.

"Ponyboy is smart."

"OK, then Brittany, how do you know that Ponyboy is smart?" I ask, encouraging Brittany to support her thinking with reasons.

"I know Ponyboy likes to read, skipped a grade in school, and gets A's and B's on his report card."

"Very good. OK class, we need to pull from our graphic organizer [Figure 10.1] another reason that supports why we think Ponyboy will continue to rise above his circumstances." Alex raises his hand. "OK, Alex, what can you say?"

"Uh, well, another reason why Pony could get out of his social class is because of his big brother Darry."

"What about Darry?" I prompt.

Alex replies, "Even though Ponyboy's parents are dead, his older brother Darry loves him and helps him out."

"Oh, so Ponyboy has the support and maybe guidance of his older brother, Darry," I clarify. I encourage others to join in the dialogue here. "From our graphic organizer or other thoughts you may have, how do you know that Darry cares about Pony?"

"Well," Arif volunteers, "Darry gets all upset at Ponyboy when he comes home late and doesn't use his head."

"Yes," I say.

Arif continues, "That shows that Darry loves him—because if he didn't he wouldn't get all upset."

"OK, how else might we know that Darry loves, guides, and supports Ponyboy?"

Anika volunteers another example. "Well, Darry works two jobs so Pony can eat, and maybe they can all save money and move or something."

"OK, Anika, how else do we know that Darry acts as a good parent to Ponyboy?"

"Umm," stammers Jacob, "well, he did give up a football scholarship to stay home and take care of Pony and the other brother, Sodapop."

"Good, Jacob. So, let me see if I understand. You are saying that

Darry must love and support Pony because he gave up something that he, himself, really wanted?"

"Yeah," clarifies Jacob.

The discussion continues. "Class, now we have three examples that show how we know Darry supports Pony. Let's move on to the third and final block on our argumentation map. We need to come up with a third reason why we think that Pony can rise above his circumstances. To review here, we have listed two reasons supporting our proposal. What is our proposal, class?"

At this point, the class recognizes the invitation to chorally state: "*Ponyboy will be who he wants to be.*"

"OK, so now what is our third reason for thinking this?" We continue on with the third reason and examples.

On another day, we repeat the process, this time considering the other point of view or counterargument: Ponyboy will remain a Greaser and not rise above his circumstances. Anyone who works with middle school students knows that little cajoling is needed to summon a viewpoint that opposes that of another classmate. When I model development of counterarguments, I can always count on someone to raise a hand and offer a starting point—a voice that so often is lacking in students' writing. I think the trick is to model how students must consider (and include in their writing) this opposing point of view might answer the proposed questions, without getting caught up in the battle of who is right and who is wrong.

After we complete two argumentation maps, I pair students and instruct them to create the argumentation maps on their own. I divide the class in two and invite one side to produce the counterargument to the proposal. For example, the opening question this time might be as follows: "Do you agree or disagree with Pony when he says, 'Things are tough all over'?"

Keep in mind all of the modeling and conversation that has taken place, and still I have not assigned a formal essay to students—yet. We are spending about 1 week thinking about content through lots of conversation, modeling as a potential scaffold, and grouping learners in simulations for more discussion. Notice how I have not geared students' writing toward assessing whether they have read the book, and I have not assigned essays designed around questions that everyone, having read the book, would answer the same way. For example, I am not asking students to write about what happens to Ponyboy on the way home from the movies, or what vision Ponyboy has as he wakes up in the church. This results in essays that make teachers want to poke their eyes out with sticks. You get what you ask for in terms of student writing.

Research on Using Templates for Writing

One reason we advocate writing as a means of learning is that, in construction of a useful argument, students are doing more than demonstrating that they've already read through the textbook. Rather, students arguing a position must return to the texts, notes, and summarizations while making new connections and reexamining the terrain over which they've roamed. In argumentation, adolescent writers are presented with an opportunity to construct understanding, if the classroom structures permit it. Some classroom structures that promote or constrain learning through writing include grading or evaluation, purposes for writing, and skills in writing. Argumentation is a window on thinking that is as effective in exploring literature as it is in science or math. In the previous section we explored how argumentation might be taught and employed in the service of learning. Now we turn our attention to the fine points of writing one's ideas while working in a world where others' ideas are the context for creating our own understanding. In constructing a written argument, teachers can show students the moves that a writer makes to put his or her ideas within the context of what others have said about the topic. For this framework, we have drawn heavily on the work of Graff and Birkenstein (2006). Table 10.1 illustrates the moves that a writer might make to weave his or her thoughts with those of others. These moves, if taught explicitly, help students learn to identify what they bring to the discourse, what contributions may be made by others, and how they may respond to the contributions of others.

The Teacher's Voice: Helping Adolescents Use a Template for Argumentation

Once we have completed argumentation maps based on classroom discussion, in-class reading, and writing, how do we then teach students to

TABLE 10.1. Moves or Navigation

Recognize the contribution of others.
  Summarize the point of others.
  Quote others.

Respond to the contribution of others.
  Show how your point of view is different than that of others.
  Anticipate objections.
  Indicate why the topic matters.

draft actual writing from our collaborative learning? The opportunity arises to show students how to navigate the waters between their own ideas and those of others.

Let's refer back to the completed argumentation maps I (Kelsey) created with my students (Figure 10.2). Looking at our thesis—"Ponyboy will be who he wants to be"—and drawing upon our many discussions leading up to the essay and reading from the critiques of Hinton's (1967) work, I show a template that may be used successfully to introduce the debate, such as the following one developed by Graff and Birkenstein (2006, p. 164):

In discussion of _____, one controversial issue has been _____. On the one hand, _____ argues _____. On the other hand, _____ contends _____. My own view is _____.

I encourage the class to volunteer responses for the template. We eventually form the beginning of an essay, which might look something like this: "In discussion of the book *The Outsiders*, one controversial issue has been: Will Ponyboy always remain a Greaser? On one hand, some readers argue that he will not be able to rise above his circumstances; on the other hand, some readers contend that Ponyboy will improve his social status and not be limited by the hard times he has faced."

After we complete the template for stating our goal or thesis, students usually are successful in taking the reasons from our argumentation map and including them in the essay. For example, one student writes, "The first reason that I think Pony will not always be a Greaser is because he is a smart boy." Students often run into trouble when incorporating facts and examples into their essays. I usually try to have them find dialogue or commentary from the actual text that supports our facts and examples, as written in the graphic organizers. Using the template, I show students various ways of introducing and explaining ideas other than their own. For example, once again referring to our argumentation map, under facts or examples, we read, "He [Ponyboy] earns A's and B's on his report card." I challenge students to review the text and show with dialogue or commentary how they know this is true. I may say, "Find the fact or example in the chapter between pages 15 and 16 that supports our reason: 'Ponyboy is smart.'"

Caesar raises his hand, "*On page 15 Ponyboy talks about how Darry insists on better grades*" (Hinton, 1967).

"Great, Caesar," I reply. "Now let's look at some ways we can incorporate into our essay our facts and examples to support one of our main reasons, 'Pony is smart,' in our thesis." I then provide another template (Graff & Birkenstein, 2006, pp. 66–67).

_____ himself exclaims, _____. In making
this comment, Pony indicates that _____.

As a class, we complete this template, which might look like this: "While Pony is arguing with his older brother Darry, Pony exclaims, 'If I brought home B's he wanted A's, and if I got A's he wanted to make sure they stayed A's" (Hinton, 1967, p. 15). In making this comment, Pony indicates that he makes good grades (such as A's and B's). We continue to practice navigating between students' ideas and those of Hinton with our three main reasons and supporting facts or examples, until we come to the crafting of our conclusion. I have found that if I don't explicitly teach writing conclusions using templates and common transition words, students tend to skip writing the conclusion all together. I stress to students the importance of restating the original thesis and the three main reasons that support the thesis.

Research on Feedback on Student Writing

When writing is viewed only as an evaluation of learning, teachers may assign written work only as homework. If, instead, writing is a means of learning, we think of it as a classroom activity. Schools in Los Angeles (Hernandez, Kaplan, & Schwartz, 2006) and Tempe, Arizona (Schmoker, 2007), make time for discussion, reading, and writing in class. It's only during class that students have time for sustained exploration of important, content-related topics and time to write well, with support from peers and teachers. Just as important, students who use time in class to write have the support of their teachers.

Feedback during Writing

Important scaffolding interactions between teacher and student must occur while the writing is in progress (during class). In education, we sometimes call such interactions *feedback*. Table 10.2 categorizes feedback along three dimensions: purposes, types, and qualities (Wolsey, 2008). In this chapter, we emphasize the idea that writers, whatever their age, do not intentionally trample conventions and ignore concepts. Student work should be treated as a sincere effort to communicate. To that end, the purposes, types, and qualities of feedback in Table 10.2 may help teachers frame responses to student writing. The framework suggests that teachers' comments should primarily be useful and compassionate.

TABLE 10.2. Feedback

Purposes	Types	Qualities
Feed back (How am I going?)	Affirmations (simple and complex)	Identified positive aspects of the work
Feed up (Where am I going?)	Clarifications	Explains rather than labels
Feed forward (where to next?)	Observations	Perceptive
	Corrections: content	Corrective
	Corrections: mechanics, usage, spelling	Compassionate
	Questions	Useful
	Exploratory	Timely
	Personal	Linked to specific criteria
		Expands, clarifies, elaborates

Note. Data from Wolsey (2008).

Once teachers devote time for writing in class, feedback becomes a regular and meaningful feature in the lives of young writers. Effective feedback takes three forms (Hattie & Timperley, 2007) that are expressed as questions:

1. Feed up helps the student answer the question "Where am I going in relation to the goal for this task?"
2. Feed back (the space is intentional) helps the student answer the question "How am I going?"
3. Feed forward helps the students answer the question "What next?"

Although peer groups can provide important information about another student's writing, in this chapter, we focus on the interactions between teacher and student. If the objectives are aligned with the assessment criteria, scaffolding student writing is easier, because teacher and students have a clear idea of what the writing will look like when it is finished. Much of the feedback, then, revolves around these criteria. However, thinking about the purpose of the feedback can help students to make better use of the information: "What is next?"

The Teacher's Voice: Feedback during Writing

At the beginning of my career, I (Kelsey) offered little feedback to my writers and failed to set clear student expectations in terms of a published piece. I am afraid that expectations, rubrics, anchor papers, and evaluations remained unknown to those students. Through experience I learned that important scaffolding interactions between teacher and student must occur while the writing is in progress (during class). What I learned after a few years of teaching is that it is never too early to give students feedback on their writing. This, of course, is accomplished by holding many teacher–student writing conferences.

When I first began offering feedback to adolescent writers, I waited until students had more or less completed a first rough draft. In those days, much of my *feedback* merely comprised making mechanical corrections and revising student sentences.

Using Prompts and Rubrics for Writing Assignments

Two important tools for teachers and their students are prompts and rubrics. A *prompt* is little more than a direction for writing, but thoughtful prompts do more than tell students, "Please write an essay comparing democracy with another form of government. Due Tuesday." *Rubrics* identify important characteristics of the writing to be done and gradations of quality against which a student or teacher can measure progress. Teachers can attend to four features of prompts, as arranged in Table 10.3, when designing writing tasks for students (Hillocks, 2002).

Prompts may include many variations on these four features, but what students are given to consider often determines how well they can write about a topic or in a given discourse type (e.g., letter, essay, story, newspaper article). What the prompt asks students to do guides what they will write. For example, consider this prompt:

> In an essay (**discourse type**), consider the ramifications of General Lee's decision to have General Pickett lead a massive charge against the center of the Union lines on Cemetery Ridge at Gettysburg (**topic or subject**). Use information from the textbook, the Official Records of the War of the Rebellion (*www.civilwarhome.com/records.htm*), and the PBS website (*www. pbs.org/civilwar/war/map14.html*), in addition to any other reliable sources (**data, specified**). Your essay will explain for your teacher and classmates

---

TABLE 10.3 Features of Prompts

- Discourse type or structure
- Topic and/or subject matter
- Data (specified, not specified, provided)
- Audience (mentioned, general, specific)

(**audience, general**) how Pickett's charge was a turning point in the battle at Gettysburg and subsequently in the Civil War itself.

The prompt might also specify length; we agree with Benjamin (1999) that giving page or word length requirements can often undermine our goals. Word length requirements tend to encourage young writers to add unnecessary wording to their work, and page length requirements just encourage students to use large fonts or wide margins. Instead, a specified number of paragraphs (minimum) is more likely to result in good writing. Of course, your students will need to know what a well-developed paragraph looks like. Later, teachers might ask students to rely on their experience of past writing assignments to decide for themselves how many paragraphs might make up a writing task.

Rubrics are often presented as matrices with gradations of qualities. If students are to succeed with writing tasks, our guidance as teachers should be clear and aligned. By this, we mean that the objective and standards for the lesson directly inform the type of writing task assigned in the prompt, and that task is reflected in the rubric. In secondary schools, generic rubrics that don't reflect the specific objective of the lesson or the writing task may result in generic results. A rubric that only refers to "well-developed content," or "marginally developed content" is unlikely to be much of a guide for students as to what is expected. Grisham and Wolsey (2005) found that students, preservice teachers, and teachers in a graduate program had similar ideas of the general criteria that describe good writing; therefore, attention to content learning targets may be helpful. Your students will be able to help you develop prompts and rubrics, and learn more about the content and writing as a result.

The Teacher's Voice: Assessing Writing

As a middle school student, I (Kelsey) vividly remember watching my English teacher madly scribbling comments with her favorite green pen across our essays. "Oh," I thought, "What would it be like to be in charge of that green pen!" I lived for the day. Well, that day arrived as my first-year students completed their very first essay. But finally taking charge of the green pen proved not to be so glamorous. Often, throughout my career, I have fantasized about returning as a seasoned teacher to my very first class of writers. I would do so many things differently, especially in the area of assessment.

First, I believe that writers deserve to know up front how and what pieces will be assessed. For example, will rough drafts be assessed, along with the final copy? What are the criteria for each? What will the teacher look for in terms of new skills and knowledge?

Second, it is never too early to start assessing. Sometimes, teachers make the mistake of waiting until the essay is about to be published or submitted to find evidence of learning. I have found that the process of assessing as a student moves along in a piece proves much more valuable in helping the writer to grow. Let me put it this way: If you do not practically have the student's piece memorized by the time the final copy is due, then not enough assessing has occurred along the way.

A system that really keeps the writers and the teacher on track is the process of turning in new or revised writing frequently. I use the voice and text annotation features of word processors, like Microsoft Word (e.g., Jago, 2005; Wolsey & Bostick, 2008), to provide comments to students, if they submit electronic files. Frequent assessment really helps writers to stay focused and prevents them from repeating the same errors throughout a piece.

Third, probably the most challenging task as a writing teacher is to learn the skill of assessing a writer's piece through an objective lens. Although we may not like to admit this as writing teachers, assessing another person's writing will always be somewhat subjective, based on the biases and preconceptions of the evaluator. I liken it to people reading the same book and disagreeing over strengths and weaknesses of an author. Making sure that you have established criteria through the use of prompts and rubrics can make the assessment process more objective. Finally, as a beginning teacher, it is so important to remember that the infamous green, purple, or even red pen should work toward helping students grow as writers, not just criticizing their work.

Concluding Thoughts

Good writing, like good ideas, is the result of consideration, deep thought, and patience. Author Ray Bradbury wrote of his naive belief, early in his career, that one "could beat, pummel, and thrash an idea into existence. Under such treatment, of course, any decent idea folds up its paws, turns on its back, fixes its eyes on eternity, and dies" (1957, p. vii). Our students are not yet expert writers, but they need not try to thrash an idea into existence either. Instead, through considered thought, ample resources, and time to think through an argument, teachers can guide students toward becoming effective writers and efficient thinkers about content.

Questions for Reflection

1. Think about a unit of study that you have either planned or observed. What complex aspects of the unit might students grasp more readily if they write as part of the unit's instructional tasks?

2. With your chosen unit of study, create a prompt that includes elements discussed in this chapter. How would you guide students to learn about the topic through writing?

3. In this chapter, the teacher uses class discussions and students refer to the novel to provide evidence to support their claims. What instructional ideas and resources might you include in your chosen unit of study to encourage learners to apply the principles of argumentation?

References

Applebee, A. N. (1984). *Contexts for learning to write: Studies of secondary school instruction.* Urbana, IL: National Council of Teachers of English.

Atwell, N. (1987). *In the middle: Writing, reading and learning with adolescents.* Portsmouth, NH: Heinemann, Boynton/Cook.

Benjamin, A. (1999). *Writing in the content areas.* Larchmont, NY: Eye on Education.

Bradbury, R. (1957). *Dandelion wine.* New York: Bantam Books.

Day, A. G. (1947). Writer's magic. *AAUP Bulletin, 33,* 269–278.

Elbow, P. (1973). *Writing without teachers.* New York: Oxford University Press.

Emig, J. (1971). *The composing processes of twelfth graders.* Urbana, IL: National Council of Teachers of English.

Fearn, L., & Farnan, N. (2007). The influence of professional development on young writers' writing performance. *Action in Teacher Education, 29*(2), 17–28.

Gleason, M. (1999). The role of evidence in argumentative writing. *Reading and Writing Quarterly, 14,* 81–106.

Graff, G., & Birkenstein, C. (2006). *They say, I say: The moves that matter in academic writing.* New York: Norton.

Grisham, D. L., & Wolsey, T. D. (2005). Improving writing: Comparing the responses of eighth graders, preservice teachers and experienced teachers. *Reading and Writing Quarterly 21*(4), 315–330.

Hattie, J., & Timperley, H. (2007). The power of feedback. *Review of Educational Research, 77*(1), 81–112.

Hernandez, A., Kaplan, M. A., & Schwartz, R. (2006). For the sake of argument. *Educational Leadership, 64*(2), 48–52.

Hillocks, G. (2002). *The testing trap: How state writing assessments control learning.* New York: Teachers College Press.

Hinton, S. E. (1967). *The outsiders.* New York: Dell.

Kintsch, E. (1990). Macroprocesses and microprocesses in the development of summarization skill. *Cognition and Instruction, 7,* 161–195.

Jago, C. (2005). *Papers, papers, papers: An English teacher's survival guide.* Portsmouth, NH: Heinemann.

Langer, J. A., & Applebee, A. N. (1987). *How writing shapes thinking: A study of teaching and learning.* Urbana, IL: National Council of Teachers of English.

Moss, B. (2004). Teaching expository text structures through information trade book retellings. *Reading Teacher, 57,* 710–718.

Nagin, C., & the National Writing Project. (2003). *Because writing matters: Improving student writing in our schools.* San Francisco: Jossey-Bass.

Newell, G. E. (2006). Writing to learn: How alternative theories of school writing account for student performance. In C. A. MacArthur, S. Graham, & J. Fitzgerald (Eds.), *Handbook of writing research* (pp. 235–237). New York: Guilford Press.

Rinehart, S. D., Stahl, S. A., & Erickson, L. G. (1986). Some effects of summarization training on reading and studying. *Reading Research Quarterly, 21,* 422–438.

Rose, D., & Meyer, A. (2002). *Teaching every student in the digital age: Universal design for learning.* Alexandria, VA: Association for Supervision and Curriculum Development. Retrieved on July 25, 2008, from *www.cast.org/teachingeverystudent/ideas/tes/index.cfm.*

Schmoker, M. (2007). Reading, writing, and thinking for all. *Educational Leadership, 64*(7), 63–66.

Toulmin, S. (2003). *The uses of argument, updated edition.* New York: Cambridge University Press.

Wolsey, T. D. (2008). Efficacy of instructor feedback in an online graduate program. *International Journal on e-Learning, 7*(2), 311–329.

Wolsey, T. D., & Bostick, P. (2008). The C in ICT: Communication at the heart of literacy learning. *California Reader, 41*(2), 33–39.

Zull, J. (2002). *The art of changing the brain: Enriching the practice of teaching by exploring the biology of learning.* Sterling, VA: Stylus.

CHAPTER 11

How Can Content-Area Teachers Differentiate Instruction for Their Students to Improve Student Learning?

DEANNA BIRDYSHAW
LISA HOFFMAN

CLASSROOM PORTRAIT

Every time I try to do the reading the right way, it takes too much time. So I just ... I just read it. I don't understand it, but I have to read it.

—DANIEL, ninth grade

I don't have time to question and comment and go back ... I have to finish the sheet and even that is sometimes too much.

—JENNY, ninth grade

Both Jenny's and Daniel's frustrations with their content-area reading assignments reflect those of the majority of their classmates. Often overwhelmed by the large amount of reading assigned in their high school content-area classes, as well as the textual demands of those assignments, Jenny, Daniel, and their classmates find themselves reading a given section of text solely to find answers to the questions provided at the end of the chapter or by their instructors. This, according to them, is the only "way to get it all done."

Reading for answers to assigned questions worked well for Jenny and Daniel during the first couple of weeks of their ninth-grade school year. It helped them fulfill their beginning-of-the-school-year resolution to complete all of their homework assignments. However, as their content-area classes continued, Jenny and Daniel noticed that the assignments became more complex and took more and more time to complete. The worksheets contained references to prior topics and questions asking them to connect data across units, and often had much larger vocabulary demands; because they struggled with reading the texts, Jenny and Daniel started losing points on these assignments and informal assessments of their learning.

Unfortunately, just as Jenny and Daniel began to lose ground and fall behind their classmates in their content-area coursework, summative assessments in these classes began. In Daniel's social studies class, the tests featured dense, text-laden, multiple-choice sections that pushed him not only to process information from the assignments he had completed earlier but also to analyze the text within the questions themselves, and to synthesize both before attempting to select an answer. Jenny's biology teacher often asked her to write short answers to demonstrate understanding of given concepts in real-world situations, which required a much deeper understanding of concepts than Jenny had acquired from her *reading*.

Although they were beginning to slip behind, Jenny and Daniel got much higher grades on their homework than on their class tests. The disparity frustrated them and caused their teachers concern about Jenny's and Daniel's abilities to succeed in their courses. Jenny and Daniel, however, had entered their freshman year of high school wanting to get all A's and B's on their report card, trusting that if they worked hard, then they would succeed. When their test scores remained low, Jenny and Daniel began to question themselves as learners, blaming their poor test scores on "being dumb" or "not studying enough." As the term progressed and their scores continued to decline, Jenny and Daniel began to miss school, exhibiting a not uncommon pattern of avoidance in the behavior of struggling readers.

Though their teachers clearly observed both Jenny's and Daniel's decline in enthusiasm and drive, large class sizes and curriculum demands prevented them from spending large amounts of time to provide extra assistance to these two students. In essence, Jenny and Daniel began to "fall through the cracks" in their content-area classes. So did many of their classmates.

Although Jenny's and Daniel's experiences are all too common in American high schools, their story, unlike those of other struggling students across our nation, has a happy ending. In this chapter, we describe how a secondary English teacher, with an extensive literacy background, and content-area teachers worked together to create a learning environment in which Jenny and Daniel received differentiated instruction that facilitated their development of metacognitive awareness, helped them take charge of their learning, and enabled them to succeed in understanding the essential content of their coursework.

The first part of this chapter provides an overview of obstacles to differentiating instruction in secondary schools and a description of a literacy course developed to support struggling readers as they enter high school. The second part of the chapter, told by a secondary English teacher, describes how she, a social studies teacher, and a science teacher took on the challenge of using assessment results to differentiate instruction for Jenny and Daniel. The chapter concludes with a discussion of what we have learned about differentiating instruction for struggling learners in secondary classrooms.

The authors of this chapter enjoy a collaborative relationship that focuses on integrating research and practice. Deanna Birdyshaw teaches reading and writing in the content areas at the University of Michigan and conducts research in areas related to differentiating instruction and learning from records of practice. Lisa Hoffman, an English teacher in a suburban high school, takes on an informal coaching role with colleagues who are interested in addressing the needs of struggling readers in their content-area classrooms. Although she is a trained, professional literacy coach, Lisa does not work as a formal coach in the district, because the role does not yet exist officially at the secondary level.

The Case for Differentiated Instruction in High School Classrooms

Tomlinson and Eidson (2003) define *differentiation of instruction* as "a systematic approach to planning curriculum and instruction for academically diverse learners" (p. 3). The purpose of differentiated literacy instruction is to provide instruction that is aligned with the learning needs of individual students to maximize the potential for learning success. Although differentiated instruction has been a recommended practice for elementary learners for a long time, the need for differentiated literacy instruction at the secondary level has for the most part not been addressed, even though literacy data point to increased diversity in the literacy achievement of secondary learners. Biancarosa and Snow (2004) report that approximately 70% of older readers require some degree of literacy support, especially in the area of reading comprehension. The problem lies in secondary teachers' perception that it is not their responsibility to teach literacy. They believe that their focus should be on teaching their content curriculum (O'Brien, Moje, & Stewart, 2000).

The importance of differentiating instruction is well accepted in elementary classrooms, in which the curriculum is designed to reflect the reality that students enter a classroom reading at various levels and require individualized instruction that addresses their developmental needs. Many elementary teachers assume that they will need to use small-group instruction to provide the type of targeted teaching needed to help students develop skills and deepen their understanding of content knowledge. This view finds support in several recent studies, including one by Taylor, Pearson, Clark, and Walpole (2000), who discuss the importance of establishing learning objectives that are aligned with the learning needs and profiles of members of small groups. An essential aspect of targeted small-group or individualized instruction is assessment-driven decision making; teachers need sufficient information about their students to make informed decisions about what type of instruction and level of complexity is most appropriate for particular students, or groups of students (Connor, Morrison, & Katch, 2004; Connor, Morrison, & Petrella, 2004; Wharton-McDonald, Pressley, & Hampston, 1998).

Although the body of research regarding the effectiveness of differentiated instruction in elementary classrooms is growing, there is very little research on its effect in secondary classrooms. The books of Tomlinson (1999) are often cited by secondary teachers who are interested in differentiated instruction, because she offers practical suggestions for matching instruction to the needs and interests of students in content-area classes. Although teachers find these professional development books very useful, they do not provide the needed research base or theoretical foundation to support differentiation in the secondary classroom.

The theoretical foundation for differentiating instruction is related to the research on responsiveness, or the practice of providing instructional assistance to learners at levels just above that at which learners might be expected to accomplish a learning task independently (Vygotsky, 1962). As MacGillivray and Rueda (2003) point out, "Instruction that ignores what students already know or can do, or that is too difficult, does not represent effective pedagogy" (p. 1). Translated into the world of adolescents, this means that one-size-fits-all instruction cannot be effective for all students. Differentiating instruction, therefore, requires that teachers in middle and secondary classrooms attend to the developmental nature of the skills and conceptual knowledge included in their disciplinary curricula and provide scaffolded instruction that anchors learning in their students' zones of proximal development (Vygotsky, 1962). Although this sounds reasonable, it is not a common practice among secondary school content-area teachers.

Guided Academics: A Reading Support Class for Struggling Ninth Graders

As a high school English and biology teacher in a Midwestern suburban city, Lisa Hoffman has observed many of her students struggling with texts in their content-area classes. She also has spent a large amount of time working with colleagues, primarily through informal conversations, but also through more structured literacy coaching–type sessions. During these sessions, Lisa and her colleagues discuss the textual demands placed on students and work together to best tailor their instruction to improve the literacy practices of their students, while still achieving their content standards. These conversations take place in Lisa's and her colleagues' spare time. To further facilitate students' learning directly, Lisa, along with her district colleagues, now teaches a reading support class aimed at giving struggling high school students the experiences with texts and the comprehension tools that should make them more successful readers; the class is titled Guided Academics.

Guided Academics was designed by the district to develop the reading skills of incoming high school freshmen in response to district data identifying disparities between adolescents' reading abilities and their actual grade levels. This Midwestern school district recently switched to a 12-week trimester schedule, allowing freshmen and selected sophomores to take Guided Academics in the fall, before taking the majority of their core classes. Most students who enrolled in the course take one content-area course (either science or social studies) concurrently with dual enrollment in Guided Academics and a math class. Their schedules also include two additional classes, typically electives.

To be placed in the Guided Academics class, students needed to meet a number of criteria. Most students were placed in the class based on the recommendations of their middle school teachers and their scores on the Qualitative Reading Inventory (QRI) assessment (Leslie & Schudt Caldwell, 2006). The majority of the pool from which the students were selected did not include those certified for special education services; these students received support from special education teachers. For the most part, students who enrolled in Guided Academics had basic reading skills but performed far enough below their classmates' level on reading tasks and assessments that their teachers thought extra literacy support and instruction would make the students more successful in their content-area classes. Students who were recommended for Guided Academics often were reported by their teachers to be struggling more with expository and content-area reading tasks than with narrative texts. The overarching goal of Guided Academics was to improve the critical reading abilities of students, thus improving their text comprehension and promoting their success in content-area subjects.

In Guided Academics, the curriculum focused primarily on strategy and skills development, especially text structure analysis and critical reading activities that improved students' abilities to read critically content-area texts of all types: narratives, poems, speeches, letters, telegrams, photographs, graphs and charts, expository texts, textbooks, and so forth. Over the course of the first few weeks of the term, students were immersed in reading strategy instruction and analysis of the behaviors of successful readers. The strategies were modeled for them by the instructor, and students were given ample time to work with the strategies on a wide variety of texts, both at their reading level and at a more complex level, such as the ones exhibited by their content-area texts. Later in the course, students worked with language and began to define what made texts and language hard for them individually. They also analyzed text structures of narrative and informational texts, and work with Web-based texts as well. Students participated in a number of writing activities that allowed them to develop their skills in creating supported and well-developed responses to various content-area activities, and that also allowed their instructor to have informal assessments that demonstrated the students' knowledge of the concepts studied and depth of thinking. In some Guided Academics classrooms, students had opportunities independently to read narrative texts that were grade-level appropriate and reflected their interests, such as this term's selection of Ishmael Beah's *A Long Way Gone: Memoirs of a Boy Soldier* (2007). Students not only were given an environment in which reading was supported but they were also asked to discuss the texts with their peers and to present monthly book talks. In many Guided Academic classrooms, ways to share texts became part of the classroom culture, along with read-aloud time, in which the instructor read a text aloud in class and used the reading strategies discussed in class to deepen discussions and understanding.

The extensive amount of one-on-one, personalized instruction provided in Guided Academics made it a very unique experience for students. The course was capped at approximately 20 students, allowing the teacher to get to know students on a far more personal level than in most content-area classes, where enrollment can exceed 30 students. This smaller class size also allowed the instructor to conduct numerous formal and informal assessments on a daily basis and to use the assessment data to design differentiated instructional activities. The students also had numerous opportunities to work in cooperative groups on reading activities and were able to facilitate each other's learning based on their own strengths and weaknesses.

From an affective perspective, the class emphasized self-advocacy in learning. Students assessed themselves as learners and readers, they discussed their goals and the influences that often get in the way of achieving these ambitions, and they were given a place where personal reflection is not only mandatory but also critical to their success. The course created a network of support for the students through increased parent and content-area teacher contact. This network allowed for open and constant communication.

A closer look at Daniel and Jenny in their Guided Academic's and content-area classes provides an opportunity to better understand some of the challenges and possibilities for differentiating instruction for struggling adolescent readers. In the following sections, Lisa describes Daniel's and Jenny's performance in her Guided Academic class, and how she collaborated with their content-area teachers to support their learning.

Differentiating for Daniel:
A Fast Reader Who Does Not Always Win the Race

An Asian American freshman, Daniel came to my Guided Academics class as a self-proclaimed "fast reader." Although his performance on the QRI indicated that he read at an eighth-grade level, he tested at between a sixth- and seventh-grade level on the Gates–MacGinite Reading Assessment. The discrepancy in grade levels is due in part to the nature of the assessments. The QRI, which is administered orally to individual students, measures their performance in reading and comprehending increasingly more difficult text, until they reach their frustration level. The Gates–MacGinite, a quantitative standardized assessment tool, is given to groups of students; it provides grade levels for students based on previously established norms. The discrepancy in Daniel's grade-level scores may also result from his desire to read fast; he finished the Gates–MacGinite well ahead of his classmates and may not have concentrated sufficiently to answer items correctly.

Daniel professed to me on the first day of school that he "loved to read" and proceeded over the course of the term eagerly to sign out texts available to the students in class for outside reading. Titles he selected included *Anansi Boys* by Neil Gaiman, *The House of the Scorpion* by Nancy Farmer, and *Rumble Fish* by S. E. Hinton. Daniel chose to read texts of high interest to him but not demanding. On Fridays during book talk, Daniel often wanted to share his reading experiences with the class; he did twice the number of book talks over the course of the term than the other students. He demonstrated no problems with comprehending the plot of the texts but often struggled with offering an in-depth opinion regarding his analysis of the piece. David enjoyed books that "moved really fast" and "had a lot of action," but he could not comment on his feelings toward characters or understanding of thematic elements. He said that he just "read to read," not to think about his interpretation of the author's message or his response to characters' actions as he went through the narratives. When pushed to think more deeply about these things, Daniel would bury his head in his hands and say, "I don't know, I ... I read really fast. It was just a ... good book."

When working with informational texts, Daniel often skipped information in articles or textbook passages to finish first and to appear to be the best reader to his classmates. When he completed a reading, Daniel would proudly announce that he was done, then struggle with assignments, because he would fail to comprehend the text effectively. It quickly became clear to me that Daniel, like many of his classmates, liked to reinforce what he did well or felt that he could control, but he avoided reading behaviors that challenged him. He used his speed in reading novels to boost his self-image as a reader and receive recognition from his classmates. He tried to hide his weaknesses and avoided experiences that required him to read challenging text or take a visible role in talking about the meaning of text.

My focus for Daniel included talking to him about the importance of being an active reader. Differentiating instruction for Daniel involved modeling active reading behaviors that required him to pause as he read to reflect on the content, make predictions, access prior knowledge, draw conclusions, and make connections within and across texts. His resistance was obvious, but as Daniel became more successful in completing assignments that required critical thinking and complex understandings, he began voluntarily to employ strategies that helped him slow down and focus on the meaning of text.

DIFFERENTIATING FOR DANIEL IN AN ACADEMIC CLASS

In his content-area classes, Daniel's poor reading and thinking habits did not exhibit themselves as clearly as they did in Guided Academics. Daniel was one of 30 students in his social studies classroom. Because of Daniel's positive attitude, his social studies teacher, Mr. Cramer, initially thought that Daniel had a good grasp on the class content. Daniel participated frequently and paid close attention when taking notes. During lectures, he had no problem asking for things to be repeated or reworded. Because of his participation and relative success on class assignments that focused on factual information that was easily found in lecture notes or in short readings designed to reinforce information provided in lectures, Mr. Cramer was relatively unaware of Daniel's reading difficulties. It was not until assignments began to involve longer readings as the conveyors of content information, as opposed to lectures, that Mr. Cramer noticed Daniel struggling. Then Daniel's test scores dropped, and he exhibited observable signs of frustration during in-class work time.

Daniel's self-confidence quickly eroded. Not only did he express aggravation to Mr. Cramer, but he also expressed his feelings of being "dumb" and "just stupid" when he and I talked during our regularly scheduled conferences in Guided Academics. As the term progressed, he showed physical signs of frustration: burying his head in his hands, removing his glasses, and frequently slamming his pencil on his desk.

Daniel needed coping mechanisms for overcoming his anxiety when faced with informational texts, as well as the patience to employ the tools that he knew would assist him in comprehending his reading-based assignments in academic subjects. To do this, Daniel and I worked extensively in Guided Academics on the use of chunking (Myers, 1984) and questioning strategies (Beck, McKeown, Hamilton, & Kucan, 1997; Raphael, 1986; Lewis & Reader, Chapter 5, this volume), while reading texts to allow Daniel the opportunity to slow down in his reading, reflect on the texts, and process the information presented. We began with narrative texts, which did not cause Daniel anxiety. He and I would "chunk" the text by breaking it up into smaller portions. Daniel would periodically record questions, comments, and thoughts regarding a particular portion of text on sticky notes or in a notebook. This was incredibly helpful; Daniel could now process the narrative texts that he previously read far too fast for deep comprehension. Once Daniel reflected on a given narrative text and discussed the entries on his sticky notes with his classmates and me, we would reflect on the process of "chunking" the text, and how it helped Daniel better understand the text. He often questioned why a given event occurred early in the story, and as we continued to use these strategies, he began to question why the authors made particular choices in their writing.

Once Daniel felt comfortable with the strategies and found relevance in their use, we began applying them to informational texts in Guided Academics: magazine and newspapers articles at first, then textbooks. I talked to Mr. Cramer about Daniel's need to use strategies that focused his attention on meaningful chunks of texts, and Mr. Cramer encouraged Daniel to use his chunking and questioning strategies in his class as well. In Mr. Cramer's class, Daniel found that he chunked much smaller portions of text, and that many of his questions focused on clarifying things he did not understand. In fact, many of his notes simply read "I really don't get this" or an emphatic "What?!" In the past, Daniel said that he skipped over passages that he did not understand, but over time, he began to use a variety of coping mechanisms to better understand the more challenging sections of text: rereading, analyzing pictures and graphics, breaking down the passage into even smaller parts, and asking for help.

The facilitation of Daniel's development as a reader and thinker was not something that could be done in Guided Academics class alone. Mr. Cramer offered to work with us in differentiating his instruction to meet Daniel's needs as a learner. Though he did not have the classroom time to get to know Daniel on the same level as I did, Mr. Cramer was more than open to developing a partnership that would unite the Guided Academics, literacy-focused curriculum, and his content-area instruction, thus helping Daniel perform better in class, and improve his reading and thinking skills.

Prior to our work together, Mr. Cramer had followed a standard pedagogical approach that was representative of the practice of other social studies teachers in his department. He would give his students a review sheet of bulleted terms before starting a new unit, then lecture for the majority of class time on new concepts. Students were expected to take notes as he lectured; the lecture was sometimes supported by a PowerPoint slide show. Oftentimes, the students would be assigned textbook reading after the lecture to review the new concepts. When students finished reading, Mr. Cramer would ask them to answer the questions at the end of the assigned section of text.

Surprisingly, in spite of these efforts to address students' reading needs and an awareness of the complexity of the discipline, Mr. Cramer's exams were incredibly text-dense; most questions were several sentences long and featured multiple-choice answers that also contained a large number of words and complicated syntax. Mr. Cramer understood the need to simplify his exams for some students. In fact, for students receiving special education accommodations, he created more thorough notes than provided by the review sheet of bulleted terms, and he modified his exams to feature fewer multiple-choice options and easier phrasing. Seemingly, he had not been able to differentiate for his general population due to the fast-paced nature of the class and the large number of students he taught on a daily basis.

After Mr. Cramer and I began to talk about Daniel, Mr. Cramer inquired about the reading abilities of other students in his classes and how he could better facilitate their understanding of text-based assignments. As a first step, Mr. Cramer and I developed a self-assessment for his general education students to fill out (Figure 11.1).

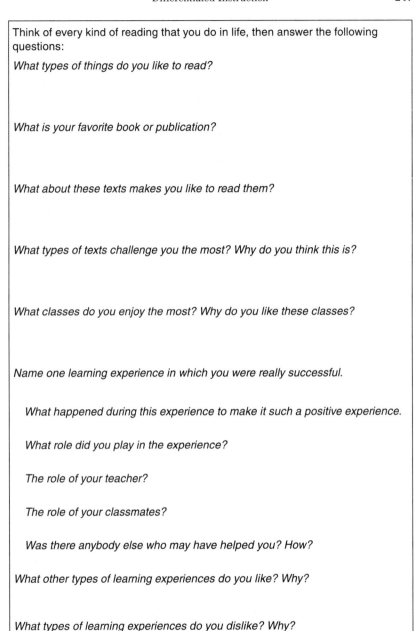

Think of every kind of reading that you do in life, then answer the following questions:

What types of things do you like to read?

What is your favorite book or publication?

What about these texts makes you like to read them?

What types of texts challenge you the most? Why do you think this is?

What classes do you enjoy the most? Why do you like these classes?

Name one learning experience in which you were really successful.

What happened during this experience to make it such a positive experience.

What role did you play in the experience?

The role of your teacher?

The role of your classmates?

Was there anybody else who may have helped you? How?

What other types of learning experiences do you like? Why?

What types of learning experiences do you dislike? Why?

FIGURE 11.1 Reading self-assessment: Fall 2007.

As can be seen, the assessment featured a variety of questions that asked the students to consider themselves as readers: what types of things they liked to read, what challenges they faced as readers, what classes they enjoyed, what types of learning experiences they considered to be the most positive and negative, and how they learned best. Following our review of Mr. Cramer's students' self-reporting of their reading behaviors, he and I analyzed their scores on the Gates–MacGinitie Reading Assessment (MacGinitie, MacGinitie, Maria, & Dreyer, 2000). The majority of his ninth-grade students scored between an eighth- and ninth-grade level. Though, initially, Mr. Cramer knew very little about the meaning of the reading scores or how to use the results to plan instruction, we worked together on a biweekly basis to analyze his current instructional practices and design strategies that he might use to differentiate instruction and accommodate the needs of other students like Daniel.

Mr. Cramer identified the need to make reading a more central practice in his classroom. By modeling how to read the textbook, as well as other, more complicated reading assignments, he thought that his students, especially students like Daniel, would develop an awareness of what a reader in the field does when approaching a social studies text. We discovered during conversations that Daniel thought taking notes, asking questions, and pausing while reading was something that only "bad readers" did. Because we were collaborating closely, Mr. Cramer and I were able to convince Daniel that these were the behaviors of good readers, especially good readers of social studies texts. Daniel's familiarity with the strategies allowed him to take a leadership role in Mr. Cramer's class; he could now demonstrate the active reading strategies that Mr. Cramer had begun to discuss with his students.

Though Mr. Cramer did not have time to model reading for the students more than once a week, he did make it a point to start the week with this practice, often previewing a section of text that the students were assigned to begin reading that night. In this way he modeled for students how to read the texts effectively and was also able to give a preliminary introduction to complex topics that would be presented in upcoming lectures. He would make sure to touch base with Daniel periodically during class, especially before the class ended, and ask Daniel to reflect on his learning that day and plan for his evening work. This personal connection helped Daniel to focus on the main learning objectives for each day's lesson and reduced the anxiety he often felt when faced with a reading-based assignment. It also motivated Daniel to plan for his reading and learning, and to attempt the homework. Therefore, Daniel was better prepared for the next day's class, and increased his learning success.

Throughout the week, in class and in homework assignments, Mr. Cramer also began to ask other struggling students to chunk texts and to record their comments, thoughts, and questions as they read. Their questions became the basis of class discussions the following day in class rather than their sole focus on answers to the questions at the end of the section of the textbook. Daniel benefited greatly from this pedagogical shift. He now had the opportunity to use the same strategies in his content-area class that he was learning to use in his Guided Academics class, and he used his social studies text to model active reading strategies in his Guided Academics class. Daniel said he began to see the purpose in slowing down when reading, texts became "easier to understand," and often he really enjoyed feeling like an expert on the topic covered in the text. Because of the extra time to engage with the texts in Guided Academics, Daniel often entered his social studies class with a complete understanding of the words on the page, as well as a deeper knowledge of the concepts presented.

As the concepts became more complicated and abstract in Daniel's social studies class, so, too, did the texts. Rather than return to primarily lecture-style instruction, Mr. Cramer wanted strategies through which the class could do more with texts and less with lecture. He noticed that as texts became more complicated, Daniel came in with more sticky notes, more questions, and more comments that needed to be addressed to fully comprehend the coursework. Mr. Cramer began to use some of the strategies he developed to differentiate instruction for Daniel with more of his students, and as a guide for how he might improve instructional planning. These included the sticky note–based questioning and monitoring, the various note-taking strategies that Mr. Cramer modeled, and the organizational impromptu conferences.

One such unit that illustrates the change taking place in Mr. Cramer's social studies class focused on the Civil Rights Movement. In the past, Mr. Cramer sent students home with not only textbook reading but also excerpts from the U.S. Constitution, as well as monumental court battles that influenced the time period, such as *Plessy v. Ferguson* (1896) and *Brown v. Board of Education* (1954) (Figure 11.2).

Mr. Cramer prided himself on the complexity of this lesson. Although students often struggled with the language, he felt a sense of accomplishment when his students finally figured out the ideas in the texts. After designing ways to differentiate instruction for Daniel, however, Mr. Cramer indicated to me that he no longer wanted simply to send all students home with the packet and have them answer the questions that followed the readings. He said that this "would cause more frustration" than was necessary on the part of some students. Instead, he modeled and encouraged students to use the "chunking" strategy.

From *Brown v. Board of Education* (1954)

—In approaching this problem, we cannot turn back the clock to 1868, when the Amendment was adopted, or even to 1896, when *Plessy v. Ferguson* was written. We must consider public education in light of its full development and its present place in American life throughout the nation.

—Today, education is perhaps the most important function of state and local governments.... In these days, it is doubtful that any child may reasonably be expected to succeed in life if he is denied the opportunity of an education. Such an opportunity, where the state has undertaken to provide it, is a right which must be made available to all on equal terms.

—We come then to the question presented: Does segregation of children in public schools solely on the basis of race, even though the physical facilities and other "tangible" factors may be equal, deprive the children of the minority group of equal educational opportunities? We believe that it does.

—To separate [children in grade school] from others of similar age and qualifications solely because of their race generates a feeling of inferiority as to their status in the community that may affect their hearts and minds in a way unlikely ever to be undone.... Segregation of white and colored children in public schools has a detrimental effect upon the colored children. The impact is greater when it has the sanction of the law; for the policy of separating the races is usually interpreted as denoting the inferiority of the Negro group. A sense of inferiority affects the motivation of a child to learn. Segregation with the sanction of law, therefore, has a tendency to [slow] the educational and mental development of Negro children and to deprive them of some of the benefits they would receive in a racial[ly] integrated school system. Whatever may have been the extent of psychological knowledge at the time of *Plessy*, this finding is amply supported by modern authority. Any language in *Plessy* contrary to this finding is rejected."

—We conclude that in the field of public education the doctrine of "separate but equal" has no place. Separate educational facilities are inherently unequal. Therefore, we hold that plaintiffs and others similarly situated ... are, by reason of the segregation complained of, deprived of [equal protection].

Sample Question

1. What does the Supreme Court in *Brown v. Board of Education* say has changed in the nearly 60 years since *Plessy* was decided? How do these factors affect the *Brown* Court's decision?

FIGURE 11.2. An excerpt from Daniel's social studies teacher's original assignment. Used with the permission of Mr. Cramer.

He also modified his assignment, asking students to pause at specific points throughout the excerpts and evaluate the language. Students were asked to share their thoughts periodically, first with a partner, and then to share their thoughts voluntarily with the whole class (Figure 11.3).

Mr. Cramer allowed students to work in pairs during class and provided support when he detected misunderstandings or frustrations. Paired activity enabled Mr. Cramer to provide differentiated support. While observing his students working, Mr. Cramer noted that some pairs

---

—To separate [children in grade school] from others of similar age and qualifications solely because of their race generates a feeling of inferiority as to their status in the community that may affect their hearts and minds in a way unlikely ever to be undone....

Reading pause: What words are key to this statement? What words challenge your thinking? Discuss as a pair how you feel about this statement.

—Segregation of white and colored children in public schools has a detrimental effect upon the colored children....

Reading pause: What does the word detrimental *mean in this passage? Do you agree or disagree with this statement? Why?*

—The impact is greater when it has the sanction of the law; for the policy of separating the races is usually interpreted as denoting the inferiority of the Negro group. A sense of inferiority affects the motivation of a child to learn. Segregation with the sanction of law, therefore, has a tendency to [slow] the educational and mental development of Negro children and to deprive them of some of the benefits they would receive in a racial[ly] integrated school system....

Reading pause: Summarize this passage in your own words. What reactions do you have to this passage, both the way it is written and what it is saying?

—Whatever may have been the extent of psychological knowledge at the time of Plessy, this finding is amply supported by modern authority. Any language in *Plessy* contrary to this finding is rejected....

Reading pause: Think back to Plessy. *What are the writers saying changed?*

—We conclude that in the field of public education the doctrine of "separate but equal" has no place. Separate educational facilities are inherently unequal. Therefore, we hold that plaintiffs and others similarly situated ... are, by reason of the segregation complained of, deprived of [equal protection].

Reading pause: What are the key terms in this passage? What are your feelings on how the case was resolved?

FIGURE 11.3 An excerpt from the new assignment with "chunking reading pauses" added. Used with the permission of Mr. Cramer.

needed little or no clarification to interpret the text, but others required encouragement and additional guidance as they worked through the complexities of the text. In fact, Mr. Cramer encountered a "teaching moment" when he noticed Daniel and his partner struggling with the four questions he had given students to answer. The questions were long and had complicated syntax. Mr. Cramer sat down with Daniel and his partner, and modeled how to read the first question. He talked about possible confusion with the question and how he would approach developing an answer. Daniel and his partner followed Mr. Cramer's example and proceeded to have a rich discussion that led to a strong answer for each question. After this lesson, Mr. Cramer commented that his struggling students seemed to have a much better understanding of the material than they had demonstrated in previous classes.

Addressing his students' difficulties with the text-based questions prior to the final, Mr. Cramer modeled how to read these questions and multiple-choice options more effectively. He also had students develop a new study guide for the unit based on what they felt were the most important concepts, questions, and discussions raised in class. Students' points took a more chronological form than they had in the instructor's previous study guides, and the process allowed Mr. Cramer to gather information about areas that caused struggling readers difficulty, and how he might differentiate instruction in the future.

After testing his students on the Civil Rights unit, Mr. Cramer told me he saw a 15% improvement on the average test score, compared to the results of the same exam the year before. Daniel also talked about the success of the unit. He referenced that this unit "made me think" and he really thought he understood his reading.

To further differentiate for Daniel, Mr. Cramer and I sought ways to increase Daniel's self-confidence and participation in discussions in Mr. Cramer's class. First, Mr. Cramer and I made sure Daniel was prepared to answer questions regarding the next day's class readings. Mr. Cramer would alert me to the kinds of questions he would ask the class, and I would make sure Daniel paid close attention to the information that would help him answer the questions. Later we organized opportunities for Daniel to lead a discussion group in Mr. Cramer's class. On days when Daniel knew he would be leading these groups, he often read the texts twice and would come to class prior to school to talk with Mr. Cramer or me about any questions that he still found challenging to understand. In preparing for the discussions, Daniel developed deeper levels of understanding than he had previously. He was also able to lead subject study groups in Guided Academics and to provide his classmates with tutoring because he had a better understanding of the text. He also benefited greatly from the previously mentioned partnership between Mr. Cramer and myself because he received similar embedded strategy instruction in both his content-area class and his Guided Academics class.

Differentiating for Jenny: A Student Overwhelmed by Anxiety and Self-Doubt

Unlike Daniel, Jenny entered my Guided Academics class with a very different mindset. Almost daily she arrived at our first-period class 20 to 30 minutes early to chat about her prior evening. Though she seemed like an incredibly positive, nice student with a very supportive family, Jenny ended the majority of her stories about her frustrating nights working on biology and algebra homework with statements such as "but that makes sense, because I'm stupid" or "it really didn't surprise me … I'm just dumb."

Though it seemed at first that Jenny was looking for someone to disconfirm her self-doubt, after a few conversations with her, her parents, and her biology teacher, Mrs. Rossi, I realized that Jenny's self-doubt and low self-esteem were major obstacles to her learning. In addition to expressing self-doubt, Jenny experienced panic attacks. When speaking during discussions, giving book talks, and, most dramatically, when she needed to present final projects, Jenny broke down. Because of her anxiety over speaking in class, Jenny often shut down and failed to participate in activities that required her to share knowledge of what she read in class, be it in research for project or smaller reading activities.

Jenny only completed reading one narrative text during the entire term of Guided Academics, because she "just didn't get it." She began works such as Laurie Halse Anderson's *Prom* (2005) and *Catalyst* (2002), Alice Sebold's *The Lovely Bones* (2002), and Stephenie Meyer's *Twilight* (2005), but she never finished them. Jenny said that reading just "really stresses me out." This is understandable. She reads two levels below grade level, according to the QRI, and almost three levels below grade level on the Gates–MacGinite. When I interviewed Jenny about her reading, she explained that she approaches every text the same way, whether the piece was a narrative or an informational text. She began with the first word in the body of the text but only got through the first few words before she became incredibly stressed and realizes she did not understand what she was reading.

This problem most affects Jenny in her biology course, a class that because of rigorous state standards moves at an exceptionally quick pace, and student learning depends quite heavily on informational texts both inside and outside of class. Much of class time is spent on interactive labs and going over exploratory assignments that students often do in groups. The biology course is required in our district. Large class size, coupled with our trimester organization, makes it very difficult for instructors to get to know their students. According to the biology teachers, the range of ability levels is far greater now than in previous years.

For a student like Jenny, these issues quickly became detrimental to her academic success. To help, Jenny and I devised a plan in Guided Academics that would allow her to achieve her goal to become a less anxious reader. At first, our plan was implemented as an addition to her biology instruction, because of Mrs. Rossi's need to adjust to the trimester schedule and her class sizes. Later, even though Jenny still felt overwhelmed by the outside factors affecting her pedagogical decisions, Mrs. Rossi worked more closely with us in achieving Jenny's academic goals.

Jenny's first goal was to be able to read a text without experiencing an overwhelming sense of anxiety. Initially, Jenny's comprehension depended on the questions at the beginning and end of the chapter, but because of the vocabulary demands, these questions alone caused Jenny to have panic attacks. Rather than diving into a piece of reading, with my guidance, Jenny worked extensively in Guided Academics when she approached both narrative and informational texts, using prereading strategies such as accessing her prior knowledge, and using titles, subtitles, covers, graphs, and pictures. Thanks in large part to my background as biology instructor, I was able to create protocols for Jenny to complete prior to reading sections of her biology texts that pushed her to use the text features, including boldface vocabulary words and graphics, to build understanding of key concepts and terms prior to reading the actual texts. Jenny wrote her predictions, questions, and vocabulary words on the left-hand side of a sheet of paper, and filled in the right-hand side with answers, definitions, and comments as she read (Figure 11.4). Having content-area knowledge was exceptionally helpful in guiding Jenny to develop an understanding of these terms.

The protocols also required Jenny to make predictions based on text features and to develop her own questions that she hoped to answer as she read. The protocols, according to Jenny, were critical in preparing her to read assignments. Once Jenny had completed the protocol, she and I would discuss her questions and predictions. These conversations pushed her to think of real-world connections and her prior experience with the information, making the task of learning the vocabulary a "little easier" to understand before she actually read the body of the text. In observing Jenny's subsequent reading of sections, her physical appearance did seem to relax a bit after she went through the protocol; she also made it through entire sections of texts and did not experience anxiety attacks with the same frequency as she had before. Another factor in Jenny's success was that the protocol was developed in such a way

Vocabulary that looks challenging or unfamiliar	Vocabulary definitions
Predictions (based on headings, subheadings, photographs, charts, graphs, etc.)	Validate your predictions
Questions (both those that arise before your reading and as you read)	Answers

FIGURE 11.4. Reading protocol designed for Jenny in Guided Academics class.

that as Jenny filled out the prereading activities, she also prepared to take notes while reading the body of the text. This note-taking strategy greatly assisted Jenny, who often lost 3 × 5-inch flashcards but could keep her notes in a binder. The notes made it not only acceptable but also almost required Jenny to ask questions and admit to her confusions with the texts in both Guided Academics and biology class. Jenny frequently brought these questions to me, not with her usual "I'm so stupid" remarks, but with the attitude that she realized it was more than acceptable to be confused.

As the school year settled down, Mrs. Rossi and I were able to discuss Jenny's work and attitude; Mrs. Rossi also began asking Jenny about her notes and questions. In fact, as time went on, Mrs. Rossi also asked me for assistance in developing minilessons to assist her other students with textual understanding. Now, despite the newness of both the trimester schedule and pressure from the state curriculum standards, Mrs. Rossi plans on working more with analyzing the texts presented in her classroom and discovering ways they might challenge her students as they attempt to gather knowledge.

Collegial Collaboration

Although I (Hoffman) was not given time to work officially with classroom teachers in a coaching capacity, I talked informally with the teachers of the students enrolled in my Guided Academics class. We talked during lunch, and during common planning periods and professional development meetings. Many of the teachers were interested in the strategies their students were learning in my Guided Academics class and asked how they could support use of the strategies in their classrooms. A few teachers, including Mr. Cramer, joined me in an informal study group that met once a month to investigate literacy strategies that might facilitate the learning of struggling readers. In the beginning, I brought resources to the meetings, such as articles from professional journals and examples of literacy strategies to serve as conversation starters. Sometimes I brought samples of student work from my Guided Academics class and talked about what we could learn about the students' literacy skills by examining the work samples. Teachers participating in the study group began to bring examples of strategies they were using in their classrooms and samples of student work to share with the group. There were times that we focused on a particular student, who was enrolled in more than one of the teachers' classrooms. The teachers shared their experiences and talked about how they might develop consistency in how they addressed the students' literacy needs. Attendance at the study group meetings varied, but interest in the group grew as teachers shared stories about their struggling readers' increasing achievements.

What We Are Learning
about Differentiating Instruction

The most important conclusion we can draw from our experiences is that teachers who work with adolescents have the desire to differentiate instruction, but they may need help identifying how to do this within the constraints of teaching an ever-expanding curriculum to a large number of students. Many content-area teachers feel that they do not have the time to create a variety of activities to address individual students' learning needs. One lesson to take from Mr. Cramer's and Mrs. Rossi's classes is that it is not necessary to design elaborate alternative activities to provide differentiated instruction. Being responsive to students is the key. Mrs. Rossi learned to help Jenny by asking her questions that activated prior knowledge or focused her attention on important content information. While circulating around the room when students are working on experiments or reading a text, Mrs. Rossi could sit for a few minutes with Jenny to focus Jenny's attention on important concepts, helping her connect new content information to what she already knew. The differentiation stems from Mrs. Rossi's knowledge of how Jenny learns and her ability to engage Jenny in targeted instructional conversation.

Teachers of middle and high school students can differentiate instruction by building upon their expert knowledge of the developmental nature of the skills and content required to construct meaning in their discipline. Both Mrs. Rossi and Mr. Cramer understand what students need to know and to be able to do to demonstrate the level of competence required in their curriculum standards and benchmarks. When they design learning activities, they can differentiate instruction for their students by providing the kind of scaffolding Mr. Cramer gave his students when he inserted "reading pauses" in his *Brown v. Board of Education* assignment. Daniel and his partner were able to gain much more from the assignment than they would have had they tried to answer the original question without the benefit of thinking about the concepts raised in the reading pauses. Furthermore, by having students work in pairs, Mr. Cramer could customize verbal interactions with students in ways that maximized their learning. The protocols that Lisa developed for Jenny and shared with Mrs. Rossi are another example of ways to scaffold learning for struggling readers. Jenny's use of the protocols helped her develop effective reading habits that transferred from one lesson to another and helped her to build confidence in her own ability to learn.

Mrs. Rossi and Mr. Cramer also shared their expertise with their students by modeling disciplinary thinking. This practice benefits all students, but it is especially effective for struggling readers. When Mr. Cramer modeled how he thought about answering questions, all of his students probably benefited, but Daniel learned essential skills that he had not previously used. Mr. Cramer was unlocking doors to literacy behaviors that Daniel had not walked through in the past. Mrs. Rossi found many occasions on which Jenny benefited from brief modeling sessions about how to activate prior knowledge or make connections to previous lessons.

We also need to consider the critical role that Lisa played in helping content-area teachers differentiate instruction for their struggling adolescent readers. Her background as a literacy specialist allows Lisa to assess students on a variety of assessment tools and share the results with her colleagues. It helps her to consult with content-area teachers to design strategies for differentiating instruction that addresses students' individualized learning goals. Lisa's tutelage was invaluable to Mr. Cramer and Mrs. Rossi, and the coordination among their teachers did not go unnoticed by Jenny and Daniel. Both Jenny and Daniel commented that they appreciated knowing that all of their teachers talked to one another, understood their challenges, and were prepared to provide the much needed individual support.

The teacher collaboration afforded by classes such as Guided Academics and literacy coaching programs are an excellent form of professional development (Bean, 2001) and are essential in making the pedagogical shift to differentiated instruction an enduring success. Guided Academics, and similar classes, provide the one-on-one interaction necessary for teachers truly to understand their students and tailor their instruction to meet students' individual needs. These changes in instruction provide opportunities for struggling adolescent learners to be more successful in class, leading to increased praise from teachers and peers, and a sense of empowerment that may make them lifelong readers and learners.

Likewise, secondary literacy coaching programs provide content-area teachers with very tailored assistance (R. Bean & Carroll, Chapter 13, this volume). When school-based literacy coaches are available to content-area teachers, the teachers receive the long-term professional development required to overcome their hopelessness and frustration when they encounter students who cannot read content-area materials (Dole, 2004; Dupuis, 1984). Furthermore, coaching programs that are integrated within a school offer teachers roles as leaders, without removing them from their classrooms; oftentimes, literacy coaches are trained staff members from within the school or district; Lisa's informal role demonstrates this.

As teachers take risks associated with integrating literacy-focused activities into their content-area classrooms, it is helpful for them to share ideas with their own content-area colleagues, as well as others throughout the school (Bean, 2001). Content-area teachers are experts within their given fields, and together with colleagues from other disciplines, are able to discuss and better understand the complexity of their various texts. When this happens, differentiation becomes a much easier practice to integrate into teachers' pedagogical beliefs. By working with colleagues, teachers learn to improve their practice, and when they belong to a learning community with a reading specialist, they are able to work in new ways to address the needs of struggling learners (Allington & Baker, 1999). Study groups that focus on a variety of issues associated with differentiating instruction and content-area literacy demands also allow educators to gain insight regarding textual difficulties that students, who often are novice readers, might face when they encounter the texts. Through these experiences, educators can find a deeper appreciation for various texts across disciplines and the challenges that the texts pose to readers, and also discuss how they can translate these issues into more effective practices in their classrooms.

Concluding Thoughts

Differentiating instruction for adolescents holds tremendous promise for struggling readers. Although we can learn a great deal from watching our elementary school colleagues engage students in guided reading groups and learning centers, we must plot our own course in middle and high schools. Differentiating instruction in these classrooms means knowing more about our students and taking time during class to model, scaffold, and engage them in conversations customized to their learning needs. It requires that we think carefully about the development of skills and conceptual knowledge that are integral to our disciplinary curriculum, and that we finally abandon our trust in a one-size-fits-all approach to instruction.

Questions for Reflection

1. The task of differentiating instruction for students is often daunting for content-area teachers, especially with the large class sizes and wide variation in literacy skills among secondary students. What support is necessary to enable teachers to analyze their students' performance and to plan effective instruction for individual students?

2. The Guided Academics class taught by Lisa offered a large amount of structure and guidance, especially for Jenny and Daniel early in their school year. How might features of this course be integrated into content-area classes if your school doesn't have such a class? What types of roadblocks would teachers face, and what possible solutions might be proposed in integrating these features?

3. Many of the pedagogical decisions made by Mrs. Rossi and Mr. Cramer were designed to improve the academic success of Jenny

and Daniel, and to increase their confidence as learners. What strategies might you use to build your students' learning confidence?

References

Allington, R. L., & Baker, K. (1999). Best practices in literacy instruction for children with special needs. In L. B. Gambrell, L. M. Morrow, D. S. Strickland, L. C. Wilkinson, S. B. Neuman, & M. Pressley (Eds.), *Best practices in literacy instruction* (pp. 292–310). New York: Guilford Press.

Anderson, L. A. (2002). *Catalyst.* New York: Viking.

Anderson, L. A. (2005). *Prom.* New York: Viking.

Beah, I. (2007). *A long way gone: Memoirs of a boy soldier.* New York: Farrar, Straus & Giroux.

Bean, R. M. (2001). Classroom teachers and reading specialists working together to improve students achievement. In V. J. Risko & K. Bromley (Eds.), *Collaboration for diverse learners: Viewpoints and practices* (pp. 348–368). Newark, DE: International Reading Association.

Beck, L. L., McKeown, M. G., Hamilton, R. L., & Kucan, L. (1997). *Questioning the author: An approach for enhancing student engagement in text.* Newark, DE: International Reading Association.

Biancarosa, G., & Snow, C. E. (2004). *Reading next—a vision for action and research in middle and high school literacy: A report to Carnegie Corporation of New York.* Washington, DC: Alliance for Excellent Education.

Brown v. Board of Education of Topeka, 347 U.S. 483 (1954). Retrieved from *www.nationalcenter.org/brown.html.*

Connor, C. M., Morrison, F. J., & Katch, E. L. (2004). Beyond the reading wars: The effect of classroom instruction by child interactions on early reading. *Scientific Studies of Reading, 8*(4), 305–336.

Connor, C. M., Morrison, F. J., & Petrella, J. N. (2004). Effective reading comprehension instruction: Examining child by instruction interactions. *Journal of Educational Psychology, 96*(4), 682–698.

Dole, J. A. (2004). The changing role of the reading specialist in school reform. *Reading Teacher, 57*(5), 462–471.

Dupuis, M. M. (Ed.). (1984). *Reading in the content areas: Research for teachers.* Newark, DE: International Reading Association.

Leslie, L., & Schudt Caldwell, J. (2006). *Qualitative Reading Inventory–4.* Boston: Allyn & Bacon.

MacGillivray, L., & Rueda, R. (2003). *Listening to inner city teachers of English language learners: Differentiating literacy instruction.* Washington, DC: Office of Educational Research and Improvement. (ERIC Document No. ED479982)

MacGinitie, W., MacGinitie, R., Maria, K., & Dreyer, L. (2000). *Gates–MacGinitie Reading Tests* (4th ed.). Itasca, IL: Riverside.

Meyer, S. (2005). *Twilight.* Boston: Little, Brown.

Myers, M. (1984). Shifting standards of literacy–the teacher's catch-22. *English Journal, 73*(4), 26–32.

O'Brien, D. G., Moje, E. B., & Stewart, R. A. (2000). Exploring the context of secondary literacy: Literacy in people's everyday school lives. In E. B. Moje & D. G. O'Brien (Eds.), *Constructions of literacy: Studies of teaching and learning in and out of secondary schools* (pp. 27–48). Mahwah, NJ: Erlbaum.

Plessy v. Ferguson, 163 U.S. 537 (1896).

Raphael, T. E. (1986). Teaching question–answer relationships. *Reading Teacher, 39,* 516–520.

Sebold, A. (2002). *The lovely bones: A novel.* Boston: Little, Brown.

Taylor, B. M., Pearson, D. P., Clark, K., & Walpole, S. (2000). Effective schools and accomplished teachers: Lessons about primary-grade reading instruction in low-income schools. *Elementary School Journal, 101*(2), 121–165.

Tomlinson, C. A. (1999). *The differentiated classroom: Responding to the needs of all learners.* Alexandria, VA: Association for Supervision and Curriculum Development.

Tomlinson, C. A., & Eidson, C. C. (2003). *Differentiation in practice: A resource guide for differentiating curriculum grades 5–9.* Alexandria, VA: Association for Supervision and Curriculum Development.

Vygotsky, L. S. (1962). *Thought and language.* Cambridge, MA: MIT Press.

Wharton-McDonald, R., Pressley, M., & Hampston, J. M. (1998). Literacy instruction in nine first-grade classrooms: Teacher characteristics and student achievement. *Elementary School Journal, 99*(2), 101–128.

CHAPTER 12

How Can Assessment Evaluate Student Learning, Inform Instruction, and Promote Student Independence?

VICTORIA RIDGEWAY GILLIS
LEIGH HALTIWANGER
APRIL FICKLIN
MARY DILLINGHAM
BARBARA DAVIS

CLASSROOM PORTRAIT

Conversations in the teachers' lounge

"How many times must I teach about commas before students actually use them appropriately? I've written the same comment a half-dozen times on two papers ... and I have 150 to grade! I'll go crazy marking the same errors over and over."

—EMMA THOMAS, 10th-grade English teacher

"I've explained this assignment a dozen times, I even showed them one from last year, but they just don't get it. What is so hard about creating a quilt block and explaining the geometry in it? I thought they would really get into this project. These kids just don't care. I give up!"

—THEODORE MATHIS, geometry teacher

Conversations in the students' cafeteria

"If I get another bad grade on a paper in Ms. Thomas's class, I'll be grounded for life ... and it'll be all her fault. What difference does it make where you put the stupid comma? I never can tell; this is pointless!"
— CELESTINE STROUD, a student in Ms. Thomas's English class

"I just don't get it. ... What does he want? I drew a quilt square—it's a dumb assignment, but I did it. When am I ever going to use this stuff? Men don't quilt! Useless! I did it, and he gave me a C ... and mine looked just like the one he showed us!"
— FRANK AGATI, a student in Mr. Mathis's geometry class

Conversations like these occur in countless middle and high schools across America among teachers who are frustrated by repeated student errors, and students who are frustrated by a perceived capriciousness on the part of their teachers: two players in the game of school at cross purposes, each wondering about the intentions of the other. English teachers, in particular, spend hours grading student papers and marking errors, a job that is perhaps more appropriate for an editor than a teacher. Math, science, and social studies teachers using alternative assessments—assessments other than the familiar multiple-choice, fill-in-the-blank, true–false, and essay formats—are frustrated when students don't seem to understand the requirements of the assignment, even when they share *rubrics*, or scoring guidelines, before students begin work and show students model assignments from former students.

Despite years of instruction in the use of commas and other punctuation, students continue to make errors, and teachers continue to mark them on students' papers. The same holds true for content-area reading assignments. Even with rubrics shared before students complete alternative assignments, students misinterpret those rubrics and fail to appreciate connections between these alternative assignments and the concepts they assess, and the world in which they live. What can we do so that students better understand their assignments, and how can we as teachers help students become more independent as learners and achieve greater success in our classrooms? One answer we have found is to involve students more completely in the assessment process. Students who take more responsibility for assessment become more actively engaged in their learning and develop skills and strategies that serve them long after they leave our classrooms.

We have participated in a statewide, long-term professional development effort, the South Carolina Center of Excellence for Adolescent Literacy and Learning (CEALL), for 3 years. When we first began working together, Leigh Haltiwanger, who has a master's degree in math education, was a middle school math teacher. Now a regional math coach, she is responsible for training local math coaches in elementary and middle schools. Mary Dillingham and April Ficklin taught just across the road from Leigh at the high school; Mary, who has a PhD in chemistry, taught Advanced Placement and regular science courses, and continues to do so. April, who has a master's degree in English, taught English to ninth- and 11th-grade students, but has since taken leave for the birth of her first child and is currently an adjunct English teacher for a local college. Barbara Davis, who is currently working toward her master's degree, taught science at a high school about 2 hours away. Victoria Ridgeway Gillis, the director of CEALL, taught science in middle and high schools for 20 years before returning to graduate school and becoming a professor of literacy education. She made regular visits to all four teachers' classrooms during their first year of involvement in CEALL and helped to lead the workshops that form the central activities associated with CEALL. During the third year of CEALL, these four teachers, designated Teaching Consultants after 2 years of training with CEALL, were asked to serve on the Leadership Team to assist with workshops and to mentor participants. All of us have used student self-assessment in a variety of forms, across a wide range of content areas and grade levels. All of us have seen the benefits of involving students in the assessment process.

In this chapter, we present assessment *for* and *as* learning: involving students in peer- and self-assessment, as well as co-creating rubrics for evaluating their work. First, we address the general topic of assessment, drawing from research on self- and peer-evaluation. Next, we describe the processes of assessment *for* students' learning in science classrooms, using peer- and self-assessment as students completed research projects and lab reports. In both science examples, students used teacher-developed evaluation criteria to assess themselves and their peers. Following this discussion, we turn to assessment *as* learning, drawing from an English/language arts class for an example. In this class, students created a rubric, collaboratively with their teacher, that was then used to assess their public speaking performance. Finally, we explore self-assessment for teachers involved in professional development efforts aimed at improving student math achievement. We hope that readers will be able to see their students and themselves in assessment *for* and *as* learning.

Assessment *of*, *for*, and *as* Learning

Assessment is most often used to summarize what students have learned in a particular class and usually involves multiple-choice, fill-in-the-blank, matching, short answer, and/or essay test questions. High-stakes assessments measure the sum of student learning and determine whether that learning is sufficient to move to the next grade level, to graduate, or to gain admission to college or university. These examples of assessment *of* learning, also known as *summative* assessment, are the kinds of assessment most often encountered in schools. Currently, schools, districts, and states are focused on assessment of learning as a result of *No Child Left Behind*. Stiggins (2002) calls the current obsession with standardized assessment "assessment as reward and punishment" and elaborates on using assessment to help our students want to learn. Stiggins focuses on assessment *for* learning, pointing to specific benefits of student self-assessment; he includes student self-assessment using teacher-created rubrics, as well as assessment instruments co-created with teachers. Brownlie, Feniak, and Schnellert (2006) differentiate between assessment *for* learning, which involves student self-assessment, and assessment *as* learning, which includes students creating the assessment by which they are evaluated and that reflects their learning.

In this chapter, we adopt Brownlie and colleagues' (2006) use of assessment *for* learning and assessment *as* learning to depict more clearly teacher practices described here. It is daunting to think about including students in the assessment process, because it involves giving up some teacher control of the classroom. In many classrooms, teachers control virtually everything, from where students sit to how students' learning is assessed; giving students an opportunity to provide input into the assessment process through self-assessment means that teachers give up part of that control; however, research indicates that student gains far outweigh any loss of control the teacher feels, and we have found this to be true in our own classrooms (Shepard, 2000).

Assessment *for* learning involves students in self-assessment, and ranges from *think writes* (Mayher, Lester, & Pradl, 1983) that informally ask students to assess their understanding of concepts being studied, to more formal self-assessment using teacher-created criteria and rubrics. When students are asked to explain a newly introduced concept to a student who was absent from class, they are given an authentic audience and a specific task that requires them to think about what they know about the topic, and how they might convey that information to a peer. When students who are given a rubric then engage in self- and/or peer assessment using the instrument, they gain a clearer understanding of the content, as well as the requirements, of the project or activity being assessed. Self-assessment fosters student ownership of learning, develops intrinsic motivation (Cassidy, 2007), and has been associated with self-regulated learning and metacognitive skills development (Kirby & Downs, 2007).

Assessment *as* learning involves students in creating the standards and/or criteria by which to judge their work, then applying the criteria (Brownlie et al., 2006). Research on self-assessment has not consistently separated the two processes of generating and applying criteria, but it emphasizes that involving students in co-creating criteria and standards facilitates the development of student beliefs about their competence (Pintrich & de Groot, 1990) and, as such, influences students' perceived control over their school success and failure.

There is a rich research base supporting student self-assessment in higher education across a variety of disciplines (Cassidy, 2007; Hudd, 2003; Kirby & Downs, 2007). There is also evidence supporting the use of self-assessment in K–12 educational settings. Obach (2003) conducted a longitudinal–sequential study of self-assessment in middle-school-age students, grades 5–8. Sixty percent of Obach's participants, who were enrolled in a parochial school, were members of a minority, and 55% were female. Obach followed the students for 3 years and found no significant differences related to grade in students' ability to self-assess their academic competence, although there were increasing linear trends as students moved through the middle school grades. No significant differences were found between male and female participants. Obach's study, together with others investigating student self-assessment in K–12 settings (e.g., Chen, 2006), provide support for the use of self-assessment in middle and high school.

Assessment *for* Learning in Science Classrooms

We turn now to a consideration of assessment *for* learning in science. In this section we describe two uses of student self-assessment, both of which involve the use of teacher-created rubrics. One example involves students in self-assessment and revision prior to peer assessment; the other example involves students in self- and peer assessment prior to a final chance for revision.

Student Learning and Assessment in Barbara's Biology Class

Barbara teaches biology in a small rural high school in South Carolina. In one of the projects she uses to foster student learning about genetics, students create brochures about genetic disorders that are suitable for local doctors' offices. Students conduct research on the Internet, determine the value of various websites, and ultimately evaluate themselves and their peers as they present the results of their research, which are incorporated into the brochures placed in local doctors' offices. Before they begin the research process, students are given the project description and requirements, as well as a rubric with assessment criteria. Barbara provides students with an initial set of questions to answer for each of the genetic disorders under investigation. Together Barbara and her class then generate additional questions of interest, as illustrated in Table 12.1.

Students use library resources and Internet sites to find answers to their questions. As they prepare to present the information to peers and to the community, they design a PowerPoint presentation for their classmates and brochures suitable for doctors' offices. They present their findings about the genetic disorder to the class, and their peers use the rubric (Figure 12.1) to evaluate presentations for organization, mechanics and spelling, use of PowerPoint, the content presented, and presentational skills. Student evaluations become part of students' overall grade for the project. Barbara builds group interdependence by making students responsible for information related to all the genetic disorders presented in class, thus putting a premium on paying attention to peer presentations.

Preparing students to engage in peer evaluation requires patience and time, but it is time that Barbara considers well spent. If it is to

---

TABLE 12.1. Questions for the Genetics Project in Biology

Medical issues

1. How is the disorder inherited? Is it a dominant or recessive trait?
2. On what chromosome is it located, and what are the possible genotypes?
3. Is there a family pedigree or visible family tree illustrating how it is inherited?
4. Does it affect a certain population or ethnic group? Cite statistics.
5. Are there physical symptoms?
6. Does it affect the person mentally or intellectually?
7. Is there treatment? If so, what is it?
8. Life expectancy?
9. How is it diagnosed?

Personal issues

1. Describe everyday life.
2. What is the quality of life?
3. What help can a family or the person receive from organizations?
4. Limitations of the person.
5. Is there a cure in the present time or in the future?

	Unsatisfactory (1 pt)	Satisfactory (3 pts)	Good (4 pts)	Excellent (5 pts)
Grammar/ Spelling	Presentation had 4 or more spelling or grammar errors.	Presentation had 3 spelling or grammar errors.	Presentation had no more than 2 spelling or grammar errors.	Presentation had no spelling or grammar errors.
Organization	Audience cannot understand the presentation because there is no sequence of information.	Audience has difficulty following, topics jump around.	Logical sequence, audience can follow.	Logical, interesting sequence that audience can follow.
Slide Show	Transitions are not used, slides have major technical mistakes. Slide too busy—hard to read.	Bullets and transitions are used ineffectively, or are distracting. Hard to read.	Bullets and transitions used, but there are some problems with flow.	Bullets and transitions used effectively, presentation flows smoothly.
Information 1	Presentation has major gaps in knowledge, audience is not likely to leave with useful information.	Presentation has some major gaps in knowledge, or is presented in such a way that the audience has trouble understanding.	Presentation provides information on the topic, some elements are missing (see questions).	Presentation provides a wealth of information on the topic, all questions are answered in a way the audience can understand.
Information 2	Information too technical for an average person to understand, information is cut/pasted from sources.	A majority of the information seems copied from sources.	Some information seems cut and pasted from sources, too technical for a layperson to understand completely.	Information in the author's own words, with consideration of the audience.
Speech	Speech was not well presented, seems confused or lost. Failed to answer the audience's question.	Seemed confused, not well versed about some issues. Does not speak clearly.	Vague about some issues, or questions were answered inaccurately. Difficult to understand speech sometimes.	Appeared to understand the issues of the topic. Questions were answered accurately. Articulates well.

FIGURE 12.1. Genetics project individual student evaluation form: Grading rubric.

be effective, peer assessment necessitates a classroom atmosphere of mutual respect. Barbara begins to develop this atmosphere on the first day of class, so that students are comfortable with each other and with Barbara when they begin the genetics project. Students prepare to use the rubric to assess others by first applying it to their own work, then making revisions before presenting it to their classmates. This gives students practice with improving their presentations and develops their understanding of and familiarity with the rubric. Shifting part of the assessment responsibility to the students requires trust on the part of both teacher and students, but the rewards far outweigh the additional time required for peer assessment.

Mary's Advanced Placement Biology Class

Mary's advanced placement (AP) biology class in a large rural high school in South Carolina also uses rubrics for self-assessment. She chose to develop the rubric by adopting a one-page lab report instead of the lengthier forms she had seen and used when teaching college chemistry to freshman. The short format removes the focus on the length of the report and places the emphasis on data, analysis, and discussion instead of procedural details. She needed a lab report format for AP biology class that would hold students accountable and help them crystallize their thinking. The one-page format helped to place the emphasis on student thinking. See Figure 12.2 for the one-page lab report format.

Mary discusses the teacher-constructed rubric in class before students are required to write their lab reports. Based on student need, she sometimes provides one of her own lab reports as an exemplar. Her students really like seeing an example that she has written, but familiarity with the rubric is just the beginning for students. They need practice to become proficient at analyzing data generated from experiments. Mary's students express their difficulty in getting started and knowing what to include in the lab report, especially at the beginning of the course. To help, Mary has them complete analysis questions provided in each lab, before the lab report is due, and students discuss them in class to uncover questions and misconceptions. One common misconception is that when water (H_2O) boils and changes state from liquid to gas, it breaks down to become hydrogen gas (H_2) and oxygen gas (O_2). This is not the case, because a chemical formula does not change with a change in the state of matter.

The lab reports are completed in two stages. Students first hand in typed rough drafts, which may be missing formal data tables, diagrams, or graphs, but include all required categories of information, including procedures, results, analysis, and conclusion (Figure 12.2).

Name _____ Date _____ Lab # _____

Group members (if any) _____

Title: (one complete sentence describing the lab)

Objective statement/hypothesis: (One to three sentences) What question are you attempting to answer and what is your expected result?)

Procedure: (Be brief, and reference standards procedures where possible, noting any changes from standard in a brief comment).

Results: What did you observe? What did you measure? Tables of data belong in this section and may be attached on separate pages.

Discussion/Analysis: What does this information tell you about the experiment? What does it mean? (Graphs belong in this sections and may be attached on separate pages.) Evaluate your data by describing all possible problems with procedure, observations, data, and data collection. "Human error" is NOT acceptable. Be specific to the error and to the experiment.

Conclusion: (2–3 sentences) Did your data support or refute your hypothesis? Were your data of sufficient quality that you feel confident your conclusion is correct?

FIGURE 12.2. AP biology laboratory report format.

Mary then randomly redistributes the reports to students, who then use the rubric to grade the rough draft (Figure 12.3). She directs them to be as strict and tough as possible, following the rubric. When students have evaluated the lab reports, grades are recorded and each report is returned to its author. The author of a lab report is allowed to ask the peer grader for clarification on both content and format. The students have assessed their own work with the rubric, had their work reviewed by a peer, and have had an opportunity to experience peer teaching when asking–answering questions about the rough draft. Then they can revise their own work in all aspects of the report, both scientific content and formatting.

Advance preparation and explanation of the rubric for students, set due dates for both the rough draft and final report, and announcing these in advance works very well, because students know the expectations "up front." Having students grade rough drafts in class, then turn them in to the teacher, so that she can both determine that the feedback is thorough and record the evaluation, saves a huge amount of time and gives students immediate feedback and an opportunity to revise their work. Answering each other's questions helps students learn to teach each other and to become more independent learners as they identify their own questions.

Many labs have three or four separate procedures for testing different aspects of a concept. Most of the time, a short lab report format is suitable only for a single segment of the long AP biology labs. Mary had to be willing to focus on one segment of the lab for the report. Preparing for AP biology labs can be very labor intensive. The shift to shorter lab reports and the focus on one lab segment results in more lab time for students and less time grading lengthy reports for Mary.

To help students understand how to develop reports and use the rubric, Mary uses a report that she wrote, although on a different topic, thus modeling her own struggle with issues related to the lab report to show how she improved it and to illustrate the revision process. Mary wrote her report to fulfill requirements for the AP biology teacher preparation course. Students enjoy knowing that even teachers work on improving their knowledge and skills, get graded on their work, and benefit from these experiences.

Mary's students submit their revised final report several days after the rough draft is completed and assessed. She uses the same rubric (Figure 12.3) to score the final draft, but its grade counts twice as much as the rough draft. In this way, Mary emphasizes the revised work rather than the first attempt. The rough draft and its scored rubric are handed in to Mary, along with the final draft.

Category	Scoring Criteria	Points	Teacher Evaluation	Points Lost
Title	Name, date, and descriptive and interesting title of lab in the heading of a word document. Title should engage the reader and hint as to why the lab was performed.	1		
Objective Statement	Hypothesis is clearly stated and a brief description of what is to be done is included. For the physiology experiment, you should predict your own fitness rating.	1		
Procedures	In paragraph form, accurately describe how the lab was done. All descriptive units should be included. For the physiology experiment, use the information provided in class to help you be brief in this section.	2		
Results	The Data section should only include important data, be relevant to the objective statement, and be in a format that is most easily understood and most informative (charts, graphs). A brief narrative should accompany the data and succinctly explain what the data show.	2		
Discussion/ Analysis	Summarize the essential purpose of each component of the lab; describe how the data found apply to the objective and specifically cite the evidence that supports your analysis (i.e., What do the data mean, and why do you think so?).	3		
Conclusion	State which objectives we have met for this lab by examining the list of objectives on the lab handout and determining which we accomplished to the best of our ability so far. **Did your data support your hypothesis or not?**	1		
Total Score		10	**Student Final Score**	

FIGURE 12.3. AP biology lab report evaluation rubric.

The process of peer assessment and revision also provides an opportunity for teachers to assess students' motivation and commitment. Occasionally, students do not improve from the rough draft to their final report, earning a low grade in spite of being given a chance to improve their work. Mary addresses this issue during individual conferences, analyzing with each student the rough draft and rubric alongside the final version of the lab report. Suggested edits focus on the content of the lab report, such as what students have emphasized in their report. Usually they spend a lot of space on procedure and little on analysis of results and discussion. Mary suggests important lab ideas and concepts that students should address, referring to the already answered Analysis Questions, to help students grasp what they should include in the report. She also questions them about the "what ifs"—what might have gone wrong—to lead them to Error Analysis. Mary's purpose is to move students past the notion that the Error Analysis means they did something wrong.

Parents also like specific information about how their children can improve, and the rough draft and final lab reports can serve as a vehicle for teachers to share with parents their observations about a student's motivation and academic commitment. This strategy works for any science class and any lab report format. Even for cases in which students do not write formal lab reports, but instead complete analysis questions, an opportunity to revise their work after peer review can be very helpful.

Assessment *as* Learning: Preparing a Speech in an English/Language Arts Class

One of the most effective and underused ways to implement assessment *as* learning is collaborative development of assessment criteria between teacher and students. Students experience anxiety when it is finally time for them to perform—write a paper, take a test, complete a difficult homework task, or finish a project. Similar feelings occur for teachers as they get ready to grade these assessments; often teachers think, "Why did I assign this again? Why have students strayed so far from what I had hoped for on this assignment?" Often difficulties and low grades are the result of initiating the paper, test, homework, or project, with neither student nor teacher being really clear about what was expected.

As a classroom teacher, nothing is more important than establishing clear expectations for the instructor, for the class as a whole, and for individual students. Though developing expectations is a part of class activity, the most effective time to include students in determining appropriate expectations occurs with assessment of their work. Typically, student anxiety results from tests and grades—areas of a course in which students usually have little input and understanding of the ultimate objective. Stress occurs when teachers realize that they have not been really clear in their own goals for the assignment. However, if teachers alter the way they create assessment by involving students directly, confusion, student–teacher barriers, and habitual low scores can be eliminated, or at least diminished. Development of criteria may be accomplished in a variety of ways and for an assortment of assignments, but it is often easiest when creating a rubric for a test or project. Rubrics are vital in a performance assessment, such as public speaking.

Such clarity changes the dynamic of the teacher–student relationship, from a power struggle to a partnership in which all parties have a fair chance for success. The biggest advantage of including students in establishment of grading standards is that it provides a feeling of ownership. Usually, the most ambiguous part of a classroom for adolescents is assessment, but when they understand up front the standards expected, they feel like the playing field is level. Otherwise, students often feel like they are playing games in the teacher's world, with no way to know how to satisfy the instructor. Developing criteria together allows students to see the teacher as a collaborator instead of simply a judge, and creates more student cooperation before and after assessment. This changed spirit is an extra benefit for the teacher as well, because students are forced to be more accountable for their ultimate performance.

Assessment as *Learning in April's Classroom*

April teaches nontraditional students who are returning to a small university after several to many years in the work force. Her students are career changers who need help in developing their academic skills and knowledge to be successful. April has found great success within her classroom, working as a team leader with her students collaboratively to determine requirements that best exemplify a good speech. Although this example is drawn from higher education, we have all developed criteria for projects with adolescents in much the same manner described here. What follows is an outline of a lesson designed both to teach content and to engage students in designing a rubric for public speaking assignments. In this lesson, assessment is a tool to encourage comprehension and application rather than merely a measure of final success.

The initial activities of the lesson help to improve students' ability to identify main ideas in a textbook reading assignment about effective public speaking. After reading the assigned text, students focus on a specific section of the reading, and each student identifies the five most important details in the text, forcing students to review independently their comprehension of the reading and their understanding of significant ideas about effective public speaking. Similar to a *think–pair–share* (McTighe & Lyman, 1988) activity, students then join with a partner and discuss the similarities and differences in their selections. Such collaboration helps struggling readers see the ideas of other classmates and reinforces the skill of finding the main idea, allowing all students to review their own thinking.

Once students have determined the main points in their text section, they defend their selected ideas, while remaining open to other opinions. To further distill the information, student partners work to reach consensus on the three most important ideas from the text. The negotiations that take place during this part of the assignment are a great time for teachers informally to assess student text understanding and cooperation. At this point in the process, students have reviewed the material several times and have discussed the information with a peer. Conversations among students offer insight about individual comprehension and preparedness.

After locating significant details, April's class moves to more challenging thinking, wherein they group specific ideas under larger, more general concepts, in preparation for giving a speech based on the article. Once they agree on the three main points of the text, partners share their findings with the entire class. They explain their decisions, and April provides any additional details needed. This activity produces an unorganized list that, once refined, includes the elements in an effective speech. The next task is to organize the information into several superordinate concepts. The class members work together to organize the details into overarching groups; this pushes students to think more critically. As students discuss the speech elements and categories, April has a chance to explain further the main points and to evaluate student understanding of the information; students have the opportunity to make connections and ask questions about confusing areas. Eventually students turn a whiteboard full of random qualities of a speech (eye contact with audience, attention-grabbing subject, and knowledge of material) into organized categories (organization, content, delivery, and preparation). At this point, though they do not realize it, students have created a skeleton rubric outlining the criteria for their upcoming assignments.

After students have demonstrated an understanding of the major attributes and specific details of an effective speech, they must determine the most significant concepts about public speaking. Students in small groups work to place these concepts according to their order of importance, then share their rankings, so that the class can come to consensus, finalizing the organization of the future rubric. This step is not only crucial in the structure of the grading tool, but it is also most significant, because the end result points students to areas with which they should be most concerned, giving them more concrete guidance for their speech preparation. Having the class come to consensus about the most important elements of a speech lessens student confusion and eliminates opposition to final grading decisions. This point in the process of determining criteria gives students the strongest feeling of power and involvement.

Following this step, April gives the students one more chance to show their understanding of the text information and of the final goals. Students reconvene in their small groups one last time. Each group is assigned a particular overarching concept, and the final task is to use the details identified earlier to create a written explanation of excellence. Students must explain the requirements for each detail of the concept to receive full credit on this phase of speech preparation. This written expression of expectations is the final agreement concerning the standard by which students will be held accountable—a standard created, stated, and affirmed by the students themselves. Finally, April gathers the explanations and physically creates the rubric for all subsequent speeches (see Figure 12.4).

The initial rubric-making assignment usually occurs within one or two class periods, depending on time; however, an ongoing step in the process is also helpful. Because student understanding of speech making becomes more sophisticated as the course progresses, April often returns to the rubric for reevaluation and revision. Until students form a solid knowledge base, some criteria (e.g., demonstrating a confident flow, with clear transitions) would be unfair in the beginning, yet once students' content knowledge becomes more extensive and complex, the quality of work should evolve. Therefore, the rubric becomes a dynamic entity, changing when necessary to fit the growing comprehension and performance of students. These revisions, resulting in increased expectations, are made in concert with students. In the end, the procedure offers clarification, socialization, and empowerment.

April originally began creating criteria with her students to establish clear assignment goals, but the results were much more far-reaching. Although her students clearly understood the most important elements of speech preparation, their understanding encompassed much more. The gains in knowledge, changed attitudes, and opened minds were far more important than any of April's assignment expectations. After receiving student feedback, she realized that such uses of assessment are rare in the classroom. Most students confessed that this was the first

Preparation (25)

To receive full credit, the speaker must ...
  choose a topic that is interesting to the audience
  demonstrate a confident flow with clear transitions, but few pauses and distractions
  display deep knowledge of topic

Content (20)

To receive full credit, the speaker must ...
  present appropriate details and evidence
  choose relevant material

Organization (20)

To receive full credit, the speaker must ...
  create a clear central idea/purpose statement
  create a beginning, middle, and end
  demonstrate a logical order

Know Audience (15)

To receive full credit, the speaker must ...
  present ethical material
  present material that is interesting to the audience at hand
  adjust to audience feedback

Presentation (10)

To receive full credit, the speaker must ...
  show confidence through body language
  connect with audience
  speak using the appropriate volume

Visual Aid (10)

To receive full credit, the speaker must ...
  use visual aid to present relevant material
  use visual aids that do not distract from the presentation

Name of Speaker _____

Final Grade _____

Comments: _____

_____

_____

FIGURE 12.4. Speech and communication rubric.

time an instructor had ever consulted them about learning goals. Their reactions were overwhelmingly positive. Student responses reminded April that assessment *as* learning may be the most effective tool in fostering both learner independence and a team spirit, because students were forced not only to examine their own command of information but also to compare and reconcile it to the ideas of other classmates and of the teacher.

Although the attributes of autonomy and cooperation are essential characteristics of a good student and citizen, April's class was most impacted by the opportunity to have ownership in the assessment process. She suspects that students in many classrooms often see assessment through tests, homework, and projects as punishment, torture, and a form of teacher control. Letting students own some of the assessment development offers both accountability and a new sense of confidence. Teachers also benefit by trusting students to take more responsibility for their own assessment. Classrooms become partnerships between students and teachers.

Assessment *as* Learning for Teachers

Students who are skilled at self-assessing their learning are in better positions to become independent, lifelong learners (Black & Wiliam, 1998). In the same way, teachers who assess their teaching practices are in better positions to develop into flexible, lifelong learners that are more enthusiastic about making changes in their teaching to ensure student success. Change is difficult for students and teachers alike. Teachers who risk modeling self-assessment encourage similar reflective behaviors from students.

Before beginning the journey of self-assessment, teachers must have clear, measurable, and explicit criteria defined for themselves, and for the lessons they teach, including a well-defined set of student expectations that encompass what we expect students to know and be able to do when they fully comprehend and are able to apply their learning. Without clear criteria and expectations, we have nothing against which to measure the success of our teaching.

After we have identified the criteria against which to judge our teaching success, we can begin to reflect deliberately on ourselves as teachers. One of the most valuable gifts we can give ourselves is the gift of time—time to consider our teaching, and time to learn and grow professionally from our experiences and what we are learning about ourselves through our reflection. One way to monitor our teaching is to keep a professional journal. It is critical that our journal writing focuses not only on *what* happened, but also on *why* things that happened are important, and how we will *use* what we learn as a result of our reflection as we plan future lessons. Hence, there are three main components to our professional journal writing: (1) summarizing *what* happened; (2) examining the events to determine *why* they unfolded in the way they did, and why they are important to consider; and (3) forming thoughts about how we can *use* what we have learned from reflecting on the events.

This last component, forming new learning from reflection about events, is the most important and the most overlooked element of reflective self-assessment. Many teachers get stuck in the "summarizing" component and find it difficult to move to the "forming new learning" component. Without movement into new learning, however, teachers have not truly reflected on their teaching; they are not learning. Only when we are able to transform our thinking and examine how to use what we have learned through our experiences will we be able to assess our own teaching practices. Self-assessment of our own teaching helps to guide our planning for future lessons.

Leigh's Reflections on Her Teaching

As a math teacher in a small rural middle school, Leigh kept an extensive journal of her strategy use. Her journal entries provided a window on her thinking about teaching, and about her students' learning. In her current position as a mathematics specialist, Leigh helps elementary and middle school teachers become reflective practitioners. As a middle school teacher, Leigh regularly wrote her reflections in her professional notebook. In the following journal entry, Leigh reflected on the use of a literacy strategy in her math class. The strategy she is thinking about is an *anticipation guide*, which is a series of statements (English, science, or social studies) or mathematical expressions (math) that prompt student thinking about a topic under study (see Lewis & Jones, Chapter 1, this volume). She writes:

Thursday, Algebra Classes

I used an anticipation guide—solving linear equations with variables on both sides of the equal sign. Goal—to get the kids to see that the first step should be to get the variable on one side first. On the anticipation guide, I included statements about the steps involved in solving multistep linear equations—true-or-false statements. Prior to the actual lesson, students were to indicate whether they agreed or disagreed with each statement. I thought my anticipation guide looked great and would work great. However,

I now see that maybe this is a difficult concept to grasp without having first seen the lesson. Students worked hard to fill out the sheet, but I feel like they didn't really understand it. I went over the sheet with them, but I could tell they weren't "getting it" as well as I wanted.

So here's what I should have done:

- Anticipation guide must have a *before* and *after*—let them fill it out before and after the lesson has been taught.
- I could also have used a discussion web here—this might be a strategy that would really help students grasp the concept of solving multistep equations.

Leigh clearly identifies what she did (used an anticipation guide) and her expectation for the strategy ("I thought it looked great and would work great."). She also reflects on student response to the strategy—students didn't "get it." At the very end, Leigh lists the revisions (the now what) she feels are needed for this strategy to be more effective, and also extends that thinking to another strategy with which she was experimenting.

Leigh's experience as a mathematics specialist working with math coaches has led her to another form of self-assessment: rating herself on a teaching rubric that *she* developed. Producing a more structured form of self-assessment, instead of a journal, forces us to think about desired outcomes for our teaching practices. To develop such a rubric, however, we must first have clearly defined criteria and expectations for ourselves and for our students' learning—not only for one teaching experience but also for our teaching experiences for the school year. Once it is created, we may use this self-assessment rubric repeatedly to reflect on our teaching.

When developing a rubric for self-assessment, we must be prepared to reflect on the entire teaching cycle: planning, teaching, and reflecting. Reflecting on the planning we have done and the actual teaching of the lesson asks us to consider *what* happened. Next we shift our thinking to reflecting on *why* things happened and in what ways we will *use* what happened to plan for future lessons. In designing the reflection piece of our self-assessment rubric, we need to make sure we craft questions that help us reflect on *why* we learn and the ways we *use* what we have learned (Costa & Garmston, 2002) (Figure 12.5).

Because teaching is an all-absorbing creative activity, self-assessment can be difficult after the lesson. Teachers we know have videotaped their own teaching to have an opportunity to see the lesson as a third party might see it. After viewing the lesson video, a teacher can use the

Planning

Defining Explicit Criteria and Identifying Standards
1. What are the goals/criteria for a successful lesson?
2. What standards will be addressed?

Markers for Student Success
Identify what might be some of the markers for student success (how will you know students can successfully apply their new learning?).

Steps for Implementing the Lesson
What steps might you take in ensuring students successfully meet the outlined goals?

Teaching

Describe the implementation of the lesson. Consider the following:
• Do the tasks of the lesson align with the goals of the lesson?   • Did the lesson flow as planned, or were adaptations needed?   • What evidence do you have that students successfully met the goals of the lesson (refer to the markers for student success)?

(continued)

FIGURE 12.5. Teacher self-assessment rubric. Adapted by permission from Costa and Garmston (2002); revised by Ellison and Hayes (2007). Copyright by the Center for Cognitive Coaching.

Reflecting

In what ways did you meet your goals?
What evidence do you have to verify that your goals were met or not met?
What are some ways that this lesson will affect future lessons?
What are some things you will do differently as a result of this lesson?

FIGURE 12.5. *(continued)*

self-generated teaching rubric and/or write his or her reflections in a professional journal entry. Either form of reflection helps us as learners to focus on the important elements of our teaching, so that we can learn what goes right in the lesson, as well as what goes wrong.

Students and Self-Reflection

Like many teachers, Leigh believes that students can also benefit from reflective thinking about their learning, and Brownlie and colleagues (2006) assert that this reflective thinking is the essence of assessment *as* learning. Having students regularly reflect on their own learning through informal think writes (Mayher et al., 1983) about *what* they are learning, and *how* they are accomplishing the process and how successful it is, then *re-visioning* their learning as a result of the *think write*

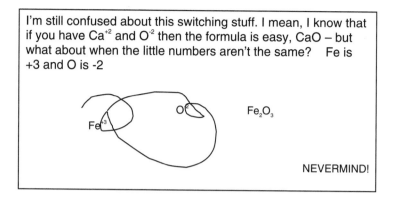

FIGURE 12.6 Student response to think write.

process helps them to clarify their own thinking and helps teachers to identify areas of instruction that need revisiting.

Victoria recalls an event in the mid-1980s involving a student's response to the following prompt:

Finish one of the following sentences: "Now I understand ... "

"I'm still confused about ... ."

She was teaching physical science and had just introduced a new concept [writing chemical formulas when valences are not equivalent]. One student wrote the response shown in Figure 12.6. In his attempt to explain his confusion, this student figured it out himself. It gave Victoria a window on her students' thinking, and provided an opportunity for them to clarify their own understanding.

Concluding Thoughts

Currently, high-stakes, multiple-choice assessments receive much attention, but teacher-constructed classroom assessments have more impact on student learning (Hargreaves, Earl, & Schmidt, 2002). We have described three types of teacher-constructed assessment. Assessment *of* learning typically measures what students have learned at the end of a unit of study. Assessment *for* learning is used to measure student knowledge during the learning process and can help students clarify what they know and do not know about concepts under study. Assessment *as* learning involves student self-assessment and plays a dual role: to promote metacognitive thinking, and to shift the responsibility for learning to the students.

As we reflect on our own experiences with peer- and self-assessment, we have come to see that the reflective process is valuable in a variety of ways for both students and teachers. Students benefit through increased ownership of the learning process, resulting in increased understanding and improved metacognitive skills. Teachers' benefits related to student peer- and self-assessment include increased student achievement, fewer conflicts over grades, and ultimately less time spent grading papers and projects. In addition, teachers who regularly engage in reflective self-assessment improve their own learning and that of their students through more effective instruction. Isn't it time for teachers to take control of their learning and to help students do the same?

Questions for Reflection

1. How might you begin to involve students in peer- and self-assessment?
2. What curricular changes would you have to make in classrooms where you have taught or where you have been a student to accommodate student self-assessment?
3. How might you begin your own journey into reflective thinking?
4. Talk with some experienced teachers. How do they make time for reflective teaching and learning in their classrooms? What have you learned from these conversations that you can apply to your own teaching?

References

Black, P., & Wiliam, D. (1998). Inside the Black Box: Raising standards through classroom assessment. *Phi Delta Kappan, 80,* 139–148.

Brownlie, F., Feniak, C., & Schnellert, L. (2006). *Student diversity: Classroom strategies to meet the learning needs of all students* (2nd ed.). Markham, ON, Canada: Pembroke.

Cassidy, S. (2007). Assessing inexperienced students' ability to self-assess: Exploring links with learning style and academic personal control [Electronic version]. *Assessment and Evaluation in Higher Education, 32,* 313–330.

Chen, P. P. (2006). Relationship between students' self-assessment of their capabilities and their teachers' judgments of students' capabilities in mathematics problem-solving. *Psychological Reports, 98,* 765–778.

Costa, A. L., & Garmston, R. J. (2002). *Cognitive coaching: A foundation for renaissance schools.* Norwood, MA: Christopher-Gordon.

Ellison, J., & Hayes, C. (2007). *Cognitive Coaching Foundation seminar learning guide* (7th ed.). Highlands, CO: Center for Cognitive Coaching.

Hargreaves, A., Earl, L., & Schmidt, M. (2002). Perspectives on alternative assessment reform. *American Educational Research Journal, 39,* 69–95.

Hudd, S. S. (2003, April). Syllabus under construction: Involving students in the creation of class assignments. *Teaching Sociology, 31,* 195–202.

Kirby, N. F., & Downs, C. T. (2007). Self-assessment and the disadvantages students: Potential for encouraging self-regulated learning? [Electronic version]. *Assessment and Evaluation in Higher Education, 32,* 475–494.

Mayher, J. S., Lester, N., & Pradl, G. M. (1983). *Learning to write: Writing to learn.* Portsmouth, NH: Heinemann.

McTighe, J., & Lyman, F. T. (1988). Cueing thinking in the classroom: The promise of theory-embedded tools. *Educational Leadership, 45*(7), 18–24.

Obach, M. S. (2003). A longitudinal–sequential study of perceived academic competence and motivational beliefs for learning among children in middle school. *Educational Psychology, 23,* 323–338.

Pintrich, P. R., & de Groot, E. V. (1990). Motivational and self-regulated learning components of classroom academic performance. *Journal of Educational Psychology, 82,* 33–40.

Shepard, L. A. (2000). The role of assessment in a learning culture. *Educational Researcher, 29*(7), 4–14.

Stiggins, R. J. (2002, June). Assessment crisis: The absence of assessment FOR learning. *Kappan Professional Journal, 83*(10). Retrieved December 19, 2007, from *www.pdkintl.org/kappan/k0206sti.htm*

PART III

Building School Communities
for Adolescent Literacy Instruction

■ ■ ■

CHAPTER 13

What Do Middle Grades and High School Teachers Need to Know about Literacy Coaching?

RITA M. BEAN
KATHRYN E. CARROLL

CLASSROOM PORTRAIT

Latasha was so excited about her new position as a middle school language arts teacher. She had just been assigned to her school and was eager to start working with students. She prepared hard to get her classroom environment just the way she wanted it. She planned what she thought were fun activities for the first day of school to help her get to know the students. Her first day, however, did not go as well as she had hoped. She reflected on the day and planned for her second day, which went much like her first. In fact, her first 2 weeks followed a similar pattern despite the long hours Latasha spent reflecting, planning, and making changes she thought would help her better manage and instruct her students. She struggled through her classes each day. She resisted asking for help because she was afraid other teachers would see her as a "weak" teacher. However, one morning, as she was sitting in the teachers' lounge looking at her lesson plan book, Kelly, the literacy coach, sat down to chat with her. Kelly asked how everything was going. For some reason, Latasha felt free to tell Kelly how frustrated she was. Kelly asked if she could help, and with a great sigh of relief, Latasha opened up. They talked about what Latasha was doing and why she thought she was experiencing difficulties. Together they came up with several ideas: First, they brainstormed some specific changes that Latasha could make to engage students more actively; second, they actually planned the next day's lesson together; and third, Kelly

---

> agreed to go into the room to observe a lesson, after which she and Latasha
> would talk about what happened and possible adjustments. As she walked
> back to her classroom, Latasha felt comforted by her conversation with the
> literacy coach and excited about the ways they might work together.

Too often, new teachers become discouraged when the reality of the
classroom hits them; they are not certain of where to go for support or
how their requests for help might be viewed. The preceding Classroom
Portrait describes the ways a literacy coach can provide needed support
for new teachers. In many middle and high schools, such coaches are
available to work with all teachers, administrators, and students in ways
that improve classroom instruction and student learning. In this chapter, we introduce the notion of literacy coaching, then describe the work
that literacy coaches may do to facilitate the work of teachers.

We recognize, to quote H. L. Mencken, that "There is always an easy
solution to every human problem—neat, plausible, and wrong" (1949,
p. 443). In today's secondary schools, teachers are often introduced to
a literacy coach, an individual who is there to support teachers in their
efforts to improve instruction. And teachers are asking questions:

What does "support instruction" mean?
What *is* a literacy coach?
What does the literacy coach do?
How am I supposed to work with the coach?

Often, educators write about coaching from the perspective of coaches,
and although these materials are useful to coaches, it may be that such
perspectives provide a simplistic view that does not address what teachers need to know about coaching. By viewing coaching from teachers'
perspectives, we hope to be able to help them better understand and
accept coaching as a positive approach to school improvement.

In this chapter, we discuss the role of the literacy coach through
the lenses of teachers, addressing issues about the coach's role, coach–
teacher relationships, and ideas about how teachers might work with
coaches in their schools. By responding to questions that teachers ask,
we hope to provide a better understanding of how the coach fits into the
culture of the school and how teachers might develop more effective
working relationships with him or her. In this chapter, then, we address
the following questions:

What is a coach, and what do teachers of adolescents need to know
    about coaching that will increase their comfort level and facili-
    tate the coaching process?

What can a coach do that will help teachers be more effective and enable students to be more efficient learners?

Both the authors of this chapter have had considerable experience with literacy coaching. Rita Bean served in the role of coach (K–12) in a public school and has also worked as an external coach for several professional development initiatives focused on literacy instruction. She has also conducted research and written extensively about the leadership role of the reading specialist and literacy coach. Kathryn (Katy) Carroll, a literacy coach in a variety of settings on and off for the past 6 years, currently works as a coach in both an elementary and a middle school setting. During her 18 years in education, all spent in an urban school district, she has worked at various grade levels.

We begin this chapter by sharing and summarizing the research about coaches' work with teachers. We then discuss variations in teachers' willingness and readiness to work with coaches, their knowledge of literacy, and how these various dimensions play a role in establishing an effective coach–teacher relationship.

What We Know about Coaching

Recently, many books have been written about coaching that highlight the rationale for coaching as job-embedded professional development. The literature is clear. Effective professional development must be meaningful and relate to the classroom needs of teachers. It should involve active learning on the part of the teacher. Moreover, it should be long term rather than "drive by" or "flavor of the month" (American Educational Research Association, 2005; Anders, Hoffman, & Duffy, 2000; National Staff Development Council, 2001).

Joyce and Showers (2002) have provided a thoughtful framework for understanding professional development and its various components. They suggest that if the goal of professional development is to provide teachers with the ability to transfer what they are learning to the classroom and to ensure student learning, four components of professional development are essential. Teachers must understand why the specific program, initiatives, or strategies are important; that is, they need to understand the underlying theory. They must see how it works; that is, they should see it modeled. They should have opportunities for practice. Finally, coaching should provide an opportunity for support and feedback. New teachers especially desire this type of feedback, which helps them become more proficient in using various skills and strategies (Johnson & Kardos, 2002; Kohler, Crilley, Shearer, & Good, 1997).

Coaching Is a Powerful Professional Development Tool

Those who write about professional development are not proposing that schools no longer bring in speakers or have workshop sessions. What they do propose is that teachers be given follow-up support through coaching, so that they can successfully implement the suggested program or innovation. In other words, regardless of the quality of a particular innovation, the real key to success is its implementation. Teachers need ongoing support, guidance, and feedback that enable them to use the strategies effectively. One can compare this to a novice golfer or tennis player who seeks out a coach to provide the essential feedback: Am I holding the club or racket correctly? What does my swing really look like? Do I follow through? The very best golf or tennis players routinely seek the advice of their personal coaches as they strive to become the very best at what they do. Also, there is currently a trend for individuals to seek out a personal trainer as a means to ensure good health and remind them about adequate exercise and good eating habits. One teacher who worked with a literacy coach referred to that coach as her "personal professional development trainer."

Although we currently lack conclusive evidence that coaching can ultimately effect student achievement given the newness of this type of support for teachers (Snow, Ippolito, & Schwartz, 2006), some studies show that coaching can and does influence teacher practices. For example, Neufield and Roper (2003), in discussing the coaching model in Boston Public Schools, indicated that teachers who were coached were more likely to try out the new ideas they learned. Likewise, Knight (2004) indicated that a larger percentage of teachers who were coached implemented teaching practices they had learned in a summer workshop compared to those who did not work with a coach. Also important is that coaching appeared to have a positive impact on teacher collaboration (Schwartz & McCarthy, 2003). In a recent study, Gibson (2006), in a report on the work of one coach in a school, indicated that although she saw some changes in teacher instructional practice, these changes were small; she acknowledged, therefore, that coaching is a slow and not linear process. Bean and Zigmond (2006), in their study of Reading First coaches, reported that many teachers indicated they valued the coach in their schools as a source of professional development. In an evaluation report issued by Research for Action (Brown, Reumann-Moore, Hugh, du Plessis, & Christman, 2006) about the secondary coaching project in Pennsylvania, it was reported that teachers valued coaching and felt that the various strategies suggested by coaches increased student active engagement and helped students gain a better understanding of how to be effective independent readers. Teachers were also positive about the effect of coaching on their teaching; as a teacher in one of the secondary level project school stated to Rita, "Coaching has made me want to stay in teaching; I wasn't burned out, but I was crinkly around the edges." As research evidence continues to accumulate, we are learning more about the value of coaching and how it can be an effective tool in the school for promoting teacher learning and student achievement.

Definitions of Coaching and School Models of Coaching Vary

As we already noted, although coaching is a powerful tool for professional development, we acknowledge that coaching is implemented in different ways in some schools; therefore, at times, coaching descriptions may be akin to blind men describing an elephant. Each views the elephant from a different perspective and, in a similar manner, those who write about coaching view it differently. Toll (2007), for example, discusses five different perspectives related to coaching: coach as technician, service provider, supervisor, professional developer, and what she terms a "fresh alternative" (p. 13). Whereas the coach as technician has been designated to be responsible for helping teachers implement a specific program or innovation as accurately as possible, the coach as service provider supplies teachers with the materials or resources they need to do their job. The coach as professional developer is similar to what we described earlier. The coach as supervisor, in our view, is not consistent with what is suggested about successful coaching; that is, coaching should not be an administrative line position designed to evaluate teachers. We acknowledge, however, that in some schools, such a perspective exists. Toll's definition of coaches as a "fresh alternative" is based on the notion that coaches "help teachers to go where they, the teachers, want to go.... They work with all teachers.... They initiate coaching conversations, convene teacher teams, and propose study groups" (p. 13). We contend that this view of coaching is indeed refreshing, but we caution that individuals in coaching—and the teachers with whom they work—will confront the need to juggle the individual desires and goals of teachers with the recognition that schools also have accountability mandates and standards that must be achieved. We also believe that the effective coach can work with teachers in ways that address and respect individual needs and goals, and at the same time help teachers meet goals and standards set by schools.

Successful Coaches Establish Good Working Relationships with Teachers

Effective literacy coaches recognize that the goal of coaching is to increase literacy achievement of students. They also acknowledge and appreciate the fact that teachers are the key to student learning, and that the role of the coach is to facilitate teachers' work. According to Hasbrouck and Denton (2005), coaching is "a cooperative, ideally collaborative relationship, with parties mutually engaged in efforts to provide better services for students" (p. 22). Thus, these authors recognize that the most effective teacher–coach relationship would be one based on collaboration, wherein they work together on an issue of importance to both. But they recognize that not all coaching relationships are collaborative and that, at worst, the coach and teacher cooperate for the benefit of the students. If teachers understand that the goal of the coach is to enable them to do their jobs better, which may result in greater self-confidence and satisfaction, they will be more inclined not only to accept but also to celebrate the presence of a coach in the school.

The effective coach must focus on building trust with classroom teachers to engage in the in-depth conversations that address the specifics of instruction. Building these relationships takes time. In their study of three coaches in urban schools, Lowenhaupt and McKinney (2007) remind us that until these relationships are established, coaches will not be able to fulfill their responsibilities. Moreover, trust is established more readily when the culture of the school is one in which teachers have a common vision and similar goals for students, work well as a group, and have leadership that understands and supports the notion of coaching (Bean, 2007).

Effective Coaches Differentiate Their Work, but Are Available for All Teachers in Their Schools

One of the most important tasks of coaches is to help teachers understand that they are in the school to improve the learning of all students in all classrooms. Although some teachers—and some coaches—believe that coaches are there to help teachers who are experiencing difficulty, school improvement can only occur if there is a schoolwide effort to improve instruction. Therefore, all teachers, from novice to experienced, should think about how coaches can facilitate their work. For novice teachers, the coach can prevent problems by providing support when they have difficulties with an unfamiliar approach to teaching, a new textbook, or a specific student experiencing difficulties in the classroom. Coaches can support experienced teachers in several ways:

problem solving with these teachers about various issues, working collaboratively to implement specific programs or approaches, or providing the reinforcement we all need for doing a good job! In other words, coaches and teachers working together, in different ways, can lead to better instruction and enhanced student learning. The bottom line is that education changes rapidly, and new knowledge helps teachers improve their work in the classroom. The needs of students change; thus, educators need to be lifelong learners. Coaching can facilitate that process.

Given the differences in teachers' needs and expertise, coaches must offer different services to teachers. In 2004, Bean identified three levels of coaching that may help teachers understand the possible roles or tasks of coaches (see Figure 13.1). Coaches may function at what

Level 1 (informal; helps to develop relationships)

Conversations with colleagues (identifying issues or needs, setting goals, problem solving)
Developing and providing materials for/with colleagues
Developing curriculum with colleagues
Participating in professional development activities with colleagues (conferences, workshops)
Leading or participating in study groups
Assisting with assessing students
Instructing students to learn about their strengths and needs

Level 2 (more formal, somewhat more intense; begins to look at areas of need and focus)

Coplanning lessons
Holding team meetings (grade level, reading teachers)
Analyzing student work
Interpreting assessment data (helping teachers use results for instructional decision making)
Individual discussions with colleagues about teaching and learning
Making professional development presentations for teachers

Level 3 (formal, more intense; may create some anxiety on part of teacher or coach)

Modeling and discussing lessons
Coteaching lessons
Visiting classrooms and providing feedback to teachers
Analyzing videotape lessons of teachers
Doing lesson study with teachers

FIGURE 13.1. Coaching activities (levels of intensity). From Bean (2004). Copyright 2004 by the California Reading Association. Reprinted by permission.

Bean labels Level 1, serving as a resource, providing materials, or meeting with teachers to discuss students about whom they have concerns. Any teacher, at any given time, may want to consult with a knowledgeable colleague, such as the coach, to talk about how to adjust or modify instruction for a specific child, or to find specific materials to enrich a specific topic or skills being taught. The coach might also be a member of, or lead, a study group in which several teachers meet to discuss a specific article or book. In one middle school, teachers met to discuss an article about discussion in the classroom (Connolly & Smith, 2002) given their interest in improving the way they held discussions in their English classrooms.

Other teachers may want to work with coaches in what Bean labeled Level 2 activities. At this level, the coach might coplan a lesson with a teacher (e.g., help a social studies teacher build a lesson that teaches students to engage in "before reading" activities). The coach and teacher might meet to review the chapter and select activities that are appropriate. The teacher would teach the lesson, then meet with the coach later to discuss what went well and what questions or problems arose. Other examples of Level 2 activities include holding team meetings with teachers, problem-solving with individual or groups of teachers, or analyzing test data across a curricular area or grade level. For example, in one urban high school, 11th-grade teachers from several content areas met frequently with their coach to discuss the study habits of their students and to plan ways that the coach and teachers could help to prepare these students not only to take the upcoming state test but also to develop study habits to facilitate their work across subjects. These teachers, then, shared a common language—and designed common activities—that they implemented, so essential for improving achievement in all subject-area classrooms in the secondary schools.

Level 3 includes those activities that most educators associate with coaching: modeling, coteaching, or observing teachers either in the classroom or via videotape. It is this level that often has created concern, anxiety, and controversy in schools. Teachers are not accustomed to being observed, or if they are observed, the observation typically served an evaluative purpose. One of the most important tasks of the coach, in fact, is to dissuade the faculty from this belief about the coach's role! There are several reasons why this classroom work is important. First, thinking back to what we said earlier, the coach is there to provide the modeling or observation that helps teachers really understand and be able to implement a new strategy. So, for example, if the school has decided that teachers should use small-group instruction to facilitate active engagement of students, the coach can model or coteach, helping the teacher see how such instruction can be implemented effectively.

Second, teaching is such a demanding responsibility. Think about it: one teacher and 25 (or more) students, each with different needs, skills, and levels of interest. Teachers must think on their feet to respond to comments and ideas that come from students. There is little opportunity to reflect on whether a specific response was successful or not successful. Coaches provide a "mirror" for teachers (Robbins, 1991). In other words, they reflect back to teachers what occurred to facilitate discussion, build on strengths, and address any changes that might need to be made. Often these changes come from teachers themselves, who, when provided the opportunity for reflection, quickly identify how they might adjust what they are doing to facilitate student learning. Earlier in this section we discussed a coach coplanning a lesson with a social studies teacher. Once trust is established, this teacher may ask the coach to coteach or observe the lesson in which he or she teaches students how to engage in "before reading" activities. Level 3 also includes lesson study (Stigler & Hiebert, 1999) or videotaping of lessons for review by a group of teachers. In one high school in the Pennsylvania Coaching Initiative, the two coaches (math and literacy) met with a small group of volunteer teachers (e.g., psychology, foreign language, English, and business) who had agreed to have their lessons videotaped for review and to participate in a follow-up discussion. The goal was to help teachers move from a more lecture-type format to discussion, which facilitated active engagement of students. To begin this project the assistant principal agreed to model a lesson that was then videotaped and reviewed by this group.

Coaches and teachers may move between and among the three levels, and work with individuals and groups of teachers. What is important is that everyone realize that coaching differs, depending on teacher and student needs, the newness of the coach, the culture of the school, and even the time of year! Although coaches support teachers, it is critically important to realize that coaches also need the support of teachers. They cannot be effective without teachers' support and cooperation. And teachers need to remember that coaching is a relatively new phenomenon in schools; therefore, coaches are struggling to identify the most effective ways to do their work.

In the following section, Katy provides scenarios that illustrate the four different types of teachers. Each is a composite of middle school teachers with whom she has worked throughout her years as a coach. The scenarios illustrate four different kinds of teachers with which coaches are likely to come into contact in their work: an experienced, knowledgeable teacher; an eager and enthusiastic teacher attempting some new approaches to literacy instruction; a somewhat reluctant teacher; and, finally, a teacher that is resistant to coaching. We encourage readers to think about the category into which they would fit—and how they would respond to coaching.

The Literacy Coach's Voice: Acknowledging the Need for Variation in Coaching

In this section, I (Carroll) describe my work with four categories of middle level teachers and offer scenarios to illustrate how they responded to my coaching. I provide background information about each teacher, explain the work we did together, and elaborate on how our work relates to the intensity levels (Bean, 2004). I share lessons learned from working with each teacher at the end of each scenario.

Scenario 1: Expert to Expert

James has been a teacher for more than 10 years. He has attended many professional development workshops, training sessions, and classes since finishing his master's degree. He brings to his teaching a deep understanding of children and how they learn. Application of that knowledge is crucial to the success of his students. James consistently reflects on his teaching and often makes changes based on what he sees when working with students. James was previously an elementary school teacher, but he recently began teaching language arts in a seventh-grade classroom.

After I talked to James and briefly observed his classroom, I decided that he was not a person who needed my help. I thought I had more pressing issues to deal with within the school. But soon after my visit, James came to me. He wanted to work with me on a writing program for his students. He said that the new district curriculum was weak in the area of writing, and that was not an area in which he felt particularly strong, so he wanted to work collaboratively to create a nurturing writing program in his classroom.

I first gathered all of the information I could on adolescent writing: successful programs, district-level handouts, articles and books about teaching writing to adolescents, and a list of websites that might be helpful for our work.

James and I set up our first planning session during his lunch period, the third week of school. Without any prompting from me, James had also gathered materials about writing and the adolescent learner. Because we were both knowledgeable about how children learn and what he wanted to do with his students, through the course of our conversation we were easily able to set long- and short-term instructional goals, plan a tentative schedule for classroom work, and determine what each of us needed to do to prepare for our next meeting 2 days later.

Over the next 2 days, we separately read an article about adolescent writing. The next time we met, we talked about the article and how it related to James's students and his goals for them. This reading and the conversation helped further to shape his thinking, and it solidified our plans for collaboration.

James is not afraid to take a risk. During our meeting he asked me to come into his room the next day and observe as he taught writing. He had many questions that he wanted me to help him answer. We identified two big areas on which I would focus during my observation. Our postobservation conference was a discussion of those areas, as well as new questions and ideas that came to both of us during the observation.

Our work continued like this for 2½ months. We met often to talk about what James was seeing in his students. We looked at student work to identify gaps in student learning and talked about how James could address those needs. We would stop each other in the hallway for a brief conversation about an idea, question, or resource that one of us had recently discovered. There were times when James asked me to model a writing strategy, or just to teach so that he could observe the children at work. We also did some coteaching. When we saw that different students had different needs, we did small-group instruction, teaching simultaneously, feeling that through differentiation the students would learn more quickly and efficiently.

Toward the end of November, it became quite clear that James could handle the writing program on his own. At this point, I moved on to work with other teachers. I did, however, continue to check in with James, and our hallway conversations continued. He knew that I was available for any questions, comments, or concerns he had. I continued to provide new ideas, suggestions, and support from outside the classroom.

This scenario illustrates how James and I moved among all three levels of intensity (Bean, 2004). Level 1 activities included having many, many conversations about adolescent literacy and learners, as well as individual students. We also discussed the curriculum and what needed to be done to supplement what was already there, based on the needs of his students. Within Level 2, we coplanned, analyzed student work, used assessment data—anchor papers, grammar assessments, and work the students did when completing daily language activities—to drive James's instruction and, again, had many discussions about teaching these middle level learners. Level 3 activities included coteaching, modeling, classroom visits, and feedback to James about a variety of topics.

The biggest lesson I learned from working with James is that first impressions can be deceiving. Although I never thought James would need my assistance, because of his background knowledge and level of expertise, our partnership was very important for both of us. It was an opportunity to try different approaches and strategies, and to participate in reflecting on our work together and on our own. We both knew we were working in an environment where we could take risks and not be judged by the outcome. That enabled us both to enrich our knowledge of children, deepen our understanding of the strategies we tried, and strengthen our belief in the importance of self-reflection as a means to achieve more growth.

Scenario 2: Eager Learner

Samantha had been teaching for only a few years. She had been moved from school to school and from grade level to grade level during her first years of teaching. This was her first permanent assignment, teaching social studies to all of the middle school students, and she was very excited about that!

The first time I met Samantha, she had 100 questions for me. She wanted to know about her curriculum, ideas for room arrangement, how much homework she should give, and anything else she could think to ask every time she saw me. There were times when I was a bit overwhelmed by her questions. Often I had to admit that I did not know the answers, and that I would get back to her. I must confess that there were times when I sent her e-mails instead of answering her questions face-to-face, because I was not ready to handle the new barrage of questions she had for me. So our relationship really began through the computer. She sent me e-mails late at night that often began, "I can't sleep because I was thinking about ... " I would try to answer her questions, give her ideas, share insights, or provide whatever she needed when I received her e-mails.

Samantha attended every available afterschool and Saturday training that she could. One Saturday she attended a district-sponsored workshop that introduced teachers to a new writing curriculum we were adopting. Coaches had attended the professional development workshop on this curriculum, but the only teachers who currently used it were middle school science and social studies teachers. Samantha was so excited about what she learned during that introductory session that she wanted to implement the system in her classroom the following Monday. But she did not know how. She e-mailed me Saturday evening all excited and, of course, with many questions. I asked whether we could meet on Monday during her preparation period to talk about it, because there was just too much to discuss in an e-mail. She agreed, so our meeting was set, and our collaboration in her social studies classroom began.

I had not used the writing curriculum before, so Samantha and I learned it together. I brought to our first meeting a three-inch binder I had been given at a workshop. To understand Samantha's goals for her students, I asked many questions at that first meeting and, based on her answers, asked some more. We talked so much during that period that we decided to meet again the next day to create a plan for our work together.

At our second meeting we discussed how Samantha wanted to approach our work. Specifically, what did she want to try on her own, without my presence in her classroom? What did she want me to observe to provide her with feedback? What did she want me to model? Samantha decided that she wanted to struggle through it mostly on her own. She did ask for my help in securing all of the necessary materials she would need to "do it right," and I was able to do that within 3 days. After I gave Samantha the supplies to get started, she immediately began her work with the students.

I checked in with Samantha at the end of each day. Some days she was so excited about what happened that she could barely get everything said. On other days she had more questions for me to answer and/or to think about, including questions about the social studies curriculum, how to deliver the materials to students, struggles with particular students and, at times, questions about writing in general. Many days she was not happy with the way things had gone during her lesson, and she wanted to debrief to learn why she had envisioned it going one way and it had not happened that way at all. It was on one of those days that I suggested I could be more helpful to her if I could actually see the lesson while it was happening. She agreed to let me come and watch.

That began a series of classroom visits. I would watch her teach, and we would talk later that day about what I saw. Based on these conversations, on several occasions she asked me to do a model lesson to help her better understand my comments. Because she taught more than one section of social studies at each grade level, I would do the model lesson in the morning, then come back to watch her do the same lesson with another group of students in the afternoon. We always debriefed at the end of the day.

Samantha continued to attend professional development workshops, provided by the district, every time they were offered. Once she felt comfortable with the writing program, she was ready to move on to other areas in which she felt her students were struggling. Her enthusiasm and openness with her students and about herself as a learner seemed to help them face challenges in their own learning.

As with James in the previous scenario, Samantha and I moved among all three levels of intensity (Bean, 2004). She drove much of our work together, because she was curious and eager to use what she had learned with her students. She was more than willing to have goal-setting or problem-solving conversations. She was eager to coplan, look at student work, and hear feedback from me after a classroom visit. Although we talked about possibly video- or audiotaping her and analyzing it together, we never did so.

Samantha was fun, and it was easy to work with her. There were times, however, when I did feel overwhelmed by her enthusiasm. I learned early on that I could not remember all of her ideas and/or concerns, which is why I asked her to write them down for me. I think that was the key to our relationship at the beginning. I could then be certain I was addressing everything she wanted or needed from me. It also gave me time to think about my answers and always to know that I was giving her the most accurate information available. I made sure that my answers were as thoughtful as her questions. Over time, it became easier for me to have the conversations with her face-to-face. I derived pleasure from actually seeing her thought processes, her genuine interest in learning, and the way she truly cared about each of her students. She taught me that it is OK with some teachers to hang back for a time and be their support, without having to be in the classroom every day. I also learned that teachers at times have so much enthusiasm and excitement about their learning that a coach may not be able to address all that teachers want to do—so coach and teacher need to set priorities. The question that needs to be asked is: What is most important to you and your students at this time?

Scenario 3: Reluctant Teacher

Kendra, a sixth-grade teacher, was relatively new to teaching. It seemed that she felt a bit unsure about herself and her abilities, because she was very quiet around me. She never said a word at our staff meetings, and she seemed to want to hide at our team-level or content-area meetings. When asked a direct question by a colleague or by me, she often answered, "I'm not sure."

Although Kendra was not a particularly active contributor at our team meetings, I knew that she was observing and listening to all interactions. She took careful notes; she could repeat what had been said at previous meetings. She also kept all artifacts from the meetings. Because she and James were on the same team, I would often see her standing in his doorway, watching him teach, and talking to him at lunchtime, as well as before or after school. When I would walk by her room, she was always engaging the students in rich conversations.

Because Kendra was a newer teacher, the principal asked me to work closely with her. I knew that if I wanted to establish a mutually positive working relationship, I could not force myself into her classroom. I had to move slowly and gradually build her trust in me, and in the work we could do together.

I began by going to her room every day at times when the students were not there. I would ask her how things were going ("Fine") and whether she needed anything ("Nope"). After several weeks of this, I told her about the work James and I were doing together, and invited her to observe in his classroom if she'd like. Although she did not come into the classroom, I noticed her walking by the door several times throughout the lesson. James told me that, later that day, she asked him several questions about his collaboration with me. I knew she was considering how she and I might be able to work together.

I resumed my daily drop-in but lingered a bit longer, asking Kendra questions about the progress of particular students in her class. She still gave short answers. I also continued to talk about the activity in James's room, and again invited her to watch.

The next day, Kendra sat in the back of the room and observed about half of the lesson. She took notes the whole time and left without saying a word to anyone. First thing the next morning, Kendra stopped me in the hall, saying she had to ask me a question. Something she saw me do with a student in James's room contradicted what she had learned in college, and she wanted to know why I had done it that way. I explained my thinking and my reasoning. She thanked me and left. Later that day, I received an e-mail from her, with more questions about her work with her students. I replied immediately but did not hear anything from her for several days. I was out of the building for training, so I did not see her for the rest of that week.

When we returned to school on Monday, Kendra said she had been waiting to see me. She wondered whether she, James, and I could have lunch together "to talk" sometime that week. Both James and I agreed, so we ate lunch together that day. Kendra's questions were about the new curriculum she was using, and also some of the materials that were listed as core curriculum materials but missing from her classroom. James was very helpful in allaying many of Kendra's fears. She seemed a bit unsure of herself when we first sat down, but as the conversation began to flow easily, she became relaxed and was able to ask and to answer questions quite freely.

Two days later, she asked whether we could meet during her preparation period. This time she had an assessment to show me. She could not understand why her students had done so poorly on the assessment, when she had done everything in the manual to teach the concept. I told her that another teacher in seventh grade had asked me the same type of question. I asked Kendra whether she would be willing to share her concerns with the group at our next content-level meeting the following afternoon. She agreed. Thus began our work together.

The next day, Kendra shared the results from her assessment with the group of five teachers at the meeting. She had made copies of the students' work, and we all looked at it and talked about ways Kendra and the other teachers could reteach for understanding. We agreed, as a group, that certain skills might require teachers to teach more than what is in the curriculum. After that group meeting, Kendra and I adapted the curriculum and coplanned lessons to meet the needs of her students. Our cycle of work included meeting to plan, then meeting again, after Kendra had taught the lesson, to look at the work her students produced. After analyzing the work and seeing what was there and what was missing, we planned the follow-up work she should do with her students. There were several times that Kendra brought this work to a content-level meeting to share with the other teachers and get their reactions. At the same time, however, although I offered to come into her room to model particular strategies or to watch her teach and provide feedback, she always declined.

It was obvious from the work she was bringing to our meetings that Kendra was reflecting on and improving her teaching. Student products continuously showed more depth and understanding. Her questions and comments were always thoughtful and revealed an ever-growing knowledge of the adolescent learner.

Kendra and I interacted on only two levels of intensity. Although she was willing to share the work of her students with me, she was not willing to allow me into her classroom to observe her teaching. As a result, we engaged in a great deal of informal dialogue to establish our relationship; this led to the more formal processes at Level 2, in which we analyzed student work, had conversations about their learning, and coplanned her lessons.

My approach with Kendra had to be slow and steady. If I had rushed her in any way or forced myself into her classroom, she would have shut down and not have allowed me to assist her at all. Because I let her take the lead and make decisions about what we could or could not talk about or do, she was willing to sit with me and consider her practice through her students' products. I know she learned a lot about teaching through our conversations. She needed to take baby steps and feel like she was in control of the situation. From this experience I learned that by taking a slow, relaxed, almost hands-off approach, coaches can sometimes move further than they ever would by pushing a teacher who is not ready to be pushed. Kendra also had to develop trust in me; it took some time for the two of us to learn how to have a successful and productive professional partnership.

Scenario 4: Resistant Teacher

Cathy had been a teacher for over 15 years when I met her. The majority of her work had been in high school language arts classes. She saw herself as an excellent teacher—better than most of the teachers in her building. She described herself as demanding and as having very high expectations for her students. Her philosophy of teaching was that she would not begin teaching a new concept until all of her students had mastered the one she was currently teaching. She currently teaches eighth-grade language arts.

At the end of every unit of the core curriculum there is an assessment that teachers have to administer. The answer sheets are scanned at the school and the results are compiled in a computer program to which the principal, coach, and district-level officials have access.

It became clear after the second benchmark assessment that Cathy's students were not progressing as expected. The principal asked me why the students had not done well on the benchmark. I told her that I would talk to Cathy and get back to her.

When I approached Cathy, she told me that the problems were the curriculum—it was going too fast, the students—they were not grasping the concepts she was teaching, and the home—the parents never made the students do their homework and return it to the school. She blamed everyone and everything she could, while insisting several times throughout our conversation that she would not move on to a new concept until everyone in the class had mastered it.

I asked her what concept or concepts were causing difficulty for the eighth graders. She told me she had been working on simple and complex sentences for a month and a half. I asked to see some of the work the students had produced during that time. She showed me workbook page after workbook page in which many of the students answered every item correctly and others had missed only a few. I then asked her whether students had done any authentic writing to show their knowledge of sentence structure. She was unsure of what I meant. I also asked her during that conversation whether she ever grouped the learners according to what they were producing on her assignments. Might it be possible for her to give the students who had shown mastery of the topic a different assignment, while she taught those students who were still struggling with the concept? Again, Cathy said she was unclear about what I was suggesting she do. I then offered to do a model lesson for her to make my point clear. Cathy agreed.

We started planning for the next day's lesson. Through the course of that conversation, we agreed that because I could not get everything done in one day, I would teach in her room for 2 days.

When I began my lesson the next day, Cathy was sitting at her computer taking attendance. I asked Cathy to sit at a student desk, so she could be part of our learning. She told me she would be there in a minute, but as she was finishing her computer work, a student was brought to the room by her parent. Cathy had a 22-minute conversation with the parent, while I taught. Apologizing when she returned to the room, Cathy explained that she had been trying to reach that parent for a long time and desperately needed to talk to her.

By this time, I had grouped the students and was sitting with the struggling readers. I asked Cathy to circulate among the other groups to be certain they were on task, and to listen to the conversations. I requested that she not interrupt them because of the directions I had given. She ignored my request, asking several students for their homework. When it was clear that they did not have it, she made them leave their group work, go to their lockers, and get their homework. After she circulated the room and got homework, she sat at a student desk near a group and began to check it. Before I left the room that morning, I asked whether we could meet later that day to debrief the morning. She happily agreed.

At our debriefing meeting, I tried to explain tactfully that the purpose of my modeling was for her to watch, not to be doing other work or conversing with parents. Cathy said she knew that, but she had already done what I was showing her, so she could pay attention to me while getting other things accomplished. I queried as to why we had planned that particular lesson, if she had already done it with her students. I was under the impression that these were things she had not tried. She explained that she must have misunderstood what we were talking about when we planned the lesson, because she thought it was going to be different.

Our attention then turned to the plans for the next day. I made certain that she knew exactly what I was going to be modeling, and that these were things about which Cathy had genuine questions and wanted/needed to be shown how to use them with the students in her classroom. She agreed.

Before I began my lesson the next day, I gave Cathy an observation sheet. At the top of it I had Cathy's questions from our conversations and places where she could keep track of what I was doing, as well as space for any questions or comments she had during the lesson. I gave her a specific place to sit and made sure she had no other materials with her. She seemed a bit annoyed when the lesson started, and jokingly said she felt I was treating her like a child. But she did what I asked—for about 10 minutes.

Just as I was placing students into their groups and explaining how the period was going to go, Cathy stood and walked to her desk. I stopped and asked her what was wrong. She said, "Nothing. Just keep going. I just need to check on something. I am still listening." I thought about telling her that we would wait, but I did not want to have a confrontation with her in front of the students.

I tried to redirect Cathy throughout the time that students were working in small groups, but she always managed to find an excuse to go to her desk and begin her own work. At one point, she walked out of the room. I caught up with her in the hallway, and she told me she would be right back; she had to check on something in the office.

When we met to debrief the second day, she talked and talked about how beneficial the modeling had been for her. She had learned so much. She was going to try some of the strategies I had shown her for grouping students. Basically, she was a changed teacher.

I went back to visit her classroom a few days later. She was instructing all of the students in a whole group about simple and complex sentences. I heard her say to the students, "I'm sorry that we have to do this, but I refuse to move on until I am sure you all understand. Take out the worksheet I gave you as you walked into the room and let's try this again."

Although it seems like Cathy and I worked among all three levels of intensity, we really didn't. I did have conversations with her and seemed to coplan, and I did model lessons in her room, but what I really did was give her several extra preparation periods over those 2 days. It was obvious from her actions during the lessons, and the lack of even a hint of change in her approach to teaching or grouping the students, that she had gotten nothing from our work.

The lesson I learned from Cathy is that coaches are not always successful with all teachers. Cathy came to content-area meetings but did not want to participate in self-reflection, planning, or sharing of ideas and strategies. She always had excuses for why things were not working, and it was never her fault. She also was not willing to try a new suggestion from a colleague or a strategy from something we had all read, because she had "already done it," and it did not make any difference. I believe that because I was her colleague, and not in any kind of position of authority, she thought she could use the situation however she wanted. I had to turn my attention away from her and concentrate my efforts on teachers who were genuinely ready to work with me. I could not, however, give up completely. I tried reaching out to Cathy several times throughout the year, using different ways to approach her. Sadly, nothing ever worked. I was reminded, then, that a coach may not be able to reach 100% of the teachers, that teachers have to be willing to meet the coach halfway—or at least to start down the road. There is room for variety in how teachers work with coaches, but if a teacher refuses the partnership—passively or aggressively—probably little will happen.

What I've Learned

Certainly, each teacher is different, as is each coach, but the four scenarios I have provided illustrate how four different teachers viewed and worked with me. I have found that the resistant teacher is a rarity. Almost all teachers have some needs, interests, and ideas that they would like to discuss with the literacy coach. It is obvious that the first three teachers did make use of my services—although in very different ways. Time was an essential in establishing trust, building relationships, and moving from Level 1 to Level 3 for those teachers. Although I was not successful in establishing a collaborative or cooperative relationship with the fourth teacher, I recognize that many factors may have influenced why it did not work. In spite of this experience, however, I always offer my services and continue to hope that every teacher decides to partner with me.

Teachers Speak: What the Coach Can Do for Teachers

Middle school teachers who are currently working with coaches have provided us with a list of their ideas for how teachers can effectively use the services of a literacy coach.

- "Test preparation ... helping me align my materials and instruction to the content and standards on the state test."
- "Providing me with materials and other resources to help me differentiate instruction (e.g., obtain the novels or supplement materials that I need)."
- "Helping me make decisions about what to teach (streamlining the curriculum so that I focus on the big and most important concepts)."
- "Assisting me with selecting reading strategies for students (e.g., helping students move to more fluent reading and writing)."
- "Helping with specific analyses of data, so that I can use specific strategies to move from point A to point B."

- "Coplanning lessons with me, especially when we are instituting a new instructional approach."
- "Assisting with differentiated instruction and flexible groups by modeling and coteaching."
- "Just a different point of view—offering suggestions for improvement and SUPPORTING ME!"
- "Offering a more experienced source to bounce ideas 'off of.'"

Concluding Thoughts

Coaching has the potential to be a wonderful resource for middle grades and high school teachers. Coaches can assist them in their efforts to change or improve the way they structure their classrooms, plan, and implement instruction. There is no single model for how teachers and coaches work together. Indeed, there are opportunities for many different models—from situations in which the coach serves only as a "sounding board" for teachers to classrooms in which the coach and teacher, at least for a short time, work together to plan and implement a specific approach or instructional strategy. Coaches may work with teachers one-on-one, or they may work with teachers in group settings, such as a specific content area or grade level, to identify common goals or experiences for students. They may serve as leaders or participants in professional development activities that enable all to become more knowledgeable about how to improve the literacy abilities of students in the middle or secondary school. The message is this: Coaching is a model that reinforces the view that teachers need to be reflective decision makers. Coaches are there to help teachers make that a reality.

Questions for Reflection

1. Given what you have learned about coaching in this chapter, what are some ways you think a coach could work with you to "support instruction"? With which activities identified in Figure 13.1 would you be most comfortable? Which would be most useful to you?

2. What qualities of a coach do you think would be most important to you as a teacher? Any thoughts about the qualifications and experiences that you think would be essential for effective coaches?

3. Think about Cathy, the resistant teacher, described in this chapter. Are there things that Katy, the coach, might have done to help that teacher work more effectively with her? What are your thoughts

about how this teacher might be helped to become more effective? Should the administrator be asked to address concerns about this teacher's instruction? Why or why not?

References

American Educational Research Association. (2005). *Research points: Teaching teachers: Professional development to improve student achievement* (Vol. 3, Issue 1) [Brochure]. Washington, DC: Author.

Anders, P. L., Hoffman, J. V., & Duffy, G. G. (2000). Teaching teachers to teach reading: Paradigm shifts, persistent problems, and challenges. In M. L. Kamil, P. B. Mosenthal, P. D. Pearson, & R. Barr (Eds.), *Handbook of reading research* (Vol. III, pp. 719–742). Mahwah, NJ: Erlbaum.

Barkley, S. G. (2004). *Quality teaching in a culture of coaching.* Lanham, MD: Scarecrow Press.

Bean, R. M. (2004). Promoting effective literacy instruction: The challenge for literacy coaches. *California Reader, 37*(3), 58–63.

Bean, R. M. (2007, Fall). The promise and potential of literacy coaching. *PASHCI Portfolio Report*, pp. 2–3. Also available on www.pacoaching.org.

Bean, R. M., & Zigmond, N. (2006). *Professional development role of reading coaches: In and out of the classroom.* Paper presented at the IRA Reading Research Conference, Chicago.

Brown, D. C., Reumann-Moore, R. J., Hugh, R., du Plessis, P. L., & Christman, J. B. (2006, September 1). *Promising inroads: Year-one report of the Pennsylvania High School Coaching Initiative.* Philadelphia: Research for Action.

Connolly, B., & Smith, M. W. (2002, September). Teachers and students talk about talk: Class discussion and the way it should be. *Journal of Adolescent and Adult Literacy, 46*(1) 16–29.

Gibson, S. (2006). Lesson observation and feedback: The practice of an expert reading coach. *Reading Research and Instruction, 45*(4), 295–318.

Hasbrouck, J., & Denton, C. (2005). *The reading coach: A how-to manual for success.* Boston: Sopris West.

Johnson, S. M., & Kardos, S. M. (2002). Keeping new teachers in mind. *Educational Leadership, 59*(6), 12–16.

Joyce, B., & Showers, B. (2002). *Student achievement through staff development.* Alexandria, VA: Association for Supervision and Curriculum Development.

Knight, J. (2004). Instructional coaches make progress through partnership. *Journal of Staff Development, 25*(2), 32–37.

Kohler, F. W., Crilley, K. M., Shearer, D. D., & Good, G. (1997). Effects of peer coaching on teacher and student outcomes. *Journal of Educational Research, 90*(4), 240–250.

Lowenhaupt, R., & McKinney, S. (2007). *Coaching in context: The role of relationships in the work of three literacy coaches.* Paper presented at the American Educational Research Association Conference, Chicago.

Mencken, H. L. (1949). The divine afflatus. In *A Mencken chrestomathy* (pp. 442–475). New York: Knopf.

National Staff Development Council. (2001). *Standards for staff development* (rev. ed.). Retrieved August 6, 2008, from *www.nsdc.ord/standards/index.cfm*.

Neufeld, B., & Roper, D. (2003). *Expanding the work: Year II of collaborative coaching and learning in the effective practice schools.* Cambridge, MA: Education Matters. (ERIC Document Reproduction Service No. ED480874)

Robbins, P. (1991). *How to plan and implement a peer coaching program.* Washington, DC: Association for Supervision and Curriculum Development.

Schwartz, S., & McCarthy, M., with Gould, T., Politiziner, S., & Enyeart, C. (2003). *Where the rubber hits the road: An in-depth look at collaborative coaching and learning and workshop instruction in a sample of effective practice schools.* Boston: Boston Plan for Excellence.

Snow, C., Ippolito, J., & Schwartz, R. (2006). What we know and what we need to know about literacy coaches in middle and high schools: A research synthesis and proposed research agenda. In *Standards for middle and high school literacy coaches* (pp. 35–49). Newark, DE: International Reading Association.

Stigler, J. W., & Hiebert, J. (1999). *The teaching gap: Best ideas from the world's teachers for improving education in the classroom.* New York: Free Press.

Toll, C. A. (2007). *Lenses on literacy coaching: conceptualizations, functions, and outcomes.* Norwood, MA: Christopher-Gordon.

CHAPTER 14

■ ■ ■

What Is the Role of the Reading Specialist in Promoting Adolescent Literacy?

PAMELA A. MASON
JACY IPPOLITO

CLASSROOM PORTRAIT

The seventh/eighth-grade English language arts (ELA) teacher introduced me (Jacy Ippolito) to Anthony on my first day at the school. The cheerful eighth-grade African American boy smiled and shook my hand as I told him that I would be working with him one-on-one that year. The ELA teacher informed me that despite his positive attitude toward school, Anthony had not read a book since fourth grade. She was concerned that he would not make it through the advanced texts that the eighth graders were going to read as a class that fall—*To Kill a Mockingbird, Johnny Tremain*, and *The Crucible*. As the brand-new reading specialist assigned to work with the fifth- to eighth-grade students and teachers, it was clear to me that both the principal and the middle school teachers were hoping I could quickly "fix" the roughly 25% of students reading below grade level.

After administering a battery of informal reading inventories, I determined that Anthony was reading independently at a fourth-grade level. I quickly introduced him to Jerry Spinelli's high-interest, fourth-grade-level book *Crash*, about a sometimes-insensitive, adolescent sports hero who grows into a reflective friend. Anthony and I began meeting three times a week in the mornings. We would take turns reading together and working on vocabulary, fluency, and comprehension strategies, such as questioning, summarizing, and inferring. Progress was slow but steady. By the end of the year, Anthony was reading at a sixth-grade instructional level. Although he still needed a great deal of support to keep up with his class assignments, Anthony was reading, enjoy-

---

ing, and completing a greater number of texts—books at his instructional and independent level that were helping him to build fluency.

Years later, as I work with new students, I always think back to Anthony and his eagerness to read and to feel successful despite his impoverished skills. I see my role of middle school reading specialist as helping students overcome barriers to accessing and enjoying texts. It has always been important for me to remember that most struggling adolescent readers are eager and able to improve, when given the proper support.

But how many Anthonys receive the support of a reading specialist at the middle school level? This is one of the questions that brought us together to write this chapter. Pamela Mason is the director of the Language and Literacy master's program at the Harvard Graduate School of Education and supervises reading specialist interns in their practicum placements in the Cambridge Public Schools. Jacy Ippolito is a doctoral candidate at the Harvard Graduate School of Education and a former reading specialist and literacy coach in the Cambridge Public Schools. Our common investment and experiences in the preparation of reading specialists and literacy coaches brought us to question their role at the middle and high school levels.

As reading specialists and literacy coaches are increasingly placed in middle and high schools to address the literacy needs of underperforming students, the pressure to provide one-on-one interventions for students, as well as instructional support to teachers, is immense. Can one person meet all of these very real and very important needs and expectations? In this chapter, we suggest that one person cannot, and should not, address all of these student- and teacher-level needs. By working in tandem and collaboratively, the middle and high school reading specialist and literacy coach can effectively help students and teachers to improve student achievement.

In this era of high-stakes testing, school-level accountability for literacy achievement, and state sanctions for not achieving appropriate levels of student progress, increased attention is being paid to the intersection of adolescent literacy research, policy, and practice. The nation's report card, the results of the National Assessment of Educational Progress (NAEP; 2005), has demonstrated that U.S. students, especially at middle and high school levels (grades 5–12), have not performed better than previous years' cohorts in reading and writing skills over the past three decades (Perie, Moran, & Lutkus, 2005). Skills that are the foundation for entering institutions of higher education, for attaining employment above the minimum wage, and for engaging actively in civic life and labor markets are not being attained by significant numbers of adolescents (Levy

& Murnane, 2005; Murnane & Levy, 1996). The discrepancies between the performance of our European American, African American, Asian American, and Latino/a students is a stark reminder that there are still two Americas, with divisions according to race, class, home language, and disability (Snow & Biancarosa, 2003). Differences are exacerbated by the increased demands of academic language, the introduction of specialized content vocabulary, and the variations in text structures at the secondary level that challenge all adolescents, especially those who may be marginal readers from the outset. As noted in earlier chapters in this volume, the assumption that skilled reading at the elementary level automatically results in skilled reading at the secondary level has not been supported by the realities faced by students, and new answers to the question "How do we adequately prepare adolescents for college and the workplace?" are being sought. If our children are truly our future, then they need better literacy education that starts in early childhood settings and extends through middle and high school coursework.

Middle and high schools are beginning to address the needs of their underperforming adolescents in various ways. Some are purchasing literacy programs that can be implemented by ELA teachers (e.g., the Reading Apprenticeship's Academic Literacy course). Some are restructuring the school schedule to provide for more instructional time in ELA classes. Some are instituting cross-disciplinary, schoolwide professional development, following the often-quoted mantra "All teachers are teachers of reading." Some are hiring literacy coaches and/ or reading specialists both to directly instruct students and to provide literacy-oriented professional development for teachers. This urgency to address the literacy needs of adolescents, in the face of assessment data that indicate little or no improvement over the last three decades for this age group, is appropriate and welcome in the literacy community.

Given the clear need for increased literacy instruction and achievement at middle and high school levels, we believe that the reading specialist has an important and growing role in addressing the literacy needs of students in grades 5–12 (middle and high schoolers). Before elaborating on our premise, we would like to establish a common understanding of terms to distinguish between literacy coaches, discussed in the previous chapter, and reading specialists, discussed here.

Of Specialists and Coaches: Major Differences and Why Both Roles Are Critical

As noted in the previous chapter, literacy coaches play an important role in middle and secondary schools, primarily by providing professional development for classroom teachers. What, then, do reading specialists do? In reviewing the growing literature on *reading specialists* and *reading/literacy coaches*, one is confronted by the differences in titles and responsibilities. Dole, Liang, Watkins, and Wiggins (2006) conducted an extensive survey of 48 state departments of education, inquiring about the job title, prerequisite requirements, and typical roles/duties of these literacy professionals. The variation was astounding. To summarize their findings briefly, *reading specialists* mostly address the needs of underperforming students and provide some mentoring and professional development for teachers. Meanwhile, *reading/literacy coaches* mostly address the needs of teachers by providing mentoring and professional development, and provide some direct instruction to underperforming students.

According to the International Reading Association (IRA), a reading specialist can and does serve three essential roles: reading intervention teacher, reading or literacy coach, and reading coordinator/supervisor. As the reading intervention teacher, the reading specialist uses formal and informal assessments to diagnose and remediate individual students with reading difficulties in individual or small-group settings. As the reading or literacy coach, the reading specialist provides professional development to teachers in the form of peer observations, model teaching, coplanning and coteaching, and study groups. As the reading coordinator/supervisor, the reading specialist monitors and evaluates the effective implementation of the schoolwide reading program. However, at this point in time, the roles of the reading specialist as coach and supervisor are increasingly being assumed by literacy coaches, who may or may not have acquired licensure/certification as a reading specialist.

Although it may initially seem that the roles of *specialist* and *coach* are identical, the largest differences in these two positions lie in whom they *primarily* serve (students or teachers) and their academic preparation. The order of the duties we reported earlier are important, with reading specialists focusing, first and foremost, on student learning, and coaches, on teacher learning. This difference, though perhaps subtle to policymakers and administrators, is quite large in terms of how reading specialists and coaches approach their work and actually operate in schools. In terms of training, by and large, reading specialists hold a graduate degree in the areas of reading or language and literacy (IRA, 2006), whereas literacy coaches are currently far less consistently prepared for their roles as professional developers and reading instructors. The role and preparation distinctions between reading specialists and literacy coaches are differences that have serious implications for those schools in need of literacy professionals to work directly with students, providing tailored assessment and remedial literacy instruction.

For the rest of this chapter, we use the following definitions for literacy professionals working in middle and high schools. *Reading specialists,* as indicated by the standards published by the IRA (2004a), hold a graduate degree and are licensed as such by their state department of education. In the 2004 revision of its standards, the IRA included that graduate candidates must demonstrate the ability to assist and support classroom teachers and paraprofessionals; however, we do not view this ability as overlapping with coaching roles and responsibilities, which primarily focused on teachers' professional development. In contrast, few states currently have formal licensure requirements for literacy coaches, and although many literacy coaches are experienced teachers, recognized for their effectiveness in teaching literacy, few are licensed reading specialists (Frost & Bean, 2006). While the IRA (2004b) has taken the position that literacy coaches ideally should hold a license as a reading specialist ("the gold standard" according to Frost & Bean, 2006), this recommendation has not been widely implemented due to the newness of the position, the sudden and large demand for coaches, and the fact that coaches with reading specialist training and certification often require higher salaries than grants or public funds currently allow.

In response partly to the adolescent literacy crisis (Biancarosa & Snow, 2004), and partly to shifts in federal funding (Dole, 2004), the trend in middle and high schools across the country is toward hiring literacy coaches in place of reading specialists (Shaw, Smith, Chesler, & Romeo, 2005). In some cases, currently employed reading specialists have been asked to assume the roles and responsibilities of coaches, working more frequently with teachers, as opposed to working directly with students (Dole, 2004; Shaw et al., 2005). Collaborating with classroom teachers and providing a moderate amount of literacy-focused professional development is clearly part of the reading specialist's role (Bean, 2004; IRA, 2004a, 2004b); however, it is worth noting that many middle and high schools nationwide may soon be forced to choose between funding of reading specialists and of literacy coaches. Given that literacy coaches at the middle and high school level are increasingly expected to hold many of the qualifications of reading specialists, as well as additional qualifications as content-area experts (IRA, 2006), is the role of the reading specialist at middle and high school levels becoming obsolete? Should schools be asked to make a choice between coaches and reading specialists?

We answer both questions with a resounding no: reading specialists make a unique contribution to secondary school settings, above and beyond the work of literacy coaches. Hiring a literacy coach and a reading specialist should not be an either–or decision. We believe that there has never been a time when reading specialists are more needed at secondary levels, and instead of replacing reading specialists with literacy coaches, we argue that both reading specialists and literacy coaches should be contributing to students' and teachers' literacy work. State-, district-, and school-level leaders need to consider how to support simultaneously the work of reading specialists and literacy coaches, if they wish to see systemic improvement in teachers' literacy instruction and students' literacy achievement.

Given the similarities and differences between reading specialists and literacy coaches, we maintain that despite any current overlap in the roles, and despite increased interest and funding for literacy coaches nationwide as a solution to poor adolescent literacy achievement, reading specialists have much to offer adolescents and secondary school teachers. Below we outline the major ways that reading specialists contribute to middle and high school settings.

How Reading Specialists Can Support Literacy Instruction in Middle and High Schools

The reading specialist can and should serve many roles in the secondary school setting (Bean, 2004; IRA, 2004a, 2004b). The reading specialist is an expert on research-based literacy programs and practices that can be implemented across the disciplines and in every classroom. He or she can address the needs of teachers and students through individual interventions, grade-level/department support of teachers, and whole-school initiatives. The reading specialist should be the person who makes connections between students and their literacy skills and challenges, between teachers and their content standards, and between materials/programs and their efficacy. Below, we elaborate on four distinct ways in which reading specialists contribute uniquely to middle and high school settings:

1. Supporting adolescents through assessment-based individual and group instruction.
2. Supporting content-area teachers.
3. Supporting the instruction of students with learning differences.
4. Supporting the acquisition, dissemination, and implementation of literacy materials and programs.

Supporting Adolescents through Assessment-Based Individual and Group Instruction

Student achievement has become the top priority of every school, and the No Child Left Behind Act of 2001 (NCLB) has focused national attention on student literacy achievement at the secondary level. According to NCLB, all students must be assessed in reading/writing and mathematics annually in grades 3–8 and at one grade level in high school. Therefore, the responsibility of literacy instruction rests with all teachers, K–12, in all schools. The reading specialist can serve students by providing and interpreting student assessment data for teachers, as well as by providing remedial instruction for students deemed to be at risk.

Student assessment data can come from large-scale testing, using nationally norm-referenced instruments that the reading specialist administers. The most recent data available from the National Center for Education Statistics (NCES; 2005) indicate that most states are using a standards-based instrument for students at the middle and high school levels to determine adequate yearly progress (AYP), as required by NCLB legislation. The reading specialist working in a middle or high school can assist teachers in developing an item analysis of these standards-based tests that could help to identify the strengths and challenges for students in a particular grade level or class. These student strengths and challenges can be aligned with the curriculum standards for the school, so that teachers and specialists can focus on areas that have not been well addressed. This analysis highlights areas in which the curriculum standards are and are not being met by students.

Using this information, the reading specialist can then develop a two-prong approach. First, the specialist can work directly with small groups of students, implementing a remedial intervention for those who did not attain a passing score, as defined by the state. Second, the specialist can work with groups of content-area teachers to identify effective, literacy-based instructional strategies that can help struggling students learn and meet the curriculum standards in each of their subjects. Content-area teachers must be encouraged to determine how their students can master disciplinary content through the effective use of literacy strategies (see Lewis & Reader, Chapter 5, this volume).

For students who are assessed as being "at risk," based on large-scale test (norm-referenced or standards-based) results, the reading specialist is in a unique position to administer individual and small-group assessments. Such targeted assessment uses student and specialist time efficiently, and maximizes the information gained from further testing. The results of this small-group and individual testing can be used by the reading specialist to recommend and model teaching strategies to content-area teachers. This process serves to capitalize on students' strengths and address students' needs, providing the literacy scaffolding for students to access the content-area curriculum.

It may be determined from this individual assessment that a student requires remediation in reading and writing. The reading specialist's training makes this possible. With growing numbers of English language learners in our secondary schools, this remediation might be focused on oral language development, academic vocabulary, and/or reading fluency. The improvement of these skills will support increased reading comprehension and writing achievement.

Although a two-prong approach to improvement (i.e., remediation with students and professional development with teachers) must be implemented nationwide, there is an immediate need for reading specialists at the middle and high school levels to work directly with students on basic and advanced literacy skills. Reading specialists are trained specifically to attend to students' literacy needs in one-on-one and small-group contexts. Working directly with struggling readers and writers, one-on-one and in small groups, is a much-needed activity in middle and high school settings, where explicit literacy instruction is often absent. For example, one local middle school reading specialist worked collaboratively with an eighth-grade science teacher who was teaching a unit on bridges. The performance outcome for the students was a written report on one bridge construction type (e.g., suspension, beam, cantilever). This project placed many literacy demands on the students: selecting appropriate and reliable texts, reading expository text, synthesizing information from multiple sources, and executing the writing process. The reading specialist worked with small groups of students (struggling and proficient) on reading and writing strategies, and the science teacher taught the physics and engineering aspects of bridge construction. The final student projects exceeded the science teacher's expectations, and now she looks forward to collaboration with the reading specialist.

This science teacher was unaware of the literacy demands that "reading and writing like a scientist" placed on her students. The reading specialist was able to make these demands more transparent to the students and to their teacher, using the schoolwide state testing data to inform his interventions. Thus, if a middle or high school selects a literacy coach without the training and expertise of a reading specialist, then the school's capacity to meet the needs of individual students at risk through one-on-one or small-group assessment and instruction may be compromised.

Supporting Content-Area Teachers

Integrating specific disciplinary literacy skills with content instruction, such as science, math, and social studies instruction, is increasingly becoming the work of all middle and high school teachers (Lewis
& Reader, Chapter 5, this volume), yet, as a nation, we cannot afford
to neglect the pressing need for individual and small-group literacy
instruction in grades 5–12, which often cannot be provided in content-
area classes due to both schedule conflicts and lack of content teachers'
training in literacy. Middle and high school teachers, who increasingly
encounter students with learning disabilities, with English as a second
language, or with poor elementary-grade literacy instruction, must certainly develop strategies to work on reading and writing skills in their
content-area classes; however, reading specialists can provide the necessary one-on-one or small-group remediation for those students most in
need, thereby alleviating some of the burden on content-area teachers,
who may already serve more than 100 students daily.

Unfortunately, there are so many adolescents who need *some* read-
ing/writing support, it is not feasible for reading specialists at the middle and high school levels simply to teach *all* struggling readers/writers
in individual pullout, or push-in, small-group settings. Beyond providing direct individual and small-group instruction with students, reading
specialists necessarily must collaborate with content-area teachers, as in
the previous example with the eighth-grade science teacher. Reading
specialists (treading lightly into coaching territory) may collaborate by
providing professional development workshops, modeling instruction,
and coteaching in classrooms. The Standards for Reading Professionals,
developed by the IRA and the National Council of Teachers of English
(NCTE), call on reading specialists to assist content-area teachers in
building a better understanding of the relevance of reading to their
discipline, using their textbooks effectively, and implementing effective
literacy strategies (IRA, 2004b, p. 2).

The reading specialist is trained in a variety of research-based
instructional strategies that may be the basis of well-planned, consistent, professional development activities for middle and high school
content-area teachers. Guskey (2000) reviewed the professional development literature and identified important characteristics of effective
professional development that apply to the work of both literacy coaches
and reading specialists working in secondary settings (Snow, Ippolito,
& Schwartz, 2006). The reading specialist is well positioned to provide
some of the ongoing professional development that is procedurally
embedded in middle and high schools (Guskey, 2000). Topics for such
professional development might include vocabulary development strate-

gies, text structures as support for reading comprehension, and reading like a historian (Snow, Griffin, & Burns, 2005).

As part of a well-conceived professional development plan (and depending on whether the school also employs literacy coaches), the reading specialist might model and/or coteach these strategies in content-area classes. Such models of collaboration have been demonstrated to be effective in changing and sustaining teachers' implementation of new techniques (Guskey & Huberman, 1995; Huberman, 1995). Most certified reading specialists have had prior teaching experience; thus, they understand the teaching–learning process, the challenges of classroom management, and the pressures of covering the curriculum. This prior experience lends credence to the reading specialist's suggestions and credibility to the techniques being implemented. Specialists can also assist content-area teachers in differentiating their instruction for the wide range of adolescent learners in the classroom. As a colleague, and not a supervisor, the reading specialist can also be a sounding board for teachers when the implementation of literacy techniques varies in effectiveness. The reading specialist and the teacher can conduct peer observations and debriefing sessions to identify the strengths and weaknesses of the implementation of new instructional strategies. Adult learning and professional development literature demonstrate that this type of ongoing, supported professional development helps teachers make effective and lasting modifications in their craft (Guskey, 2000, 2002). Although professional development lies squarely in literacy coaches' territory, reading specialists, too, can share their expert knowledge of literacy instruction with peers. Delivering professional development may become a secondary goal of the reading specialist working in a school where a literacy coach is also employed, but it is still important to see professional development as one of the roles that specialists play.

Supporting the Instruction of Students with Learning Differences

Another role that the reading specialist plays at the secondary level is that of a coteacher with learning disability specialists for students with identified learning differences. Most students with an Individualized Education Plan (IEP) are challenged with respect to reading and writing tasks, whether or not this is their primary, identified specific learning disability. The reading specialist can work with homogeneous and/or heterogeneous groups of students, teaching, reinforcing, and applying literacy skills to new materials. As a coteacher in an inclusion model, students' needs may be addressed in the least restrictive environment, as mandated by the Individuals with Disabilities Education Act (IDEA) in 2004. In addition, the reading specialist can coordinate literacy instruction with learning disability specialists or resource room teachers to provide consistency of individualized instruction across a student's academic schedule.

Middle and high school teachers, who routinely teach large numbers of students on a daily basis, may not have the time or expertise to conduct individual informal and formal reading assessments. Thus, when a student is struggling with reading and/or writing, a classroom teacher or literacy coach may not be able to assess accurately whether the student's difficulty is the result of improper literacy instruction, lack of motivation or engagement, lack of background knowledge, impoverished vocabulary, or a reading-based learning disability. Making these distinctions is quite important, because each difficulty (or combination of difficulties) may need to be addressed through different instructional courses of action. At the extreme, a student might need to be referred for special education services, so that a learning disability may be identified and accommodated. Secondary schools without reading specialists run the risk of both under- and overidentifying adolescents for special education services. Both situations are harmful to students and to the school as an organization.

Reading specialists are experts in administering a host of informal and formal assessments[1] that help to distinguish between typical and atypical reading development. This is a much-needed service in the middle and high school setting, for students arriving from a wide range of local or distant elementary school environments may not bring with them a clear school record of previous literacy achievement. Without these records, middle and high school teachers may not be able to determine whether a student's current reading/writing difficulties stem from contextual or developmental factors (or both). Reading specialists are able to identify both typical and atypical reading development in adolescent readers, which is one of the first steps in providing the necessary support that all students need in transitioning to work with advanced disciplinary texts. After identifying students' particular literacy needs, reading specialists are then able to design individual instructional plans to respond to particular difficulties (e.g., impoverished vocabulary, comprehension difficulties due to nonstrategic reading). These instructional plans not only benefit individual students but they also provide

---

[1]Formal assessments range from the Woodcock–Johnson tests, the Peabody Picture Vocabulary Test (PPVT), and the Test of Word Reading Efficiency (TOWRE), to informal assessments, such as the Developmental Reading Assessment (DRA), the Qualitative Reading Inventory (QRI), and the Writing and Reading Assessment Profile (WRAP).

teachers with clear strategies for contributing to students' reading development.

Finally, reading specialists work closely with learning disability specialists and often collaborate with teams of teachers, specialists, and administrators who review individual students' needs and make referrals for special education services as needed. By employing a reading specialist at the middle and high school levels, schools are better able to provide services to students who might otherwise slip through the cracks, whether those students need just a little bit of additional literacy instruction or much more intensive one-on-one or small-group special education services. With the national move toward response-to-intervention models, the role of the reading specialist as a support to classroom teachers (Tier 1) and to individual students (Tier 2) is essential in avoiding the rush to referral for special education services (Tier 3) (Fuchs, Fuchs, & Vaughn, 2008). The IRA position paper (2003) on the overidentification of minority students in special education alerts reading specialists, classroom teachers, and administrators to such cautions.

Supporting the Acquisition, Dissemination, and Implementation of Literacy Materials and Programs

Armed with detailed knowledge of the strengths and challenges of their student population from the analysis of literacy assessment data, reading specialists in middle or high schools can recommend scientifically based reading research (SBRR) materials and programs. Although a growing number of instructional and intervention programs are designed to meet the literacy needs of adolescents (Deshler, Palinscar, Biancarosa, & Nair, 2007), not all are well suited to particular student, teacher, or school contexts. Reading specialists, who have expert knowledge of students' needs and program selection, may determine which literacy programs will best meet student, teacher, and curricular needs. Beyond material and program selection, reading specialists are then in a unique position to assist in the implementation of any adopted programs. Specialists can support student instruction and the ongoing professional development that is required to implement these programs.

Once new materials and/or programs have been implemented, the reading specialist can design a process to evaluate the efficacy of the program using data gathered from student work samples and from large-scale testing that may be administered on an ongoing basis at the school or district level. Reading specialists can engage content-area teachers in the formative assessment of an intervention by sharing student work samples and using them to determine benchmarks for improvement in student achievement. As the facilitator for this process, the reading specialist can help to establish a collaborative community of teachers (Robinson, Egawa, Buly, & Coskie, 2005). The performance-based assessments that are administered to meet the NCLB requirements are also a source of valuable data in assessing the effectiveness of program implementation.

In their seminal report *Reading Next* (2004), Biancarosa and Snow identified 15 important factors to consider when creating and evaluating effective literacy programs for adolescents. These factors were divided into instructional and infrastructure improvements. Among the instructional improvements cited, direct and explicit comprehension instruction, effective instructional principles embedded in content, and strategic tutoring are all well within the role and expertise of a reading specialist.

The reading specialist, who is trained specifically to address the literacy learning needs of a wide range of students, who has experience working with content-area teachers, and who is knowledgeable about scientifically based reading materials and programs, has an important and integral role to play in the middle and high school setting. However, these are heavy demands to place on one professional's shoulders. Working in tandem with a literacy coach whose primary responsibility is the professional development of content-area teachers through small-group and individual mentoring, the reading specialist can focus more exclusively on working with adolescents who are most in need of explicit literacy instruction.

Challenges in Urban Settings

Having enumerated several of the unique contributions of reading specialists in middle and high school settings, it is important to acknowledge some of the major challenges these professionals face, particularly in urban settings. We have arranged these into two broad categories: student-level and organizational-level challenges.

Student-Level Challenges Facing Reading Specialists

Reading specialists in urban middle and high schools face a wide variety of challenges at the student level. First and foremost, middle and high school reading specialists in urban settings increasingly work with students who speak (and possibly read and write) in home languages other than English. In the Cambridge Public School District, where we have done most of our work with/as reading specialists, there are more than a dozen different home languages. With limited English as a second language (ESL) services available in the public schools, the responsibility of providing individual literacy instruction for second-language learners often falls on reading specialists. Specialists trained in fostering bilingual literacy acquisition are a particular commodity in middle and high school settings, especially because middle and high school classroom teachers often have limited time to devote to ESL instruction. Reading specialists not only help teachers consider the needs of ESL students and advocate for differentiated instruction across content areas, but specialists also work with ESL students to foster independent reading and transfer of language skills. Recognizing, identifying, and helping such students understand language, dialect, and cultural differences is partly how reading specialists help adolescent readers become more independent. Fostering independence is one of the keys to helping adolescent readers/writers successfully navigate the myriad classrooms and assignments they encounter.

Beyond language differences, middle and high school reading specialists encounter learners possessing great variations in background knowledge and vocabulary skills. Background knowledge and vocabulary are built slowly over time and, for many adolescents in urban settings, these skills are impoverished due to a lack of rich literacy experiences in school and at home, as well as transience within and across school districts. Reading specialists can build adolescents' background and vocabulary skills in one-on-one and small-group settings, providing some of the skills that students need to survive and thrive in content-area classrooms.

Beyond teaching discrete literacy skills, reading specialists can foster adolescents' motivation and engagement, reorienting reluctant or resistant adolescents toward reading and writing activities. One of the persistent recommendations related to adolescent literacy is to encourage motivation and engagement; although older readers often can *decode*, or sound out words in text, they are often unable to read fluently and comprehend text, because of a lack of practice born of years of frustration and subsequent negative attitudes about reading. Reading specialists can help on this front by focusing on changing adolescents' attitudes about reading. For those adolescent readers who struggle and view reading as a frustrating experience, a reading specialist can provide insight into specific roadblocks (e.g., lack of vocabulary, lack of strategic processes, lack of practice) and work collaboratively with students to develop individual reading plans that include both traditional and nontraditional texts (e.g., graphic novels, video game magazines, manga) that connect directly with students' interests. When given concrete strategies to improve reading, adolescent readers have a greater chance to engage with texts and practice the skills needed to make reading enjoyable and meaningful.

Organization-Level Challenges Facing Reading Specialists

Beyond student-level challenges, reading specialists in urban settings also face a number of challenges at the organization level. The first and most common challenge we have noted is the school schedule. Middle and high school schedules, particularly in urban settings, are often frenetic, with dozens of transitions for both students and teachers throughout the school day. For reading specialists looking to find time to work with students, it can be quite difficult to schedule one-on-one or small-group instructional time that does not conflict with content-area class work. Although in-class support of students can be productive, finding time for pullout services is critical for those students in greatest need of individual literacy instruction.

Reading specialists at the middle and high school levels need to work closely with content-area teachers, other specialists, and school administrators to coordinate instructional efforts and carve out time for individual services. One common solution to the scheduling challenge is to provide small-group instruction opposite elective courses, such as world language classes (e.g., Spanish, French, Mandarin). This option allows students—many of whom might already be native speakers of a language other than English—to hone their English speaking, reading, and writing skills at a time when other native English speakers are working on their own second-language skills. In addition to their regular ELA course, a second common option is a "reading course" that students can take as an elective, led by a reading specialist. Such a reading elective course allows groups of students to experience explicit literacy instruction, including reading comprehension strategies, vocabulary acquisition skills, and disciplinary literacy skills that students can transfer into their content-area courses. Neither option is perfect, and both limit the amount of time that reading specialists are able to spend in content-area classrooms supporting teachers and students; however, both options allow for a great deal of narrowly tailored literacy instruction.

A second organizational challenge faced by middle and high school reading specialists is competition for students' time. At the secondary level, many students who are most in need of literacy instructional support also need second-language instructional support, special education services, and perhaps even other, more specialized support (e.g., speech and language support, social–emotional counseling, occupational therapy). Particularly in urban settings, students' multiple needs may necessitate that several specialists vie for an individual student's time, and this can create tension among adults in the school, if a clear system for sharing instructional time is not agreed upon early. When an individual student needs to see multiple specialists every week, reading specialists might wisely opt to support that student during content-area classes, study halls, or even after school. Another option is for a reading specialist to work closely with other specialists, so that literacy instructional strategies are included in other specialists' work.

The challenges facing middle and high school reading specialists in urban settings can be overwhelming at first, and we have only mentioned the most salient challenges here. However, the challenges are not insurmountable, and they are best met with frank conversations about scheduling and coordination among reading specialists, administrators, teachers, and other school specialists. Below we provide a few brief case examples of a middle school reading specialist working with fifth- to eighth-grade students and teachers in an urban school.

A Day in the Life of a Middle School Reading Specialist

As a newly minted middle school reading specialist 8 years ago, I (Jacy) was told in no uncertain terms by the principal that my position had been created to address the needs of the roughly 20% of fifth- to eighth-grade students who underperformed both in their classes and on the annual state standardized test, the Massachusetts Comprehensive Assessment System (MCAS). The 400-student, K–8 urban school had greatly benefited from employing an early grades reading specialist, and it was the principal's hope that hiring a middle grades reading specialist would similarly help to improve early adolescents' reading and writing skills, strengthen reading and writing instruction across content-area classes, and ultimately result in higher annual test scores. To achieve these goals, I sat down with the principal and the middle school instructional teams, and we collaboratively designed a middle school literacy support system that included four major components: in-class support, literacy classes for small-group instruction, one-on-one tutoring, and professional support for content-area teachers. What follows is a brief glimpse of each component.

In-Class Support

I have spent roughly 90 minutes per day in other teachers' classrooms, assisting individual students, leading small-group instruction, or coteaching whole-class lessons. Over the past 8 years, our middle school ELA classes have transitioned from traditional whole-class instruction centering around one book at a time, with classic texts such as *Johnny Tremain* and *The Crucible*, to reading and writing workshop formats that rely on minilessons, independent reading and writing based on student-selected texts, and group share times. To support this transition to workshop instruction, I have spent a good deal of time in the fifth- to eighth-grade teachers' classrooms delivering minilessons and assisting students individually during independent work sessions. Serving in teachers' classrooms has allowed me to tailor instruction to particular students' needs. Two examples of how I work alongside teachers in classrooms include my experiences with Tatiana[2] and with small groups that were writing opinion essays.

Tatiana, an eighth-grade African American girl, was reading at a fifth-grade level. I began providing assistance as a reading specialist to Tatiana when she was in sixth grade—in large groups, small groups, and also one-on-one. Over the 3 years I worked with her, I got to know Tatiana fairly well, and I was eager to help her overcome her anxieties about not reading and writing as well as her peers. Besides receiving reading specialist services from me, Tatiana also met with several learning disability specialists during her time at our school. However, despite a great deal of in-school support, Tatiana's erratic home life, including having to take care of several younger siblings on her own, while her single mother worked days and nights at a hospital, did not allow her much room outside of school to practice literacy skills. I assisted Tatiana, one-on-one, with vocabulary and fluency skills while she was in sixth and seventh grade, but when she reached eighth grade, our instructional team decided to limit the amount of time Tatiana was pulled out of core courses. As a result, I chose to work side by side with Tatiana twice a week during her ELA class. The bulk of my work entailed helping Tatiana to focus and correctly interpret the daily minilessons on reading/writing strategies, but I sometimes needed to repeat or rephrase the minilessons for her, while the rest of the class began their reading/writing tasks. I sat next to Tatiana and quietly helped her apply the reading/writing strategies introduced by Carlos (Tatiana's ELA teacher) in her independent work—including rereading, summarizing, questioning, paraphrasing, note taking, and making inferences. Perhaps most satisfying for me was helping Tatiana with her writing, such as her biography about Dr. Martin Luther King, in which she expressed astonishment

---

[2]All names are pseudonyms, and all cases are composites to protect participants' privacy.

at Dr. King's bravery in the face of adversity. Although Tatiana would become frustrated quite easily when she could not find the right words to express her opinion (which sometimes would lead Tatiana to disrupt the entire class with angry outbursts), when I sat with her and talked through ideas as she wrote, the sentences always seemed to flow a bit more easily.

Teaching Tatiana over several years gave me a great deal of satisfaction, in that it was always clear to me that she was able to produce higher-level work with my assistance. However, I was always quite conscious of the fine line between helping Tatiana to achieve more independence as a reader/writer and making sure that she did not become too dependent on adult specialists for help. I was very careful not to spend entire class periods with Tatiana. I would always begin and end the class by her side, but in between, I would move around the room and assist other students, giving Tatiana time to reflect and to work independently. As a reading specialist, I am always concerned about moving students gradually toward more independence.

A second example of working in classrooms is an opinion essay project I led with Carlos's seventh graders. Carlos expressed concerns that he was not reaching the most proficient writers in his seventh-grade classes, and he asked me to guide small groups of students in writing sophisticated opinion essays. Carlos and I combed through his students' past writing assignments, identified students who might benefit from such an experience, then asked his classes for volunteers (we did not want to exclude any students who had the motivation to undertake an advanced, independent project). Using this process, Carlos and I jointly chose a group of eight students from each of his two 25-student, seventh-grade classes. These students met with me for 1 hour, twice per week for 2 months, and during that time we looked at model opinion essays and discussed topics that were of great importance to them. The students quickly identified overarching questions that related to their interests, and that they thought fellow students would be interested in learning more about (e.g., Should guns be sold to private citizens? Should gay marriage be legalized? Are there situations in which abortion should be legal/illegal?). Over the course of the 2 months, students developed thesis statements, introductory paragraphs, supporting paragraphs filled with evidence gleaned from at least three independent sources, and conclusions that worked to convince readers of authors' opinions. As a result of these small-group assignments, the students produced essays, ranging from a decent five-paragraph essay to an astounding 10 pages. This assignment, in addition to the regular reading/writing assignments that were part of the ELA class, gave some of the most advanced seventh-grade writers an opportunity to push themselves and invest time in a topic of personal importance. In this way, Carlos and I worked to meet the needs of both the struggling and the advanced readers/writers in his classes.

Literacy Classes for Small-Group Instruction

Besides serving as a reading specialist alongside content-area teachers in their classrooms, I spent the bulk of my time teaching independent "literacy classes," in which 6–10 students from each grade-level class met with me three times per week for 45 minutes, instead of attending a Spanish elective. After all middle school students' reading instructional levels were assessed at the beginning of the year with informal reading assessments (e.g., the QRI, the WRAP, or the DRA), students who were reading one or more grade levels below average were invited to attend literacy classes. After obtaining their parents' permission, students would enroll in the literacy class elective and subsequently spend the year developing discrete reading and writing skills. I carefully designed units of instruction in coordination with the middle school curriculum, covering poetry, short stories, novels, and plays during the times of year these units were covered in ELA classes. Moreover, I also made sure to spend additional time developing students' vocabulary, fluency, comprehension strategies, and oral language skills. In the small-group setting, students felt comfortable enough to attempt reading and writing tasks that they might otherwise have shied away from in larger class settings. It was within these small literacy classes that I formed my strongest connections with students—often boys, second-language learners, and/or adolescents from homes without much parental support.

Serving as a reading specialist in a city with a diverse student population, I vividly remember teaching literacy classes during 2001. At that time, my literacy classes were attended primarily by a large number of Somali refugee students, all of whom were Muslims who had been ostracized by peers after the tragic events of September 11, 2001. One of the most powerful literacy instructional activities that year occurred in May, when I offered each student the opportunity to lead our small literacy class in a minilesson, independent writing activity, and group-share of their choosing. One boy, Abdul, led a powerful lesson, during which he wore a white prayer robe and asked the group to write the words that would first come to their minds if they saw a man dressed like him walking down the street. Students responded with words ranging from *priest* to *terrorist,* and this allowed Abdul the opportunity to present to the group a short article from a newspaper, about how Muslim students in U.S. schools were being treated disrespectfully. Students ended the class session by writing about their understandings of how life in the United States had changed dramatically for Muslim students, regardless of their country of origin or political beliefs.

Lessons such as this, which connected directly with students' lives, dominated our literacy classes and provided opportunities for struggling readers and writers to engage in meaningful literacy experiences. As a result, teachers reported noticeable changes in students' orientation toward reading and writing activities. Moreover, our school has made AYP under NCLB standards for the past handful of years in ELA, which, I believe, is partly due to our middle school team's focus on bolstering the skills of both our struggling and high-achieving adolescent readers and writers.

One-on-One Tutoring

Assisting students in their content-area classes, as well as in small-group settings, has clearly been a large part of my role as a middle school reading specialist. However, I have also spent a small, but critical, portion of my weeks working one-on-one with the neediest adolescent students. After analyzing schoolwide literacy assessment data and consulting with our school's middle school learning disability specialist and K–8 inclusion specialist, I chose several students each semester to see individually.

One memorable tutoring relationship was formed with Rudolph, a Latino boy who had failed several grades, was three times my size, and had been placed in a self-contained classroom for special education middle school students with behavioral disabilities. Assisting Rudolph was challenging, because although physically he looked like a man, he was reading on a third-grade level. Rudolph was reluctant to meet with me at first, which was understandable after experiencing years of frustration with reading and writing; however, I finally won Rudolph over with a series of *Simpsons* comic books that I kept on hand for my most reluctant adolescent male readers. I quickly discovered that Rudolph loved drawing, and before long we were writing and reading our own collaborative comic book. In between drawing and writing sessions, I worked on Rudolph's word attack skills with word sorts and flash cards, practicing long and short vowel sounds. Building Rudolph's sight-word recognition and fluency proved difficult, but by the end of the year, his QRI assessment results demonstrated that he had made modest gains in his reading skills. Such one-on-one tutoring sessions are as exciting as they are difficult, with progress often being slow but worthwhile.

Professional Support for Content-Area Teachers

I typically spent the remainder of my time as a middle school reading specialist providing support to content-area teachers. Admittedly, most of my early activity as a reading specialist was exclusively with the fifth- to eighth-grade students and ELA teachers, but over time I began to work in math, science, and social studies classrooms. One brief example of this work is my collaboration with the seventh/eighth-grade social studies teacher around homework reading and writing assignments.

The seventh/eighth-grade social studies teacher, Jonathon, approached me because he was concerned that his homework reading and writing assignments were not providing all that was needed for students actually to gain literacy and content knowledge. To address his concerns, we met regularly over the course of a semester to identify a discrete set of literacy skills that he expected students to acquire as "historians." As historians, Jonathon wanted his students to read and write in terms of *cause and effect, sequences of events,* and *relationships between important people and events.* Given these three goals, Jonathon and I cotaught a series of whole-class minilessons around these concepts. We demonstrated to students how to identify cause and effect, sequences of events, and relationships between people and events in the social studies textbook, using sticky notes and key words. We then worked to reorganize Jonathon's homework reading and writing assignments to ask students explicitly to summarize homework reading in terms of these three overarching categories. Jonathon has reported great success with these techniques over the past 2 years: Students' responses to questions are consistently more analytical and complete.

These brief examples are only glimpses into the multiple ways I have spent my days as a middle school reading specialist over the past 8 years. Ranging from classroom to one-on-one settings, from teaching students to assisting teachers, I have found great satisfaction in supporting students' and teachers' literacy work. Whether operating as a remedial teacher or as a sounding board for both students and adults, I have found my work to be helpful in creating and sustaining a larger "culture of literacy" in the middle grades. Once initiated into this culture of literacy, middle school students seem to internalize it. I know that I have been successful when students eagerly show me passages from books that they find exciting. One of my happiest moments came at the end of my first year, when an eighth-grade student admitted somewhat reluctantly that he had never finished reading a novel before having attended one of my small-group literacy classes. I like to think of my work as unlocking doors for students who, for a variety of reasons, were never given keys. If, as a middle school reading specialist, I can help students overcome anxieties and begin to enjoy reading and writing, then I will have succeeded.

Concluding Thoughts

Whether teaching students in small groups, one-on-one, or as part of a larger class, we hope that the previous case examples illustrate several ways that reading specialists encourage the growth of literacy skills in adolescents. Moreover, we hope that the case examples demonstrate that although reading specialists work collaboratively with teachers to improve literacy instruction, work with students forms the core of their support role.

As we near the end of the first decade of the 21st century, middle and high school teachers throughout the United States are facing incredible pressure to improve adolescents' reading and writing skills, and raise achievement scores on standardized literacy assessments. Reading specialists and literacy coaches are two roles that have existed in some form or another since at least the 1920s and 1930s (Bean & Wilson, 1981; Dole, 2004; Hall, 2004; Sturtevant, 2003), but in the past two decades, both roles have become more well defined and more prevalent in the United States. Due partly to an increased need for literacy support personnel in schools, and partly to broader federal funding of the roles, we are now seeing more reading specialists and coaches than ever before in middle and high schools.

It is our contention that although reading specialists and literacy coaches seemingly share a common knowledge of literacy instruction, and may even share some school-level tasks, both roles have unique contributions to secondary school settings—particularly when both roles are present in the same school at the same time. With numerous reading specialist training and licensure programs available throughout the country, reading specialists have become well known as experts in the areas of literacy assessment, identification of reading disabilities, and most importantly, the direct instruction of students in one-on-one, as well as small- and large-group settings. When allowed to serve in a school side by side with a literacy coach, a reading specialist can focus most of his or her attention on student learning, while the coach focuses primarily on teacher learning. Again, this is not to say that, when a reading specialist and a literacy coach find themselves working in a school without the other, a coach cannot assist students, or a reading specialist cannot work with teachers. However, if both roles are funded at middle and high school levels, then a great deal of literacy support for both students and teachers will be available.

Some educators may see reading specialists only as supports for primary grade children who are struggling with the earliest stages of reading (e.g., decoding text). As the body of adolescent literacy research grows, and as increasing numbers of national assessments and reports demonstrate that adolescents still need ongoing literacy instruction, we hope that this view will change and that reading specialists will become a mainstay in middle and high school settings.

Questions for Reflection

1. If you are teaching a content-area subject in middle or high school, what do you use as the basis for referring one of your students to a reading specialist?
2. Based on information in R. Bean and Carroll (Chapter 13, this volume) and in this chapter, how might reading specialists and literacy coaches at the middle and high school levels work collaboratively to meet the literacy needs of both students and teachers?
3. Given what you know about the routines, organization, and political climate of middle or high schools, what factors might help or hinder the work of a reading specialist?

References

Bean, R. M. (2004). *The reading specialist: Leadership for the classroom, school, and community.* New York: Guilford Press.

Bean, R. M., & Wilson, R. M. (1981). *Effecting change in school reading programs: The resource role.* Newark, DE: International Reading Association.

Biancarosa, G., & Snow, C. E. (2004). *Reading next—a vision for action and research in middle and high school literacy: A report from Carnegie Corporation of New York.* Washington, DC: Alliance for Excellent Education. Retrieved October 27, 2007, from *www.carnegie.org/literacy/pdf/ReadingNext.pdf*

Deshler, D. D., Palinscar, A. S., Biancarosa, G., & Nair, M. (2007). *Informed choices for struggling adolescent readers: A research-based guide to instructional programs and practices.* Newark, DE: International Reading Association.

Dole, J. (2004). The changing role of the reading specialist in school reform. *Reading Teacher, 57*(5), 462–471.

Dole, J. A., Liang, L. A., Watkins, N. M., & Wiggins, C. M. (2006). The state of reading professionals in the United States. *Reading Teacher, 60*(2), 194–199.

Frost, S., & Bean, R. (2006). *Qualifications for literacy coaches: Achieving the gold standard*. Denver, CO: Literacy Coaching Clearinghouse. Retrieved October 23, 2007, from *www.literacycoachingonline.org/briefs/LiteracyCoaching.pdf*.

Fuchs, D., Fuchs, L., & Vaughn, S. (Eds.). (2008). *Response to intervention*. Newark, DE: International Reading Association.

Guskey, T. R. (2000). *Evaluating professional development*. Thousand Oaks, CA: Corwin Press.

Guskey, T. R. (2002). Professional development and teacher change. *Teachers and Teaching: Theory and Practice, 8*(3/4), 381–391.

Guskey, T. R., & Huberman, M. (1995). *Professional development in education: New paradigms and practices*. New York: Teachers College Press.

Hall, B. (2004, Fall). Literacy coaches: An evolving role. *The Carnegie Reporter, 3*(1), 10–19. Retrieved October 23, 2007, from *www.carnegie.org/reporter/09/literacy/index.html*.

Huberman, M. (1995). Networks that alter teaching: Conceptualizations, exchanges, and experiments. *Teachers and Teaching: Theory and Practice, 1*(2), 193–211.

International Reading Association (IRA). (2003). *The role of reading instruction in addressing the overrepresentation of minority children in special education in the United States*. Newark, DE: Author. Retrieved October 23, 2007, from *www.reading.org/downloads/positions/ps1063_minorities.pdf*.

International Reading Association (IRA). (2004a). *Standards for reading professionals—revised 2003*. Newark, DE: Author. Retrieved October 27, 2007, from *www.reading.org/resources/issues/reports/professional_standards.html*.

International Reading Association (IRA). (2004b). *Teaching all children to read: The roles of the reading specialist: A position statement of the International Reading Association*. Newark, DE: Author. Retrieved October 27, 2007, from *www.reading.org/downloads/positions/ps1065_reading_coach.pdf*.

International Reading Association (IRA). (2006). *Standards for middle and high school literacy coaches*. Newark, DE: Author. Retrieved October 27, 2007, from *www.reading.org/downloads/resources/597coaching_standards.pdf*.

Levy, F., & Murnane, R. J. (2005). *The new division of labor: How computers are creating the next job market*. Princeton, NJ: Princeton University Press.

Murnane, R. J., & Levy, F. (1996). *Teaching the new basic skills*. New York: Free Press.

National Center for Education Statistics. (2005). *NAEP 2004 trends in academic progress: Three decades of student performance in reading and mathematics: Findings in brief* (NCES 2005–463: U.S. Department of Education, Institute of Education Sciences, National Center for Education Statistics). Washington, DC: U.S. Government Printing Office.

Perie, M., Moran, R., & Lutkus, A. D. (2005). *NAEP 2004 trends in academic progress: Three decades of student performance in reading and mathematics (NCES 2005-464)*. Report from the U.S. Department of Education, Institute of Education Sciences, National Center for Education Statistics. Washington, DC: U.S. Government Printing Office.

Robinson, L., Egawa, K., Buly, M. R., & Coskie, T. (2005). From the coaches' corner: FAQs about literacy coaching. *Voices from the Middle, 13*(1), 66–67.

Shaw, M. L., Smith, W. E., Chesler, B. J., & Romeo, L. (2005, June). Moving forward: The reading specialist as literacy coach. *Reading Today, 22*(6), 6.

Snow, C. E., & Biancarosa, G. (2003). *Adolescent literacy and the achievement gap: What do we know and where do we go from here?* New York: Carnegie Corporation of New York. Retrieved October 27, 2007, from *www.carnegie.org/literacy/carnegie.pdf/ALFF1.pdf.*

Snow, C. E., Griffin, P., & Burns, S. M. (Eds.). (2005). *Knowledge to support the teaching of reading: Preparing teachers for a changing world.* San Francisco: Jossey-Bass.

Snow, C. E., Ippolito, J., & Schwartz, R. (2006). What we know and what we need to know about literacy coaches in middle and high schools: A research synthesis and proposed research agenda. In *Standards for middle and high school literacy coaches.* Newark, DE: International Reading Association. Retrieved October 27, 2007, from *www.reading.org/downloads/resources/597coaching_standards.pdf.*

Sturtevant, E. (2003). *The literacy coach: A key to improving teaching and learning in secondary schools.* Washington, DC: Alliance for Excellent Education. Retrieved October 23, 2007, from *www.all4ed.org/publications/LiteracyCoach.pdf.*

Index

Page numbers followed by *f* indicate figure, *t* indicate table.